Directory of the
North Sea
coastal margin

The Joint Nature Conservation Committee

The Joint Nature Conservation Committee was established by the Environmental Protection Act 1990 'for the purpose of nature conservation, and fostering the understanding thereof' in Great Britain as a whole and outside Great Britain. It is a committee of the three country agencies (the Countryside Council for Wales, English Nature and Scottish Natural Heritage), together with independent members and representatives from Northern Ireland and the Countryside Commission. It is supported by a specialist staff.

JNCC's statutory responsibilities include:
- ❖ the establishment of common scientific standards
- ❖ the undertaking and commissioning of research
- ❖ advising Ministers on the development and implementation of policies for or affecting nature conservation for Great Britain as a whole or nature conservation outside Great Britain
- ❖ the provision of advice and dissemination of knowledge to any persons about nature conservation.

JNCC also has the UK responsibility for European and international matters affecting nature conservation.

Directory of the

North Sea
coastal margin

Edited by Dr J. P. Doody[1], Charlotte Johnston[2], and Barbara Smith[3]

[1]Coastal Conservation Branch, Joint Nature Conservation Committee, Peterborough

[2] Analytical and Environmental Services, Gregsons Building, East Howden, Wallsend, Tyne and Wear NE28 0QD

[3] Scottish Natural Heritage, Old Bank Road, Golspie, Sutherland KW10 6RS

With additional sections compiled by:
Roger Covey and Keith Hiscock, Joint Nature Conservation Committee: Marine Habitats
Colin Graham, British Geological Society: Offshore Geology
Dan Leggett, National Rivers Authority, Anglian Division: Geology and Geomorphology
Jonathan Cox and Sarah Fowler, The Nature Conservation Bureau Limited: Introduction to North Sea Habitats

Originally funded under contract to the NCC (Chief Scientist Directorate) by the UK Department of the Environment as part of its co-ordinated programme of research on the North Sea.

NB. Responsibility for the production of the Directory has now passed to the Joint Nature Conservation Committee (JNCC), following the re-organisation of the Nature Conservancy Council.

The final version of the Directory was revised and sub-edited by the Nature Conservation Bureau Limited.

Published by the Joint Nature Conservation Committee, Peterborough, UK.

Prepared in collaboration with the Department of the Environment. The Department funded much of the preparatory work.

Citation: Doody, J.P., Johnston, C. and Smith, B. (1993). *Directory of the North Sea Coastal Margin*. Joint Nature Conservation Committee, Peterborough, UK. vi + 262pp.

British Library-in-Publication Data.
A catalogue record for this book is available from the British Library.

ISBN 1 873701 54 3

Designed and produced by The Nature Conservation Bureau Limited, 36 Kingfisher Court, Hambridge Road, Newbury, Berkshire, RG14 5SJ, UK.

Cover illustration by Charlotte Matthews.

Printed by Information Press, Oxford, UK.

Available from the Joint Nature Conservation Committee Publications Branch, Monkstone House, City Road, Peterborough, PE1 1JY, UK.

CONTENTS

ACKNOWLEDGEMENTS

The Editors would like to thank the many people who have provided information for the Directory, in particular those who compiled chapters or gave editorial assistance with some technical aspects of the work. (Where appropriate, individual acknowledgements are given at the end of each section.)

Special thanks to the Marine Conservation Society and other members of the Steering Group both past and present who provided information and advice on the production of the directory. We would also like to thank them for their time.

Steering Group Members (August 1991)

Dr Pat Doody   (Coastal Conservation Branch, JNCC)
Dr Chris Reid   (Department of the Environment, London)
Mr Henry Cleary   (Department of the Environment, London)
Dr John Gamble   (Scottish Office Agriculture and Fisheries Department)
Mr Brian Spencer   (Ministry of Agriculture, Fisheries and Food, Conwy)
Mr Colin Graham   (British Geological Survey, Edinburgh)
Dr Lennox Campbell   (Royal Society for the Protection of Birds, Sandy)
Mr Ray Woolmore   (Countryside Commission, Cheltenham)
Dr Sue Gubbay   (Marine Conservation Society, Ross-on-Wye)
Dr Roger Mitchell   (Marine Conservation Branch, JNCC)
Dr Steve Bolt   (Marine Conservation Branch, JNCC)
Dr Stephen Ward   (Nature Conservancy Council for Scotland)
Dr John Baxter   (Nature Conservancy Council for Scotland)
Dr Geoff Radley   (English Nature)
Mr Mark Tasker   (Seabirds Team, JNCC, Aberdeen)

NB the following changes of location have been noted:

Charlotte Johnston   Analytical and Environmental Services, Tyne and Wear
Barbara Smith   Scottish Natural Heritage, Golspie
Dan Legget   National Rivers Authority, Anglia Region, Peterborough

PREFACE

The first discussions between the Department of the Environment and the Nature Conservancy Council about the production of a directory of information on the North Sea coastal margin took place in 1989. These followed a suggestion from the UK within the North Sea Task Force (NSTF) that the assessment of the quality of the North Sea should include resources, habitats and species along the coastal margin. At that time the concept of coastal zone management, in the UK at least, was being discussed by public and voluntary bodies in detail for the first time.

The cornerstone of coastal zone management is the development of an integrated approach to coastal management. Achieving this requires recognition that the coastal zone includes both the terrestrial coast, estuaries and the shallow seas around the coast as well as the offshore marine environment. By extending the assessment of the quality of the North Sea to include the coastal margin, the UK facilitated a wider debate, in keeping with the concept of coastal zone management.

The first stage in the development of the approach adopted for the North Sea has involved the production of a summary document providing a directory of information for the whole coastline. It provides a description of the resource which can be assessed at a geographic scale in keeping with work of the North Sea Task Force, i.e. for the whole North Sea coastline.

It is important to note that this work does not attempt to provide an explanation of the importance of the habitats and species concentrations in the North Sea nor a rationale for the selection of important sites. It does, however, provide essential baseline resource information and reference to sources of data which are important for the development of coastal zone management policies.

The continuing work on the directory includes the production of a series of regional reports which will provide more detailed resources-based information. (Currently ten volumes are in preparation for the North Sea coast.) It is envisaged that, in their turn, these will aid the development of management policies which operate at the regional

level, as, for example, in the approaches to regional coastal protection strategies being encouraged by the Ministry of Agriculture, Fisheries and Food. The Coastal Zone Management picture is completed by the implementation of site-based management plans, which are being developed by Local Planning Authorities and English Nature, amongst others.

Throughout this book, and in the regional reports which are in preparation, an attempt is made to highlight some of the human activities which affect the coastal environment. However, this assessment is relatively superficial because of constraints on time and resources. A more detailed review, which matches the resource information with an assessment of the implications of human activity on that resource, will provide a much more accurate indication of issues and management needs. To some extent the Estuaries Review and its further development within the work of the JNCC Coastal Review Unit (see Chapter 8) will provide this assessment.

It is hoped that the other North Sea states will find this approach helpful to their own needs. To some extent the North Sea Task Force, whose responsibility it is to coordinate a programme of research and monitoring as part of the assessment of the state of health of the North Sea, provides an upper level of coordination which addresses one of the principle issues affecting the environment: pollution. By developing an integrated approach at geographically small levels, the management needs of other issues which impact at the coastal margin can be addressed. These initial stages in the development of wider information collection and collation provide an opportunity to develop a cascade of approaches to management which, it is hoped, will facilitate the appropriate level of response to particular problems.

I should like to thank Chris Reid, the UK North Sea Science Coordinator, for his foresight in initiating discussions and continuing support for these initiatives.

Dr J P Doody
Coastal Conservation Branch, JNCC

Chapter 1

INTRODUCTION

1.1 THE NORTH SEA

HISTORICAL BACKGROUND

The International Council for the Exploration of the Sea (ICES) was set up in 1902 to coordinate marine research on the north-east Atlantic, including the North Sea. The Council acts as a scientific advisory body to intergovernmental fishery management organisations and to the Oslo Commission for the Prevention of Marine Pollution by Dumping from Ships and Aircraft, and the Paris Commission for the Prevention of Marine Pollution from Land based Sources. In 1967 a working group was initiated by ICES to look at pollution in the North Sea. In 1983 a separate group of experts from North Sea states and from the Commission of the European Community compiled a report on the *Quality Status of the North Sea* for the International Conference on the Protection of the North Sea, Bremen 1984 (Newman & Agg 1988). This was the first Ministerial Conference for the North Sea and was followed three years later by a second conference which was held in London in 1987.

Two documents were produced as a result of this second Ministerial Conference – an assessment of the state of health of the North Sea, as a 'Quality Status Report' and a report on the oceanography of the North Sea. Ministers suggested at this conference that a special group – the North Sea Task Force – should be established to organise a coordinated programme of research and monitoring. At the Third Ministerial Conference on the North Sea (the Hague 1990) an initiative was developed that specifically targeted wildlife and habitat issues – Third International Conference on the Protection of the North Sea, the Hague, March 1990, Ministerial Declaration issued by the Department of the Environment of the United Kingdom, March 1990.

In recognition of the wide range of human activities carried out at the interface between land and sea and the consequent threats to this environment, it was suggested by the United Kingdom at the second meeting of the North Sea Task Force that an assessment of the natural resources, habitats and species which are present along the coastal margin should form part of the next Quality Status Report on the North Sea (Anon. 1990). It is envisaged that the North Sea Task Force should coordinate and evaluate research, monitoring and conservation of the coastal margin as a further contribution to a sub-regional approach in the study of the North Sea as a whole.

DEFINING THE AREA

The North Sea basin is a shallow horn shape with a deep trough (up to 600 m) on its eastern margin. The North Sea has a surface area of 575,000 km^2 and a volume of 47,000 km^3. The water body is subject to influences from the Atlantic Ocean in the north and to a limited extent through the narrow Strait of Dover in the south. It is further affected by terrestrial inputs from the surrounding lands since the region is one of the most populated in the world, and consequently domestic and industrial waste is fed into it from bordering countries.

Within this directory the area identified as North Sea includes part of the North Atlantic shoreline and the English Channel and concurs with that defined by Ministers for the 1984 and 1987 Ministerial Conferences. This area is taken as extending from 5°W in the north, which lies in Cape Wrath, Sutherland, to 5°W on the south coast, which falls near Falmouth in Cornwall. No offshore limit has been set and information on offshore geology and marine interests, amongst other data, covers a substantial area of the North Sea.

The North Sea boundary may be defined differently in other documents, often using that identified by the International Council for the Exploration of the Sea – the North Sea Sub Area IV. In the discussion of fisheries in the North Sea, the ICES boundary has been used, since most international fishery statistics relate to this and not to 5°W.

ORIGINS AND CONTENT OF THE DIRECTORY OF THE NORTH SEA COASTAL MARGIN

A review of information relating to the location of the coastal and marine habitats and communities, protected status of individual sites and species and the factors affecting conservation in the United Kingdom was produced by the Marine Conservation Society (MCS) in 1986. The report, which drew on research undertaken by the Nature Conservancy Council (NCC) since 1974, was revised and published as a *Coastal Directory for Marine Nature Conservation* (Gubbay 1988).

The directory prepared here is intended to bring together information held within the Joint Nature Conservation Committee (JNCC) and the country agencies, and where necessary from other organisations, to provide an expansion and update of the MCS directory and a comprehensive account of the maritime and marine interest of the North Sea coastal margin from a UK perspective. This has been achieved by compiling information into three broad areas:

i)   a description of the natural environment;

ii) the current protected status of coastal and marine habitats, communities and species;

iii) an indication of activities which have an effect on the North Sea coastal margin.

The Joint Nature Conservation Committee, English Nature and Scottish Natural Heritage hold a considerable amount of information on the maritime and marine environment. Information on the nature conservation interest of Sites of Special Scientific Interest, National Nature Reserves and other protected areas is being collated by the JNCC, as part of the development of a coastal information base on behalf of the country agencies.

An attempt is made throughout the document to describe each resource and to give some indication of its importance and the range of variation around the North Sea coast. Recognising that the coastal margin should not be considered in isolation, the directory includes an assessment of other offshore interests (habitats, conservation features and resources).

REGIONAL REPORTS

As a follow-up to this directory the JNCC is preparing a series of regional reports or almanacs. These will provide more detailed, local information than the directory. The regional almanacs will include information on geology, geomorphology, coastal habitats, the marine environment and species found within each defined region. There will also be more detail on the distribution of sites of nature conservation significance as well as more up to date information on survey work.

1.2   METHODS

At the outset of the project in 1990, a small steering group was established under the direction of Dr Pat Doody (Coastal Conservation Branch, JNCC), which included staff from within the Nature Conservancy Council plus representatives from the Department of the Environment, UK Fisheries Departments, the Marine Conservation Society and other interested organisations. The steering group felt that the directory should, in addition to identifying the distribution and extent of habitats and species, describe the main interest of each and give an indication of its protected status.

A draft of the directory was produced in August 1991 and circulated to a wide range of organisations and individuals for comment. Many of these responded with both detailed and general comments. The final design and editing of the directory, taking into account the comments made on the draft, was undertaken by the Nature Conservation Bureau Limited under contract from the JNCC.

The directory aims to highlight geographical variation and to provide an indication of the factors affecting the conservation value of the natural resource. In order to describe the main features which characterise the natural environment of the coastal and inshore zones of the North Sea, it has been necessary to consult a wide variety of data sources within the JNCC, English Nature, Scottish Natural Heritage and other organisations. An initial approach has also been made to specialists within specific fields to ascertain what other information is available. Much of the detail contained within the directory was obtained by extracting from databases and reports. Wherever possible, information has been taken from the most recently published material. In some cases it was necessary to extract information directly from survey sheets. The principal sources of data which were used to compile the directory are given at the end of each section. An extensive bibliography is included, which highlights more general texts and publications.

Using geological and geomorphological features as a baseline, the environmental resources of the North Sea coastal margin have been detailed in sections which deal with the major habitats and species following a standard format. Subheadings for the sections are given below:

❖   Introduction: a brief summary of subject and the information available

- ❖ Distribution of habitat/species
- ❖ Description of resource, including regional variation on the North Sea coast
- ❖ Important sites/protected status of resource
- ❖ Impacts: an indication of factors affecting the resource
- ❖ Sources of information.

1.3 DATA SOURCES

The *Coastal Directory*, produced by the Marine Conservation Society, has been used both as a source document and as a basis for the structure of this directory.

Much additional data was obtained from the Coastal Ecology Branch of the NCC which was established in 1979. This work was continued by the JNCC Coastal Conservation Branch after the NCC was split into separate country agencies in 1991. One of the functions of the branch was to coordinate a programme of research and survey in the field of terrestrial coastal conservation. A research programme was established, which aimed to describe the size, location and quality of the main coastal habitats in Great Britain (salt marshes, sand dunes, vegetated shingle and sea cliffs). A Coastal Resource database provided summarised information based on 1:50,000 maps of the location and size of the main habitat groupings, and was used as background for a number of projects including the surveys noted below and the work referred to in Chapter 4. The major coastal surveys carried out up to 1993 are described below. (Although the results of some of this work were only just being published at the time of writing, the data were available for inclusion in Chapter 4 of this report.)

The National Sand Dune Survey of Great Britain has provided a national inventory of the range and extent of sand dune habitats in Great Britain. This allows the interest of any particular site or group of sites to be placed in a national context. Surveys have been completed for all sand dunes in England and Wales and a selection of sites in Scotland. The results are currently being published. Individual Site Survey Reports have also been published for England, Scotland and Wales (see Section 4.3). The Survey information is also held on database.

Lancaster University has surveyed a number of sea cliff habitats to produce an inventory of the vegetation. Relatively few sites have been covered and a full scale survey has yet to be undertaken (see Section 4.2).

Cambridge University, under contract to the NCC and subsequently the JNCC, has carried out a survey of the vegetation of major shingle structures, to produce site reports and to review the applicability of the National Vegetation Classification to shingle communities (see Section 4.5).

The Saltmarsh Survey of Great Britain was set up in 1981 with the aim of describing the saltmarsh resource nationwide. This survey is complete and results are contained in a main report which summarises the national results, regional supplements and county reports (see Section 4.4).

Vegetation communities on the main coastal habitats are being reviewed as part of the National Vegetation Classification (NVC). Material dealing with coastal habitats was consulted in the preparation of the directory. This information will be published in the NVC series on British Plant Communities.

The Marine Nature Conservation Review was initiated in 1987 to review additional information and to survey marine habitats around the coast of Britain in order to assess the nature conservation importance of sites and to provide a fund of information on which to base advice. Literature and survey information from this project has been used in the preparation of Chapter 5 on Marine Habitats.

Information for Chapter 3 on the geology and geomorphology of the North Sea coast includes data provided from the Nature Conservancy Council's Geological Conservation Review (GCR) and the British Geological Survey, Natural Environment Research Council (NERC).

Ornithological data was originally supplied by the NCC Ornithological Branch and subsequently by JNCC's Offshore Animals Branch. This is often based on information compiled by the British Trust for Ornithology, the Wildfowl and Wetlands Trust, the Royal Society for the Protection of Birds, the Seabirds Group and others, as well as that gathered by the NCC and the JNCC themselves. A full description of sources is given in Section 7.2.

A review of the conservation interest of estuaries in Great Britain was commenced within the NCC and is being continued in the JNCC. Its results are discussed briefly in Chapter 8.

REFERENCES

ANON. 1990. *Ministerial Declaration of the Third International Conference on the Protection of the North Sea and Memorandum of Understanding on Small Cetaceans in the North Sea*. The Hague, Ministry of Transport and Public Works.

NEWMAN, P.J. & AGG, A.R. eds. 1988. *Cetaceans in the North Sea*. The Hague, Ministry of Transport and Public Works.

Chapter 2

INTRODUCTION TO NORTH SEA HABITATS

2.1 INTRODUCTION

The coastline of Great Britain extends to 18,843 km, of which 40% lies along the North Sea margin as defined above. This geographical area includes the island groups of Shetland and Orkney. Britain has the longest North Sea coastline of any of the eight surrounding countries.

The UK North Sea coastal margin is one of great physical contrasts, ranging from the north and east of Scotland which is predominantly rocky cliffs to the south-east of England which comprises essentially flat, sedimentary, eroding coastline. The variety of natural features sustains a very wide range of habitats of nature conservation importance (Fowler 1991). This chapter provides a summary of the main features of maritime and marine nature conservation significance on the United Kingdom's coastal margin.

2.2 HABITAT FORMATION

The great diversity of the landscape and wildlife features of the North Sea coastal margin is the product of many factors, the most fundamental of which is the underlying geology which forms the very fabric of the coasts. This ranges from resilient granite to erodible clays and gravels. The resulting coastline is actively being modified by erosion and deposition, the latter forming new sediments and landforms. These processes are driven by the energy of the sea, and by wind and rain. The development of vegetation and finally human activities further modify the landforms to produce the landscape of today.

Understanding these geomorphological processes is of great importance to the way in which we manage the coastline. The nature of the rock types and their reaction to forces of change are discussed more fully in Chapter 3. However, a brief review of the main factors affecting the development of the coastline will help set the scene for the descriptions which follow.

The most important factor governing how rapidly the evolution of the landscape takes place is the nature of the rock itself. The harder the rock, the more resilient it is to change. Hence the older, harder rocks of the north and north-east of Scotland appear to change least. However, there is a slow process of erosion caused by the action of rain accompanied by frost and the continuous battering from the sea. This results in the development of the precipitate cliffs which are the home to specialist vegetation types and nesting sea birds. Some of the material derived from this erosion is transported, together with additional material brought down from the upland by rivers and originating as remains of dead animals and other sea-borne material, to provide for the growth of new land elsewhere. This results in the presence of high, steep cliffs interspersed with small pocket beaches of pebbles and/or dunes which occur in the north of Scotland and south-west England.

Where the land is low-lying with larger amounts of sediment, as in the east coast firths (Dornoch Firth, Cromarty Firth and the Firth of Forth) greater accumulations of materials are evident. Morrich More (see Section 4.3) provides a particularly fine example of the way in which the landscape can evolve as a consequence of deposition of mobile sediment. Much of Scotland is rising as a result of the removal of the ice mass which occurred at the end of the last glaciation. (The weight of the ice depressed the land which 'rebounded' when the ice mass was removed, a process known as isostatic change, which has continued over the last 10,000 years or so.) Morrich More, over a period of 7,000 years, has developed as a sequence of dune ridges which have formed progressively seaward as the sand has accumulated and the land risen. Other areas of sand dunes are found further south, for example around the Tay estuary (Barry Budden and Tentsmuir Dune systems). Associated with these areas are saltmarshes (in the most sheltered sites) and shingle bars (in more exposed areas).

Change is much more prevalent in these low-lying areas. Culbin shingle bar for example (see

Section 4.5) has been moving progressively westwards for several hundred years. Recently, in only the last 5–10 years on the high level beach, sheltered by the bar, new accumulations of sand have helped create new sand dunes and saltmarshes. These examples illustrate the way in which change occurs over different time scales with the most recent events taking place over a period of a few years.

Further south the pattern of landscape continues as a sequence of cliffs interspersed with estuaries (albeit relatively small) into northern England. However, an abrupt change takes place south of Scarborough where the accumulation of more recent and often softer geological material outcrops on the coast. These sometimes extensive lengths of easily eroded rock, such as that in the Holderness coast, result in the development of a retreating coastline. The general sinking of land in the south-east of England today, relative to sea level, further contributes to this process.

The material from these eroding cliffs is transported in a generally southward direction and helps to build up the sedimentary habitats of the Humber Estuary, North Lincolnshire coast, the Wash and North Norfolk. In some ways the whole length of coast from Scarborough to Norfolk can be considered to be one huge geomorphological system.

Throughout this coastal area and further south including the Essex and North Kent coast, resilient cliffs are virtually absent (the major exception is Flamborough Head, an outcrop of limestone). The flat landscape, particularly the fens of East Anglia, has been formed as a result of the natural accretion of sediment in response to changes in relative sea level. Human activities have taken advantage of the natural tendency of the land to accrete during periods when relative sea level has fallen to enclose the tidal land. This has left a much narrower intertidal zone in which natural geomorphological processes of erosion and deposition can take place. This appears to have disrupted the natural systems and a high proportion of the coastline is 'protected' by man-made structures (see Chapter 11), designed to prevent erosion, transport and deposition of material. It is beginning to be recognised that this interference has not always been in the best interest of human use of these areas and has had adverse environmental consequences. In addition, because relative sea level is rising, much of the south and east coasts is at risk from flooding and erosion. This has in its turn led to further demands for protection. It is not clear what the ultimate effect of this disruption of the geomorphological systems will be, but it is increasingly being recognised that understanding

their operation within sedimentary cells is important for effective management against land loss due to erosion and flooding.

2.3 SALTMARSHES

The North Sea coast has approximately 22,300 ha of saltmarsh out of a British total of 45,337 ha. The largest expanses of saltmarsh in Britain are concentrated around the Greater Thames estuary in Essex and Kent, with extensive areas around the Wash, the north Norfolk coast and in the Solent.

Saltmarsh vegetation develops between mean low water of spring tides and mean high water of spring tides where there is an accumulation of fine sediment. Some degree of shelter is required for this accumulation, so saltmarshes are found in inlets, estuaries and behind barrier islands or spits. Examples of each are found on the North Sea coast; the saltmarshes behind the barren islands on the north Norfolk coast are among the finest in Europe. In the north, Dornoch Firth provides some of the most important dunes/saltmarsh transitions with important populations of northern saltmarsh communities with *Blysmus rufus*. Plants that grow in saltmarshes have to tolerate high and often changing soil salinities as well as regular immersion in sea water. Many of the plants that are adapted to these stressful conditions are found nowhere else. Of a total of 29 rare and scarce plant species recorded from British saltmarshes, 25 occur within the North Sea coastal margin.

The saltmarshes of the North Sea coast provide a valuable habitat for feeding and breeding birds. In winter large numbers of grazing wildfowl such as wigeon feed upon saltmarsh grass, while birds such as twite and linnets feed upon the seeds of saltmarsh plants. The saltmarshes of the Wash, for instance, are estimated to attract the largest flocks of twite in Britain, with an estimated 26,000–32,000 birds. The tidal creeks that cross most saltmarshes are favoured feeding places for wading birds such as curlew and for ducks such as teal. In summer, saltmarshes provide nest sites for a variety of birds; the highest densities of breeding redshank in Britain have been recorded from the saltmarshes of the Solent and the Thames estuary. Saltmarshes also support some of the largest breeding black-headed gull colonies in Britain, with large colonies found in the Solent, around the Thames estuary and along the north Norfolk coast. This is a difficult habitat for birds to breed in, as tidal inundation can destroy large numbers of nests. The higher upper level saltmarshes, which receive less frequent inundation, are consequently of greatest value to nesting birds.

Plate 1
Warham saltmarsh, North
Norfolk, showing extensive
areas of sea-lavender
Limonium vulgare. The
complex mosaic of ungrazed
mid-upper marsh
communities supports
breeding (nesting) birds and
is rich in invertebrates.
Photo: J.P. Doody.

The invertebrate fauna of saltmarshes is composed of a mix of terrestrial, freshwater and marine species. Due to their stressful saline environment, saltmarshes tend to have a rather low faunal diversity. Those species that have adapted to this habitat are, however, quite specialised and often have a very localised distribution. Saltmarshes consequently contain numerous species of invertebrate that are considered to be rare and endangered. For example, the sea wormwood *Artemisia maritima*, a shrubby plant of saltmarshes, hosts the larvae of the scarce pug moth *Eupithecia extensaria* ssp. *occidua*, a rare species confined to only a few saltmarshes in Norfolk, Lincolnshire, Humberside and Essex.

By virtue of their high productivity in terms of biomass, some saltmarshes contribute a primary source of material for the complex food chains within an estuary. This is of particular importance to the large numbers of migratory wildfowl and wading birds which are attracted to overwinter on the highly productive mudflats of the North Sea coast.

Saltmarshes have traditionally been lost to enclosure and conversion to agriculture, although this threat has receded in recent years. They continue to be affected by various forms of land claim development through tipping and the building of roads, marinas and housing. The construction of tidal barrages and the rise in sea level predicted as a consequence of global warming also pose a threat to many of the North Sea's saltmarshes. As the evidence from Essex and north Kent shows, saltmarsh erosion here can be attributed partly to sea level rise, which is currently approximately 5 mm per year.

2.4 SAND DUNES

Sand dunes are a rare and specialised habitat. Great Britain contains approximately 56,000 ha of dunes, of which some 25,000 ha lie along the North Sea. These are scattered widely, but with particular concentrations on the Moray Firth, the Northumberland, Lincolnshire and Humberside coasts and along the north Norfolk coast between the Wash and Cromer.

Dune formation occurs where a supply of dry, wind-blown sand is trapped by an obstacle such as a shingle ridge, tidal litter or vegetation. This process often takes place above a sand flat which is exposed sufficiently at low tide for the surface layer of sand to dry out. Sand that is then moved from the upper, dry zone may be replenished by wave action on the lower shore. The dunes of the North Sea coast are characterised by the creation of front shore sand ridges formed by the opposing forces of prevailing and dominant winds which occur as offshore and onshore winds, respectively. The dunes of the west of Britain and Ireland, by contrast, extend considerable distances inland, as the prevailing winds are also the dominant ones.

The flora of dunes contains a number of specialist and often scarce species that are able to tolerate the difficult conditions for plant growth in this mobile, nutrient-poor and highly water stressed environment. The type of vegetation that develops on dunes is dependent upon the age of the dune surface and the calcium carbonate content of the beach sand. Sandwich Bay in Kent is a good example of a North Sea coast calcareous dune system, but the majority of acid dune systems and several of the largest of these in the UK are found fringing the North Sea, probably reflecting the relative lack of shell sand here. Examples include those at Morrich (Scotland), Winterton (East Anglia) and Studland (Dorset).

Some dunes also provide important breeding sites for birds, notably eider duck in north-east Scotland and shelduck throughout Britain. The beaches and bare, mobile dune ridges can also be important for nesting gulls and colonies of terns. The warm, dry, open sandy habitat provided by the dunes of the south and east of the North Sea coast are favoured by some of our rarest reptiles and amphibians, such as the sand lizard, the smooth snake and the natterjack toad. This same combination of physical features attracts a diverse and specialist insect fauna, particularly on the south coast. This fauna is characterised by the abundance of rare and endangered species of burrowing bees and wasps.

In the past, large areas of dune habitat have been lost to afforestation, usually with introduced species of pine. In more recent years, dunes have been threatened by housing, recreation, industry and intensive agriculture, including overgrazing. A more insidious threat comes from the rise in sea level, particularly in the south-east, leading to an increase in wave attack and dune erosion. Few dunes in Britain are now actively prograding (creating new dunes to the seaward of existing ones). Most appear to be fossilised in their present location or retreating landwards.

2.5 COASTAL GRAZING MARSHES

Coastal grazing marshes are areas of flat, low-lying grassland drained by a network of brackish or freshwater drainage ditches. Most originated through the enclosure of estuarine saltmarsh for agricultural purposes by the construction of an embankment. The most extensive areas of grazing marsh are found in south-east England on the coasts

Plate 2
The sand dune system which forms Scolt Head, a National Nature Reserve on the north Norfolk coast, protects the coastline and harbour behind it and enables a saltmarsh to become established away from the full force of the North Sea.
Photo: J.P. Doody.

Plate 3
The Swale, Kent, is an important area of coastal grazing marsh. Arable intensification can not only result in a loss of much of the grassland interest of this habitat, but frequently also degrades the nature conservation importance of the drainage ditches through agricultural run-off and eutrophication.
Photo: J.P. Doody.

of Essex and north Kent, though they also occur in small areas around all our major estuaries.

The flora of these grasslands is not generally species-rich but contains an abundance of one or two scarce species such as hairy buttercup *Ranunculus sardous* and strawberry clover *Trifolium fragiferum* which gives these grasslands a distinctive appearance. In the more saline-influenced parts, species of the upper saltmarsh can be found which may be rare or absent from the adjoining tidal saltmarsh. The ditch system of grazing marshes can be extremely important, containing large numbers of rare and endangered plants and animals. The species diversity of these is often increased by gradations from brackish to fresh water along the ditches. Surveys have shown that for some grazing marsh ditch systems, up to 22% of the invertebrate species identified were nationally rare or scarce.

Grazing marshes are also important for a number of breeding birds including several rare species afforded protection under the Wildlife and Countryside Act. In addition, they act as valuable winter roosts and feeding sites for internationally important numbers of waterfowl.

In recent decades, coastal grazing marshes have come under increasing pressure from improved deep drainage schemes and conversion to arable or intensive grassland management, while other large areas have been lost to industrial and residential developments. These pressures have resulted in the considerable reduction in the overall extent of grazing marsh in many parts of the country, including an overall loss of 60% of this habitat on the Thames Estuary. In other grazing marshes, the aquatic ditch flora has declined due to pollution of water supplies, with excess nutrients from sewage discharges and agricultural run-off being the most likely cause. The protection of the surviving areas of high quality grazing marshes in Britain is thus an urgent priority.

2.6   COASTAL SALINE LAGOONS

Until recently, saline lagoons were poorly understood, but some comprehensive surveys undertaken during the 1980s have revealed the importance of these coastal habitats. Saline lagoons in Britain occur mainly on the east and south coasts. They consist of shallow, open bodies of brackish or saline water, partially separated from the adjacent sea by shingle, sand or artificial structures such as a sea wall or tidal sill. Although all coastal saline lagoons retain water at low tide, they exchange water with the sea via percolation, overtopping or via a direct inlet to the sea.

Some 220 lagoons have been identified from the coast of Britain, although only fourteen are considered to be of importance to nature conservation, all of which occur on the North Sea coastal margin. The largest and most notable of these is the Fleet, in Dorset. Thirty-eight species of plant and animal have been defined as being more characteristic of saline lagoons than of freshwater, estuarine brackish water or the sea. This includes a total of ten species protected under the Wildlife and Countryside Act, 1981. Lagoons are a priority habitat under the EC Habitats Directive (see section 10.2).

Coastal saline lagoons are susceptible to damage from the construction of coastal defences, isolation from the sea to form freshwater lakes and dredging to form marinas and harbours. They are also particularly vulnerable to pollution. In the north Atlantic natural saline lagoons are a relatively short-lived coastal feature as they go through the natural processes of succession to become freshwater lakes, fen or carr woodland. New lagoon formation is now very restricted due to the lack of suitable sites, and hence the natural rate of lagoon creation will inevitably be insufficient to replace those that are lost. Whereas man-made coastal saline ponds are susceptible to damage by development and engineering works, they are more easily protected from the natural processes of coastal habitat succession. Such lagoons can also be artificially created and, if suitably managed, form a habitat which is indistinguishable from the naturally formed lagoon.

2.7 SHINGLE

Shingle beaches are widespread around the coast of Britain, but vegetated shingle structures are rare, covering only some 4,200 ha. Shingle structures develop on high energy coasts, and many are highly mobile. Some shingle beaches formed at the end of the last Ice Age and are now covered in sand dunes while other shingle areas are associated with saltmarshes and other coastal habitats such as saline lagoons.

Five of the seven nationally important British shingle structures occur on the North Sea coast. Dungeness, Kent, is perhaps the largest shingle structure in Europe and, despite extensive gravel quarrying, is still of international importance for its wildlife.

As with saltmarshes and dunes, shingle is an environment hostile to the establishment of plants. Those that do manage to survive the nutrient-poor, often disturbed and arid conditions found on shingle beaches, are very specialised and virtually confined to this habitat. Five nationally rare and scarce plant species are associated with shingle on the North Sea coastal margin, including the little-Robin *Geranium purpureum* ssp. *forsteri,* which is confined to shingle beaches in the Solent, and the scarce oysterplant *Mertensia maritima*, found at Hunterston Sands, one of a small number of sites in Scotland.

Plate 4
Vegetated shingle on the cuspate shingle foreland at Dungeness, Kent. This is the single most important shingle feature in the British Isles (notable for its plant communities, invertebrates and geomorphology) and has been extensively studied. The site has suffered from gravel extraction, vehicle damage associated with military activity and the development of the power stations (shown in the background). Beach feeding is necessary to protect developments at this site, including the nuclear power station.
Photo: J.P. Doody.

Plate 5
The sea cliffs of the Scottish North Sea coast support internationally important seabird colonies and examples of vegetation types which are tolerant of almost continual wetting by salt spray. Where natural habitats are still present on the cliff-top, as is the case here at Foulsheugh in north-east Scotland, examples of the full zonation from maritime to terrestrial vegetation can still be found, although agricultural intensification has truncated this zonation along many other sections of coast.
Photo: J.P. Doody.

The invertebrate value of shingle structures is largely associated with the specialist flora. The invertebrate fauna consequently contains a number of species which are confined to this habitat. For example, the rare micro-moth *Aethes margarotana* lives in the roots of the sea holly *Eryngium maritimum* (also found on mobile dunes), itself a scarce plant, and is now only known from the shingle beach at Thorpeness, Suffolk.

The nature conservation importance of stable vegetated shingle structures lies in their unique plant communities. Most notable among these are lichen-dominated communities and the mostly single-species stands of plants adapted to growing just above the most mobile parts of the shore. The larger shingle structures, such as Orfordness (East Anglia) and Chesil Beach (Dorset) are also of considerable geomorphological importance.

The biggest threat to important vegetated shingle sites is from disturbance of the surface shingle. The tracks from one passage of a vehicle over a long-established area of shingle vegetation will remain visible indefinitely. Extraction of shingle for construction and coast defences destroys shingle features and its vegetation. As with other sedimentary habitats, understanding of the origins and development of each site is essential if long-term damage is not to be caused by inappropriate coastal 'protection' measures.

2.8   SEA CLIFFS

Along the North Sea coastal margin there are approximately 850 km of cliffs over 20 m in height (11% of the North Sea coastline), the majority along the coast of northern Scotland. The form and height of these cliffs depends upon the type of rock of which they are composed.

'Hard' rock cliffs, comprised of granite, sandstone or limestone, are resistant to wave attack and weather only slowly. These characteristics create near-vertical cliffs where only ledges or crevices that accumulate soil can support vegetation. By contrast, cliffs composed of sand, clays and marls regularly erode and slump; these 'soft' rock cliffs are predominantly found on the south and east coasts of Britain, with examples including Folkestone Warren in Kent and the Axmouth to Lyme Regis section of the western Channel coast. They are subject to far greater rates of erosion, and it is this which determines the ability of plants to colonise them. Although sometimes forming vertical bare cliff faces, soft rock cliffs often form a vegetated coastal slope.

The vegetation that develops on hard rock cliffs is determined by the underlying rock type (acidic or calcareous) and the degree of exposure, and consists of a relatively stable vegetation on thin soils which shows a zonation from exposed maritime vegetation, with salt-tolerant species, to more terrestrial vegetation of heathland or calcareous grassland. In the north the hard rocks and extreme exposure have resulted in the development of extensive maritime heath, notably at Strathy Point and on Orkney, where some of the most important sites occur. On softer cliffs, exposure is less of an influence and the vegetation that develops is often inland in nature. Despite this, a rich diversity of plant communities can develop in response to changes in rock type, the presence of cliff face spring lines and the stability of the cliff face.

Of a total of twelve nationally rare and scarce plant species that are confined to the coastal cliffs in Britain, seven are found along the North Sea coastal margin.

The sea cliffs of the North Sea coastal margin of Britain are internationally important for their colonies of nesting sea birds and provide nest sites for over one-tenth of the world's population of gannets and razorbills and more than 1% of the world's population of guillemots, fulmars, kittiwakes and puffins. These colonies are mainly concentrated in the north, but include an important site at Bempton Cliffs in east Yorkshire. Sea cliffs also provide important nest sites for birds of prey such as the peregrine falcon.

Cliff caves on the south coast are important for roosting and hibernating bats including some, such as the greater horseshoe bat, which are among Britain's most endangered species. Although not comprehensively studied, the invertebrate fauna of cliffs also contains a number of nationally rare and notable species. On the warm cliffs of the south coast, a variety of habitats favouring specialist insect species occur, including the only location for the Glanville fritillary butterfly *Melitaea cinxia* in Britain.

The hard cliffs of the North Sea are subject to few threats. In places, the zonation from maritime to terrestrial vegetation has been truncated by cultivation of cliff-top vegetation. On the south coast other areas of cliff-top grassland have suffered a decline in species diversity due to a lack of grazing pressure from domestic stock. On some cliffs disturbance to cliff-nesting birds from recreational activities such as abseiling and rock climbing can have an impact. Soft rock cliffs tend to be adversely affected mainly by coastal protection works. These stabilise the foot of naturally eroding cliff faces, resulting in a loss of scientifically important rock exposures and also the plant and insect communities which are dependent upon the unstable cliff face environment.

2.9   COASTAL WOODLANDS

Wooded coastlines are rare on the North Sea coast. Locations where woodland (particularly ancient, semi-natural woodland) extends down to the sea are

Plate 6
Coastal woodland at Curbridge, on the Hamble Estuary, Hampshire. Here mature woodland rises steeply from reedbeds, saltmarsh and tidal mudflats. This is a rare example of a location where the natural transition still exists between woodland and marine or estuarine conditions, and is a Hampshire Wildlife Trust Reserve.
Photo: D. Bright.

Plate 7
Chalk cliffs are a very
characteristic feature of the
English North Sea coast.
Coastal chalk outcrops
extend intermittently from
Dorset in the south-west,
through the well-known
white cliffs of Dover in Kent,
to this northernmost outlier
at Flamborough Head, North
Humberside. The chalk is
very hard here and forms
extensive wave-cut platforms
with rockpools off the tip of
the Headland, as seen at
Thornwick Nab in the
foreground, large caves, and
very high cliffs at Bempton,
in the distance. The Bempton
cliffs are well-known for
their breeding sea birds, and
are the only mainland gannet
colony in Britain.
Photo: S.L. Fowler.

concentrated around the estuaries and along soft, eroding earth cliffs of the south coast, in particular the Solent. These woodlands tend to be of great antiquity, being located on nutrient-poor clays and gravels that appear never to have been cleared for agriculture. They support an extremely rich woodland flora, including many species indicative of ancient woodland such as the wild service-tree *Sorbus torminalis* and nationally scarce species such as the narrow-leaved lungwort *Pulmonaria longifolia*.

The natural transition from these woodlands to swamp and saltmarsh formerly present on the flat alluvial plains of East Anglia has been lost as a result of land enclosure and is now a very uncommon feature along the North Sea coastal margin. Where it does exist, it provides a valuable habitat for a variety of rare and uncommon species of insect, including a very diverse hoverfly fauna.

2.10 MARINE HABITATS

The British North Sea coast and inshore waters are of particular environmental importance within Europe because of their biogeographical location and high habitat and biological diversity. The British Isles lie across three major marine biogeographic provinces; centred within the Boreal (cold temperate) province, but also extending to the boundaries of both the Lusitanean (warm temperate) and the Boreal-Arctic provinces in the south-west of England and Shetland/north-east mainland Britain respectively. This biogeographic position results in the occurrence of characteristic species of the northern and southern provinces reaching the limits of their geographical range on the British coast; frequently in the English Channel or on the east coasts of Scotland and England.

The coast and inshore waters also have a high habitat diversity, including the exposed, rocky shores and deep, sheltered sea lochs and voes of northern Scotland, numerous estuaries on the east and south coasts, the fully marine inlets and harbours of the south-west and the English chalk coasts of the south and east. As a result of these factors, Britain has the most diverse and biologically rich coastline of all the North Sea countries.

2.11 ROCKY COASTLINES

Rocky shores and cliffs along the North Sea coast are mainly confined to the northern and southern areas of Britain. They range in character from the extremely wave-exposed coasts of Orkney, Shetland and south-west England to the very sheltered margins of the Shetland voes and marine inlets in south-west England. Unusual rocky shore features include large caves (such as those of Flamborough Head), geos in the north-east, rock pools and underboulder habitats. All these increase the diversity of rocky shore communities and often hold marine species more commonly recorded below the low water mark.

About 16–20% of the world population of grey seals breed on the British North Sea coast, where they tend to be confined to exposed rocky coasts, with a few exceptions where small colonies are associated with sandbanks in estuaries. The Orkneys and the Farne Islands hold particularly important colonies of this species, which is steadily increasing in numbers in Britain. Few sightings are made of grey seals between Norfolk and Cornwall.

Common seals also pup on rocky shores in the Northern Isles, with Orkney holding the largest breeding population on the coast (following the phocine distemper epidemic). The British North Sea coast as a whole supports about 3% of the world population of this species. It is only very rarely recorded south of Essex or in the Channel.

The more exposed and remote rocky coasts of the North Sea margin are not usually subject to many impacts. Oil pollution poses a potential threat and there may be an immediate impact on seabird and marine mammal populations, as was illustrated by the *Braer* oil spill on Shetland in January 1993. At more sheltered sites, oil pollution and other impacts such as contamination by diffuse pollutants and sewage outfalls, dumping, collection of bait or food species and coastal development and protection works have a greater effect on marine flora and fauna. Such impacts tend to be more widespread in the densely populated east and south where very few areas of coast are not affected to some extent by development or other activities.

2.12 SEDIMENT COASTS AND ESTUARIES

The British North Sea margin includes a very wide range of sediment habitats, from the extremely sheltered muds of voes, estuaries and harbours, to the coarse sands and shingles of the open coast. The richness of the associated marine communities decreases both with increasing exposure to wave action and falling salinity. The richest shores are those of the fully saline sheltered marine inlets of the south-west, which have a wide range of habitats and species, including some Lusitanean species near the edge of their range, and beds of eelgrass. In contrast, very clean, coarse sands and gravels on open coasts support a very sparse fauna.

Muddy shores have a very high biomass of invertebrate infauna, even where the species diversity is low in estuaries, and many sites are of national and international importance for their breeding, migrating and wintering coastal wading

Plate 8
Mud and sand banks, sculpted by the falling tide, seen during low water in the Moray Firth near Ardersier, Scotland. The Moray Firth is a very important over-wintering site for wading birds, which are dependent upon the invertebrates of these muddy sediments for food, and also a significant site for breeding birds in saltmarsh and grassland habitats. The Firth supports over 20,000 waterfowl each January and its national and international importance for bird conservation is recognised by its inclusion in the site network of Ramsar and Special Protection Areas. *Photo: R. Mitchell.*

Plate 9
Grazed kelp stipes *Laminaria hyperborea* and bedrock dominated by pink encrusting coralline algae, photographed at the Farne Islands, Northumberland. This community is very characteristic of shallow sublittoral rock on the British North Sea coast, where heavy grazing by sea urchins *Echinus esculentus* and molluscs prevents the establishment of a diverse community of foliose algae and sessile fauna.
Photo: S. Hiscock.

birds and wildfowl populations (see Section 7.2). These sites are particularly valuable in winter when the invertebrates of many other North Sea shores are made inaccessible by icing in cold weather. The most important wader wintering site is the Wash, on the east coast, but others of international importance include Scottish firths in the north-east, the Humber Estuary, smaller estuaries in Suffolk, Essex and North Kent, and the Solent. The south-eastern sites are the most important staging areas during migration. In total, the British North Sea coast is used by about 40% of the wading bird population which winters along the Atlantic shores of Europe (60% of those which overwinter in Britain). It also supports 16% of the north-west European population of wintering wildfowl (25% of those overwintering in Britain).

The Wash, Dornoch Firth and north Norfolk coast support populations of most of the species of wader found on the British North Sea coast. Few wildfowl breed on the coast, other than eider and shelduck. There are some important breeding colonies of common and grey seals on east coast sediment shores, including common seals in the Wash (the most important site for this species prior to the phocine distemper epidemic).

The sheltered sediment shores of estuaries and other inlets, particularly in the densely populated east and south, are frequently sites targeted for coastal development, whether for industries, ports, agricultural improvement or urban and recreational purposes. Land claim is the single largest source of habitat loss and has reduced the local extent of sediment shores, habitats and species on the North Sea coast. Associated impacts include pollution from onshore industries, marinas and domestic sources, maintenance dredging and dumping of spoil, aggregate extraction onshore or nearshore, construction of barrages, and coastal defence works. Pollutants, including oil spills, are very slow to disperse from sheltered sediment shores. Fisheries for bivalve molluscs and bait digging are examples of other activities commonly occurring on sediment coasts. Overall, the most important sheltered sediment shores of the North Sea coastal margin are targeted by the greatest range of human activities.

2.13 SUBLITTORAL ECOSYSTEMS AND OFFSHORE AREAS

A wide range of sublittoral rocky and sediment habitats have been recorded from the nearshore waters of the British North Sea coast, but surveys are still underway to complete the task of describing the marine ecosystems around the coast, identifying sites of nature conservation

15

importance and assessing the impacts on these ecosystems and sites, as described in following sections. The offshore communities of the North Sea are also reviewed from the literature. No attempt is made to summarise these in this introductory chapter, but it is apparent that they are extremely diverse and that the offshore areas are among the most productive in the world. As with inshore areas, this diversity and high biomass of marine life supports internationally important bird and marine mammal populations as well as extremely valuable fisheries, the latter heavily exploited by all bordering countries.

Most offshore and nearshore areas of the North Sea are regularly fished, with effects on target and non-target species, marine habitats and the ecosystem as a whole. Yields are falling in many fisheries.

Other important activities in offshore areas include oil and gas extraction, waste disposal and aggregate dredging. In contrast to fisheries, these are restricted to relatively small areas, but can result in pollution with a more widespread effect. Nutrient enrichment from land-based and atmospheric sources may be responsible for the increased frequency and extent of plankton blooms at sea and in coastal areas.

ACKNOWLEDGEMENTS

This chapter was produced by Jonathan Cox (coastal habitats) and Sarah Fowler (marine habitats), with additional contributions by Pat Doody.

REFERENCE

FOWLER, S.L. 1991. Conservation of the coastal and estuarine zones of the North Sea. *Ocean and Shoreline Management*, **16**: 349-358.

Chapter 3

GEOLOGY AND GEOMORPHOLOGY

3.1 INTRODUCTION

To appreciate the general geology and geo-morphology of the North Sea coastal margin it is necessary to review the geological history of Britain.

The oldest rocks in Britain are of the Precambrian age (2,800–700 million years ago) and consist of strongly metamorphosed sediments and igneous rocks. Subsequently, the Caledonian Orogeny (500–380 million years ago) folded the thick pile of Cambrian to Silurian sediments to produce mountains in north and central Wales, the Lake District and Scotland with a structural grain in a south-west/north-east direction. In Scotland, terrestrial deposition of Old Red Sandstone followed during the Devonian Period (405–355 million years ago). The sediments have not been strongly metamorphosed, particularly in the Orkneys and the north-east Scottish coast. In south-west England the Devonian marine sediments were folded and metamorphosed during the later Hercynian Orogeny.

After the Caledonian Orogeny the Carboniferous Period (355–290 million years ago) saw deposition of limestone and deltaic sediments, with marine sediments in south-west England. This produced extensive Carboniferous Limestone Coal Measures which are presently exposed roughly north-west of a line from the Tees to the Exe rivers. These Carboniferous rocks are exposed on the coast between the Tees and Scottish borders and along the margins of the Firth of Forth. Simultaneously the Hercynian Orogeny folded rocks in south-west England to produce the typical east/west 'Variscan' structural grain of the area. The folding metamorphosed the sediments and led to emplacement of granites to produce typical 'hard' rock coasts along the south-west coast of England between Falmouth Bay and the Exe.

During Permian and Triassic times (290–205 million years ago) deposits of thick red sandstone and mudstone were laid down. These 'New Red Sandstones' were laid down by wind (aeolian) and water (fluviatile) processes in terrestrial conditions. The sediments are exposed on the coast approximately between the Exe and Bridport and around the mouth of the Tees.

The Jurassic Period (205–135 million years ago) saw fluctuating sea levels and deposition of marine, semi-marine and lagoonal limestones and clays. During the Cretaceous Period (135–65 million years ago), Wealden clays and sands were laid down, and are succeeded by the Cretaceous Chalk and Greensand which were deposited in shallow seas. Jurassic and Cretaceous rocks form 'soft' rock coasts whose structural grain is locally determined by folding associated with the later Alpine Orogeny. This orogeny tilted and folded the Tertiary fluvio-marine deposits of south-east England into the typical east/west 'Alpine' structural grain.

The London and Hampshire depositional basins were formed during the early Tertiary and the associated uplift of the Weald led to erosion of the rocks in its core.

The sequence of folded Jurassic, Cretaceous and Tertiary sediments form the coast from Bridport to the Thames and from Flamborough to the Tees. Along the intervening section of the coast these rocks are marked by a covering of more recent Quaternary deposits.

Most of the cliffs of Holderness, Lincolnshire and Norfolk were formed by glacial deposits laid down in the Quaternary Period. During this period, advancing glaciers eroded the underlying rocks to produce many of the land forms along the coastal margin of the North Sea, north of Lowestoft approximately. Many of these landforms are formed of the deposits, till or boulder clay, that were deposited at the base of the flowing ice sheets or left when they melted and retreated.

The geological development of Britain plays an important role in determining the form and scale of the present coastal margin. The structural grain and strength of the rocks are important factors controlling the detail of the coastal morphology, but the gross form of the coast is determined by the degree of uplift, or subsidence, which it has suffered over the last few million years. Where uplift has been substantial, the modern coastal processes have

Figure 3.1.1
Geological timescale.

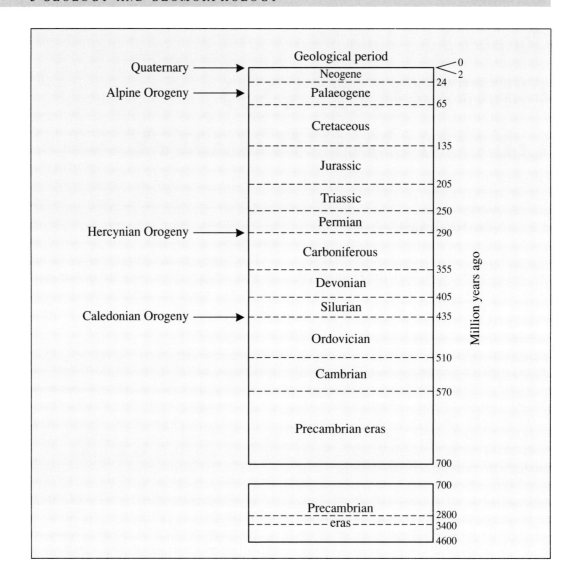

incised the coastal margin to form steep cliffs, like the Chalk cliffs of Sussex, but where the coast is subsiding, such as in the Thames Estuary, cliffs are absent or very low.

The present geomorphology of the coastal margin is therefore largely a function of its inherited geological history which may be made up of a number of episodes, each of which has a distinctive imprint on the form of the modern coast (Figure 3.1.1).

The simplest subdivision of the coast is into those formed of 'soft' and 'hard' rocks. These terms are used subjectively, but form a useful means to classify the coasts of the North Sea margin. In general terms, hard rocks are classified as pre-Permian rocks and soft rocks as post-Permian rocks. However, notable exceptions must be borne in mind. For example, some of the post-Permian rocks — the Jurassic limestones — are hard and durable, and where they are exposed at the coast may form steep cliffs.

3.2 SOFT ROCK CLIFFS

INTRODUCTION

When considering the geomorphology of the coastline, the term 'soft rock cliff' does not relate to a strictly geological distinction, but to the physical properties (mainly strength) and reaction to the processes of marine erosion. Along the North Sea coastal margin soft rock cliffs are mainly formed of post-Triassic sedimentary rocks.

Soft rock cliffs are subject to high erosion rates as a result of failure by flowing, slipping or slumping. Coastal wave processes remove the debris from the cliff base and also directly erode the cliff. Quaternary deposits, which are the most susceptible to erosion, account for the greatest length of soft rock cliffs on the North Sea Coastal Margin. In some areas the cliffs are formed of material of variable 'softness'. Where softer sediment underlies harder sediment, mass movement processes are enhanced; where softer sediment overlies harder sediment a distinct cliff morphology may be formed.

Distribution of soft rock cliffs along the North Sea coastal margin is shown in Figure 3.2.1.

SOFT ROCK CLIFF PROCESSES

There is no precise definition in terms of strength or geological age of the rocks and sediments that form soft rock cliffs. They erode rapidly, but both the rate of erosion and their physical strength may vary spatially and temporally (depending on external factors). The cliffs of Holderness may flow and slip under saturated winter conditions but undergo block failure by way of tension crack development in summer (Valentin 1954).

Mass movement processes are normally associated with soft rock cliffs. Failures are directly linked to differences in permeability, rock strength (hard over soft), or to where bedding or joint planes in the rocks dip seawards and readily facilitate sliding (Trenhaile 1987).

Slides tend to occur over bedding planes, as at Newhaven within the well-bedded Woolwich and Reading beds and the Thanet Sands. This location also demonstrates the importance of cliff toe erosion. The building of Newhaven Jetty caused the development of a wider, stable beach and protected the cliff toe. This stabilised the cliff and further failure was precluded. Conversely, at Folkestone Warren longshore drift was intercepted by the construction of a harbour, leading to beach depletion and cliff toe erosion. This enhanced the cliff failure through a series of rotational slips within the Chalk and Upper Greensand which overlay the saturated Gault Clay.

Folkestone Warren and Ventnor on the Isle of Wight are classic examples of cliffs that are as strong as their weakest component (Trenhaile 1987). At these locations water permeates and percolates through the Chalk and Greensand down to the impervious Gault Clay. The boundary between the Greensand and the Gault Clay becomes saturated and failure takes place through rotational slips. Tides may also influence rock failures by increasing pore water pressures, or actually buoying up the cliff toe at high tide to generate a slip plane. Slip planes also develop along bedding planes between different lithologies of Liassic rocks in Lyme Bay and along the North Yorkshire coast (Steers 1948). The gently dipping bedding planes form slip planes and this can produce a stepped profile in the cliffs.

Soft rock cliffs do not tend to develop long-term equilibrium forms where the material is semi-homogeneous, as in cliffs formed on glacially deposited sediments (Guilcher 1958). The glacial deposits that are eroded into cliffs a few metres high in Norfolk and Holderness are all being rapidly eroded and are highly unstable. However, there may be a short-term dynamic equilibrium of cliff profile over a period of a century (Chambers 1976) involving failure, removal of the material and shore platform lowering to reproduce the original profile. Many bays are incised into soft rock and have a soft rock cliffed surround which, in many areas, is unstable. At Robin Hood's Bay in North Yorkshire the erosion rate in the bay backed by till cliff is 2–3 times that of the Jurassic rock headlands (Agar 1960), indicating that erosional equilibrium has not yet been achieved. If an equilibrium had been reached, the retreat rate of the headlands and till cliff would be similar.

In North Yorkshire there are soft rock cliffs in till overlying harder rock cliffs formed of Jurassic well-bedded shale, limestone and sandstone. Here the harder rocks control the erosion rate and the softer rocks above maintain their natural angle of repose of 45° (Steers 1969). This forms a bevelled profile to the cliff which is maintained over time. The upper part of the profile is controlled mainly by subaerial erosion and not coastal erosion.

Coastal processes are the key to recurrent failures by enabling the cliff to steepen, and the steeper the cliff, the more prone it is to failure. Once failed, the fallen cliff material is re-worked by marine and subaerial erosion. This normally removes all the failed material but sometimes a lag deposit remains of much coarser sediment. At Goldencap on the Dorset coast a fringe of submerged boulders remains in a semicircle in front of the cliff, delimiting the edge of a previous failure (Bird 1985).

The soft rock cliffs of the North Sea margin are all prone to high rates of erosion. With rising sea levels, soft rock cliffs would erode even more rapidly than at present due to the enhanced buoying up of cliff toes, increased removal of failed material and more effective wave erosion of the cliff face.

REGIONAL VARIATION

The most significant section of soft rock cliffs on the North Sea coast is found between Flamborough Head and Lowestoft, where the coast is formed of glacial deposits. Other limited sections can be found on the south coast, where harder rocks have been breached by the sea to reveal soft clay deposits, and north of Flamborough Head, where there are isolated pockets of glacial deposits from the coast.

Figure 3.2.1
Distribution of soft rock
cliffs along the North Sea
coastal margin.
Based upon the 1975 Ordnance Survey
1:1,250,000 map with the permission
of the Controller of Her Majesty's
Stationery Office © Crown Copyright.

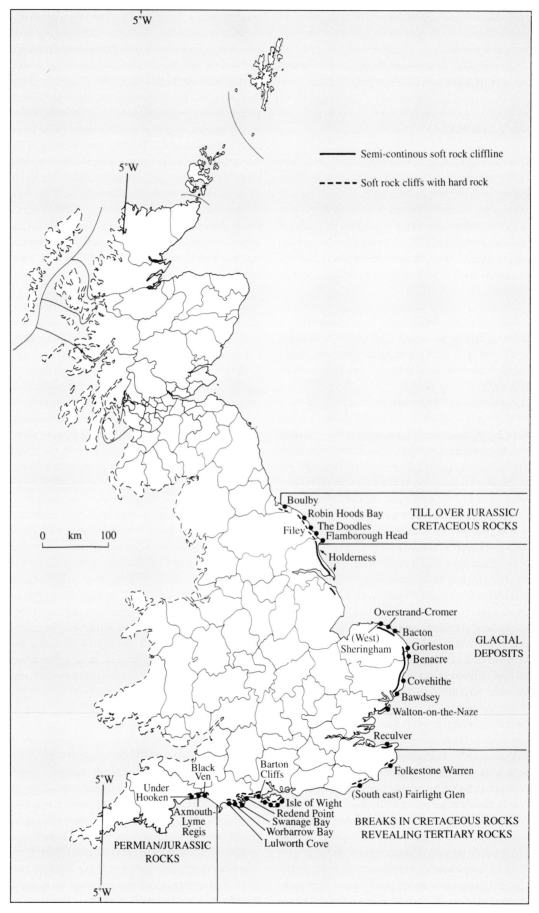

Northumberland – Scottish coast

This section of coast is predominantly made up of hard rock cliff exposures. It should be noted, however, that till locally forms cliffs down to sea level. Perhaps more significant is that the cliffs in this region are invariably capped by till and soliflucted deposits.

Flamborough Head to Cleveland

The cliffs in this region are composed of Permo-Triassic to Cretaceous sediments, usually overlain by till. Flamborough Head is perhaps the classic composite, bevelled cliff with a basal, near vertical section formed of Chalk and a more gently sloping till section above. Further north, the lithology of the unit making up the basal part of the cliff changes, but the till cover remains a common denominator. At Filey Bay subaerial erosion predominates on the cliffs, producing an expanse of gullies and arêtes. At Runswick Bay, cliff slumping and flowage takes place by basal erosion of Liassic shales.

Lincolnshire and Humberside

The Lincolnshire coast is devoid of cliffs except at Cleethorpes where they are protected from erosion by Holocene sediments. These cliffs are incised into the till deposit which is backed up against the old coastline of the Yorkshire and Lincolnshire Wolds. The cliffs of Humberside to the north, along the Holderness coast, generally decline in height southwards from Flamborough Head to Spurn Head. They are subject to possibly the highest rate of coastal erosion in Britain, averaging 1.75 m per year (Valentin 1954). This figure masks the episodic nature of erosion, with some areas retreating tens of metres in a single slump of cliffline and then not eroding again until this material has been removed. Geomorphological activity on the Holderness coast also varies on an annual cycle. In summer the cliffs are relatively dry and stable with a high beach protecting the toe, but tension cracks develop along the cliffline. In winter the cliffs can become saturated and subject to mass movement failures. Simultaneously, beach levels are lowered due to storms, exposing to erosion the toe and platform in front of the cliffs. This allows the cliff to steepen, and with high pore water pressure the cliff fails along the line of weakness formed by the tension crack.

These processes have been responsible for the loss of more than 80 square miles of land since Roman times (Steers 1969) and the loss continues. The erosion causes small headlands and bays to form all along the coast as differential (wave) erosion affects the cliffs. This area represents the finest example of a continuous soft cliffline covered in Quaternary sediments along the North Sea coast.

Reculver – Sheringham

The cliffs of this coast are incised almost exclusively into soft rocks. Although Chalk does underlie them locally, the key feature is rapid coastal erosion.

West of Reculver, the Eocene Woolwich and Reading Beds are subject to severe erosion. The cliffs have a relatively high angle but are soft enough to be rapidly removed by marine processes. From Clacton to Covehithe the London Clay is overlain by Pliocene Crag. At Walton-on-the-Naze and Bawdsey there are cliffs of Red Crag overlying London Clay.

Along the Suffolk coast there are cliffs a few metres high formed of Pliocene and Quaternary sands and gravels. These cliffs erode rapidly, with the Crag eroding more regularly than the London Clay, which erodes by flows and slumps.

From Benacre to Sheringham glacial deposits (particularly till and sands and gravels) tend to repose at a 45° angle, with frequent slips and flows being continuously removed by the sea. Erosion of the sand and gravel cliffs between Sheringham and Trimmingham is severe. This entire stretch of coast has cliffs of variable height, and in long sections the cliffs disappear, to be replaced by either sand dune systems, the Norfolk Broads or large ness features. A particularly interesting example of coastal erosion is found at Gorleston where a southward longshore drift of sand was interrupted by the building of a breakwater. As a result, the beaches at Gorleston have become depleted, whilst those at Yarmouth increased in size to the north, allowing greater wave attack at the cliff base at Gorleston and a reduced attack at Yarmouth. This has caused a step in the coastline and highlights the effect of man-made modification to the coast and the important control of toe protection upon cliff erosion.

Sussex – south-east Kent

Much of this coastline comprises soft rock cliffs formed of Cretaceous sediments, but large-scale coastal development has led to the isolation of the cliffs from the processes of coastal erosion. Two areas show active erosion of soft rock cliff, namely south-east of Fairlight Glen and Folkestone Warren. The former shows partial slipping of Ashdown Sand and Fairlight Clay on a gentle slope and demonstrates the influence of gravity on soft rock failure. Where cliffs are shallow in angle the potential for failure is reduced; if the cliff angle here were steepened by toe erosion, total failure would probably take place. At Folkestone Warren successive failures have occurred with the gently dipping Chalk slipping over the underlying Gault Clay. This site has multiple rotational slips and demonstrates that cliffs are as strong as their weakest element. Folkestone Warren is now protected from further marine erosion and the landward-dipping slopes of the previous, successive cliff failures have been infilled to produce a more regular profile in a similar fashion to Ventnor on the Isle of Wight.

Isle of Purbeck – Isle of Wight

From Lulworth to Swanage Bay the coastline is dominated by Jurassic and Cretaceous sediments, but at Lulworth Cove and Worbarrow Bay erosion of the Chalk has exposed the softer, underlying Wealden Clays. The width of the Wealden Clay outcrop controls the size of the bays. The clays support reasonably stable, low-angled, vegetated cliffs. Swanage Bay is incised into Wealden Clay, but there the coast is perpendicular in orientation to that at Lulworth. Kimmeridge Bay and the Kimmeridge Ledges also show gradual erosion, with the bedding planes in the Kimmeridge Clays, which make up the cliffs and foreshore, playing an important part in the detailed morphology of the coastline.

The borders of the Solent are formed of Oligocene and Eocene sediments which are easily eroded, but much of this coastline has been protected by man-made structures. The south coast of the Isle of Wight is one of the key areas for the study of mass movements in soft rock cliffs in the British Isles.

The southern coast of the Isle of Wight is formed of Wealden Clay and Greensand. These sediments display large-scale mass movement and are traversed by ravines ('chines') cut by streams descending steeply to the sea. Large-scale rotational slips also occur where the Chalk overlies the weaker, and less permeable Greensand and Gault Clay, as at Ventnor. Here, later slips have smoothed the profile of the cliff by infilling the backslopes produced by earlier slips. There are also terraced cliffs formed due to lithological variation in the sediments making up the cliff. Shelves may develop in the cliffs and the lower shelf is often masked by talus from the upper levels, and may be covered by mudflows produced by the natural drainage of the island.

In contrast to the very active cliffs described above, at Redend Point in Studland Bay, Dorset, a cliff formed of London Clay is progressively failing, though movement is so slow that trees migrate down-slope while remaining in a vertical growing position. The small tidal range and the protection afforded by an adjacent headland limits wave erosion, and cliff toe erosion is slow. Because of the limited wave energy, this cliff deforms and fails plastically, rather than by catastrophic rotational failure as described for the Isle of Wight.

South-east Devon and west Dorset

The dip of the Jurassic, Triassic and Permean sediments making up the cliffs in this area is nearly horizontal, leading to numerous failures in the cliffs along bedding planes. The erosion of Triassic sandstones in the area provides an important supply of sediment to the local beaches.

At Under Hooken there are important areas of undercliff formed of Cretaceous rocks which have been much disturbed by slumping. This material affords protection to the true cliff base. A landslip high upon the cliff has produced pillars of Cretaceous chalk which will degrade over time.

The cliffs at Lyme Regis, Axmouth and Black Ven have experienced major landslips. The well-bedded nature of the Liassic clays and muddy limestones forming the cliffs near Lyme Regis have resulted in multiple failures of the cliffs. At Axmouth, Dowlands Chasm was formed in a catastrophic event in 1839 which followed a long period of rain and storms, and formed a '...new inland cliff 210 feet high...backing a chasm into which some twenty acres of land had subsided' (Steers 1960). Black Ven, to the east of Lyme Regis, has seen more continuous sliding seawards of Greensand and Gault over Lower Lias clays and limestones.

FACTORS WHICH MAY INFLUENCE THE EROSION PROCESSES ON SOFT ROCK CLIFFS

Human action on soft rock cliffs may lead to inactive cliffs becoming active or *vice versa*.

1. Stabilisation

In many areas where the soft rock cliffs are being eroded rapidly, man has put in place protection schemes in an attempt to arrest the process. Such schemes are usually found where the erosion threatens buildings, man-made facilities or valuable agricultural land. The schemes, which may consist of beach nourishment, cliff grading and hard coastal defence schemes, are designed to stop the active erosion of the cliff and, in time, lead to vegetation cover on the previously eroding shelf.

Cliffs may also be graded for recreational purposes. Access to beaches, and beach hut and chalet developments all alter the natural condition of soft rock cliffs. Associated with such development may be drainage of the cliffs and tree/shrub planting to encourage stabilisation.

Dumping at the cliff base may also stabilise the cliffs by preventing toe erosion. The protection of the cliff toe may also take place as a result of the construction of pipelines, jetties or groynes on the foreshore, to promote the trapping of sediment from longshore drift.

2. Destabilisation

Whereas interception of longshore drift may stabilise a section of soft cliff, the starvation of sediment down-drift may enhance erosion or reactivate a previously stable cliff. Such effects may also follow natural depletion of beaches or increased wave energy either due to rising sea level or to the normal fluctuation in wave energy in the historic time-scale.

The drainage of inland areas may also cause cliff destabilisation. Field drains, the clearing of trees and shrubs, or increased runoff due to urbanisation may lead to increased water levels in cliffs, and can cause destabilisation and enhanced erosion.

Minor destabilisation may be caused by fencing along cliff tops (causing artificial tension cracks), downward pressure on the cliff by vehicular or foot traffic and disturbance of cliff faces by commercial or amateur fossil or coloured sand collectors.

SOURCES OF INFORMATION

The Geological Conservation Review (GCR) has identified key sites of geological interest along the North Sea coast. These volumes do not constitute a definitive survey of the extent and nature of soft rock cliffs. Information is scattered through various coastal texts; the work of Steers (1969, 1973) is particularly useful for this purpose. Local geological groups may also have extensive site-based information. The maps produced by the British Geological Survey contain a wealth of data on the rocks and sediments forming the cliffs. These maps and associated memoirs are the main source of information for any detailed geological investigation of the cliffs.

The GCR is being published by JNCC. Information relevant to soft rock cliffs will be contained in the following volumes:
- ❖ *Quarternary of East Anglia*
- ❖ *Quarternary of Northern England*
- ❖ *Quarternary of the Thames*
- ❖ *Cretaceous: Portlandian – Wealden*
- ❖ *Jurassic: Oxfordian – Kimmeridgian*
- ❖ *Lower Jurassic*
- ❖ *Marine Permian*
- ❖ *Coastal Geomorphology of Scotland*
- ❖ *Coastal Geomorphology of England and Wales*
- ❖ *Mass Movement.*

3.3 HARD ROCK CLIFFS

INTRODUCTION

The hard rock cliffs of the North Sea coast are cut into pre-Permian rocks; the cliffs may be near-vertical in profile and locally up to hundreds of metres in height. Such cliffs erode more slowly than those incised into soft rocks, but they may erode rapidly in areas with extensive structural weaknesses such as joints or shear planes. Failure of hard rock cliffs is usually through 'cliff falls' or block failure.

Along any coast, the form of the more resistant units or rock masses determines the gross morphology. This applies to the soft rock cliffs in Dorset, where the harder limestones usually form distinctive features (e.g. Durdle Door) and to the hard rock cliff where more resistant igneous rocks or more lithified sedimentary units may form upstanding features.

Distribution of hard rock cliffs along the North Sea coastal margin is shown in Figure 3.3.1.

PROCESSES AND GEOMORPHOLOGY

The form of hard rock cliffs is more controlled by the geological structure of the coast than is the case with cliffs incised into soft rocks. In this respect, the direction of bedding and joint planes, faults and lithological variation play an important role in determining the topographic detail of the cliffs and foreshore.

The key elements controlling this variability of hard rock cliffs can be summarised as: the morphology of the hinterland inherited from the Holocene transgression; climate and aspect determining the degree of subaerial weathering and vegetation; the effects of fluvial, periglacial, chemical and biological erosion; the wave climate and tidal regime; sea level change; and the geological structure and lithology of the rocks (Trenhaile 1987).

There are a number of specific geomorphic features associated with hard rock cliffs. These include bays and headlands, coves, caves, blowholes, geos, stacks, arches and wave-worn stumps on which 'there is still a surprising lack of information on the development, distribution and form ...' (Trenhaile 1987).

Figure 3.3.1
Distribution of hard rock cliffs along the North Sea coastal margin.

Based upon the 1975 Ordnance Survey 1:1,250,000 map with the permission of the Controller of Her Majesty's Stationery Office © Crown Copyright.

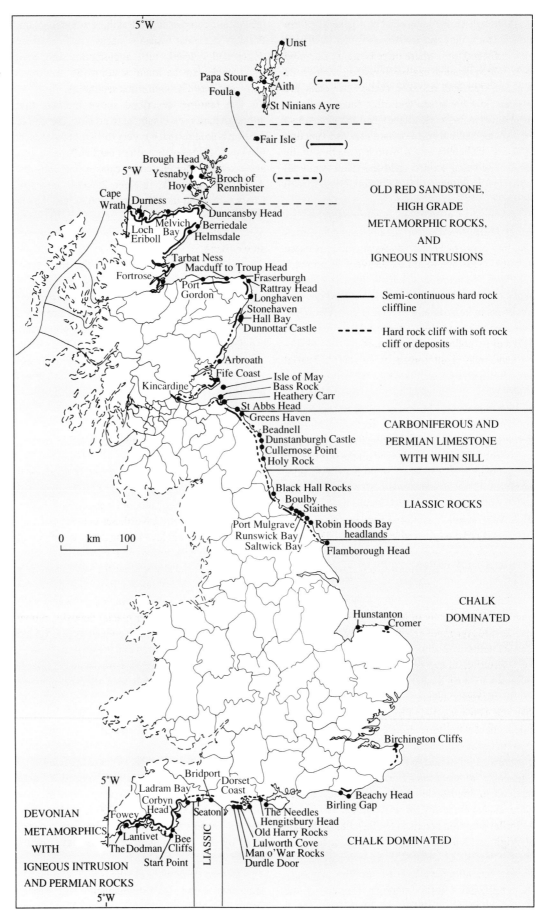

Although it is true to say that bays generally form in softer rock, they can also be associated with hard rock cliffs and form where there is highly fractured rock which erodes easily. Igneous, high-grade metamorphic and massive carbonate rocks are resistant to wave attack and often form headlands such as Start Point. Headlands and bays may also form along coasts formed of hard rock as a function of variations in cliff height, with lower cliffs of the same rock being eroded (and the talus removed) more rapidly, ultimately to form small bays (Small 1970).

Mechanical wave erosion commonly exploits joints, faults, fractures or zones of shattered rock resulting in caves, arches, stacks and other isolated features. Geos are found extensively in northern Scotland. These are long, narrow inlets with near-vertical sides formed along vertical planes of weakness in horizontally bedded hard rocks. They may also be formed by preferential exploitation of dykes or by collapse of cave roofs.

Caves may result from the exposure of terrestrial passages such as near Flamborough Head (Steers 1960); however, the morphology of marine caves is related mainly to jointing. Where jointing is horizontal, flat-roofed, wide, rectangular caves develop. The best example of this is Fingal's Cave on Staffa but others can be found on the south coast of Cornwall. Vertical jointing tends to form thin, tall caves; for example, the Isle of Thanet has caves which extend several metres above the high tide mark. Where caves develop, waves may cause air to be trapped and compressed in an upward direction. This causes shock waves and collapse of the cave roof inland from the cliff edge to form a blowhole such as the one at Flamborough Head.

Old Harry rocks in Dorset demonstrate the final stages of development of arches and stacks. Caves may develop on opposite sides of a headland (along a fault) and may ultimately join to form a tunnel. The resulting arch continues to erode until it collapses to leave a stack.

Most arches develop in rocks dipping at less than 45° (Fleming 1965) but stacks may develop independent of the dip within the rock. At Duncansby Head in north-east Scotland, water penetrates deep into vertical joints and chemically erodes the rock. This leads to the removal of large, rectangular sections of lime-sealed Flagstone, which leaves more resistant sections to survive as isolated stacks. A similar situation occurs at the Needles of the Isle of Wight, which are formed of the more resistant parts of the Chalk outcrop which previously formed a ridge extending westwards into Bournemouth Bay. Ephemeral stacks may be formed by the excavation of relict solution pipes which have been infilled and compacted, such as those at Sheringham. Perhaps the most resistant stacks are formed by dykes and volcanic tuff, agglomerate and lava. Such stacks can be found south of St. Andrews, emplaced into Carboniferous sediments.

The features described above indicate that although hard rock is subject to erosion, the rate of erosion is so slow that it is very difficult to measure. Data on the rates of erosion of hard cliffs is scarce, and erosion is dominated by catastrophic failures. At St. Margarets Bay in Kent, 254,000 tonnes of Chalk failed and travelled up to 360 m into the sea (Hutchinson 1972). Falls occur in well-fractured rock, particularly where a wave-cut notch creates an overhang.

The type of fall depends on the rock type. Massive, cohesive rocks undergo 'slab fall'; 'flexural toppling' occurs from cracked columnar rocks and 'block toppling' occurs where sections split away from the cliff and rest on previously toppled material (Trenhaile 1987).

The geomorphic form and morphology of hard rock cliffs are controlled by structural and lithological variations within the rock mass.

REGIONAL VARIATION

Hard rock cliffs dominate the coast of south-west England and north-east Scotland which are formed of highly resistant igneous and metamorphic rocks. The rest of the Scottish North Sea coast is made up of similar rocks, but lower lying expanses of gravel and mud form intervening soft rock coasts. A similar situation occurs locally between the Scottish borders and Flamborough Head where the cliffs of Carboniferous to Jurassic strata are locally very low and covered by softer glacial deposits, blown sand or estuarine mud. The south coast of England is significantly different in that the hard chalk cliffs have been breached by marine erosion to reveal soft rocks, and the coastline has been affected by large-scale coastal development.

Orkney, Fair Isle and Shetland

The more interesting cliffs of these islands occur on their west coasts which are exposed to large Atlantic waves. This high-energy environment maintains vertical cliffs up to 200 m high on Fair Isle, while on Orkney the cliff tops are scoured away by the spray produced as the waves break against them.

Orkney demonstrates the same geological sequence as the Scottish mainland with Upper Devonian volcanic rocks at Too of the Head, lavas and tuffs on Hoy and flagstone and Old Red Sandstone at Yesnaby and Gaulton. The sandstones are particularly prone to arch, stack and cave formation with the famous Old Man of Hoy being a classic example.

On Shetland, a similar suite of features can be found. Papa Stour has cliffs, caves, blow holes, geos and stacks particularly well-developed on the rocky north-west coast. These features are less well-developed on the more sheltered south-west side, demonstrating the control that the degree of exposure to wave erosion has on cliff development. The 300 m high cliffs around Foula, exposed to the full force of Atlantic waves, are the highest cliffs on the North Sea coast. Lower cliffs are found in the more sheltered inlets such as St. Ninians Ayre and the Broch of Rennibister, and their scale is in part determined by the local seaward dip of the major structural planes in the rock mass.

St. Abb's Head – Cape Wrath

The Scottish hard rock cliffs are formed mainly in Old Red Sandstone and Dalradian rocks, the latter containing numerous igneous intrusions. In these areas there are long stretches of semi-continuous cliffs with a cover of variable thickness of glacial deposits. The sweep of hard rock cliffs is locally terminated by low-lying coastal sites backed by actively eroding soft rock cliffs.

St. Abb's Head and Heathery Carr have spectacular cliffs incised into Silurian rocks. These rocks are highly folded and produce cliffs of variable height and slope with large volumes of talus at the cliff base. These contrast with the Old Red Sandstone cliffs of St. Abb's Head and account for the rectangular plan form of this part of the coast.

Bass Rock and the Isle of May demonstrate the durability of igneous rock cliffs. The former displays cliffs of phonolitic trachyte which rise from the seabed; the latter is formed of a doleritic sill which generates vertical cliffs of variable height.

From Kincardine to Stonehaven Old Red Sandstone, volcanic rocks and other igneous rocks are inter-bedded with, or intruded into, sediments. The Old Red Sandstone forms cliffs with caves, stacks and blowholes such as at Arbroath, St. Cyrus and Dunnottar Castle. Being weaker than the volcanic rocks, the sandstone also tends to form embayments such as at Dunnottar Castle and Hall Bay.

The igneous and volcanic rocks tend to be harder than the Old Red Sandstone and form headlands with geos such as Red Head (70 m high basaltic cliffs) or Stonehaven.

Longhaven has granite cliffs which are not susceptible to marine erosion. However, subaerial erosion and chemical weathering has produced a blocky surface to the cliffs and has flattened the cliff profile.

From Fraserburgh to Portgordon the cliffs are formed mainly of Dalradian rocks, but there are impressive Old Red Sandstone cliffs between Pennan and Gardenstown. The morphology of the Dalradian coastline forming headlands and bays is more a function of rock structure than lithology. Structural control on the coastline is also demonstrated in the Old Red Sandstone coastline between Fortrose and Tarbat Ness. The coastline here marks the position of the Great Glen Fault, separating the Old Red Sandstone onshore from the Jurassic rocks preserved offshore in the Moray Firth Basin.

Between Helmsdale and Berriedale the Old Red Sandstone cliffs are of uniform height with flat tops which have been planated by an episode of marine erosion prior to emergence of the present cliffs.

The coast between Duncansby Head and Skirza is formed of flagstone of Old Red Sandstone age. The fine detail of these cliffs is controlled by the dip, fault and joint patterns and resistance to erosion of the soft rock mass. There is a clear difference between the high flagstone cliffs, locally eroded into geos, and the less steep, more friable sandstone cliffs, which have alternating rock buttresses and vegetated scree slopes. At Duncansby Head the geological control is further highlighted by the existence of pyramidal stacks, demonstrating that the subaerial weathering is less effective on the flagstone than the marine undercutting.

The rocks forming the coast become older and more metamorphosed from Melvich Bay to Cape Wrath. The Moine rocks between Melvich Bay and Loch Eriboll demonstrate differential erosion, forming numerous bays and headlands, while the Lewisian Gneiss of Cape Wrath produces spectacular vertical cliffs controlled, in plan, by the rock structure.

Filey Brigg – Green's Haven

This coastline is carved into sediments ranging in age from Upper Jurassic at Filey Brigg to extensive stretches of Carboniferous rocks in the north to Green's Haven. Locally, dolerite sills are exposed at the coast in the northern part of the area. North Bay at Scarborough has a Jurassic sandstone promontory, but between there and Filey the cliffs are mainly of softer Jurassic rocks. From

Scarborough to Whitby the cliffs reach some 200 m in height and are formed mostly of Middle Jurassic Sandstone and mudstone. Northward the Liassic rocks form cliffs at Boulby, Staithes and Port Mulgrave. These are capped by boulder clay to produce a bevelled profile, although at lower levels, resistant benches cut into the bedrock form a stepped profile. These rocks have a near-horizontal dip and slight variations in this dip control the vertical inclination of the cliffs. Talus accumulates extensively at the base of the cliff; this further reduces the inclination of the cliff and protects the cliff toe.

From the Tees to Green's Haven the coast is made up primarily of Permian sediments and Carboniferous Coal Measures which are intruded locally by dolente sills. The morphology of the Permian coast is similar to that of the Purbeck coast with vertical cliffs, arches and stacks developed at Marsden Bay and Black Hall Rocks. The limestones of Holey Rock have numerous caves with rectangular cross-sections and flat roofs. These are likely to develop into arches and ultimately, stacks. The stacks of Black Hall Rocks are being eroded down into wave-worn stumps, highlighting the continuing erosion of this coastline.

Cullernose Point is formed from columnar dolerite and is part of the Whin Sill which extends north to Budle Point via the Farne Islands. The sill is inclined to the north-east, causing the more prominent cliffs to face south. The changing dip of the sill controls the cliff height but they tend to have flat tops as a result of earlier marine planation. At Cullernose Point the columnar nature of the rock results in fine examples of block toppling.

The cliffs from the Holy Island to Green's Haven are formed of Carboniferous Limestone.

Birling Gap – Flamborough Head

This extensive section of coast has few hard rock cliffs, though Cretaceous chalk forms cliffs along some stretches of the coast. Between these cliffs are soft rock cliffs, formed of Tertiary and Quaternary sediments and low-lying beach, dune and saltmarsh systems.

The chalk cliffs along the south coast of England may be up to 100 m high and are near vertical. Wave erosion maintains the near-vertical slope of the cliffs and their characteristic white appearance. The cliff sections at Overstrand show large blocks of chalk have been incorporated into the Anglian till by an ice sheet.

The cliffs at Hunstanton are formed of red and white chalk and the underlying Carstone. The chalk is relatively easily eroded but maintains a near vertical face, and slabs of Carstone are produced by wave action at the cliff toe.

At Flamborough Head and the coast immediately to its north, steep cliffs occur with arch and stack formations. The upper part of the cliff is formed of till which erodes to produce a different cliff morphology compared to the underlying chalk. A blow-hole at Flamborough Head is associated with the collapse of a cave roof.

Seaton – The Needles

Chalk and Purbeck limestone dominates the hard rock cliffs along this part of the coast, which includes examples of classic cliff formations and coastal morphology, such as The Needles, Old Harry Rocks, Lulworth Cove and Durdle Door. The near-vertical cliffs (of variable height) display caves, arches, stacks and wave-worn stumps. Notching of the cliff toe is common and cliff falls supply flint and chert to the beaches. This section of coast from The Needles westward to Swanage represents a once-continuous ridge which has been eroded to reveal the underlying softer rocks. At isolated points, such as Stair Hole, contorted folding (The Lulworth Crumple) is exposed in the cliff face. The folding and jointing of the rocks controls the finer form of features such as Old Harry Rocks and Durdle Door. Old Harry was formerly attached to the mainland by an arch which has since collapsed to leave it isolated. Considering the commonly recognised importance of this section of coast there is little specific information on erosion rates and the time-scale of coastal development. However, the rates are much slower than along the soft rock coasts of eastern England. Erosion has resulted in little measurable change in historic times, the exception being areas of active landslipping where major changes in coastal form have occurred within the last 200 years.

Ladram Bay – Dodman

The western section of this coast is dominated by Devonian rocks with igneous intrusions. These pass westward into strongly metamorphosed Devonian sediments and eastwards into Permian sandstones and conglomerates.

The gneissic rocks exposed at Start Point are the oldest and hardest in the area. These control the coastal plan as the intervening slates and sandstones in Start and Bigbury Bay have been more readily eroded. Local folds and faults within the rocks control the finer detail of the coast. The flooded valleys (rias) along this coast trend approximately north–south across the structural grain of the country rocks. The Dart, Tamar and Fowey estuaries are fine examples of rias. The generally accepted view is that the ice sheets associated with the Quaternary glaciations did not reach the southern coast of England. However, some geologists have speculated that the ice sheets flowed up the western English Channel to abut against the coast. Till is absent from southern England but many of the cliffs are covered by a thin layer of soliflucted, weathered soil termed 'head'.

Cliff profiles in this area suggest that subaerial erosion has controlled the form of the upper cliff and marine erosion has controlled the form of the lower cliff. Wave erosion is severe along the foot of many of the cliffs and this has helped to maintain their very steep lower profile. The dominant structural control within this metamorphosed rock mass is the cleavage.

In the Permian rocks of Corbyn and Ladram Bay caves, arches and stacks have developed in the horizontally bedded strata. These rocks form steep cliffs, as subaerial processes are less significant than wave erosion in maintaining their profile.

FACTORS WHICH MAY INFLUENCE EROSION PROCESSES ON HARD ROCK CLIFFS

Hard rock cliffs erode at a much slower rate than soft rock cliffs, and, for this reason, the perceived threat from coastal erosion is less and development may safely take place nearer to the cliff edge. However, a problem may exist if such development takes place on soft, glacial deposits (covering the harder rock beneath) which may erode and fail easily. This may lead to the need for hard coastal defence to reduce erosion, or cliff-top protection schemes to reduce subaerial weathering, both of which may mask these visually and geologically interesting hard rock cliffs.

Hard rock cliffs may also be threatened by pipelines disgorging into the sea. Outfall pipes require a slope to empty their contents into the sea and may be positioned where there is a natural low point in the cliffs. However, these low points may be due to some structural control, such as a fault line, and construction of the pipeline may cover up such a feature. The reverse may also be true; the construction of such a pipeline may lead to new exposures of what otherwise might be covered by superficial deposits.

Commercial mineral extraction can also be a threat to hard rock cliffs. Mineral deposits may be removed by dynamiting the cliff. This destroys the natural state of the cliffs and may diminish their

mineralogical interest. Conversely, creating new exposures may increase their mineralogical interest, but it does destroy their natural state.

Other minor damage may be caused by man creating access to beaches down hard rock cliffs (this may be in the form of cut or wooden steps fixed to the cliff). Increased pollution may also cause increased erosion, particularly the effects of acid rain on carbonate rocks which may lead to their surfaces becoming unnaturally honeycombed. Recreational activities such as rock climbing may also cause damage to cliffs and their associated stacks and arches.

SOURCES OF INFORMATION

The sources of information are the same as those for soft rock cliffs but Trenhaile's (1987) work is of particular relevance. The relevant GCR volumes are:
- ❖ *Tertiary: Palaeogene-Pliocene*
- ❖ *Marine Cretaceous*
- ❖ *Jurassic: Bathonian – Callovian*
- ❖ *Jurassic: Aalenian – Bajocian*
- ❖ *Lower Jurassic*
- ❖ *Permian – Triassic*
- ❖ *Marine Permian*
- ❖ *Carboniferous: Pennsylvanian*
- ❖ *Carboniferous: Mississippian of N Britain*
- ❖ *Carboniferous: Mississippian of S Britain*
- ❖ *Marine Devonian*
- ❖ *Silurian*
- ❖ *Ordovician*
- ❖ *Cambrian*
- ❖ *Pre-Cambrian of England and Wales*
- ❖ *Caledonian Structures*
- ❖ *Variscan-Alpine Structures*
- ❖ *Tertiary Igneous Rocks*
- ❖ *Permian – Carboniferous Igneous Rocks*
- ❖ *Caledonian Igneous Rocks*
- ❖ *Igneous Rocks of SW England*
- ❖ *Coastal Geomorphology of Scotland*
- ❖ *Coastal Geomorphology of England and Wales*
- ❖ *Moine*
- ❖ *Torridonian and Lewisian*
- ❖ *Dalradian*

3.4 FORESHORE EXPOSURES

INTRODUCTION

In some areas there are shore platforms incised into the cliff or coast which are higher than the modern platform. These raised platforms were formed when sea level was higher than at present or are the result

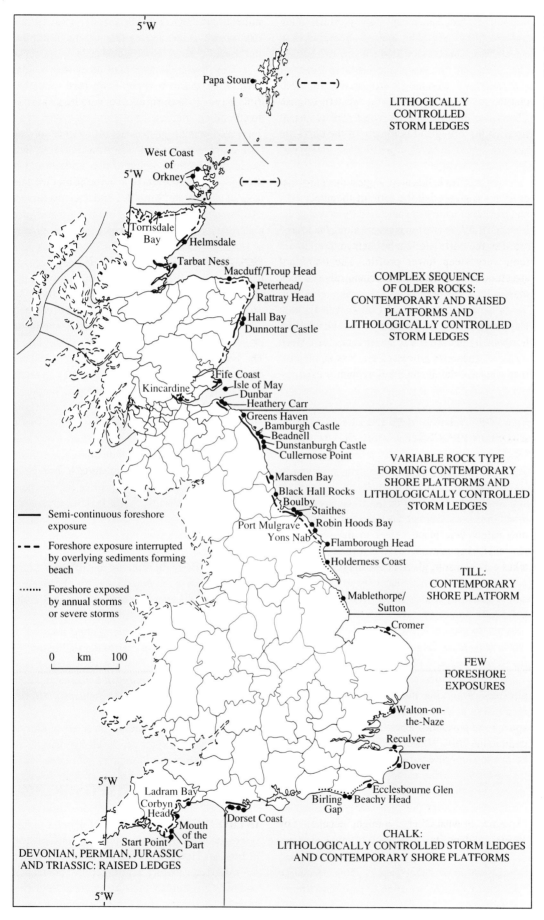

Figure 3.4.1
Distribution of foreshore exposures along the North Sea coastal margin.
Based upon the 1975 Ordnance Survey 1:1,250,000 map with the permission of the Controller of Her Majesty's Stationery Office © Crown Copyright.

LITHOGICALLY CONTROLLED STORM LEDGES

COMPLEX SEQUENCE OF OLDER ROCKS: CONTEMPORARY AND RAISED PLATFORMS AND LITHOLOGICALLY CONTROLLED STORM LEDGES

VARIABLE ROCK TYPE FORMING CONTEMPORARY SHORE PLATFORMS AND LITHOLOGICALLY CONTROLLED STORM LEDGES

TILL: CONTEMPORARY SHORE PLATFORM

FEW FORESHORE EXPOSURES

CHALK: LITHOLOGICALLY CONTROLLED STORM LEDGES AND CONTEMPORARY SHORE PLATFORMS

DEVONIAN, PERMIAN, JURASSIC AND TRIASSIC: RAISED LEDGES

Papa Stour (- - - -)

West Coast of Orkney (- - - -)

5°W

Torrisdale Bay
Helmsdale
Tarbat Ness
Macduff/Troup Head
Peterhead/Rattray Head
Hall Bay
Dunnottar Castle
Fife Coast
Isle of May
Kincardine
Dunbar
Heathery Carr
Greens Haven
Bamburgh Castle
Beadnell
Dunstanburgh Castle
Cullernose Point
Marsden Bay
Black Hall Rocks
Boulby
Staithes
Port Mulgrave
Robin Hoods Bay
Yons Nab
Flamborough Head
Holderness Coast
Mablethorpe/Sutton
Cromer
Walton-on-the-Naze
Reculver
Dover
Ecclesbourne Glen
Birling Gap
Beachy Head
Ladram Bay
Corbyn Head
Dorset Coast
Mouth of the Dart
Start Point

Semi-continuous foreshore exposure

- - - Foreshore exposure interrupted by overlying sediments forming beach

······ Foreshore exposed by annual storms or severe storms

0   km   100

29

of uplift of the land since their incision. The platforms may have been incised about 125,000 years BP when the sea level was a few metres higher than at present. Along much of northern England and Scotland the shore platforms incised immediately after the end of the last glaciation have been raised due to the land rising following the removal of the ice loading. This isostatic readjustment is especially pronounced along the east coast of Scotland.

Distribution of foreshore exposure along the North Sea coastal margin is shown in Figure 3.4.1.

PROCESS AND GEOMORPHOLOGY

The morphology of foreshore exposures is the product of a complex inter-relationship between geology, erosion, land and sea level changes and tidal elevations. Each of these elements has different degrees of importance depending upon the particular location. Some workers have found that headlands have higher platforms than embayments (Bartrum 1935; Wright 1970) while others have found the opposite (So 1965; Wood 1968). The degree of exposure to erosive forces has commonly been used to explain such differences whilst the geological (lithological and structural) differences have largely been neglected. Only on major headlands/bays such as Flamborough Head is the degree of exposure to erosion important, but even here the geological controls cannot be isolated as the headland is formed of slightly more resistant rocks than the embayment to the south. Foreshore exposures can be generalised as sloping, planar surfaces of the 'bay-head ramp' type (Hills 1972). It has been suggested that they have an upward concave profile (King 1959) where tidal range is great. The foreshore of most of the coast of the region has a linear profile (Wright 1967), though that at the Isle of Thanet is convex (So 1965). Concavity only occurs on the North Sea coastal margin where there has been ramp development, such as at Seven Sisters in East Sussex. Ramps tend to have slopes of 4–8° and have two separate sections to the profile to yield the observed concavity.

In most cases where concavity might develop, the variability of the rock strata making up the foreshore precludes it. Variations in rock strength account for much of the morphological detail of foreshore exposures. This controls the detail of the platform, and leads to the formation of steps and slight changes in gradient of the foreshore. Tides also control the morphology of the foreshore. The mean tide elevation on a platform often exhibits a flat profile because of the concentration of

storm wave attack at that level (So 1965). The overall slope and profile of the foreshore platforms becomes modified if the tidal range is over 3 m (Trenhaile 1971). In areas with a tidal range of less than 3 m, wave energy is concentrated in a narrow zone creating foreshore exposures of low gradient.

It has been suggested that a low cliff may be formed at low water mark where the tide remains at the same level for a period of time and erosion is concentrated. While there is no evidence of this form of cliff on the North Sea coast, such a feature has been recognised where raised foreshore platforms have undergone renewed erosion, such as at Homerell Hole in North Yorkshire (Trenhaile 1971). Low tide sections displaying steeper slopes have been identified, however, particularly on the northern coast of the Isle of Thanet (So 1965).

Platforms of low slope may be quickly covered by debris from cliff erosion. Debris tends to be coarse, except where the supply is from chalk cliffs. The coarser material produces steeper foreshore slopes as the platform gradient adjusts to an angle adequate to remove the covering debris. Similarly, where the rate of debris input from the cliffs is relatively high, the platform will tend to have a steeper slope. Classification of foreshore exposures by morphology or process would be highly intricate and problematical, and therefore it has been suggested that a genetic classification is more logical (Trenhaile 1971). It is also clear that different classes of platform will exist in juxtaposition. However, the classification is still of value:

i)   Contemporary shore platform – a planar surface up to 400 m wide, sloping seawards between 1° and 3°, and well adjusted to present processes.

ii) Lithologically controlled storm ledges – these are less than 30 m wide, sloping both shore normal and shore parallel (the inclination of which is controlled by the rock strata), and formed in low, dipping rocks. Resistant strata are necessary to form the ledges (Trenhaile 1971).

iii) 'Raised' shore platforms – these are platforms related to a previous sea level, the margins of which are subject to modern processes. They tend to terminate seawards in a pseudo low-tide cliff.

iv) 'Raised' storm ledges – these are higher than 'raised' platforms and formed under a higher sea level to produce a stepped, coast-normal profile (Trenhaile 1971).

A further category that could be included is foreshore exposures which are revealed following storms. These are covered by sediment under summer conditions but become exposed by major winter storms such as occurred in 1953 and 1978 (Steers *et al.* 1979).

REGIONAL VARIATION

Scotland

The foreshore platforms of Scotland are formed of a wide range of lithologies ranging from Lewisian gneisses at Cape Wrath to Jurassic shales at Brora in the Moray Firth.

The Dalradian rocks from Hall Bay to MacDuff form platforms up to 50 m wide that demonstrate lithological control of the foreshore morphology. Around Rattray Head the foreshore platform is of the raised ledge type.

Although much of the coast of Scotland is formed of Old Red Sandstone, it forms few foreshore exposures as it abrades easily and is covered in beach deposits, for example between St. Cyrus and Inverbervie. However, where platforms do develop they are extensive. The Brock of Rennibister has a raised platform up to 300 m wide. Similar features (of narrower width) can be seen in Torrisdale Bay and at Helmsdale. At Dunsar there are three raised platforms in addition to the active shoreline platform. The lowest of the raised platforms correlates to the main rock platform of west Scotland whilst the upper platforms were incised during older marine erosional phases. On the west coast of Orkney, bedding planes in the Old Red Sandstone control the morphology of the platforms and the cliffs.

Flamborough Head – Green's Haven

Along this stretch of coast the rocks range in age from Late Cretaceous at Flamborough Head to Early Carboniferous to the north at Green's Haven. A wide range of lithologies are exposed in the foreshore, ranging from chalk in the south to massive limestones with isolated igneous intrusions in the north.

Flamborough Head has a narrow platform less than 30 m wide, similar in morphology to that of the south coast of England, but to the north of the headland the foreshore becomes much wider. At Robin Hood's Bay the platform is 300 m wide with a slope of less than 4° with minor topographic domes across it and a ramp at its landward margin. The Liassic rocks of this coast are eroding vertically by 0.1–2 mm per year (Robinson 1977). At Port Mulgrave a low-tide step is apparent and the platform is undergoing abrasion by marine sand (King 1959).

The Carboniferous Magnesium Limestone at Green's Haven and Beadnell produces lithologically controlled storm ledges. The Limestone is highly contorted and synclines are clearly exposed. Exposure and erosion of the vertical bedding produces a sawtooth profile to the platform. At Beadnell the different rock types produce a fine example of a storm ledge which contrasts to the harder exposure of the Whin Sill.

Lincolnshire and Holderness coasts

The foreshore platform along this coast is covered by a thin layer of mobile sediment. This sediment may be removed during storms to reveal the underlying till platform. Along the Holderness coast, 25% of the material eroded from the cliff is sand and gravel which is suitable for building up the beach; the rest is mud which is carried away by the sea. The beach thickness varies over the course of a year and under north-easterly winter waves may be entirely removed. The till platform when exposed is seen to be highly dissected by channels, but when subject to direct erosion by waves it becomes planated. It is possible that the channelled form develops by water draining through the beach, but this process has not been observed in the field.

Cromer – Reculver

The few foreshore exposures of Quaternary and pre-Quaternary sediments that occur along this coast form contemporary shore platforms. The Woolwich and Reading beds at Reculver form a very low-angled platform (less than 1°) between mid and low tide. The platform of London Clay seaward of the cliff around Walton-on-the-Naze is only exposed during severe storms. Near Cromer, an isolated chalk foreshore platform is exposed, displaying flat-bottomed pools. *Pholas* species can lower the chalk platform (by boring) up to 13 mm per year (Trenhaile 1987).

Dover – Dorset coast

Along this section of coast a Chalk platform is found seaward of the 'white cliffs of Dover', from Beachy Head nearly as far as Bognor Regis, and locally west of Lulworth in Dorset. The platforms display sharp pinnacles near to low tide (lapies), flat-bottomed pools around mid-tide and fine pitting near high tide. These features are associated with the chemical erosion of the Chalk by solution.

Along the Dorset coast and Isle of Thanet, horizontal bedding and thin cover of beach sand allows a rate of vertical erosion of up to 25 mm per year. At Beachy Head and Dover, higher wave energy levels tend to keep the platform clear of sediment but biological grazers and borers may lower the platform; for example, at Dover *Patella* species have been measured boring into the Chalk up to 15 mm per year (Trenhaile 1987). It is also important to note that the platforms seaward of the exposed headlands have a steeper slope than these of the protected bays and all foreshore exposures are relatively narrow.

Falmouth Bay – Ladram Bay – Start Point

From Falmouth Bay eastward to Start Point, the Devonian rocks produce narrow foreshore exposures of the raised ledge type. The ledges form part of a series of platforms along the coast which extend offshore to form submerged cliffs. The intertidal platforms are dissected frequently along the coast by river valleys which may be traced offshore to a depth of nearly 40 m. These platforms contrast with those cut into Permian, Jurassic and Triassic rocks to the east which have a steep section at the cliff base where they have been protected by detritus from cliff erosion. Along the southern coast of the Isle of Wight where Greensand is exposed in the foreshore, small, conical cylinders and pits are formed by crystallisation from salt spray (tafoni). Locally this platform is lowering in the spray zone by 0.55–0.64 mm per year (Mottershead 1982).

EFFECTS OF MAN ON FORESHORE EXPOSURES

Most of the man-made modifications to soft or hard rock cliffs would also have an impact on an exposed foreshore platform.

Coastal defence may directly destroy foreshore platforms or cover them in sediment. Mining activity (such as mineral extraction) damages the foreshore by exposing the rocks to wave erosion, while dumping of material masks the platform and may cause it to abrade. Any man-made change to the beach will alter the natural equilibrium of the platform but removal of material is by far the most damaging.

3.5   FORMER SHORELINES

INTRODUCTION

The North Sea coastal margin contains widespread evidence of sea-level changes reflecting the combined effects of isostatic (land-level change)

and eustatic (sea-level change) controls. The most detailed information is available for changes during and since the period of wastage of the last ice sheet (about 18,000–10,000 years BP), notably in Scotland. However, a few sites are known where older interglacial changes are recorded, notably on the south and east coast of England.

The geological evidence for sea-level change is based on an examination of coastal sedimentary sections. Multiple or individual raised beaches, i.e. former beaches which are now higher than the contemporary shoreline or platforms, may produce a stepped or staircase profile to the coast. These features are higher than their modern equivalents, implying a higher sea level during their formation. Raised beaches may preserve relict features such as storm ridges, bars or sand dunes. There is the evidence for shoreline change in deposits below present sea-level and this indicates where coasts have been submerged since the sediments were laid down. A detailed record exists for sea level changes across the North Sea coastal margin over the last 10,000 years (see Shennan 1987).

The dating of the various shoreline levels and landforms is often problematic, requiring consideration of the conditions under which they were formed. The combination of eustatic and isostatic controls means that many former shorelines of the same age are not horizontal and some can be proved to be tilted. For example, a platform formed during the Loch Lomond Stadial (glacial period) is now at -7 m OD at St. Andrews, -3 m OD in the Tay estuary and 0 m OD at Inverness (Gray 1985). This tilting is the result of differential isostatic uplift across the region related to rebound following the melting of the Scottish Ice Sheet.

REGIONAL VARIATION

Scotland

In Scotland the evidence for former sea-level changes is represented both in raised shorelines and buried in beach and estuarine deposits. Late glacial and Holocene raised beaches and shorelines occur along the coast from Holy Isle to south-east Caithness. Their pattern of occurrence and variations in altitudes reflect the interplay of isostatic and eustatic controls. Key areas where detailed studies have been completed include the Forth, Tay and Ythan estuaries, the Montrose area, the Beauly Firth and Dornoch Firth. In each of these areas both surface landforms and sedimentary sequences provide detailed records of late glacial and Holocene changes in relative sea level. The geomorphological features that reflect these changes include the staircases of raised shorelines that occur widely on the east coast of Scotland, the more extensive shingle spreads, for example at Spey Bay and Loch Fleet, and the massive sand foreland at Morrich More.

In Orkney and Caithness isostatic effects are diminished due to the rebound following the retreat of the Scottish Ice Sheet. However, submerged peat and buried gravel deposits near shore in these areas demonstrate that sea levels were much lower between about 18,000 years BP to about 5,000 years BP.

East Anglia and eastern England

On the coast of East Anglia Holocene sea-level changes are similarly widely recorded in the sediments buried along the coast, most notably in the Essex chenier plane, the Fens, along the north Norfolk coast, in the Broads area and at Orfordness. Intertidal peat beds exposed on the coast of eastern England, for example at Chapel Point and Hartlepool, indicate a lower sea level at about the mid-Holocene time, while relict cliffs can be found behind the Roman-aged saltmarshes of Norfolk.

South coast

This coastline has fossil shorelines preserved in and on the Mesozoic rocks at the coast at -7 m, -3 m, 3 m, 4.5 m, 30 m, 35 m and 40 m OD. The precise sequence of these levels is unknown but the relict coastline found behind Slapton Ley (Start Bay) is Ipswichian in age (128–122 thousand years ago). The massive shingle structures at Chesil beach and Dungeness provide the principle evidence for Holocene sea level change in the area. Sequences of sediments behind these structures provide a detailed record of sea-level changes over the last 7,000 years, as do the sediments infilling the lower parts of several valleys draining into the English Channel in Sussex.

THE EFFECTS OF MAN ON FORMER SHORELINES

Relict cliffs and platforms are naturally denuded over time, destroying their morphology and precluding accurate measurement of their elevation. They may also provide a suitable site for building, providing a reasonably level platform in areas of otherwise steep terrain. The greatest threat to former beaches is sand and gravel extraction; the key sites containing information on Holocene sea level change are either peat, sand or gravel and once disturbed or removed the evidence for interpreting sea-level change is lost.

SOURCES OF INFORMATION

There are numerous articles addressing the sequence of shoreline development along the North Sea coastal margin. The work of Gray (1985) provides a useful bibliography of work on shoreline changes in Scotland whilst Ward (1922) and Shennan (1987) provide a broad overview of coastline development. The relevant GCR volumes are:
- ❖ *Quarternary of East Anglia*
- ❖ *Quarternary of Northern England*
- ❖ *Quarternary of the Thames*
- ❖ *Quarternary of South West England*
- ❖ *Quarternary of Southern and South East England*
- ❖ *Coastal Geomorphology of Scotland*
- ❖ *Coastal Geomorphology of England and Wales.*

3.6 OFFSHORE GEOLOGY AND GEOMORPHOLOGY

BATHYMETRY

The sea floor on the continental shelf of the North Sea is mostly very flat. Average gradients across the shelf are between 1:3,000 and 1:500, and water depths gradually increase northwards in the North Sea, westwards in the English Channel and north-westwards to the north of Scotland. Superimposed on this overall trend, however, is a complex distribution of large- and small-scale topographic features with either positive or negative relief (Figure 3.6.1). In the north, the shelf edge occurs in depths of between 160 m and 220 m and, beyond this, the sea floor slopes relatively steeply into the Faroes–Shetland Channel (100 km north-west of Shetland) to a maximum depth of over 1,600 m.

On the shelf north of Scotland, there are large, low-amplitude, topographic depressions and rises with a relief of about 20 m, and more localised features with a relief of about 60 m. These local features include bathymetric highs, which rise above sea level locally to form the islets of Sule Skerry and Stack Skerry, and elongate, north–south trending deeps west of Orkney and Shetland. Farther east, water depths in the region of Orkney, Fair Isle and Shetland are generally shallower than 100 m, and around Shetland the bathymetry is complex with large, irregular ridges and nearshore deeps exceeding 150 m.

Figure 3.6.1
Bathymetry of the North Sea (adapted from British Geological Survey map).

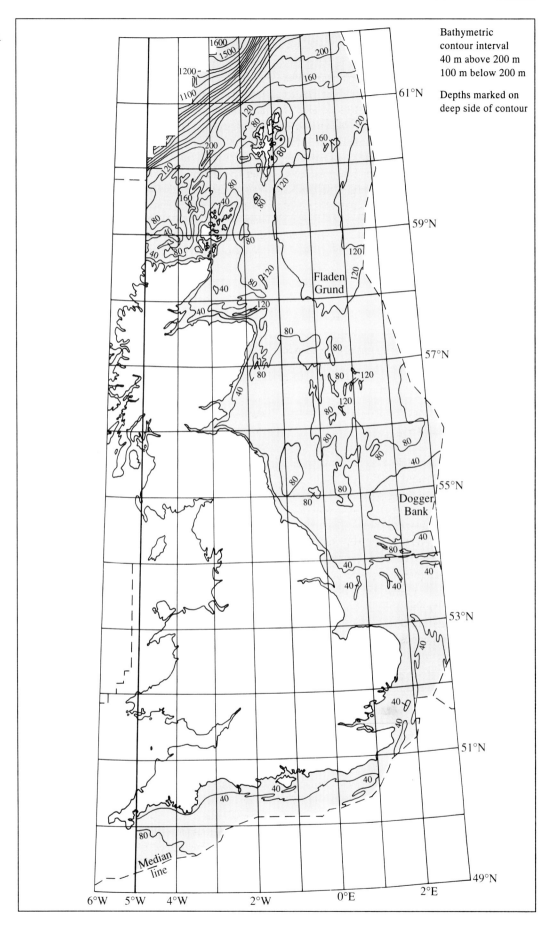

The North Sea is generally an area of low, hummocky relief. Several broad, bathymetric depressions deeper than 140 m occur in the north, and there is a conspicuous zone of linear deeps arranged in a semi-circular belt around the Fladen Grund, a large depression centred 150 km east of the Moray Firth. The Dogger Bank (100 km north-east of Flamborough Head) is a major positive feature in the south, rising from about 60 m to less than 20 m, and the adjacent Outer Silver Pit is an elongate depression with maximum depths of over 80 m. Between East Anglia and the Straits of Dover, the most significant topographic features are the large, tidal sand ridges which are up to 40 m in height.

The English Channel is mainly an area of low relief, deepening from about 40 m in the east to over 80 m at the western limit of the area. The most conspicuous features are two linear, east–west trending troughs. St. Catherine's Deep, south of the Isle of Wight, has depths of over 60 m in places, and the larger Hurd Deep in mid-channel exceeds 160 m.

SEABED SEDIMENTS

The sea floor of the North Sea is covered by a thin layer of unconsolidated sediment which has accumulated during the post-glacial period (spanning the past 10,000 years). In many areas these sediments are less than 1 m thick and the underlying glacial deposits or bedrock are exposed locally. The sediments consist of a mixture of terrigenous material (mainly quartz sand, lithic fragments, silts and clays) derived from the underlying deposits, and shell debris which has accumulated during the post-glacial period. The proportions of terrigenous and shell material are very variable. The main accumulations of shell debris tend to occur in the nearshore, with the largest concentrations occurring in the region around Orkney and Shetland.

The sediment distribution (Figure 3.6.2) reflects a complex process of erosion, transportation and deposition related both to the hydrodynamic conditions at the sea-floor and to the supply of sediment. Tidal currents are the most important factor determining sediment mobility, and the main sand transport paths are aligned parallel to the directions of maximum tidal flow. The strongest tidal currents occur in the English Channel and around Orkney and Shetland, and are weakest in the northern and central North Sea. The sediments are also subject to wind-induced, oscillatory currents created during gales and storm surges.

Sediments with a high gravel content occur on bathymetric highs, in areas of extensive rock outcrop and in areas of strong bottom currents. The largest concentrations occur in the English Channel, the Thames Estuary, east of the Humber and on the shelf north of Scotland. Sands are widespread, largely very mobile and tend to accumulate in areas of moderate to strong tidal currents. Tidal sand ridges up to 50 km in length and 40 m in height occur in the southern North Sea and in the Straits of Dover. Muds tend to occur in areas of weak tidal currents, in bathymetric deeps and off estuaries in the nearshore. The largest accumulations occur in the bathymetric depressions in the northern North Sea.

SEABED ROCK AND GEOLOGY

The geological history is complex and spans over 2,500 million years. The main offshore geological features consist of sedimentary basins containing rocks which in general decrease in age away from the coast (Figure 3.6.3). These basinal areas are bordered by upstanding basement areas which consist of older and more resistant metamorphic, igneous and deformed sedimentary rocks.

Basement areas mostly occur north of 55°N, where they form a large proportion of the onshore geology. They usually extend for only a short distance offshore, although basement ridges do occur farther offshore, both east and west of Orkney and Shetland. The rocks, which range in age from Precambrian to Lower Palaeozoic (2,500–400 million years BP), were deformed and metamorphosed during the Caledonian Orogeny (a period of structural deformation, igneous activity and mountain building which lasted from about 500–380 million years BP) and retain the characteristic Caledonian north-east–south-west structural trend. Separated from these is the Cornubian basement block in the extreme south-west which is formed mainly of Devonian and Carboniferous strata (405–290 million years BP) deformed during the Hercynian Orogeny (370–280 million years BP). There are also some small blocks of older, Precambrian basement rock in this area.

Devonian (Old Red Sandstone) continental sediments extend as a broad belt northwards from Caithness and Orkney to Shetland, and occur inshore around the north and east Scottish coastline. Carboniferous, marine and deltaic sediments also occur in the nearshore, forming a link between the onshore Carboniferous basins of central Scotland and north-east England.

Permo-Triassic and Mesozoic sedimentary rocks (280–65 million years BP) occur on the

Figure 3.6.2
Seabed sediments in the
North Sea (adapted from
British Geological Survey
map).

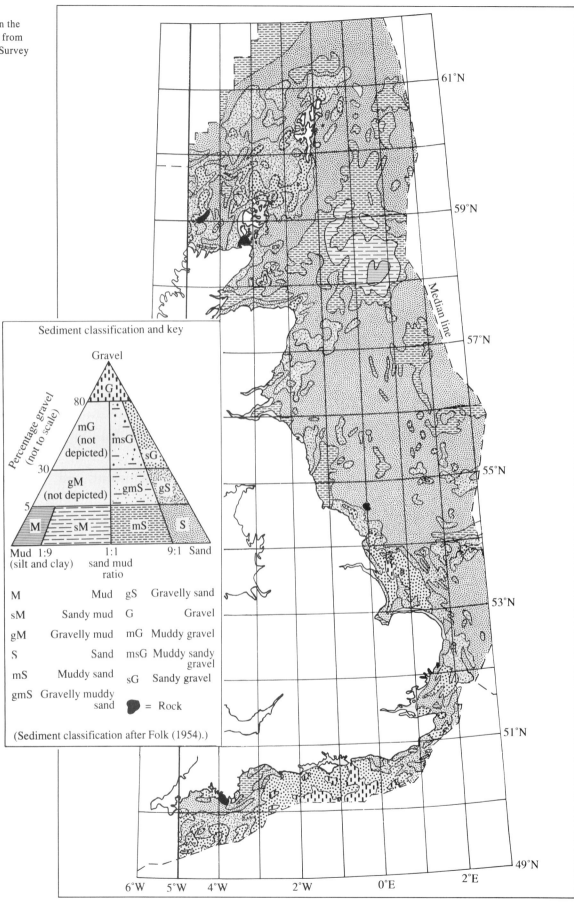

Sediment classification and key

M   Mud   gS   Gravelly sand
sM   Sandy mud   G   Gravel
gM   Gravelly mud   mG   Muddy gravel
S   Sand   msG Muddy sandy
                             gravel
mS   Muddy sand   sG   Sandy gravel
gmS Gravelly muddy
            sand   = Rock

(Sediment classification after Folk (1954).)

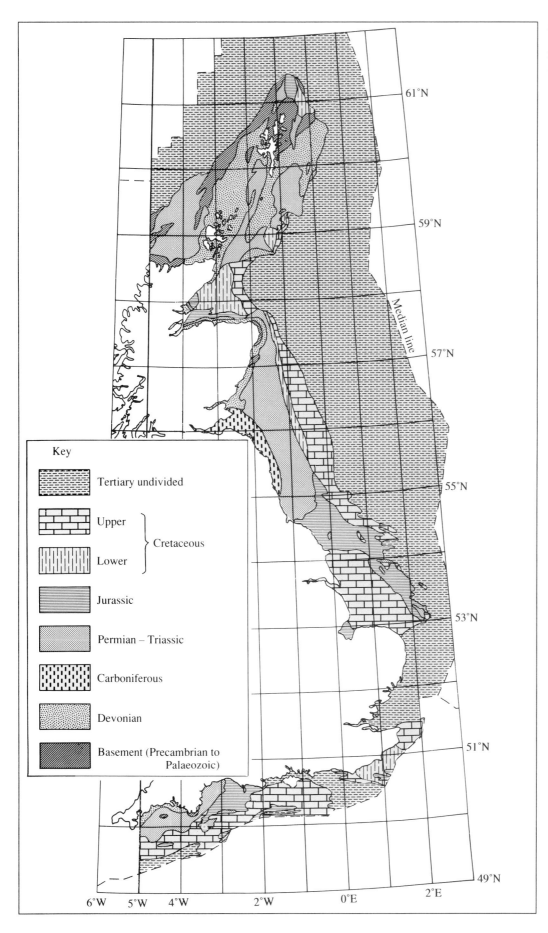

Figure 3.6.3
Seabed geology (adapted from British Geological Survey map).

Key

Tertiary undivided

Upper ⎫
⎬ Cretaceous
Lower ⎭

Jurassic

Permian – Triassic

Carboniferous

Devonian

Basement (Precambrian to Palaeozoic)

north-west shelf, locally around Shetland, in the Moray Firth and as a broad, offshore zone on the western side of the North Sea. This zone widens in the southern North Sea, extending onshore over most of eastern and southern England, and continues into the English Channel. Rock types vary considerably. They include Permian and Triassic continental deposits, Jurassic marine and deltaic sandstones and deep water shales, and Upper Cretaceous Chalk which occurs on the coast in Norfolk, Kent, the Isle of Wight and Dorset.

Tertiary and early Pleistocene sediments (65 to less than 1.8 million years BP) occur continuously from the outer continental margin in the north-west to the southern end of the North Sea. Tertiary sediments also extend onshore in the south-east and occur in the English Channel. The sediments mainly consist of marine sandstones and shales with some deltaic sandstones.

During the Pleistocene (which lasted until about 10,000 years BP), successive glaciations accompanied by large rises and falls in relative sea-level have had a profound influence on the geology, causing intense erosion of the basement areas and the margins of the sedimentary basins. As a result, thick sequences of glacial and glacio-marine sediments were deposited in the North Sea and on the outer continental shelf. Isostatic uplift, centred on the Scottish Highlands, has occurred in the post-glacial period, in response to the melting of the thick ice cover. This has been accompanied by subsidence of peripheral areas away from the centre of uplift. These isostatic adjustments, together with eustatic changes of sea level, have been important factors in the development of the present-day coastline and the sedimentary environment offshore.

AGGREGATES AND MINERALS

Areas of gravel and sand on the seabed are important sources of industrial aggregate for use in concrete production and land claim, with the main market in the south-east. Due to the lack of sufficient supplies from land sources, extensive dredging for gravel and sand has occurred around the UK, and 18.4 million tonnes (14.6% of the annual requirement) were extracted from marine sediments in 1991. 1.9 million of these were used for contract fill and beach nourishment to improve coast defences. Another 4.6 million tonnes were exported to the continent in that year. Aggregates are currently extracted in the southern North Sea from the gravel areas east and south-east of the Humber Estuary, off East Anglia and the Thames Estuary. The main

extraction areas in the English Channel occur in the areas of gravel to the south of the Isle of Wight.

There are large deposits of very pure shell sands and gravels in certain areas which could be exploited offshore in the future. This material is not suitable for aggregate use. The sea floor around Orkney is a major centre for high latitude, carbonate production with estimated rates of formation on the shelf north-east of Orkney of about 125 g/m^2/year. The carbonate material has been concentrated by strong tidal currents into sandwaves and sandbanks. At present the demand for industrial carbonate is small.

There is a general lack of known placer deposits (concentrations of heavy ore minerals resulting from fluvial or marine sedimentary processes) on the UK shelf, and very few potential economic deposits have been found. It is possible, however, that the offshore Quaternary sequence, which contains beach deposits as well as fluvial and glaciofluvial deposits, may have areas of suitable high mineral concentrations. Known, relatively high concentrations of minerals include cassiterite (tin) off the Cornish coast and magnetite (iron) east of Shetland. A systematic study of heavy mineral distribution in the North Sea between 54° and 59°N by the British Geological Survey showed that concentrations of heavy minerals are generally greater near the coasts than in areas farther offshore.

RESEARCH TO SUPPORT PLANNING FOR OFFSHORE SAND AND GRAVEL UTILISATION

Sand and gravel deposits on the seabed around the UK are shown by the British Geological Survey offshore geological mapping programme to be extensive. However, this impression is to some extent misleading in relation to assessing potential sources for extraction, as the grading criteria used to define the different sediment types on the BGS maps do not correspond to the classification system used by the aggregates industry and, in addition, the regional mapping programme does not provide sufficient detail to allow an adequate assessment of marine sand and gravel resources, as seabed sample sites are generally more than 5 km apart and the spacing of seismic lines is in the order of 10 km. The study commissioned by DoE on Marine Dredging for Sand and Gravel, published by HMSO in 1987, concluded that the available information on offshore aggregates resources was inadequate as a basis for planning for the future contribution to aggregates needs from the marine sector.

What is required for resource planning is a reconnaissance survey which will provide an accurate three-dimensional geological picture of the seabed at a scale which allows prediction with reasonable certainty of the locations of commercially significant resources of sand and gravel. In order to provide this information, the Crown Estate and Minerals Division of DoE have adopted a two-tier approach.

The first stage of this approach, directed and financed by the Crown Estate and carried out by BGS, is a programme of desk studies covering all offshore areas of the British Isles. These studies draw together available information concerning bathymetry, tidal current regime, solid and Quaternary geology and transportation and distribution of seabed sediments. They are aimed at summarising marine aggregates' resource potential in order to identify areas which merit more detailed assessments and surveys to define in broad terms the available resource.

The second stage consists of research to provide more detailed resource assessment surveys, targeted by the first stage desk studies, which fill a crucial gap between the BGS offshore survey mapping, which identifies general bottom conditions but gives limited indication of the resource potential, and the detailed evaluation work which the industry must undertake in specific areas to bring them into production. The detailed resource assessment research commissioned with BGS by the Department of the Environment and the Crown Estate provides information on the quality and quantity of marine sand and gravel resources for planning and resource management purposes.

The first-stage desk study programme has produced reports covering the Southern North Sea and South Coast. The other principal dredging areas will be subject to desk studies in due course.

The second stage resource assessment research has produced a detailed report of the marine aggregate resources in the area off Great Yarmouth and Southwold, East Anglia, currently the most important dredging area in terms of production and markets. The results of this work have facilitated planning for aggregates provision in the South East and East Anglia regions of England and provided a framework for resource management in the area. The results of a resource assessment study off the South Coast of England and the Humber area of the East Coast are now available from the Crown Estate. These resource surveys have been carried out by BGS. The British Geological Survey expects to extend this research to assess resources in the Bristol Channel, Liverpool Bay and the Thames Estuary.

The Department of the Environment, the Crown Estate and the BGS are making considerable efforts to identify the areas that are important in terms of their mineral resources. It is to be hoped that MAFF will put work in hand to provide data at a similar level of detail on sites of importance to fisheries.

In addition to the research into resources described above, the Crown Estate and DoE also commission research into the effects of dredging, both in terms of sediment transport and effect on coast lines and the rate of recolonisation of the sea bed by biota after dredging. The Crown Estate are also funding a joint study with SCOPAC (Standing Conference on Problems Associated with the Coast) to investigate sediment transport paths between St. Catherine's Point on the Isle of Wight and Shoreham in East Sussex from the coast to the 50 m isobath. This study is being conducted jointly by Hydraulics Research, Wallingford and Southampton University.

SOURCES OF INFORMATION

BALSON, P.S., & HARRISON, D.J. 1986. Marine Aggregate Survey. Phase 1, Southern North Sea. *BGS Marine Report,* No. 86/38.

BALSON, P.S., & HARRISON, D.J. 1988. Marine Aggregate Survey. Phase 1, Southern North Sea. *BGS Marine Report,* No. 88/31.

HARRISON, D.J. 1988. The marine sand and gravel resources off Great Yarmouth and Southwold, East Anglia. *BGS Technical Report WB/88/9/C,* Marine Geology Series.

NUNNY, R.S., & CHILLINGWORTH, P.C.H. 1986. Marine Dredging for Sand and Gravel. Department of the Environment HMSO, London.

GEOCHEMISTRY

The British Geological Survey has collected chemical data on seabed sediments since 1971. The chemical database has now been built up to cover most of the UK sector of the North Sea on a grid of approximately 5 km. Almost 9,000 samples have been analysed for 28 elements by direct reading emission spectrometry, atomic absorption spectrometry and delayed neutron activation analysis. The analyses have been carried out on freeze-dried samples of the portion of the sample finer than 2 mm (the sand and mud fractions).

The geochemical data at present exist in computer files and are now being transferred to the British Geological Survey Offshore Database (an ORACLE database). Studies are continuing on the interpretation of these data and their correlation with other geological and geotechnical information.

Preliminary distribution maps are now being prepared. It is hoped that these maps will eventually be published in a similar format to that produced by the Geochemical Survey Programme being carried out on land areas of the UK by the British Geological Survey for the Department of Trade and Industry.

ACKNOWLEDGEMENTS

This chapter was produced by Dr Dan Leggett, NCC Earth Science Division (now with NRA, Anglia Region) and Colin Graham, British Geological Survey, Edinburgh. Additional information on aggregates and minerals were obtained from Minerals Division (DoE).

REFERENCES

AGAR, R. 1960. Postglacial erosion of the North Yorkshire coast from the Tees estuary to Ravenscar. *Proceedings of the Yorkshire Geological Society, 32*: 408-425.

BARTRUM, J.A. 1935. *Shore platforms.* Proc. Aust-No. 2. *Ass. Adumt. Scl.*, *22*: 135-143.

BIRD, E.C.F. 1985. *Coastline changes – a global review.* Chichester, Wiley-Interscience.

CHAMBERS, G. 1976. Temporal scales in coastal erosion systems. *Transactions of the Institute of British Geographers*, NS1: 246-256.

DAVIS, W.M. 1912. A geographical pilgrimage from Ireland to Italy. *Annals of the Association of American Geographers*, 2: 73-100.

FLEMING, N.C. 1965. Form and relation to present sea level of Pleistocene marine erosion features. *Journal of Geology, 73*: 799-811.

GRAY, J.M. 1985. *Glacio-isostatic, shoreline development in Scotland: an overview.* Occasional Paper No. 24, Q.M.C., University of London.

GUILCHER, A. 1958. *Coastal and submarine morphology.* London, Methuen.

HILLS, 1972. Shore platforms and wave ramps. *Geological Magazine, 109*: 81-88.

HUTCHINSON, J.N. 1972. Field and laboratory studies of a fall in upper chalk at Joss Bay, Isle of Thanet. *In: Stress strain behaviour of soils*, ed. by R.H.G. Parry. Proceedings of the Roscoe Memorial Symposium, Cambridge: 692-706.

JOHNSON, D.W. 1919. *Shore process and shoreline development.* New York, Wiley.

KING, C.A.M. 1959. *Beaches and coasts.* London, Arnold.

KING, C.A.M. 1972. *Beaches and coasts.* 2nd edn. London, Arnold.

KOMAR, P.D. 1976. *Beach processes and sedimentation.* New Jersey, Prentice-Hall.

MOTTERSHEAD, D.N. 1982. Coastal spray weathering of bedrock in the supratidal zone of East Prawle, South Devon. *Field Studies, 5:* 663-684.

PETHICK, J.S. 1984. *An introduction to coastal geomorphology.* London, Arnold.

RITCHIE, W., SMITH, J.S., & ROSE, N. 1978. *Beaches of Northeast Scotland.* Countryside Commission.

ROBINSON, L.A. 1977. Erosive Processes on the Shore Platform of Northeast Yorkshire, England. *Marine Geology, 23*: 339-361.

SHENNAN, I. 1987. Holocene sea-level changes in the North Sea region. *In: Sea-level changes*, ed. by M.J. Tooley & I. Shennan. Oxford, Basil Blackwell.

SMALL, R.J. 1970. *The study of landforms.* Cambridge, Cambridge University Press.

SO, C.L. 1965. Coastal platforms of the Isle of Thanet, Kent. *Transactions of the Institute of British Geographers, 37*: 147-156.

STEERS, J.A. 1948. *A picture book of the whole coast of England and Wales.* Cambridge, Cambridge University Press.

STEERS, J.A. 1960. *The coast of England and Wales in pictures.* Cambridge, Cambridge University Press.

STEERS, J.A. 1969. *The coastline of England and Wales.* 2nd edn. Cambridge, Cambridge University Press.

STEERS, J.A. 1973. *The coastline of Scotland.* Cambridge, Cambridge University Press.

STEERS, J.A., STODDART, D.R., BAYLISS-SMITH, T.P., SPENCER, T., & DURBRIDGE, P.M. 1979. The storm surge of 11 January 1978 on the East Coast of England. *Geographical Journal 145:* 192-205.

SUESS, E. 1888. *The face of the Earth, II* (English translation by H.B.C. Sollas, 1906) Oxford, Oxford University Press.

TRENHAILE, A.S. 1971. Lithological control of high-water rock ledges in the Vale of Glamorgan, Wales. *Geografiska Annaler, 53*: 59-69.

TRENHAILE, A.S. 1987. *The geomorphology of rock coasts.* Oxford, Clarendon Press.

VALENTIN, H. 1954. Die Erde. *Zeitschrift der Gesellschaft für Erdkunde zu Berlin.*

WARD, E.M. 1922. *English coastal evolution.* London, Methuen.

WOOD, A. 1968. Beach platforms in the chalk of Kent, England. *Z. Geomorph., 12:* 107-113.

WRIGHT, L.W. 1967. Some characteristics of the shore platforms of the England Channel coast and the Northern part of the North Island New Zealand. *Z. Geomorph., 11:* 36-46.

WRIGHT, L.W. 1970. Variation in the level of the cliff/shore platform junction along the south coast of Great Britain. *Marine Geology, 9:* 347-353.

Chapter 4

COASTAL HABITATS

4.1 INTRODUCTION

The geological nature of the landform varies along the North Sea coastal margin as do climatic and edaphic factors which further influence faunal and floral community composition at any particular location. The main features which characterise the environment of the terrestrial coastal zone are described within this chapter.

Each habitat is considered separately. The distribution of the resources is shown together with a brief description of the main features of interest. The geographical variation and factors affecting the nature conservation interest of the habitat are also given.

Coastal formations included in this section are:
4.2 Sea cliffs
4.3 Sand dunes
4.4 Saltmarshes
4.5 Shingle
4.6 Coastal saline lagoons
4.7 Coastal grazing marshes.

4.2 SEA CLIFFS

INTRODUCTION

A sea cliff is defined as a break in slope between 15° and the vertical, variable in height, found at the contact with land and sea and which owes its existence in some way to the sea (Guilcher 1958). The coastline of Britain is dominated by steep cliffs, particularly in the north-west, their form and height depending on the type of rock: hard rock (metamorphic and igneous rocks) and soft rock (weakly metamorphosed sedimentary rocks and earth cliffs).

On exposed sites, salt spray is an important factor, giving a distinctly maritime flavour to the vegetation. The geology of the underlying rock, exposure and other climatic factors combine to form a wide range of variation in plant and animal communities, which is described below. Vertical hard rock cliffs, particularly in the north, also provide important areas for nesting seabirds and this interest is dealt with elsewhere (see Section 7.2). The nutrient enrichment caused by these colonies may have significant effects on the vegetation and some comment is made on this also.

DISTRIBUTION

Along the North Sea coastal margin there are approximately 850 km of cliffs which exceed 20 m in height (11% of North Sea coastline), of which 482 km occur in northern Scotland. There are only two stretches of the North Sea coastline which are largely devoid of cliffs (Figure 4.2.1). Between Flamborough Head and the Thames estuary the only cliffs are those which form low cliffs of Pleistocene sand, gravels and boulder clays near Cromer in Norfolk. The second area is between West Sussex and Dorset.

Rock type

Vertical or near vertical hard rock cliffs, composed of granite, sandstone or limestone, are resistant to the impact of waves. Weathering takes place slowly and this creates opportunities for vegetation development where ledges or crevices occur, or a break in slope allows soils to accumulate. This type of rock is found around the whole of the North Sea coast, though they are most frequent and extensive in north and north-east Scotland and in south-west England.

By contrast, soft rock cliffs, defined largely by their inherent instability, are much more limited in their distribution. Cliffs are formed from sand and clay deposits in the south and east of England and some of the softer chalk outcrops such as those on the Channel coast.

The height of sea cliffs along the North Sea margin varies, with some of the most spectacular being found in the north – Old Red Sandstone forms

Table 4.2.1
Description of sea cliffs
along the North Sea coast.

Rock type	Geology	Description
Basalt	Igneous	Fine grained, red/brown rock, sheer vertical cliffs
Granite	Igneous	Coarse grained, colour varies, steep vertical with caves
Chalk	Sedimentary	Pure soft white limestone, vertical cliffs
Limestone	Sedimentary	Calcite, soft, pale-coloured, sheer sloping cliffs with stacks
Sand and clay	Sedimentary	Very unstable, varies in colour
Sandstone	Sedimentary	Hard, coarse rock quartz, minerals, colour variable, forms stacks, ledges and gullies

a precipice on Foula, Shetland (370 m) and on Hoy in Orkney the highest vertical wall is 335 m. This rock type weathers to give steep cliffs with ledges. On the mainland, the highest cliffs are found at Cape Wrath (210 m) in Sutherland and in the south at Boulby Cliff (200 m) in Yorkshire. The cliffs at Boulby are formed of Liassic shale, sandstone and boulder clay.

In certain areas igneous rocks have formed small, isolated islands which are bordered by cliffs – Bass Rock and Isle of May, Firth of Forth. Limestone and chalk cliffs in the south of Britain also form high, vertical cliffs (Dover, Beachy Head) whereas the soft rocks along the Dorset coastline are unstable and although steep cliffs form, these are subject to considerable erosion. The main areas of this type of coast are found in the south and east of England from south Humberside to west Dorset.

The main rock types along the North Sea coastline are given in Table 4.2.1.

DESCRIPTION OF RESOURCE

Coastal cliffs provide a significant resource for wildlife conservation both in terms of their geology (see Chapter 3), seabird colonies (see Section 7.2), plant communities and associated invertebrate and other vertebrate animals. This section concentrates on the vegetation and associated fauna.

Vegetation

On hard rock cliffs the underlying rock type, notably whether it is basic or acid, helps to determine the predominant form of vegetation. Superimposed on this is variation relating to exposure (to wind and salt spray) and climatic factors. The combined effect is to support a relatively stable vegetation on thin soils which shows a zonation from the more exposed maritime vegetation with typically salt-tolerant species to essentially terrestrial types of acid heath or calcareous grassland.

Maritime cliff plant species have low growth rates compared with inland species on non-saline conditions, and are sensitive to a small temperature range. The availability of nutrients to vegetation is determined by the depth of soil and, where sea spray influence is strong, by the addition of calcium and other nutrients from the seawater. Shallow soils usually have a high salt content because of the frequent inundation by seawater and sea spray.

The vegetation types which occur exclusively on coastal cliffs are quite distinct and many include the species confined to the coastal fringe in Britain. On very shallow soils certain species have adapted to avoid summer droughts by adopting a winter annual reproductive strategy or by having thick, succulent leaves and extensive root systems. The competitive ability of inland species is reduced by high salinity, creating an environment where other species which are sensitive to competition can survive (rock samphire *Crithmum maritimum*).

The softer rock outcrops, including limestone and chalk, may form high vertical cliffs but can be too unstable to support a rich flora or fauna. Land slip is common in sand and clay deposits in the south and east of England where continuous erosion results in the formation of high sloping unstable cliffs. In these situations some of the least 'maritime' of the coastal cliff vegetation is found and may be indistinguishable from inland types.

The slumping cliff slopes show a wide diversity of vegetation types. In areas subject to recent landslip the cliffs have little or no vegetation. These areas are colonised by a succession of plant species including colt's-foot *Tussilago farfara*, kidney vetch *Anthyllis vulneraria* and creeping bent *Agrostis stolonifera*. There are few distinct maritime species although bithynian vetch *Vicia bythinica* and tufted centaury *Centaurium capitatum* are good examples

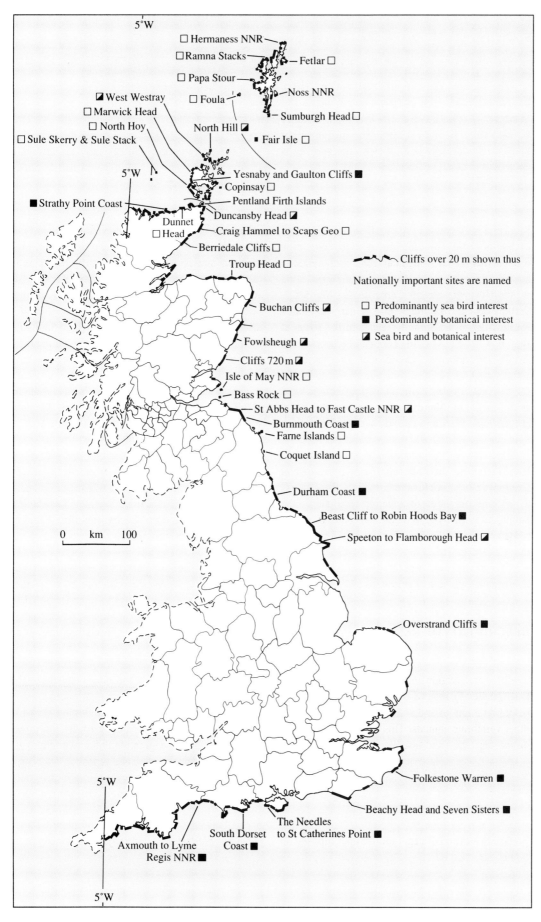

Figure 4.2.1
Distribution of sea cliffs
(>20 m height) along the
North Sea coastal margin.
Based upon the 1975 Ordnance Survey
1:1,250,000 map with the permission
of the Controller of Her Majesty's
Stationery Office © Crown Copyright.

5°W

☐ Hermaness NNR
☐ Ramna Stacks ─ Fetlar ☐
☐ Papa Stour ─
☐ Foula ── Noss NNR
◩ West Westray
☐ Marwick Head ── Sumburgh Head ☐
☐ North Hoy
North Hill ◪
☐ Sule Skerry & Sule Stack
■ Fair Isle ☐
5°W
Yesnaby and Gaulton Cliffs ■
• Copinsay ☐
■ Strathy Point Coast ── Pentland Firth Islands
Duncansby Head ◪
Dunnet ── Craig Hammel to Scaps Geo ☐
☐ Head
── Berriedale Cliffs ☐
Troup Head ☐

─── Cliffs over 20 m shown thus

Nationally important sites are named

Buchan Cliffs ◪

☐ Predominantly sea bird interest
■ Predominantly botanical interest
◪ Sea bird and botanical interest

Fowlsheugh ◪
─ Cliffs 720 m ◪
Isle of May NNR ☐
Bass Rock ☐
St Abbs Head to Fast Castle NNR ◪
Burnmouth Coast ■
Farne Islands ☐
Coquet Island ☐

Durham Coast ■

Beast Cliff to Robin Hoods Bay ■
─ Speeton to Flamborough Head ◪

0   km   100

Overstrand Cliffs ■

Folkestone Warren ■

Beachy Head and Seven Sisters ■
5°W
The Needles
to St Catherines Point ■
South Dorset
Coast ■
Axmouth to Lyme
Regis NNR ■

5°W

5°W

of scarce species associated with the soft cliffs. However, scrub and even woodland can develop on some ledges, which may remain stable for some time.

The National Vegetation Classification (NVC), has identified thirteen maritime communities and these are shown in Table 4.2.2 (from Nature Conservancy Council 1989). The influence of maritime features on coastal cliff communities is described in detail in Rodwell (1988).

Regional variation on the North Sea coast

Maritime rock-crevice and cliff-ledge. In the north of Scotland the combination of high, hard rock cliffs and exposure to wind and salt spray result in some of the best examples of maritime vegetation on the North Sea coast. Communities like MC3, dominated by roseroot *Sedum rosea* and Scot's lovage *Ligusticum scoticum*, are found on many of the vertical salt spray-drenched cliffs around the whole of the north-east of Scotland. They form fine stands on Old Red Sandstone where it is generally out of reach of grazing animals. Communities MC2 and MC3 are also usually associated with inaccessible cliffs where sea campion *Silene maritima* and thrift *Armeria maritima* are frequent. In some of the richer areas arctic alpine plants occur such as purple saxifrage *Saxifraga oppositifolia* and moss campion *Silene acaulis*.

Occupying the same zone but restricted to the south and west coast of Britain is the community identified as MC1. Rare species found there are curved hard-grass *Parapholis incurva* and Portland sea-lavender *Limonium recurvum* (see Section 7.8),

the latter being restricted to cliffs at Portland, Dorset.

On relatively sheltered, dry, calcareous cliffs on the south coast, where the community is determined more by the instability of the cliff than exposure to salt spray, wild cabbage *Brassica oleracea* is found on crumbling edges and sloping ledges (MC4). This species is rare in Britain and is found in association with other rare species such as early spider-orchid *Ophrys sphegodes* and Nottingham catchfly *Silene nutans* (see Section 7.8).

Maritime cliff and cliff-top grassland. On cliffs with less exposure to salt-laden air, particularly in the north where grazing pressure is heavy, the most common grassland community is MC10. This is especially well developed on Orkney and Shetland where sheep grazing occurs in a region of high rainfall. One rare plant found within this community, along the north-east coast of England and Scotland, is purple milk-vetch *Astragalus danicus*.

On the south coast comparable grassland communities are characterised by the constant presence of *Festuca rubra* and *Holcus lanatus* (MC9). On chalk and limestone cliffs on the south coast the community is identified as MC11, Reduction of cliff-top grazing pressure in many areas has, however, resulted in the replacement of this community with a rank *Bromus erectus* or *Brachypodium pinnatum* grassland and consequent decline of species such as white horehound *Marrubium vulgare* and bastard-toadflax *Thesium humifusum*. These communities form part of the calcareous grassland classification CG3 and CG4 respectively. The susceptibility of sea carrot *Daucus*

National Vegetation Classification Code	NVC community type	Characteristic species
MC1	Maritime rock crevice	*Crithmum maritimum-Spergularia rupicola*
MC2	Maritime rock crevice	*Armeria maritima-Ligusticum scoticum*
MC3	Maritime cliff ledge	*Sedum rosea-Armeria maritima*
MC4	Maritime cliff ledge	*Brassica oleracea*
MC5	Maritime cliff and cliff-top grassland	*Armeria maritima-Cerastium diffusum*
MC6	Seabird cliff	*Atriplex hastata-Beta vulgaris* ssp. *maritima*
MC7	Seabird cliff	*Stellaria media-Rumex acetosa*
MC8	Maritime grassland	*Festuca rubra-Armeria maritima*
MC9	Maritime grassland	*Festuca rubra-Holcus lanatus*
MC10	Maritime grassland	*Festuca rubra-Plantago* spp.
MC11	Maritime grassland	*Festuca rubra-Daucus carota* ssp. *gummifer*
MC12	Maritime grassland	*Festuca rubra-Hyacinthoides non-scripta*
SM16	Perched saltmarsh	*Festuca rubra*

Table 4.2.2
Plant communities of coastal cliffs in Great Britain (MC, maritime cliff; SM, saltmarsh communities).

carota ssp. *gummifer* to frost and to acid soils is thought to limit this species to the south.

Maritime heath. The less steeply sloping sea cliffs may also support transitions from grassland to heathland which can be very rich in species, including rarities such as Scottish primrose *Primula scotica*. This species can be found at Strathy Point, Sutherland and on the west coast of Orkney, notably at Yesnaby where transitions into typical heathland are found. In the north a maritime form of crowberry *Empetrum nigrum* heathland occurs on deep, free-draining mineral soils. On wetter soils, cross-leaved heath *Erica tetralix* may form, with heather *Calluna vulgaris* and bell heather *Erica cinerea* being found in drier areas.

This is a very rich community, though even in the north of Scotland, where it is well represented, the extent of the truly maritime zone can be small. In its most extreme form the plant communities may resemble those of saltmarshes around 'geos' where the cliff-top is drenched in salt spray.

Coastal grassland, heath and scrub. Many cliffs on the North Sea coast (particularly those which are east facing) are only marginally exposed to the onslaught of the full power of the breaking waves and salt spray. Elsewhere, either because of the orientation of the coast, the absence of a rocky foreshore against which waves can break, the presence of a high beach, or because the cliffs themselves absorb the wave energy and erode, vegetation more typical of inland types occur. These are most prevalent in the slumping earth cliffs of the south and south-east where, in their most extreme form, woodland can develop (Axmouth to Lyme Regis undercliffs). In between there may be examples of mosaics with maritime vegetation on exposed promontories. On more sheltered spots, heather *Calluna vulgaris* heathland or tall grassland with bluebells *Hyacinthoides non-scripta* and other woodland plants may form. Typically in these areas the cliff vegetation is restricted to the steepest slopes with intensive agricultural land reaching to the very edge of the cliff.

Invertebrates

Specific information on the distribution of invertebrates is not yet available, although a considerable amount of work has been undertaken which demonstrates the value of specialised cliff micro-habitats such as sand exposures and cliff seepages to them. The warm, south-facing, soft cliffs of the south coast support notable assemblages of invertebrates, in particular aculeate Hymenoptera

(bees and wasps), Coleoptera (beetles) and Diptera (flies). Many of these are recognised as being nationally rare or endangered and have been listed in the British Red Data Books. The Glanville fritillary butterfly *Melitaea cinxia* is a good example of a cliff-dwelling species being confined, in Britain, to the disturbed cliff-face vegetation of the south coast of the Isle of Wight.

Vertebrates

The sea cliffs around the British coast are internationally famous for their large colonies of seabirds (see Section 7.2). The most common and conspicuous species are guillemot *Uria aalge*, kittiwake *Rissa tridactyla*, fulmar *Fulmarus glacialis* and razorbill *Alca torda*. The steep-sided granite cliffs of the Bass Rock, Firth of Forth, hold the largest population of gannet *Morus bassanus* on the east coast. On sloping cliffs where soil has accumulated, species which prefer to nest in burrows are found in high numbers – puffin *Fratercula arctica* and manx shearwater *Puffinus puffinus*. Sea cliffs also provide nesting sites for a rare bird of prey, the peregrine *Falco peregrinus*. Raven *Corvus corax* may also nest on cliff-faces.

The short-tailed vole *Microtis agrestis* thrives on ungrazed cliff slopes. Bats use caves and clefts as roosting, breeding and hibernating sites. The caves along the Dorset coast are especially important for several species of bat including the greater horseshoe bat *Rhinolophus ferrumequinum*, Bechstein's bat *Myotis bechsteinii*, Daubenton's bat *Myotis daubentoni*, Natterer's bat *Myotis nattereri*, whiskered bat *Myotis mystacinus* and the very rare mouse-eared bat *Myotis myotis*.

Adders *Vipera berus*, common lizard *Lacerta vivipara*, and slow-worm *Anguis fragilis* are all to be found locally on broken cliff habitats. The nationally rare sand lizard *Lacerta agilis* is also found on sandy, south facing cliffs around Bournemouth, Dorset.

IMPORTANT SITES

Hard rock cliffs

Important sites which include northern elements of both maritime and para-maritime vegetation are confined to the north and north-east of Scotland including Orkney (Yesnaby and Westray), Shetland and along the north coast of Sutherland, notably at Strathy Point. The most important locations are given in Figure 4.2.1, which also gives an indication of their value botanically or ornithologically.

On the more sheltered sections of the east coast, notably south of Inverness, the areas of maritime cliff vegetation are much more restricted. The truly arctic alpine species found further north on cliffs such as Yesnaby or Strathy Point are absent and at several sites transitions to cliff-top grassland and heath are truncated by agricultural development. The most important sites are Buchan Cliffs and Fowlsheugh, Grampian. St. Abb's Head supports a limited extent of maritime vegetation and is also an important seabird site.

Hard rock cliffs do occur further south on the east coast but these support communities with little truly maritime influence. Thus, the National Vegetation Classification types are restricted to the most terrestrial part of the zonation and tall herb communities, sometimes with bluebell *Hyacinthoides non-scripta* and cowslip *Primula veris,* are often found.

Soft cliffs

Soft rock cliffs occur as mainly low features formed from Pleistocene sands, gravels and boulder clays. At Cromer, Norfolk, cliffs are formed from glacio-fluvial and aeolian drift and till deposits resting on chalk bedrock (Cooper 1988). The eroding cliffs and landslides help build the beach below, affording some protection to the cliff itself. On the south coast soft cliffs are formed from Tertiary and Cretaceous sands, clays and marls. These are also actively eroding and display a wide diversity of coastal landslip features. The most important examples of soft cliff woodland and scrub are found at Axmouth–Lyme Regis and Folkestone Warren. Examples of open vegetation occur north of Flamborough Head (Speeton Cliffs), and on the Norfolk coast near Cromer.

Limestone and chalk cliffs

Chalk and limestone cliffs on the south coast of England support a rich vegetation which is peculiar to this area. The warmer weather in the south accentuates the low moisture value of shallow, calcium-rich soils. The cliffs support a number of rare and local plants on their upper faces and slopes, including the grass *Koeleria vallesiana*, and small restharrow *Ononis reclinata*. Two rare species found on calcareous sea cliffs are sea stock *Matthiola sinuata* and hoary stock *Matthiola incana* (see Section 7.8).

At Purbeck, Dorset (Cooper 1988), the cliffs are formed from chalk and limestone with clay and sands interdigitated in the west. To the east of St. Alban's Head the cliffs are formed from Upper Jurassic limestone. Rock platforms are a noticeable feature above the high water mark. Both areas have been extensively quarried in the past, which has left a series of caves and crumbling cliff edges.

Slumping in the area has caused cliff slopes to extend over several hundred metres, almost removing cliff-top vegetation from the influence of sea spray. Cliff falls, quarrying and slumping have contributed to an intricate mix of plant communities which have established on the cliff faces, many of which are not typical of maritime cliff vegetation.

The vegetation which has developed here provides an illustration of the zonation found on the south coast. Along the dry, crumbling cliff-edge wild cabbage *Brassica oleracea* exists. This species is characteristic of southern maritime cliff-ledge communities. To the east the cliff-face is vertical and more maritime species are present with maritime grassland forming on a sloping cliff-top.

On the rock platforms the vegetation is more characteristic of maritime communities with sea thrift *Armeria maritima*, rock samphire *Crithmum maritimum* and buck's-horn plantain *Plantago coronopus* occupying varying locations.

The main area of undercliff supports hawthorn *Crataegus monogyna* scrub. This community is also common on the boulder-strewn, quarry-blasted clitter. A narrow strip of cliff-top vegetation dominated by the grass *Arrhenatherum elatius* and which includes some *Prunus spinosa-Rubus fruticosa* scrub, is bordered by agricultural land.

The Hart Warren–Hawthorn Dene coast of Durham supports the best para-maritime Magnesium Limestone cliffs in Britain. Notable populations of at least eight species of orchid occur together with other local plants such as moonwort *Botrichium lunaria*, grass-of-Parnassus *Parnassia palustris*, butterwort *Pinguicula vulgaris* and bird's-eye primrose *Primula farinosa*. Here the calcareous grasslands occur on the steep slopes and provide examples of vegetation types more typical of inland situations, but which have suffered losses due to agricultural and industrial development. The same is true of the chalk cliffs of Beachy Head, the limestones of south Dorset and the Isle of Wight.

IMPACTS ON COASTAL CLIFFS

Coastal protection

Erosion and subsequent land-slip are common features of certain types of cliff. The addition of artificial coast protection in front of unstable cliffs prevents the removal of eroded material by the sea as well as obscuring the cliff itself. This has implications for other coastal areas which rely on transported sediments to maintain their structure. The build up of scree and undercliff, where sediments are not removed, changes the composition of the vegetation which exists there.

Agriculture

Cultivation of cliff-top soils, particularly on the east coast, has modified the vegetation composition and reduced the area available to maritime species. Grazing on cliff-tops is still common practice in the north of Scotland. While it is important to the maintenance of the sometimes species-rich sward, intensive use and associated eutrophication can lead to loss of diversity with selection of resistant plant species, particularly if sheep are grazing cliff-top maritime swards. Trampling by both cattle and sheep consolidates the sward and may instigate a change in reproductive strategy in some grasses. Compaction and impeded drainage on damp soils reduces grass cover. Elsewhere on less exposed cliff-tops grazing may be a positive benefit as the grasslands or heathlands approach their inland equivalents, which are themselves dependent on grazing to support their rich and varied plant and animal communities.

Recreation

Coastal areas attract a great deal of interest. The development of holiday centres to accommodate visitors, along with the creation of cliff-top paths and steps to allow easy access to beaches and to view bird nesting sites, has led to a reduction in the visual and wildlife interest of some areas. Trampling and rock climbing destroy plant life and may lead to a loss of variety as well as disturbance to bird life.

Development

Quarrying for limestone (south coast) and the dumping of colliery waste in County Durham have locally impoverished the plant communities which exist there. The transportation of spoil along the coast may also have severe implications for other coastal habitats.

SOURCES OF INFORMATION

In 1986 the Nature Conservancy Council contracted Lancaster University to look at past and present land use on top of cliffs and to produce a handbook for the practical management of cliff-top vegetation

for nature conservation (Mitchley & Malloch 1991). As part of this contract a bibliography was also produced (Mitchley 1989) and sites have been surveyed by Cooper (1988) to assess the time-scale required to prepare an inventory of all sea cliff and cliff-top vegetation. This project forms part of the national survey of coastal habitats which was undertaken by NCC. Reports on only thirteen sites were completed and these include references to the National Vegetation Classification for maritime cliff communities produced by Rodwell 1988. Survey of the major part of the cliffed coastline of the North Sea margin remains a priority task.

The National Trust holds survey information for coastal properties in England which include cliff habitats. A list of survey reports is given in Mitchley (1989). The Countryside Commission has also surveyed those stretches of coastline identified as Heritage Coast sites (see Section 10.2).

4.3   SAND DUNES

INTRODUCTION

Sand dunes occur wherever the physical conditions allow sand to accumulate. They are important natural habitats providing characteristic succession patterns associated with specialised plant and animal species.

In Great Britain as a whole, sand dune structures represent a rare habitat of approximately 56,000 ha which includes areas affected by afforestation (14%) and other land use activities including cultivation (the machairs of western Scotland) and golf courses.

DISTRIBUTION

A recent estimate carried out by the Nature Conservancy Council suggests that there are some 56,345 ha of dune land in Great Britain, of which approximately 25,000 ha lies along the North Sea coastline. Here sand dunes are prominent features in the Moray Firth, the Northumberland coast, along the Lincolnshire and Humberside coasts and in Norfolk from the Wash to Cromer. The east of Scotland and north-east of England together account for 17,694 ha of sand dunes. Elsewhere there are a few large systems in the south and south east of England (1,602 ha), notably Sandwich Bay and Studland.

The distribution map (Figure 4.3.1) has been compiled from the Coastal Resource Survey and updated from the National Sand Dune Survey,

Figure 4.3.1
Distribution of sand dune
systems along the North Sea
coastal margin.

Based upon the 1975 Ordnance Survey
1:1,250,000 map with the permission
of the Controller of Her Majesty's
Stationery Office © Crown Copyright.

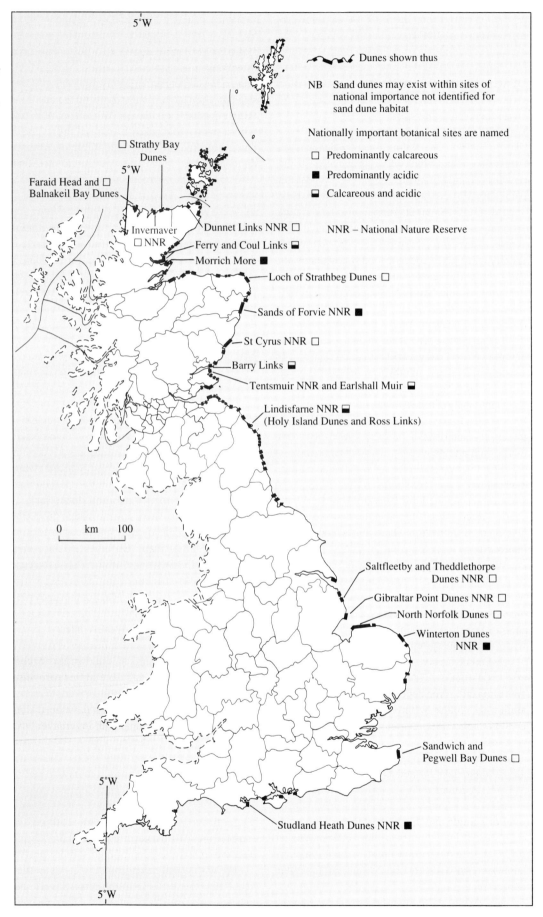

originally carried out by the NCC and now the responsibility of JNCC.

DESCRIPTION OF RESOURCE

Dune formation and type

The formation of sand dunes takes place where a supply of dry sand which is being transported by the prevailing wind becomes trapped by obstacles in its path (shingle, tidal litter and vegetation). Of these, vegetation is the most important since it both encourages further deposition of sand particles and acts as a stabiliser. Development of a sand dune usually takes place above a sand flat which is at a sufficiently high level to allow the surface layer to dry out at low tide. Sand which is removed naturally from the upper dry zone may be replenished by wave action on the lower shore.

The shape and size of the dune depends on the amount of 'dry' sand available, the direction and strength of the wind and the profile of the shore. If the coast is prograding (extending seaward), an abundant supply of sand allows a series of sand ridges to form in a time sequence, creating a front shore system characteristic of the dune types on the North Sea coastal margin where prevailing and dominant winds are in opposite directions. This is in sharp contrast to the western shores of the Irish Sea and Channel coast where the prevailing westerly and south-westerly winds are also the dominant ones. This leads to a situation where dunes tend to move landward.

Where the supply of sand is limited, the established ridge will reach a maximum height before being eroded and transported landward. On the east coast there is generally a bigger supply of sand in Scotland than in south and east England where high dune systems do not normally occur.

Sediment supply to a beach may be from cliff erosion, particularly in the soft rock areas of southeast England, river deposition, mainly in upland areas where coarse sediments are carried out to sea, erosion of existing terrestrial sand structures or from seabed deposits.

There are six main types of dune system (Figure 4.3.2) which have formed as the result of different influencing forces:

❖ offshore island dune systems – these rest on sand or shingle and are formed under high wave energy conditions, often providing sufficient shelter for mud-flats and marshland to form on their landward side: Scolt Head in Norfolk and Holkham in Norfolk

❖ prograding dune systems, ness and cuspate forelands – these build up on an open coast where there is an abundant supply of sand either from a sand flat or where sand comes to a point from two directions at once (Ness). A series of low, narrow dune ridges and intervening slacks develop. These structures are more usually found on the east coast (Barry Links, Tayside and Winterton, Norfolk) where prevailing wind blows offshore and in opposition to dominant wind. Cuspate foreland dunes also form where two sand sources meet from outer coast and inner loch shores: Morrich More, Dornoch and Tentsmuir, Fife

❖ spit dune systems – these develop at the mouth of estuaries, forming a fan-shaped series of dune ridges and intervening slacks. Examples of one of the commoner types of system are North Seaton in Northumberland, St. Helen's Common and Dunes on the Isle of Wight and South Haven Peninsula, Purbeck

❖ bay dunes – the local topography influences the distribution of a limited supply of sand between two headlands to form a single narrow strip of dune at the back of a bay: Druridge Bay, Northumberland and Blyth to Seaton Sluice, Northumberland. This type of dune system prevails along the North Sea coastal margin except on non-east-facing coasts

❖ hindshore dune systems – found on extensive sandy coasts where the prevailing wind is also the dominant wind. These feature massive ridges which reach a maximum height and then erode landward. A complex system of dunes and slacks form. In exposed locations the strong winds can drive sand landwards for considerable distances to form an extensive sandy plain. Such systems are most common on the west coast of Britain but there is a good example at Dunnet in Caithness, which occupies a west-facing bay. Much of the sandy plain at this site has vegetation which is clearly related to that of the machairs of the Western Isles.

Distinctive dune communities can be formed in more exposed sites where sand is blown up over cliffs or hills. The national sand dune survey recognises these as a distinct type:

❖ climbing dunes. They are best developed along the north coast of Scotland with Invernaver NNR being the supreme example.

Vegetation

Vegetation plays an important role in the establishment of dunes in Great Britain. Certain plants which are tolerant of high salinity provide the initial stages of development in the strandline. These and other specialist plants are adapted to trap sand and colonise the nutrient-poor environment by

Figure 4.3.2
Main types of sand dune
system along the North Sea
coastal margin.

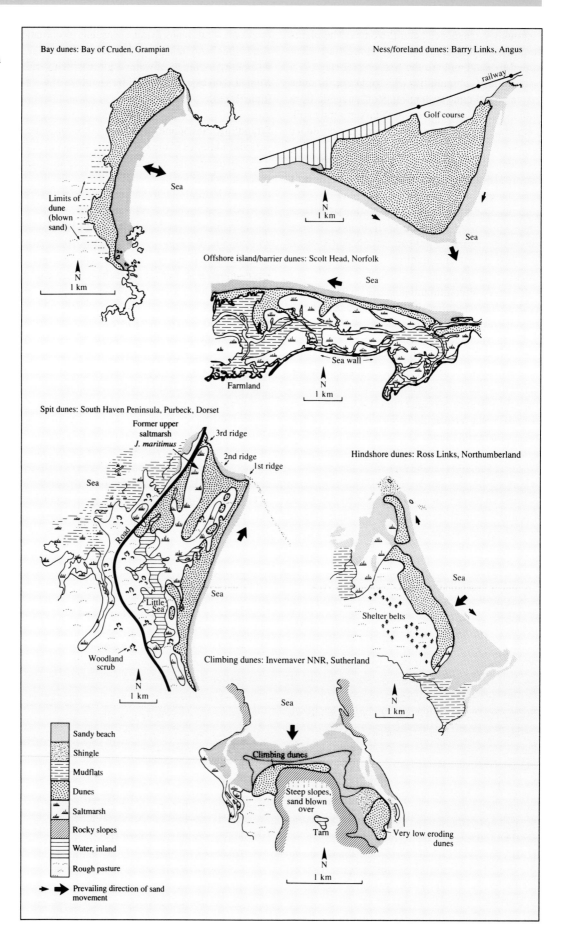

propagation from seeds and rhizomes. The plants continue to grow by vertically elongating when buried by sand and are the first crucial stage in a succession of communities which make up the dune system. Sand dune systems support endemic flora with rare or local species which favour sandy soil. Classically, community succession on sand dunes is described as strandline, foredune, yellow dune, grey dune through to heath (Figure 4.3.3), each zone being characterised by the plant species which exist there.

A number of vegetation communities which are characteristic of sand dune succession have been identified and classified as part of the NVC (Rodwell in press). These communities are listed in Table 4.3.1.

Dune heath communities are not included above as these are identified within the NVC as heath communities. Species which are characteristic of dune heath are ericaceous dwarf shrubs which form the community types H10 *Calluna vulgaris-Erica cinerea* and H11 *Calluna vulgaris-Carex arenaria*. In wetter situations *Erica tetralix* may be important. The community most often found in wetter situations is M16 *Erica tetralix-Sphagnum compactum* wet heath (a mire community).

Regional variation on the North Sea coast

The geographical range of variation on the North Sea coast is best expressed in the more stable mature stages of development. Plant communities found on sand dunes differ according to climatic conditions and underlying substratum, further influenced by the local water regime which varies from arid on exposed dune ridges to areas of water (dune lakes).

Strandline. Strandline communities occur where periodic additions of organic detritus along the tidal limit encourage the development of certain plant species. Vegetation is open and sparse and small dunes can be lost to winter storms, though succession may take place on prograding beaches. In wetter, cooler northern locations mayweed *Matricaria maritima* and cleavers *Galium aparine* (SD3 strandline) are found on sheltered strandlines where large amounts of organic debris have collected. A more widespread community which is found all along the North Sea coast has sea sandwort *Honkenya peploides* and sea rocket *Cakile maritima* as the main species (SD2).

Foredune. Pioneer species form a narrow zone above the level reached by extreme high tides. From Shetland to Northumberland, lyme grass *Leymus arenarius* is important as an early coloniser and dune builder (SD5). Marram grass *Ammophila arenaria* (SD6) largely replaces lyme grass further south. Foredune communities may also be characterised in southern locations by sea-holly *Eryngium maritimus*, absent from the north and east coast of Scotland and very sparse north of Humberside; and by sea spurge *Euphorbia paralias*,

National Vegetation Classification Code	NVC community type	Characteristic species
SD2	Strandline	*Cakile maritima-Honkenya peploides*
SD3	Strandline	*Matricaria maritima-Galium aparine*
SD4	Foredune community	*Elymus farctus* ssp. *boreali-atlanticus*
SD5	Mobile dune community	*Leymus arenarius*
SD6	Mobile dune	*Ammophila arenaria*
SD7	Semi-fixed dune community	*Ammophila arenaria-Festuca rubra*
SD8	Fixed dune grassland	*Festuca rubra-Galium verum*
SD9	Dune grassland	*Ammophila arenaria-Arrhenatherum elatius*
SD10	Dune community	*Carex arenaria*
SD11	Bryophyte/lichen community	*Carex arenaria-Cornicularia aculeata*
SD12	Grassland community	*Carex arenaria-Festuca ovina-Agrostis capillaris*
SD13	Young dune slack community	*Salix repens-Bryum pseudotriquetrum*
SD14	Young dune slack	*Salix repens-Campylium stellatum*
SD15	Dune slack community	*Salix repens-Calliergon cuspidatum*
SD16	Dune slack community	*Salix repens-Holcus lanatus*
SD17	Dune slack community	*Potentilla anserina-Carex nigra*
SD18	Dune scrub	*Hippophae rhamnoides*

Table 4.3.1
Sand dune (SD) communities.

a dune perennial which is found mainly on the south coast.

Semi-fixed dunes. 'Semi-fixed dune' vegetation is typified by marram grass tussocks. If exposed to strong winds the sand dune will remain unstable (SD6). In the north, particularly in Scotland, where the rainfall is higher, 'semi-fixed dune' vegetation is typified by the presence of *Poa pratensis* among the marram grass. Along the East Anglian coast, associated with 'acid' dune systems, the nationally rare, perennial grass *Corynephorus canescens* is locally abundant and in the south the rare sea spurge *Euphorbia paralias* and Portland spurge *E. portlandica* are present.

Small increases in organic content raise the water-holding capacity and improve the local environment for other species. To the north of the river Forth and locally in Northumberland and East Anglia the vegetation on semi-fixed dunes (SD7) is often species-poor (sub-community Typical) or characterised by the presence of the bryophyte *Hypnum cupressiforme* (sub-community *Hypnum*) which can form extensive carpets over the sand.

Elymus pycnanthus (which occurs on both sand dunes and saltmarshes) is locally abundant in Lincolnshire and East Anglia and forms a major component of the sub-community SD7e. It occurs far less frequently elsewhere on the east coast. Noticeable change occurs towards the southern half of the North Sea where restharrow *Ononis repens* dominates to produce a characteristic drought-tolerant vegetation (sub-community *Ononis repens*).

Stabilised dunes. As sand supply becomes limited, inland from the dune front, the mobile dune communities are succeeded by more stable forms. The main dune building species such as marram grass disappear and on the older, mature systems these are replaced by plant communities which reflect the geographical location of the dune and the underlying nature of the sand. Sand with a high proportion of shell fragments supports a species-rich grassland community in which red fescue *Festuca rubra* and lady's bedstraw *Galium verum* are prominent (SD8). The composition of this community is greatly influenced by the climate.

In the relatively wet, damp conditions of northern Scotland the meadow buttercup *Ranunculus acris*-daisy *Bellis perennis* sub-community (SD8d) and the selfheal *Prunella vulgaris* sub-community are widespread. Further south where conditions are drier, the field wood-rush *Luzula campestris* and *Tortula ruralis ruraliformis* sub-communities are more commonly found (SD8b and c respectively) along with a species-poor variant (SD8a) which is characteristic of undergrazed sites such as Sandwich Bay.

These sub-communities also vary regionally. Sub-communities d and e are almost totally confined to the north-west of Scotland, while a, b and c are more typical of dry conditions further south, although the nationally rare purple milk-vetch *Astragalus danicus* is to be found in dry grassland communities in the north.

The main dune grassland type in Northumberland is SD9b denoted by the presence of bloody crane's-bill *Geranium sanguineum*. This community is common north to Edinburgh but disappears south of the river Tees.

Dunnet Bay, Caithness is a bay dune system which supports calcareous species-rich links

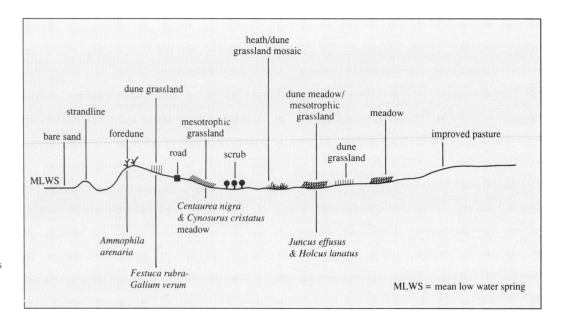

Figure 4.3.3
Succession on a calcareous dune system (species rich link grassland/machair) – Dunnet Bay, Caithness.

grassland and Figure 4.3.3 illustrates the distribution of vegetation types within such a system. One species which is restricted to the north of Scotland and occurs on calcareous dunes is the Scottish primrose *Primula scotica*. In contrast, lizard orchid *Himantoglossum hircinum* has a southern distribution and occurs in calcareous dunes in Kent (Sandwich Bay).

Non-calcareous dunes. Sand dunes which have acidic particles or where calcium has been leached from the surface tend towards acidic conditions. Acidic dunes are rare even on the east coast where dry dune communities are often rich in lichens (*Cornicularia aculeata* and *Cladonia* spp.). In the north, grassland communities are characterised by *Agrostis capillaris-Festuca ovina-Carex arenaria* (SD12) while in the south and east SD11 is more common with *Carex arenaria-Cornicularia aculeata*. Both can develop into or take over from heathland.

Dune heathland forms on the oldest and most stabilised parts of non-calcareous dunes with distinct geographical differences in the type of ericoids which develop. In the north and east of Scotland crowberry *Empetrum nigrum* dominates heath communities. Bell heather *Erica cinerea* is more common in western localities but also occurs in East Anglia and at Studland in the south. In the south and east, heather *Calluna vulgaris* persists with the sub-community *Hypnum cupressiforme* being characteristic in East Anglia.

The community on the acid dune at Barry Links is dominated by *Empetrum nigrum*, and community succession is shown in Figure 4.3.4. As a contrast, at Winterton the dune system shows

equally acidic features but vegetation has a high proportion of the rare grass *Corynephorus canescens*. The assemblage of vegetation on this system is more similar to communities found on dune systems in Denmark.

Scrub. Sea buckthorn scrub *Hippophae rhamnoides* is more abundant on the Humberside, Lincolnshire and Norfolk coasts than elsewhere. It is a natural vegetation type along the east and south-east coast but has been widely planted here and in other areas to help stabilise the dunes and act as a sea defence. Sea buckthorn fixes nitrogen from the atmosphere via root nodules and so alters the nutrient status of the dune. Sea buckthorn scrub is often associated with stands of the rather tall, rank seacouch grass *Elymus pycnanthus*. The dunes of Morrich More, Easter Ross, contain distinctive areas of wind-cut and grazed juniper *Juniperus communis* scrub which are not known from any other British dune system.

Dune slacks. Dune slack habitats are nationally rare and are especially scarce on the east coast of England. In this context Lindisfarne and Ross Links dune systems are important. A range of species, similar to those found on marsh or fen, is able to survive – marsh helleborine *Epipactus palustris* and round-leaved wintergreen *Pyrola rotundifolia*. Low shrub growth is common with either creeping willow *Salix repens* or on more acidic areas bog myrtle *Myrica gale*.

There are regional differences in flora but a number of dune constants recur all over Britain. Rare plant species which occur on sand dunes are listed in Section 7.8.

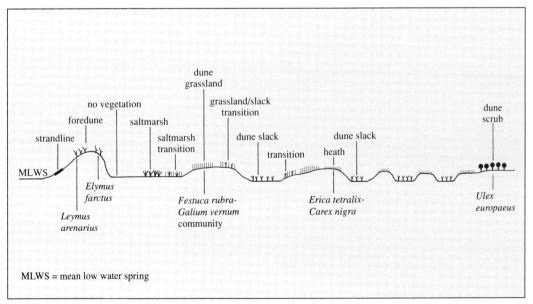

MLWS = mean low water spring

Figure 4.3.4
Succession on an acidic dune system – Barry Links, Angus.

Invertebrates

The little work which has been done on invertebrates indicates diversity within the older dunes and slacks with a wide range of insects and molluscs found in these habitats (Institute of Terrestrial Ecology 1979).

Vertebrates

Sand dunes are nationally important as habitats for certain reptiles, notably sand lizards *Lacerta agilis* on the south coast dunes and natterjack toads *Bufo calamita* on the west coast (see Section 7.6) where the combination of warm, sandy soils and shallow pools for breeding is conducive to its survival. Both these species are local in occurrence and are protected under the Wildlife and Countryside Act (1981). Adders are found on some dune systems.

Machair is very important for nesting waders (dunlin *Calidris alpina*, redshank *Tringa totanus*, oystercatcher *Haematopus ostralegus* and ringed plover *Charadrius hiaticula* (see Section 7.2) and other species which feed in the nearby marshy vegetation and shallow lagoons.

IMPORTANT SITES

Sand dune systems which exhibit topographical diversity and are associated with well developed 'slacks' are regarded as particularly important since this diversity is generally paralleled by that of the plant communities and flora. The selection of sand dune systems for statutory designation as Sites of Special Scientific Interest is determined on the basis of the representation of vegetation types from mobile foredunes, dune grassland (or heath) to dune slacks. A list of some of the more important sites is given in Table 4.3.2.

IMPACTS ON SAND DUNES

Stability

Sand dunes are an important natural form of sea defence, preventing storm waves from flooding areas of low lying land. The form and stability of individual dune systems, and the extent to which vegetation provides a protective layer, are extremely important to their ultimate conservation (Doody 1989a). Limited natural erosion helps to regenerate dune systems but where erosion is increased beyond this level the survival of the biological interest of the system and the actual structure may be at risk.

Few of the dune systems on the east coast are undergoing active net accretion. One exception is North Denes, Great Yarmouth, where several hundred metres of dune have accreted in front of the concrete sea wall built earlier this century. A rather larger number of sites appear to be in approximate equilibrium with erosion and accretion occurring at different parts of the system. Scolt Head Island, which is moving gradually westwards, is a good example. However, at the majority of

Site	Location	Status	Main botanical interest	Type of dune
Invernaver	Sutherland	NNR, SSSI	Calcareous	Climbing dune
Dunnet Links	Caithness	NNR, SSSI	Calcareous	Hindshore dune
Morrich More	Ross & Cromarty	SSSI	Acidic	Cuspate foreland
Culbin Sands	Nairn	SSSI	Acidic	Hindshore
Sands of Forvie	Grampian	NNR, SSSI	Acidic	Hindshore
St. Cyrus	Grampian	NNR, SSSI	Calcareous	Climbing dune
Tentsmuir	Fife	NNR, SSSI	Acidic	Cuspate foreland
Ross Links & Lindisfarne/ north Northumberland coast	Northumberland	NNR, SSSI	Calcareous/acidic	Offshore island/bay dune/spit
Hart Warren	Cleveland	SSSI	Calcareous	Bay dune
Saltfleetby/Theddlethorpe/ Humberside/north Lincs. coast	Humberside/ Lincolnshire	NNR, SSSI	Calcareous	Spit/offshore island/bay
North Norfolk coast	Norfolk	NNR, SSSI	Calcareous	Spit/offshore island
Winterton dunes	Norfolk	NNR, SSSI	Acidic	Ness
Sandwich Bay	Kent	SSSI	Calcareous	Hindshore/spit
Studland Heath	Dorset	NNR, SSSI	Acidic	Spit

Table 4.3.2
Some examples of nationally important sites along the North Sea coastal margin.

sites erosion appears to exceed accretion. Druridge Bay is a typical example. Two long sections of the dune front are eroding while nearly all the rest of the site is static. Accretion is only occurring in very small and localised areas. The reasons for this net erosion of dunes along the North Sea coastal margin are poorly understood but appear to be similar to those affecting other sediment coasts of Britain. Collectively these suffer from a net sediment deficiency and show a progressive narrowing and steepening of the intertidal profile. It appears increasingly likely that these effects are related to the development of extensive coast protection structures in the past century. These tend to lock sediment within a section of coast, either within a beach protected with groynes or within a cliff encased in a sea wall, and interrupt sediment supply.

Vegetation that is killed by activities taking place on the sand dune exposes the underlying sand to wind and rain resulting, particularly on the west coast, in a 'blow out' and loss of larger areas of vegetation and sand. The main problems occur in the north and west of Scotland where extreme climatic conditions increase the effect of erosion and near major centres of population, for instance in Tyne and Wear. While rehabilitation of vegetation of these exposed surfaces can be carried out it may take years for the natural variety of plants and animals to become re-established.

Grazing

Moderate grazing is necessary to maintain the diversity of species-rich calcareous grassland and to prevent the development of scrub. Undergrazing, on the other hand, due to a decline in the number of rabbits after the introduction of myxomatosis, has allowed vegetation on certain east coast dune sites to become dominated by tall, rank swards with reduced species diversity. Grazing with domestic stock can, in some cases, cause problems if not properly controlled. In the north there are serious local problems due to excessive grazing pressure. Heavy grazing by domestic stock and especially by rabbits appears to have contributed to the loss of the surface vegetation on a number of important sites in north Scotland (Doody 1989a).

In Northumberland the practice of over-wintering stock on coastal land has led to areas of grassland receiving high levels of nutrients. Feed enhancement has intensified over the last 20 years and dune grassland communities have been replaced at Ross Links and Druridge Bay by nitrophilous weeds. Dune slack areas have also become eutrophicated.

Sand extraction

Unauthorised and authorised sand extraction from beaches can reduce the already limited supply of available sediments which are necessary to maintain the natural sea defence provided by sand-flats and stabilised dunes.

Development

Pressure on older stable dune systems continues with further developments proposed, resulting in further destruction of habitat (Doody 1989a). Many dune links are now golf courses. The use of fertilisers, herbicides and irrigation to improve these facilities has a significant impact on rich dune vegetation (Marshall & Green 1984). Car and caravan parks improve access and subsequently increase trampling.

Afforestation

Afforestation over the last 100 years has covered approximately 8,000 ha of dune (14% of the estimated total resource), much of which has been planted with non-indigenous pines. The natural vegetation and associated animal life are often destroyed during planting and a secondary effect can be seen at Tentsmuir, Fife, where the water table has been lowered by greater evaporation through the canopy of planted trees resulting in the invasion of dune slack areas by birch *Betula* spp. The shading effect of the tree canopy, combined with the effects of soil acidity changes resulting from leaf and needle fall, also destroys the herbaceous dune vegetation (Doody 1989a).

Non-indigenous species

Sea buckthorn *Hippophae rhamnoides* has been used to stabilise dunes and to act as an access barrier, resulting in large areas being colonised through vigorous growth strategies. *Hippophae* frequently forms dense thickets which shade out other dune vegetation, add nutrients to the soil and limit the distribution and richness of natural flora and fauna. This species is commonest on dunes rich in calcium and *Rhododendron ponticum* appears to replace it on acidic dunes, though this is known to be a problem in only one site: Winterton, Norfolk.

The alien plant, pirri-pirri-bur *Acaena anserinifolia*, native to New Zealand, is locally abundant on less stable dunes. The extent of this alien is now too great for eradication to be contemplated.

SOURCES OF INFORMATION

In 1969 the Countryside Commission for Scotland (CCS), prompted by increasing recreational use of beaches, commissioned a study of sandy areas in the north of Scotland. The initial survey carried out was then extended to cover beaches around the coastline of Scotland (Ritchie & Mather 1984).

The Institute of Terrestrial Ecology (ITE) was commissioned by NCC to provide information on the botanical importance of particular coastal sites (Shaw, Hewett & Pizzy 1983). A second report was commissioned in 1976 to assess the scientific interest of the invertebrate fauna associated with a similar range of Scottish sand dune systems (Institute of Terrestrial Ecology 1979).

More recent survey work includes the National Vegetation Classification (Rodwell 1989) and the ongoing National Sand Dune Survey which was carried out by NCC and subsequently by JNCC. Individual site reports (including vegetation maps) have been produced for 112 sites so far; a total of 154 reports will eventually be produced. National survey reports for England, Scotland and Wales are being produced (Radley, in press; Dargie 1993; Dargie, in press).

4.4   SALTMARSHES

INTRODUCTION

Saltmarsh vegetation may develop in temperate waters between mean high water of spring tides (MHWS) and mean high water of neap tides (MHWN) where net accumulation of sediment occurs. Some degree of shelter from wave action is necessary for accumulation of sediment, so saltmarshes are found in inlets, estuaries and behind barrier islands or shingle spits. Under favourable conditions in areas with extensive tidal flats and in the absence of enclosure, large areas of saltmarsh may develop.

Different species of saltmarsh plant have different tolerances to inundation with saline water. This results in successional development of plant communities according to the inundation tolerance of the constituent species. Successional development is represented horizontally as vegetation bands orientated approximately parallel to the shoreline, and vertically as a banded record of successive sediment accumulation. This may occur with time as sediment accumulates within an area of marsh, so raising the level of the marsh. In a few areas sediment availability is limited and the successional stages occur as a transition across the shoreline.

DISTRIBUTION

The distribution of all saltmarshes of at least 1 ha (0.5 ha in Shetland) covered by NCC's survey of saltmarsh vegetation is shown in Figure 4.4.1. This represents an almost complete distribution map of saltmarshes, as only 0.8% of sites were excluded from the survey (Burd 1989). In Scotland saltmarshes are mostly small, isolated marshes scattered around the coast, the only relatively large areas on the North Sea coast being in the Firth of Tay and the Firth of Forth. By contrast, in England there are many low-lying regions with extensive saltmarsh areas, such as the Humber, the Wash, Suffolk and Essex, north Kent and the Solent.

Of the counties or districts in Britain the following counties on the North Sea coast are placed in order of size of the saltmarsh resource in Great Britain:

1   Essex   4,637 ha
2   Lincolnshire   4,223 ha
5   Norfolk   2,903 ha
7   Hampshire   2,661 ha.

The North Sea coast altogether has approximately 22,300 ha of saltmarsh, out of a British total of 45,370 ha.

DESCRIPTION OF RESOURCE

Vegetation

Plant communities found in saltmarshes in Britain have been described in the National Vegetation Classification (Rodwell in press). There are five zones of vegetation in saltmarshes in Britain. These, starting at the seaward edge, are:
Pioneer marsh
Low–mid marsh
Mid–upper marsh
Drift-line
Swamp.

Table 4.4.1 is a simplified summary of the National Vegetation Classification (NVC) of saltmarsh community types, described in their approximate successional order, from the seaward edge on mud- or sand-flats to the upper levels of the marsh and the transitions to non-saline habitats.

Transitions to non-saline habitats

Species composition of the seaward zones, from mud–sand-flats to low–mid marsh, is relatively simple with only a few species able to tolerate the stressful conditions. Species which occur in these zones, such as eelgrass *Zostera*, cordgrass *Spartina* spp. or samphire *Salicornia* spp. are often present in

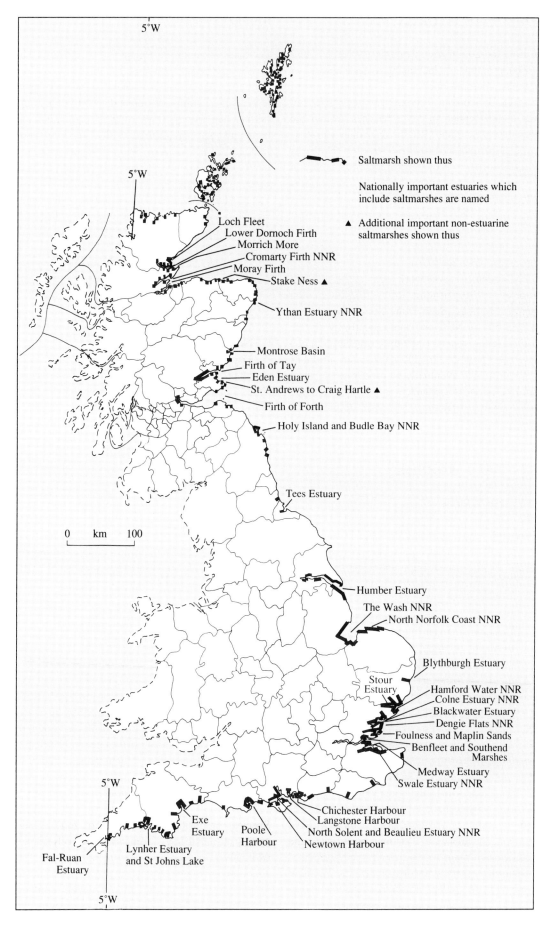

Figure 4.4.1

Distribution of saltmarshes along the North Sea coastal margin.

Based upon the 1975 Ordnance Survey 1:1,250,000 map with the permission of the Controller of Her Majesty's Stationery Office © Crown Copyright.

Saltmarsh shown thus

Nationally important estuaries which include saltmarshes are named

▲ Additional important non-estuarine saltmarshes shown thus

Loch Fleet
Lower Dornoch Firth
Morrich More
Cromarty Firth NNR
Moray Firth
Stake Ness ▲

Ythan Estuary NNR

Montrose Basin
Firth of Tay
Eden Estuary
St. Andrews to Craig Hartle ▲
Firth of Forth

Holy Island and Budle Bay NNR

Tees Estuary

0   km   100

Humber Estuary

The Wash NNR
North Norfolk Coast NNR

Blythburgh Estuary

Stour Estuary
Hamford Water NNR
Colne Estuary NNR
Blackwater Estuary
Dengie Flats NNR
Foulness and Maplin Sands
Benfleet and Southend Marshes
Medway Estuary
Swale Estuary NNR

Exe Estuary
Poole Harbour
Chichester Harbour
Langstone Harbour
North Solent and Beaulieu Estuary NNR
Newtown Harbour

Fal-Ruan Estuary
Lynher Estuary and St Johns Lake

5°W

Table 4.4.1
Plant communities of British saltmarshes (SM, saltmarsh; S, swamps).

National Vegetation Classification Code	NVC community type	Characteristic species
SM1	*Zostera/Ruppia* low marsh	*Zostera marina, Z. noltii, Z. angustifolia*
SM2		*Ruppia maritima*
SM3		*Eleocharis parvula*
SM4	Pioneer marsh	*Spartina maritima*
SM5		*S. alterniflora* with *S. anglica, Puccinellia maritima* and *Aster tripolium*
SM6		*Spartina anglica*
SM8		*Salicornia* spp.
SM9		*Suaeda maritima*
SM7		*Arthrocnemum perenne*, sometimes with *Halimione, Puccinellia* and *Suaeda*
SM11		*Aster tripolium* var. *discoides*
SM12		Rayed *Aster tripolium*
SM10	Low–mid marsh	Annual *Salicornia, Suaeda* and *Puccinellia maritima*
SM13		*Puccinellia maritima*
SM14		*Halimione portulacoides*
(SM13)	Mid–upper marsh	Sub-communities of *Puccinellia maritima* saltmarsh with *Limonium vulgare* and *Armeria maritima*
		P. maritima with *Glaux maritima* co-dominant in species-poor vegetation
		P. maritima with *Plantago maritima* and/or *Armeria maritima*
SM16		*Festuca rubra*
SM17		*Artemisia maritima* with *Festuca rubra*, or open canopy of *A. maritima* and *Halimione*
(SM16)		Sub-communities of *Festuca rubra* with *Agrostis stolonifera, Juncus gerardi, Puccinellia maritima, Glaux maritima, Triglochin maritima, Armeria maritima* and *Plantago maritima*
SM19		*Blysmus rufus*
SM20		*Eleocharis uniglumis*
SM15		*Juncus maritimus* with *Triglochin maritima*
SM18		*Juncus maritimus*
SM24	Drift-line	*Elymus pycnanthus* with *Suaeda vera* or *Inulu crithmoides*
SM28		*Elymus repens*
SM25		*Suaeda vera*
S4	Swamp	*Phragmites australis*
S19		*Eleocharis palustris*
S20		*Scirpus lacustris* ssp. *tabernaemontani*
S21		*Scirpus maritimus*

monospecific stands. However, as tidal influence lessens further up the marsh, the species composition becomes increasingly complex and more variable within a particular height band. There may often be mosaics of different community types within a small area. External influence such as grazing substantially alters species composition and overall dominance of particular species within a community type. Transitions may be to reed swamp, sand dune, shingle, freshwater or woodland vegetation types,

or the natural transition may be truncated due to construction of sea walls or other coastal defences. Where saline influence continues landwards of sea walls, coastal grazing marshes with brackish ditches may develop (see Section 4.7).

Regional variation on the North Sea coast

There are six geographical units which represent the major divisions between saltmarsh vegetation types in Britain (Burd 1989); four of these units are on the North Sea coast. The regional differences in vegetation types and proportions by area of the types within each geographical unit are described below, with National Vegetation Classification (NVC) community or sub-community types in parentheses. Factors which affect distribution of community types are mentioned where relevant to a particular geographical area.

North Scotland. In northern (and western) Scotland the marsh structure is often fairly simple, being largely dominated in the low and mid-marsh zones by *Puccinellia/Festuca* communities (SM13, SM16 and SM17, plus sub-communities), often also with large areas of *Juncus gerardii*. This is due to the general decrease in floristic diversity of many communities, inland as well as coastal, observed with increasing latitude and decreasing average temperatures.

Mid–upper marsh loch head and beach head marshes, with the turf fucoid sub-community of *Puccinellia* (SM13) are among the most important types of marsh within this region (Burd 1989).

Transition communities, particularly to grassland, are well represented and extensive in northern Scotland (Burd 1989). These are often rich in plant species, and may be of considerable importance for invertebrates. The abundance of freshwater transitions in the north of this area, compared with the almost total absence of these communities further south on the North Sea coast, is largely attributable to the wetter, more oceanic climate in northern Scotland. This more humid climate and lack of enclosure also enables more terrestrial species such as *Armeria maritima* and *Glaux maritima* to occur lower down the marsh, almost in pioneer conditions (Beeftink 1977).

There are several National Vegetation Survey plant communities and sub-communities which are not found in eastern and northern Scotland. These are:

❖ The mud–sand-flat community of *Eleocharis parvula* (SM3). The pioneer zone communities of *Spartina maritima* (SM4), *Spartina alterniflora* (SM5), *Suaeda maritima* (SM9), *Arthrocnemum perenne* (SM7), *Aster tripolium* var. *discoides* (SM11) and rayed *Aster tripolium* (SM12) are all absent from Scotland, while *Salicornia* (SM8) is absent from eastern and northern Scotland and *Spartina anglica* (SM6) occurs mainly in England.

❖ The low–mid marsh community with *Puccinellia*-annual *Salicornia-Suaeda* co-dominant (SM10) and the sub-communities of *Halimione portulacoides* (SM14) with i) *H. portulacoides* as dominant, ii) with *Juncus maritimus*, or iii) *H. portulacoides* and *Puccinellia* co-dominant, are all absent from Scotland.

❖ The mid–upper marsh sub-community of *Puccinellia* (SM13) with *Limonium vulgare* and *Armeria maritima*, and the *Artemisia maritima* (SM17) community are both absent from Scotland. The drift-line community of *Elymus pycnanthus* (SM24) is also absent from Scotland.

East and south-east Scotland. Within this region four dominant communities occur in varying proportions (Burd 1989):
i) annual *Salicornia-Suaeda maritima* (SM8 and SM9);
ii) *Puccinellia* (SM10 and SM13) communities;
iii) *Puccinellia-Festuca-Artemisia* (SM13, SM16 and SM17) communities;
iv) *Juncus gerardii* (SM16).

Transition to reed bed with *Phragmites australis* (S4) swamp is especially abundant in the Tay estuary within this region.

North-east, east and south-east England. In this region of England pioneer and low–mid marsh communities make up the largest proportion (60% by area) of saltmarsh vegetation. This is particularly evident in the counties of Lincolnshire, Norfolk, Suffolk and Essex. This preponderance of lower marsh communities is due to construction of sea walls to enclose areas of marsh for conversion to agricultural land or for development.

Although the low–mid marsh communities are dominant within this geographical area, the pioneer communities are also important. In south-east England *Spartina* is the dominant community, where some of the marshes may bear a resemblance to those of the south coast (Burd 1989). *Spartina* is also a major constituent of the marshes in the north-east around Lindisfarne.

The principal communities within the low–mid marsh in this region are the *Puccinellia maritima* (SM10 and SM13) communities, with *Halimione* (SM14) and, especially in Essex, *Limonium-Armeria* (sub-community of SM13).

In general, the mid–upper marsh communities are not well represented. In small marshes in the north-east, a fairly large proportion of the *Puccinellia-Festuca* (SM13, SM16 and SM17) community occurs, and in East Anglia *Limonium-Armeria* (SM13) is abundant. *Juncus gerardi* (sub-community of SM16) and *J. maritimus* (SM15 and SM18) are only present in very small amounts within this area (Burd 1989).

Drift-line communities, however, are well represented all along this section of the North Sea coast. These consist mainly of the *Elymus repens*

(SM24) community in the northern part of the region and *Elymus pycnanthus* (SM28) in the southern part. The *Suaeda vera* (SM25) drift-line community is abundant in Norfolk (Burd 1989).

Upper marsh swamp communities are present in small areas in the northern part of the region and East Anglia, but are almost absent south of East Anglia. The only swamp community of any significance found within this zone is *Phragmites australis* (S4).

Transition communities are almost non-existent within this region. This is because of the widespread construction of sea walls resulting in truncation of the natural succession of saltmarsh vegetation types. Upper marsh and transition communities are virtually eliminated by this. In extreme examples, such as in the Wash, the mid–upper marsh communities are also enclosed behind the sea wall (Burd 1989). In a few areas, notably the north Norfolk coast, sand dune-saltmarsh interfaces do occur, and these may be rich in unusual plants or plant communities.

Communities particular to north Norfolk are:

i) the drift-line *Elymus pycnanthus* and *Halimione* co-dominant sub-communities of the *Suaeda vera* community (SM25);

ii) the species-rich upper marsh and strandline dune transition *Suaeda vera-Limonium binervosum* (SM21) community, and the SM21 sub-community with *Frankenia laevis*.

South and south-west England. The marshes of this region are dominated by *Spartina* (SM4, SM5 and SM6), which occupies large areas in most of the counties, with the possible exceptions of the Isle of Wight and Cornwall. In the eastern part of this region, up to 63% of the total marsh area is taken up by *Spartina*. Further west the proportion is less, but is still up to 46%. The other pioneer communities of *Salicornia-Suaeda* (SM7, SM8 and SM9) and *Aster* (SM11 and SM12) are relatively uncommon (Burd 1989). The overall dominance of the pioneer marsh zones by *Spartina* (SM4, SM5 and SM6) within this region may be ascribed to the extensive spread along the south coast from the place of origin of *S.* x *townsendii* and *S. anglica* in Southampton Water (Tubbs 1984).

The low–mid marsh communities within this region are small in area when compared with *Spartina* communities. However, *Puccinellia* (SM10 and SM13) and *Halimione* (SM14) communities do occupy significant proportions of the total area in the southern part of the region, but are relatively scarce further westwards. They are replaced on the south-western Channel coast by *Puccinellia/Festuca* (SM13 sub-communities and SM16) communities.

Upper marsh swamp communities, mostly of *Phragmites australis* (S4), are more common in the south-west marshes than elsewhere on the English North Sea coast. These communities are found mainly in the Isle of Wight, Dorset, Devon and Cornwall. In Hampshire the swamp zone is less frequent (Burd 1989). Transitions to non-saline communities are uncommon but notable examples of transitions to ancient semi-natural woodland and unimproved mesotrophic grassland are found around the estuaries of the Solent.

Invertebrates

Information is available on the distribution and community structure of invertebrates in saltmarshes. Work has been carried out on particular marshes in the context of bird feeding studies, and some studies of particular marshes have concentrated on the invertebrate fauna (Frid & James 1989; Charman, Fojt & Penny 1986). The Invertebrate Site Register maintained by JNCC holds records of individual sites and the species recorded at these sites, but the information is not available for publication.

Saltmarshes tend to have a relatively low faunal diversity. They are transitional habitats between fully marine and terrestrial conditions and present difficult environments for colonisation due to changes in salinity and humidity caused by periodic tidal immersion. The fauna present is a mixture of marine, freshwater and terrestrial derived species, which have found various ways of adapting to the stressful environment. Marine species tend to occur lower down the marsh and often burrow to avoid desiccation. Terrestrial and freshwater species occur mostly in the upper marsh and transition zones, and have a variety of methods of adapting to, or avoiding, immersion in saline water. The distribution of faunal species is often determined or strongly influenced by the distribution of the vegetation. The macrofauna of all marsh zones is numerically dominated by deposit feeders, mainly infaunal oligochaetes, polychaetes, nematodes and surface-deposit feeding gastropods, with a few crustaceans and bivalves. Other fauna are herbivorous, terrestrial-derived invertebrates, making up a small proportion of the total macrofaunal biomass. They are mainly sap-sucking species, such as aphids and other hemipterans, or are chewing species such as grasshoppers, and tend to occur in the upper marsh zones.

Differences in faunal distribution up the shore have been observed, and the following is a description of invertebrate species and groups found on saltmarshes, starting on the low shore sand or mud-flats, and progressing up the shore to transition vegetation habitats.

The fauna found on sand- and mud-flats is largely determined by sediment particle size which is dependent on exposure of the site and availability of sediment. In general on predominantly muddy shores the mud snail *Hydrobia ulvae* is numerically dominant, especially where vegetation is sparse. The ragworm *Hediste diversicolor* and other small polychaetes such as *Scololepsis* spp. and *Peloscolex benedeni* are also likely to be present in large numbers. On more sandy shores the fauna is dominated by the lugworm *Arenicola marina* with the sand mason worm *Lanice conchilega* and bivalves such as *Angulus tenuis* (the fauna of these types of shores is dealt with more thoroughly in the marine section on sediment shores).

A sharp discontinuity in faunal distribution occurs at the interface between mud- or sand-flat and pioneer marsh. This is caused not only by the change in structure, microclimate and food availability, but also by a change in predation pressure from birds and fish. The fauna on flats is more diverse than that of a *Spartina*-dominated pioneer zone, but the biomass is less. This is due to increased predation pressure from wading birds such as dunlin, which tend not to feed in *Spartina* if alternative feeding areas are available (Millard and Evans, in Doody 1984).

In pioneer and low–mid marsh zones the fauna is similar to that of sand- or mud-flats, but with less dominance of species which require open sediment such as *Arenicola*. *Hediste* appears not to be affected by the presence of *Spartina* and may be frequent within both the low and mid marsh zones. Species which require the cover provided by denser vegetation, such as the shore crab *Carcinus maenas* and the rough periwinkle *Littorina saxatilis* (ssp. complex) become more common. In pools within the marsh, species such as the goby *Pomatoschistus minutus*, the shrimp *Palaemon elegans* and, in muddier sediment, the bivalve *Macoma balthica* may occur. *Arenicola* may also be common within pools.

In mid–upper marsh zones the burrowing amphipod *Corophium volutator* is often numerically dominant, and may occur at very high densities, especially where vegetation is less dense on creek edges and around pools. *Hydrobia* is also present in upper marsh zones, with various oligochaetes and polychaetes. Higher up in the mid–upper marsh zones, invertebrates of terrestrial rather than marine origin become more frequent, especially around the better drained margins of creeks. Un-vegetated areas are of importance to a number of specialised invertebrates. Adults of a number of families of beetles, most notably of the Heteceridae and rove beetles of the genus *Bledius* (Staphylinidae), burrow into sandy or clay sediments, different species preferring different particle size distributions within their substrate. These species are algal or detrital grazers, while some burrowing ground beetles of the genus *Dyschirus* are specific predators on species of *Bledius*. The detritivorous larvae of a number of flies also burrow into similar sediments, extending much further down the shore than the beetles. Fly larvae also occur on much siltier sediments of large mudflats. Particularly significant are flies of the families Dolichopodidae (marsh flies), with predatory adults, Ephydridae (shore flies) and a few species of Tabanidae (horse flies), with adults of some species feeding on the blood of estuarine birds.

It is the vegetation structure, as well as the species composition of the upper marsh and transition zones, which is important in determining the faunal composition. Large expanses of open sand-flat in the upper marsh and transition zones are required specifically by a few species. The ground beetle *Bembidion pallidipenne* and the two maritime tiger beetles *Cicindela maritima* and *C. hybrida* range very widely over extensive intertidal sand-flats backed by dunes. Grazing of upper marsh zones is highly deleterious to the invertebrate fauna, there being relatively few species able to cope with the very short, even sward that this produces. This may be in contrast to the value of the marsh for the avifauna, where grazed marsh may be very valuable as roosting or feeding grounds. The botanical species-richness and structural diversity of an ungrazed marsh produces a greater spectrum of terrestrial invertebrate niches, ranging from sites for web spinning by spiders, to habitat for specific phytophagous species, such as aphids, weevils, gall midges and Lepidoptera. The litter accumulations at the bases of plants are also important habitats for some species. Transition zones to terrestrial habitats support a number of highly specific species, notably among the two-winged flies. The fauna of brackish water reed beds is distinct from that of freshwater reed beds, and a discrete suite of species of noctuid moths, in particular species of wainscot moth, *Mythimna* spp. and others, have caterpillars feeding on and in the stems of reeds. Reeds in standing brackish water may prove more favourable for some phytophagous species, by isolating them from ground-dwelling predators which are more prevalent in tidal reed bed or reed bed with reed litter.

Strandline accumulations of drift litter of various compositions, whether with saltmarsh species growing within them or not, support various assemblages of invertebrates, dependent on the humidity and state of decay of the drift material. Accumulations of seaweed at the high water mark support a wide diversity of specialist flies, with different species inhabiting fresh, rotting or dry weed. These strandlines may occur on any intertidal habitat, but are often trapped within saltmarsh vegetation where they would be washed or blown away in other habitats. One scarce beetle, *Aphodius plagiatus*, in a genus composed otherwise only of dung beetles, is associated with rotting fungi and accumulations of plant litter in saltmarsh and dunes. Species found elsewhere in coastal habitats such as surface predators, nectar feeders, etc. often either breed in strandline material or use it as shelter.

Vertebrates

Birds are the only vertebrates which occupy saltmarsh habitat to any great extent. Most birds which use saltmarshes for breeding, feeding or roosting are not restricted exclusively to saltmarsh, but use it as part of the whole estuarine or coastal system (Davidson *et al.* 1991). However, some species use saltmarshes during particular parts of the year or for a particular purpose, as described below.

Feeding

During winter months twite and linnets, and also teal, feed on the seeds of *Salicornia* (samphire) in the lower marsh and pioneer zones. The Wash is an important area in this respect. Brent geese feed on the lower marsh plants of *Zostera* and *Enteromorpha*, as well as other saltmarsh plants. The south and south-east coast marshes are important areas for the dark-bellied form of brent geese, and Lindisfarne is important for the light-bellied form. Several other species of geese and grazing duck, such as wigeon, use upper marsh areas for feeding, eating plants such as *Plantago* and *Puccinellia*. Grazed upper marsh areas, although species-poor, provide better feeding resources for herbivorous wildfowl than ungrazed areas.

Roosting

Saltmarshes are becoming more important for roosting sites as grazing marshes are lost to more intensive agriculture or development (Davidson *et al.* 1991).

Breeding

Several species of wader or wildfowl breed on undisturbed areas of upper marsh. Redshank prefer

upper saltmarsh to grazing marsh for breeding (Davidson *et al.* 1991). Black-headed gulls also form important breeding colonies on areas of saltmarsh, for example on the north Solent shores.

IMPORTANT SITES

In terms of saltmarsh vegetation there are 33 important saltmarsh sites on the North Sea coast of Scotland and England. These are shown in Figure 4.4.1 and consist largely of estuaries or inlets, many of which may have several distinct marshes within them. Marshes within important estuaries may be valuable as part of the whole estuarine or coastal system, such as the Wash, which contains 10% of the whole saltmarsh resource in Britain. They may also be important in their own right as particularly good examples of regional variation in vegetation, or in types of saltmarsh zonation, such as the unusual type of 'beach head' marsh where sediment supply is limited, such as at Stake Ness or St. Andrews. Beach head marshes are much more common on the west coast of Scotland than the North Sea coast.

In addition to these 33 sites, other saltmarshes may also be important because of their rare or scarce flora, or as resources for other interests, such as bird feeding or roosting areas.

The geographical regions described above have varying areas of marsh protected by Site of Special Scientific Interest (SSSI) or National Nature Reserve (NNR) status. This information is presented in Table 4.4.2 by country agency administrative region, some of which are partly outside the North Sea coast as defined for this directory.

IMPACTS ON SALTMARSHES

Erosion

There are 44,370 ha of saltmarsh in Great Britain (Burd 1989). Of all the coastal habitats only vegetated shingle structures are less common than saltmarshes. There are a number of natural processes which cause significant changes in saltmarsh development, such as changes in river channels in large estuaries, which cause local cycles of erosion and accretion. Major rises in sea level will also affect saltmarshes if sedimentation rate is exceeded by the rate of sea level rise. This, combined with increased wave action and reduced availability of sediment, may result in (and may already be causing) severe erosion of saltmarshes (Burd 1989). This problem will be most acute in south and east England, where land is low lying, and the natural tilting of the British Isles resulting from the last ice age is downwards, so increasing the effects of rising sea levels from other causes.

Land claim

Saltmarsh vegetation is also affected by man's activities, such as the construction of sea walls. Historically, enclosure has had a major effect, with large areas of marsh being lost through reclamation for agricultural use. Transition vegetation to other habitat types, such as woodland, dune or grassland are most severely affected, as they occur highest up the marsh within the area which is usually enclosed. This is particularly evident in eastern and southern England, where enclosure of saltmarsh is most prevalent. Freshwater transition habitats are little affected by land claim for agriculture as they tend to be moved, or occur further up estuaries outside the sea wall, and normal dilution of seawater to brackish and freshwater conditions can still occur upstream. Freshwater transitions may be lost at the landward edge of marshes, causing a reduction in species characteristic of this habitat, such as *Oenanthe*, which is still found in Norfolk.

Development and reclamation for building, marinas, mariculture, industrial and power plants, etc. is severely damaging to saltmarshes as it results in complete removal of areas of marsh vegetation. It may also affect areas adjacent to the construction site by changing patterns of water flow and causing increased erosion or accretion. Construction of tidal barrages within estuaries or inlets for power or amenity use is also likely to cause similar problems.

Grazing

Grazing of saltmarshes by sheep or cattle does affect the vegetation types which may occur on a particular marsh, especially if grazing pressure is high. Heavy grazing generally reduces species diversity, especially for some communities dominated by *Halimione* or *Limonium*, which are intolerant of grazing. Grazing pressure is highest in the north-west of England, so is not a major factor in limiting species diversity of North Sea coast saltmarshes. Grazing pressure does not have any significant effect on the areas of saltmarsh present.

Recreation

Recreational pressure is generally minimal for saltmarshes, but there may be some erosion problems on paths if areas are particularly heavily used for access by wildfowlers, birdwatchers, walkers, etc.

Pollution

Oil pollution can severely affect saltmarsh flora and fauna, mainly by physically covering the marsh and its plant and animal populations. Some direct toxic effects are particularly likely in instances where the oil is freshly released. Some saltmarsh areas have been lost due to their use as waste disposal sites, but little work has been done to establish the effects of chemical pollution on saltmarsh species. There have been a few instances of seabird mortality in mudflat or saltmarsh areas attributed to ingestion of chemically contaminated invertebrates; however, most such bird mortalities occur as a consequence of oil pollution or feeding on coastal domestic refuse sites.

As a general rule, areas of saltmarsh affected by oil pollution should be left to degrade naturally as many of the clean up techniques can cause further damage.

In general, saltmarsh sediments act as a sink for pollutants such as heavy metals and pesticides. When sediments are eroded and these pollutants are released, they may cause recontamination.

Region	Total area (ha)	Protected area (ha)	Percentage area
North Scotland (also includes some of the north-west coast)	2,045	1,060	51%
East and south-east Scotland	1,452	1,199	83%
North-east, east and south-east England	16,163	14,417	89%
South and south-west England (also includes parts of Devon and Cornwall outside the North Sea area)	4,555	3,610	79%

Table 4.4.2
Summary of the area of saltmarsh statutorily protected on the North Sea coast.

Cordgrass

Since the turn of the century saltmarsh dominated by the recently evolved species of cordgrass *Spartina anglica* (Hubbard & Stebbings 1967) has developed around much of the coast of England and Wales and, more recently, southern Scotland. *Spartina anglica* was first recorded in Southampton Water in the late 19th century. It spreads rapidly over intertidal mudflat and in so doing raises the level of the mudflat surface by accumulating sediment around the cordgrass plants (Doody 1984). In most instances the spread of *Spartina anglica* has been facilitated by its deliberate introduction to aid in the reclamation of mudflat for agriculture. *Spartina anglica* will invade localised areas of established saltmarsh, along tidal creeks and around saltpans. The extensive monospecific stands of *Spartina anglica* saltmarsh have, however, developed on areas of intertidal mudflat. In the west and north of Britain this has caused concern about the resulting loss of important bird feeding ground. On the south coast of England where *Spartina anglica* first developed, the *Spartina* saltmarshes have, however, been dying back, exposing the accumulated sediment platforms to erosion and increasing wave attack to sea defences (Tubbs 1984).

SOURCES OF INFORMATION

An extensive survey of saltmarsh vegetation in Great Britain has been carried out by the Nature Conservancy Council and is reported in Burd 1989. There is also a considerable amount of information on the invasion and dieback of *Spartina*, summarised in Doody 1984. Information on estuarine birds using saltmarshes and mud- and sand-flats is extensive (see Davidson *et al.* 1991).

4.5 SHINGLE

INTRODUCTION

Shingle beaches are found extensively around the coastline of Great Britain. By contrast, shingle structures are rare, with only some 4,200 ha of stable or semi-stable vegetated shingle around the coast. Development takes place in high energy environments and many shingle formations, particularly fringing beaches, are highly mobile. Some shingle beaches formed in early post-glacial times are now covered by sand dunes and many small shingle features are associated with other coastal habitats, notably saltmarshes and sand dunes.

DISTRIBUTION

Much of the coastline of the North Sea is fronted by shingle fringing beaches but these are often highly mobile and may not support vegetation communities. Stable or semi-stable vegetated shingle structures are concentrated in two main areas in Shetland, Orkney and the Moray Firth and in East Anglia and along the English Channel. The majority of the more important shingle sites occur in the south-east, from Norfolk to East Sussex. Altogether there are approximately 2,754 hectares of vegetated shingle lying along the North Sea coastal margin. The east and south-east of England account for 90% (2,482 ha) of vegetated shingle. The distribution of fringing shingle beach and shingle structures along the North Sea coastal margin is given in Figure 4.5.1.

DESCRIPTION OF RESOURCE

Development of structure

The establishment of a shingle structure is dependent on the available supply of sediments with a predominant particle size of over 2 mm but less than 200 mm. This is derived from cliff erosion, transported from rivers draining highland areas or from offshore deposits of glacial material which may include erratics. In the south much of the shingle is composed of flint which eroded from glacial cliffs and was either deposited directly or reworked from offshore banks.

Waves, the most important constructive factor, determine the position of the sediment on the beach. Deposits may be reworked in front of the shore or moved in parallel to it by longshore drift before being thrown up onto the beach by storm waves. Small foreshore ridges are deposited at the limit of high tide. Ridges are the main feature of shingle beaches, and storm waves will throw pebbles into position high up on the beach where the backwash cannot remove them. Coarse sediments remain at the top of the shore while finer shingle tends to be carried back down the beach. Established ridges contain finer sediments than the intervening 'lows' and it is this pattern of alternating sediment which in part determines the eventual vegetation distribution.

According to Chapman (1964) there are five types of shingle structure. The first three are

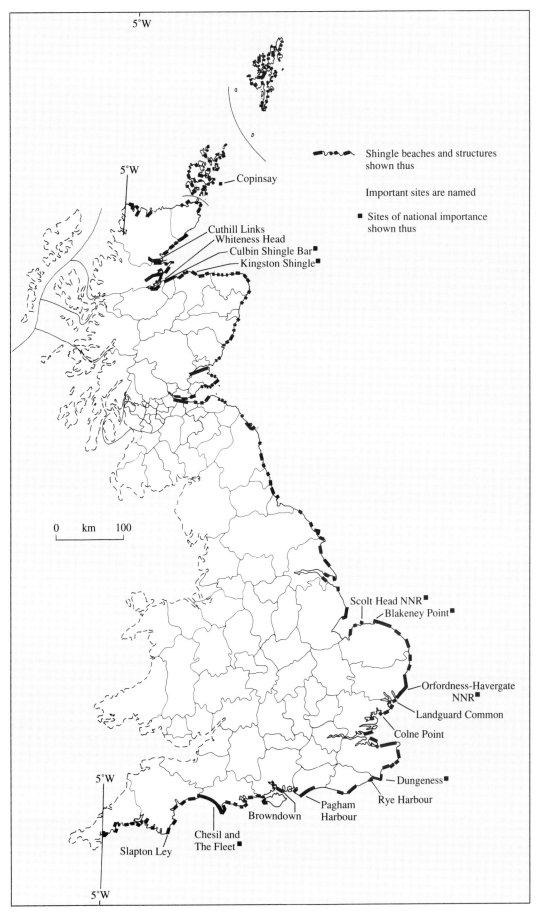

Figure 4.5.1
Distribution of fringing shingle beach and shingle structures along the North Sea coastal margin.
Based upon the 1975 Ordnance Survey 1:1,250,000 map with the permission of the Controller of Her Majesty's Stationery Office © Crown Copyright.

Shingle beaches and structures shown thus

Important sites are named

■ Sites of national importance shown thus

Copinsay

Cuthill Links
Whiteness Head
Culbin Shingle Bar ■
Kingston Shingle ■

0   km   100

Scolt Head NNR ■
Blakeney Point ■

Orfordness-Havergate NNR ■
Landguard Common
Colne Point

Dungeness ■
Rye Harbour
Pagham Harbour
Browndown

Chesil and The Fleet ■
Slapton Ley

5°W

regularly washed by spray and storm waves and vegetation is restricted. The larger, more stable structures have a more extensive cover of vegetation.

❖ Fringing beaches are the most common form, rarely developing further than a simple strand of shingle in contact with the land. These structures are mobile and vegetation is sparse but very characteristic of this type of habitat. Fringing beaches occur all around Britain but are particularly frequent on the Channel coast and in East Anglia – Brighton, Abbotsbury, West Bexington and between Shingle Street and Bawdsey in East Anglia.

❖ Shingle spits are common where coasts have an irregular outline, especially where there is an abrupt change in direction. Deflection of waves by refraction around the end of the spit allows recurved hooks and recurved distal ends to form: Blakeney Point, Norfolk. Other spits are Languard Point, Essex, and Orfordness, Suffolk.

❖ Bars/barriers form either where a spit crosses an estuary mouth or bay and ultimately encloses a freshwater or brackish lagoon: Looe Bar, Cornwall, or where shingle is thrown up along a beach front which forms a bar: Chesil Beach/Fleet lagoon, Culbin Bar, Moray Firth. In Shetland, well sorted material has accumulated in bars across narrow inlets to form characteristic features: Ayres of Swinster (SSSI).

❖ Cuspate forelands are large structures formed from a series of parallel ridges. Shingle piles up at the front of an existing spit or fringing beach then sediment is driven landward to form an apposition beach. Where there is a change in predominant wave direction there is restricted wave approach and subsequent ridges are deposited in a different alignment. In such cases, large stretches of stable shingle form a cuspate foreland: Dungeness, Kent.

❖ Offshore barrier islands are an extent of shingle deposited in shallow water and often linked to other coastal habitats: Scolt Head Island (sand dune overlying shingle structure).

Vegetation

The degree of exposure to which the beach is subjected strongly influences the development of vegetation on shingle structures. Beach composition is an important influencing factor and Randall (1989) recognises four major types of shingle beach with associated flora. Scott (1963) suggests five categories of vegetation assemblage which are related to the stability of the structure, with many high energy locations being totally devoid of all vegetation. Plants establish where they have adapted to the nutrient-poor environment or where the structure has become sufficiently stable to allow fine material to accumulate and plants to grow. Climatic variation is further responsible for differences in community composition.

The National Vegetation Classification (NVC: Rodwell 1989) has identified vegetation types found on shingle structures with the regional variation in community composition indicated where possible. There are less than 24 species of plant that are specific to shingle structures. Many species exist locally on stable shingle which are not present elsewhere within a region and shingle flora is distinctive with several rare or declining species (see Section 7.8). The principles of vegetation development are dealt with by Randall (1989).

Shingle communities identified by the NVC (Nature Conservancy Council 1989) represent only strandline flora. These are given in Table 4.5.1 and are included in the sand dune classification. A more detailed review of shingle communities has been completed under contract by Girton College, Cambridge (Sneddon & Randall 1993).

Stable shingle includes communities in which *Armeria maritima* and *Silene vulgaris* ssp. *maritima* are important components occurring within the spray zone. These communities have yet to be assigned within the NVC.

Regional variation on the North Sea coast

Pioneer communities. In Scotland the rare oysterplant *Mertensia maritima* may be found on fringing beaches (SD1), often in association with Scot's lovage *Ligusticum scoticum*. The distribution of the oysterplant is restricted on the east coast to Shetland, Orkney and a few sites on the north-east (Randall 1988).

Pioneer vegetation of maritime shingle is exemplified by that found around the warmer south coast. It is best developed on the more extensive

National Vegetation Classification Code	NVC community type	Characteristic species
SD1	Vegetated shingle beach	*Crambe maritima-Glaucium flavum*
SD2		*Cakile maritima-Honkenya peploides*

Table 4.5.1
Shingle plant communities (SD, sand dune).

spits and apposition beaches from East Anglia southwards. Characteristic of bare shingle on the open foreshore is a species-poor community dominated by sea pea *Lathyrus japonicus* (SD1b) and the nationally scarce sea-kale *Crambe maritima*. This community is restricted to sites on the south coast of the North Sea, reflecting the geographical distribution of the sea pea which has declined in recent years due to human disturbance. The endemic little-Robin *Geranium purpureum* ssp. *fosteri* is confined to this bare shingle community on the Hampshire coast.

A more closed pioneer community, found on less disturbed shingle beyond the storm crest, is identified by the constancy of yellow horned-poppy *Glaucium flavum* and curled dock *Rumex crispus* (SD1). This assemblage of species gives a highly distinctive character to stretches of bare shingle which is also the preferred habitat of sea-kale *Crambe maritima*. The northern limit of sea-kale and the yellow horned-poppy is the Forth/Clyde area. This habitat is also the preferred location of shrubby sea-blite *Suaeda vera* which is normally found on the lee of spits where shingle abuts saltmarsh. The distribution is limited to East Anglia, Kent and Dorset.

Stable communities. Maritime communities on more stable structures are rarer and the best of these occur on the exposed southern end of Orfordness. Vegetation is frequently covered in salt-spray and is dominated over large areas by thrift *Armeria maritima* and sea campion *Silene vulgaris* ssp. *maritima*. Rich, lichen-dominated communities develop on undisturbed, exposed shingle which is crucial to the survival of slow-growing, fragile lichens. Both Kingston and Orfordness have very important lichen-rich communities.

Grassland. A distinct north/south variation appears where continuous swards of vegetation develop on structures which have remained stable for a considerable time. In the north the common indicator species are the grasses *Ammophila arenaria-Agrostis stolonifera*. A highly developed lichen flora is often found in association with this community. Further south, where maritime influence may be restricted, *Festuca rubra-Poa pratensis* grass communities are common. In undisturbed areas where there is little fine material *Arrhenatherum elatius* becomes the major constituent and is commonly found in association with sea campion *Silene vulgaris* ssp *maritima*.

Heath. Mature grassland may be succeeded by heath, particularly in the north. Indicative of well-drained northern sites, heather *Calluna vulgaris*

becomes constant in association with the lichen species *Cladonia impexa* and *C. arbuscula*. In wetter areas, particularly in shallow excavations, black bog-rush *Schoenus nigricans* and crowberry *Empetrum nigrum* form significant components of the community. Within these hollows rarer plants, including coralroot orchid *Corallorhiza trifida*, are also to be found. Further south, heath is restricted. The development of acid grassland or heath on shingle is perhaps one of the rarest of plant communities in Britain.

Scrub. Scrub development is associated with many sites where a sequence of ridges supports progressively more established vegetation. Heath may become replaced by scrub dominated by gorse *Ulex europaeus* and broom *Cytisus scoparius,* although scrub develops where there is no evidence of previous heath vegetation. In areas where *Ulex* sp. is particularly successful the understorey vegetation is limited by lack of light and a species-poor community prevails.

In wet areas in the north, willow scrub *Salix cinerea* may develop and this may be the climax species of northern shingle communities. Juniper *Juniperus communis* also forms discrete patches of scrub vegetation on bare shingle at Kingston. On the Channel coast dwarf heath has developed on apposition beaches where it is eventually invaded by gorse *Ulex europaeus* and other scrub.

Wetland depressions. Natural wetland exists in depressions (pits) which are thought to have formed as the result of irregularities in the pattern of shingle deposition (Dungeness) and in the 'slack' area behind storm ridges. Pits may have either open water or peaty deposits associated with wetland vegetation. Reed swamp and *Salix* carr dominate the vegetation within the 'natural' pits at Dungeness. The slack areas are characterised by the presence of creeping willow *Salix repens* and a species-rich community prevails with silverweed *Potentilla anserina* and tormentil *P. erecta* being common. Where excavation has taken place artificial hollows have been created and plant communities exist which are characterised by sea purslane *Halimione portulacoides*. Community composition varies and reflects either the influence of moisture in wet areas in Scotland or better drainage in both northerly and southerly sites.

Species distribution

Regional differences in flora are highlighted by certain lichen species which are specific to the south-west. Randall (1989) details the distributional

Table 4.5.2
Distribution of important
shingle plants on the North
Sea coastal margin of Great
Britain (after Randall 1989).

South-east	South	North
Corynephorus canescens	*Parapholis strigosa*	*Mertensia maritima*
Parapholis incurva	*Limonium binervosum*	*Cochlearia scotica*
Limonium bellidifolium	*Rumex rupestris*	
Lathyrus japonica	*Trifolium scabrum*	
Suaeda vera	*Beta maritima*	
Frankenia laevis	*Tamarix gallica*	
Lactuca saligna	*Glaucium flavum*	
	Eryngium maritimum	
	Crambe maritima	
	Halimione portulacoides	

relationships between the major vascular plants on British shingle habitats. Table 4.5.2 outlines those species with distribution on the North Sea coastal margin which compares with the eight species which are specifically found on the south-west and west coasts.

Invertebrates

Invertebrates on coastal shingle tend to be associated with the specialised flora of shingle or to be dependent on the shelter provided by the shingle itself and the litter that accumulates on it.

The most important coastal shingle site for invertebrates is Dungeness although other southern and south-eastern shingle sites also support rich fauna.

Examples of species dependent on the specialist shingle flora include the darkling beetle *Omophlus rufitarsus,* known only from thrift *Armeria maritima* growing on shingle at the Fleet in Dorset, and the micro-moth *Aethes margarotana* (RDB2, see Shirt 1987), the larvae of which feed on the roots of sea-holly *Eryngium maritimum,* itself an uncommon plant. This moth was once known from a number of sites in southern England, but has since declined and is know only known from Thorpness, Suffolk. Another rare moth, *Pima boisduvaliella* (RDB3, Shirt 1987), has larvae that live in and feed on the pod of the sea pea *Lathyrus japonicum,* a nationally scarce plant. The rare jumping spider *Euophrys browningi* (RDB3, Bratton 1991) lives amongst litter in a few east coast shingle systems, preferentially sheltering in cast-up whelk shells on the shingle. It has the distinction also of being one of the few spiders endemic to Britain (Roberts 1985). The ground beetle *Aepus robini* lives amongst stable intertidal shingle in estuarine conditions.

Vertebrates

Few vertebrates are specifically associated with shingle structures although certain sites form an important landfall for small, migrant birds. Open shingle structures and beaches are important as breeding sites for ringed plover *Charadrius hiaticula,* oystercatcher *Haematopus ostralegus* and four species of tern (common *Sterna hirunda,* Arctic *Sterna paradisaea,* Sandwich *Sterna sandvicensis* and little *Sterna albifrons*). Little terns appear to be declining in numbers due to disturbance. All four species are protected by the European Community Council Directive on the Conservation of Wild Birds (10.2 Ramsar/SPA).

Hares *Lepus capensis* are common on shingle where they graze vegetation cover. Grey seals *Halichoerus grypus* use less disturbed beaches to haul out and as breeding locations.

IMPORTANT SITES

In Britain there are approximately 200 Sites of Special Scientific Interest (Doody 1989b) which include shingle features within their boundary. Very few of these sites contain significant areas of stable or semi-stable vegetation and only seven of the shingle areas are considered to be of national importance for nature conservation. Six of these sites are to be found along the North Sea coastal margin and these are indicated on the distribution map (Figure 4.5.1) and in Table 4.5.3. Kingston, a relatively recently discovered site, is not identified as a Nature Conservation Review (NCR) site (Ratcliffe 1977). The restricted number of sites increases the importance of this site and the others that have been selected.

Shingle sites on the northern isles are all small and have distinctive geomorphological characteristics. Structures generally form when storm beaches cut off inlets or lochs, developing single or double spits, often between islands which retain at least one opening to the sea. The shingle is composed of large-sized pebbles due to the degree of exposure experienced by the coastline.

A north/south trend in species composition has been identified (Randall 1989). The two most important shingle structures are Culbin Bar, Moray

Site	Type of structure	Status
Dungeness, Kent	Cuspate foreland	SSSI, NCR, RSPB
Orfordness-Havergate, Suffolk	Apposition beach/shingle spit	SSSI, NCR, NNR, RSPB
Blakeney Point, Norfolk	Spit	SSSI, NCR, NT
Scolt Island	Barrier island	SSSI, NCR, NNR
Chesil Beach, Dorset	Bar/barrier	SSSI, NCR
Culbin Shingle Bar, Moray/Nairn	Bar	SSSI, NCR
Kingston Shingle, Moray	Apposition beach	SSSI

Table 4.5.3
Nationally important shingle structures (after Doody 1989b).

and Dungeness, Kent, and these exemplify the difference in species composition found in the north and south. However, each of the above sites is unique in geomorphological terms and overlying this each has particular vegetation and invertebrate community compositions which are specific to the location. Much of the work on shingle structures has concentrated on Dungeness and this information has been extensively reviewed by Sneddon & Randall (1989).

IMPACTS ON SHINGLE

Causes of damage to shingle structures are varied. Reduction in the total area of habitat leads to loss of some species, and discontinuity in the plant succession can affect the life cycles of certain invertebrates which rely on a mosaic of habitats in order to complete reproduction.

Coastal defence

The value of shingle structures as coastal defence cannot be underestimated since any impact which undermines the mobility of the structure will alter its value as a natural sea defence. A reduction in available sedimentary material through coastal protection works can result in weaknesses developing in shorelines fed by longshore drift. There is concern in some localities that aggregates taken offshore might also reduce the availability of sediments for natural regeneration of shingle beaches and structures. Along parts of the south and East Anglian coasts, low-lying land is protected from flooding by shingle beaches and in these areas their maintenance is of great importance.

Recent storms required shingle structures to be repaired under emergency procedures resulting in loss of natural vegetation and integrity. Material removed from the Ness at Orford to infill other areas has restricted the width of the beach. Groynes used to retain shingle as a means of coastal defence in one area starve other parts of the coastline of their supply of beach sediment.

Aggregate extraction

Gravel extraction has affected a number of sites notably Dungeness. It remains the single most damaging activity. At Kingston, excavation has lowered a large area of shingle to within inches of the summer water table and the habitat now remains wet resulting in a different community composition. Dungeness has suffered more from gravel extraction than other sites (Ferry & Waters 1985).

Military use

Unlike the use of sand dunes by the Ministry of Defence, military activity on shingle structures has contributed to major damage, particularly at Orfordness (Fuller & Randall 1988). At Orfordness there is a much lower species diversity within the military area. The remote nature of these structures has encouraged development of radar stations and bombing ranges while construction of railways and embankments during the war destroyed large areas of shingle.

Recreation and vehicle damage

Damage to fragile surface vegetation lasts a long time. Both recreational activities and vehicle movement cause damage to shingle. Although many shingle foreshores are not safe for recreation because of deep water lying immediately offshore, certain areas are extensively used by fishermen.

Trampling has affected several plant species and Fuller and Randall (1988) attribute the decline of certain species to increased recreational pressure. Disturbance to ground-nesting birds, in particular the little tern, has led to a serious decline in numbers.

Any vehicle movement causes compaction of the shingle surface and tracks remain visible for decades. The movement of vehicles associated with the disposal of bombs and bulldozing areas of shingle have further contributed to the damage of surface vegetation. There has been extensive vehicle damage at Dungeness associated with military activity, extraction of aggregates and with the development of the power stations.

Grazing

Whilst grazing does not have a direct effect on communities it may have implications for particular species. The decline of oysterplant *Mertensia maritima* at a number of sites has been attributed in part to domestic grazing pressure (Randall 1988).

Development

The development of nuclear power stations and housing on Dungeness has contributed to damage of shingle structures (Ferry & Waters 1985). Once buildings are established, services and roads become a necessity which further destroys the surface shingle, vegetation and animal life associated with that area. At Dungeness it has been necessary to continue beach feeding to protect the developments, including the nuclear power station.

SOURCES OF INFORMATION

Much of the survey work on the habitats and communities of shingle areas has in the past been carried out on the three major sites, Dungeness in Kent, Orfordness in Suffolk, and Chesil Beach, Dorset.

A more general study of vegetation on shingle structures throughout Britain was initiated in 1987 by the Nature Conservancy Council (NCC) in conjunction with Girton College, Cambridge University. This contract was to conduct a survey of the 60 major shingle sites – 32 sites along the North Sea coastal margin have been surveyed and site reports for each area prepared (Sneddon & Randall 1993) – and to review the applicability of the National Vegetation Classification to shingle communities (Sneddon 1992).

A preliminary review of the current conservation status of vegetated shingle in Britain has been prepared by Randall, Sneddon and Doody (1990).

A review of all existing information on shingle structures is presented in Sneddon and Randall (1989). The extent of material which specifically relates to the largest shingle site (Dungeness, Kent) is contained in a separate bibliography compiled by Riley (1989).

Vegetation communities on shingle structures have recently been investigated as part of the National Vegetation Classification review (Rodwell 1989) and a detailed survey of the vegetation on Dungeness has been undertaken by Royal Holloway and New Colleges under contract to the Nature Conservancy Council. The invertebrate fauna of Dungeness has also been studied by Philp & McLean (1985) and a survey of the invertebrate fauna at Dungeness funded by NCC and the Central Electricity Generating Board (CEGB) confirmed the significance of shingle structures for conservation of invertebrates.

4.6 COASTAL SALINE LAGOONS

INTRODUCTION

Coastal saline lagoons can be defined in general terms as bodies of salt water, from brackish to hypersaline, partially separated from an adjacent sea by barriers of sand or other sediment (Barnes 1989a; Smith & Laffoley 1992). Lagoons in Britain can be divided into two types: natural features impounded by a coastal barrier, and artificial or semi-natural features resulting from sediment extraction or other human interference (Pye & French 1992). The definition of a coastal saline lagoon varies between workers, so it is difficult to assign sites to a particular lagoonal type, or to ascertain whether a particular water body may be considered a saline lagoon or not. In the context of this directory, lagoons are taken to be those sites which fit into the two above categories or contain species of animal or plant of marine origin specific to lagoonal or brackish habitats. Enclosed harbours (e.g. Poole Harbour) and disused docks are therefore excluded. British lagoons may have salinities varying from less than 1‰ to full-strength sea water at 35‰, or even be hypersaline where evaporation is higher than input of fresh or sea water.

DISTRIBUTION

Saline lagoons are rare in Britain and largely confined to the south and east coasts of England, where they are relatively transient features. This distribution is related to the prevalence here of soft coasts, storm beaches and possibly isostatic movement. Smith & Laffoley (1992) list 110 saline lagoons or lagoon-like habitats on the English North Sea coast, with a total area of 1,162 ha. Thirteen of these are found from Northumberland to Humberside, twelve in Lincolnshire, fifteen in Norfolk and Suffolk, and thirteen and ten sites in Kent and Sussex, repectively. The largest local concentration is in Hampshire,

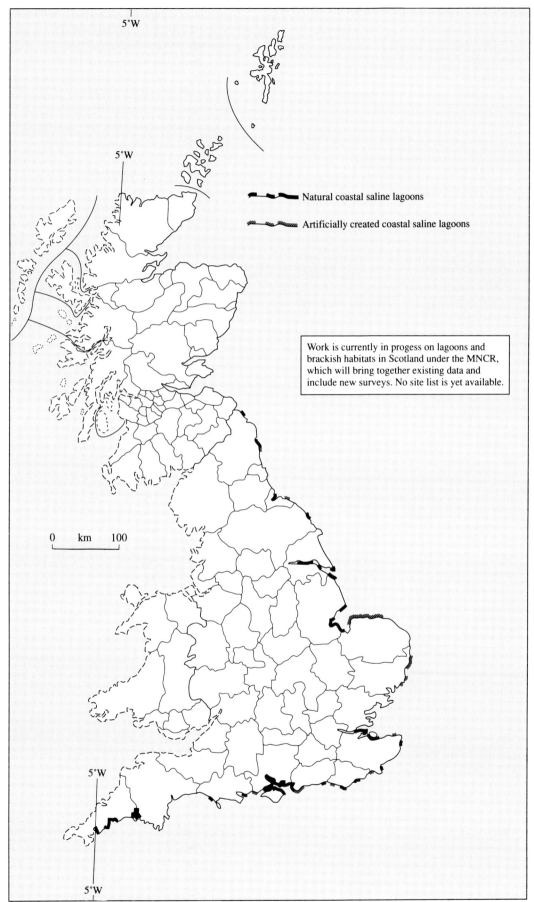

Figure 4.6.1
Distribution of coastal saline
lagoons and lagoon-like
features on the English North
Sea coast. (After Smith &
Laffoley 1992 and Barnes
1989a.)
Based upon the 1975 Ordnance Survey
1:1,250,000 map with the permission
of the Controller of Her Majesty's
Stationery Office © Crown Copyright.

Natural coastal saline lagoons

Artificially created coastal saline lagoons

Work is currently in progress on lagoons and
brackish habitats in Scotland under the MNCR,
which will bring together existing data and
include new surveys. No site list is yet available.

0   km   100

with 27 sites (and nine on the Isle of Wight). The four sites in Dorset include the largest in Britain, the Fleet. One coastal lagoon is recorded from Devon and six from the south-eastern coast of Cornwall. Information on lagoons in Scotland is very sparse; the lack of lagoonal sites in Scotland is probably not as great as it appears from the available data.

DESCRIPTION OF RESOURCE

The two types of coastal saline lagoon in Britain are as follows:

i) Natural saline lagoons. These are naturally formed, shallow, open bodies of brackish or saline water, partially separated from an adjacent coastal sea by a barrier of sand or shingle. All or most of the water mass is retained in the lagoon at low tide, and sea water is exchanged directly via a natural or man-modified channel or by percolation through, or overtopping of, the seaward sediment barrier.

ii) Artificial coastal saline ponds. This category comprises a variety of artificially or naturally formed brackish or saline water bodies which are not strictly naturally formed saline lagoons as defined by Barnes, but nevertheless have similar environmental variables and species composition (Sheader & Sheader 1989).

In reality, there is a continuum between truly natural and artificial coastal lagoons due to man's intervention in some way at most sites.

In Britain there are eight major types of natural saline lagoon, as defined by Barnes (1989a):

i)   streams ponded back by sand and/or shingle bars over which the sea occasionally transgresses (e.g. Benacre Broad, Suffolk)

ii) marine bay semi-isolated by a shingle bar or spit (e.g. The Fleet, Dorset)

iii) pool enclosed within a shingle mass (e.g. Shingle Street/Bawdsey, Suffolk)

iv) low-lying percolation pools fed from the water table within natural longshore shingle/sand barriers (e.g. Broadwater, Norfolk)

v)   natural harbour semi-isolated by the extension of paired spits across its mouth (e.g. Poole Harbour, Dorset)

vi) estuarine backwater, short-circuited by the development of a new (upstream) mouth (e.g. Elliot Links, Tayside)

vii) ponds created by marine transgression into low-lying areas (e.g. Easington Lagoons, N. Humberside)

viii) lagoon-like percolation pools fed from the water table within sea walls (e.g. Bembridge Lagoons, Isle of Wight).

There are five types of saline pond in Britain described by Sheader & Sheader (1989):

i)   pools formed by constriction of the mouth of an estuary: fresh water enters at all times; sea water enters at each tide. A salinity gradient and extensive littoral zone are present

ii) pools formed by constriction of the mouth of a sea inlet: fresh water input (other than rainfall) low; sea water entering at each tide; fully saline; extensive littoral zone (lack of sill, therefore water not retained at low tide)

iii) lagoons isolated from the sea in saltmarsh or marsh pasture: often behind sea walls; sea water/brackish water enters by ground water percolation or overtopping; salinity variable, often low

iv) percolation pools, fed from the water table, in shingle: salinity variable, mostly high; seasonal or more often tidal changes in water level; water enters by percolation or occasionally overtopping

v)   silled or sluiced ponds retaining water at all states of the tide. Fresh water input low; sea water input regular and frequent; salinity seasonally variable but usually high; very little sediment exposed at low tide.

These definitions of 'natural' and 'artificial' saline lagoons do not separate easily. Some of the categories describe the same physical situation, but one example may be naturally formed while another is man-made. Most, if not all, naturally formed lagoons have been modified by man to some extent. For example, the Fleet in Dorset is a good example of a natural lagoon formed by isolation of a marine bay by a longshore shingle barrier; however, the entrance channel to the Fleet was excavated in a new location in 1987 in order to rebuild a bridge.

Fauna and flora

There are many marine, brackish water and freshwater species which may be found in lagoons. Thirty-eight lagoonal species (i.e. species distinctly more characteristic of lagoon-like habitats than of freshwater, estuarine brackish waters or the sea) were identified by Barnes (1989a) and 23 by Bamber *et al.* (1992). These lists are combined in Table 4.6.1. Ten of these species are rare in Britain, have a south and eastern distribution, and are protected by the Wildlife and Countryside Act 1981. All ten of these rare species are found on the North Sea coast. Bamber *et al.* (1992) consider that brackish lagoons may be ranked in terms of their ecological/ nature conservation importance with respect to their biotic community and in particular its

Cnidaria	Gonothyraea loveni		Insecta	Sigara selecta
	Edwardsia ivelli**(a)			Sigara stagnalis
	Nematostella vectensis**			Sigara concinna
				Agabus conspersus
Polychaeta	Armandia cirrhosa**(a)			Berosus spinosus
	Alkmaria romijni**			Coelambus parallelogrammus
	Nereis diversicolor			Dytiscus circumflexus
				Enochrus bicolor
Crustacea	Idotea chelipes			Enochrus melanocephalus
	Sphaeroma hookeri			Enochrus halophilus
	Gammarus insensibilis**(a)			Haliplus apicalis
	Gammarus chevreuxi			Ochthebius marinus
	Corophium insidiosum			Ochthebius punctatus
	Palaemonetes varians			Paracymus aeneus**
Mollusca	Hydrobia ventrosa(a)		Flora	Chara canescens**
	Hydrobia neglecta(a)			Chara baltica
	Onoba aculeus(b)			Chara connivens
	Littorina tenebrosa			Lamprothamnium papulosum**
	Tenellia adspersa**			Tolypella n. nidifica
	Cerastoderma glaucum(a)			Ruppia maritima
				Ruppia cirrhosa
Bryozoa	Conopeum seurati			Chaetomorpha linum
	Victorella pavida**(a)			

**   Protected by the Wildlife and Countryside Act 1981.
(a)   In Britain known only from lagoon-like habitats.
(b)   Lagoonal only in England and Wales; more widely distributed in Scotland.

Table 4.6.1
Specialist lagoonal species recorded in Britain (after Barnes 1989a and Bamber *et al.* 1992).

proportion of specialist lagoonal species. They also hypothesize that such species are adapted to the stresses of a variable environment (in terms of salinity, temperature and pH) with reduced tidal exchange and survive because they are not out-competed in lagoons by less tolerant marine or estuarine species.

Regional variation on the North Sea coast

Saline lagoons, both natural and artificial, are found predominantly on the east and south coasts of England, i.e. the North Sea coast (Figure 4.6.1). The lack of recorded lagoonal sites in Scotland is probably a reflection of lower survey coverage (new survey work is in progress). 'Obs' and 'houbs' are features of the Orkney (Bullard 1972) and Shetland Islands; they are naturally formed, shallow, brackish habitats behind sand, shingle or rock barriers, but were not included in the saline lagoon reviews or surveys by Barnes (1989b) or Sheader & Sheader (1989).

The state of knowledge of other lagoonal species is not yet at a level where information on rarity or overall distribution is reliable. Many lagoonal species occur in brackish drainage ditches, saltmarsh pools and sand dune slack pools, none of which have been subject to any form of comprehensive faunal survey. Vegetation of these areas has been better studied, but has not been collated.

IMPORTANT SITES

Important lagoonal sites in England have been identified in reviews of naturally formed lagoons by Barnes (1989b), and coastal saline ponds by Sheader & Sheader (1989).

For natural coastal lagoons, those sites considered to be of regional significance are listed in Table 4.6.2. Those sites marked with an asterisk were

1 **Blakeney Spit Pools**, Norfolk

2 **Holkham Salts Hole**, Norfolk*
(low lying percolation pool in shingle mass)

3 **Broadwater**, Norfolk

4 **Benacre Broad**, Suffolk*
(ponded-back stream)

5 **Shingle Street/Bawdsey**, Suffolk*
(pool in shingle mass)

6 **Widewater Lagoon**, W Sussex
(this site has deteriorated considerably since the survey and may no longer merit this high assessment)

7 **Bembridge Lagoons**, Isle of Wight*
(percolation pool behind sea wall)

8 **Christchurch Harbour**, Dorset

9 **Poole Harbour**, Dorset*
(semi-isolated natural harbour)

10 **The Fleet**, Dorset*
(marine bay semi-isolated by shingle spit)

11 **Swanpool**, Cornwall

Table 4.6.2
Natural coastal lagoons of regional significance
(* best representatives of their type). (After Barnes 1989b.)

Table 4.6.3
Artificial coastal lagoons of
conservation significance.
*** of considerable
    conservation value
** strongly recommended
    for conservation
* recommended for
    conservation.
(After Sheader & Sheader
1989.)

1	**Easington Lagoons**, N Humberside **
2	**S. Killingholme Lagoons**, S Humberside**
3	**Humberston Fitties**, Lincolnshire ***
4	**Aldeburgh**, Suffolk ***
5	**Cliffe Marshes Lagoons**, Kent***
6	**Pagham Lagoons**, W Sussex ***
7	**Widewater Lagoon**, W Sussex *
8	**Birdham Pool**, W Sussex *
9	**Fort Gilkicker Moat**, Hampshire ***
10	**Little Anglesey**, Hampshire **
11	**Shut Lake**, Hampshire *
12	**Keyhaven–Lymington Lagoons**, Hampshire ***
13	**Brading Marshes system**, Isle of Wight ***
14	**Horsey Island Pool**, Devon *

considered to be the best representatives of their type (described above). Of these important sites, all but one were on the North Sea coast (Barnes 1989b).

For artificial lagoons, Sheader considered 135 individual coastal saline ponds in England and Wales, making a total of 35 pond systems. Twenty-three pond systems were considered worthy of conservation, all of which are on the North Sea coast. The fourteen most important coastal pond sites are listed in Table 4.6.3 and categorised according to Sheader's evaluation of their conservation value.

Lagoons are a priority habitat under the EC Habitats Directive (see section 10.2).

IMPACTS ON LAGOONS

Lagoons are naturally fragile habitats in that they are usually small, shallow and vulnerable to relatively minor changes to their containing barriers and salinity regimes. Many are vulnerable to pollution, being relatively small with a limited ability to buffer changes in water quality conditions. All are easily reclaimable by infill to form land, by isolation from the sea to form freshwater lakes, and by dredging or opening of a connecting channel to the sea to form harbours or marinas.

The type of natural lagoon formed in the North Atlantic in macrotidal conditions (i.e. where tidal range is greater than 2 m) is a relatively short lived feature, and will eventually be lost through natural processes of succession to freshwater lakes, fen and carr; or through man's activities. Areas of shingle or sand banks on the upper shore where natural lagoons have formed or would form are now largely protected by coastal defences: therefore the natural rate of formation of new lagoons by coastal sediment movement is

likely to be insufficient to replace lagoons as they are lost. Coastal lagoons as a natural physiographic feature are therefore a rare and diminishing resource in Britain.

Rising sea levels and possible increases in storminess may affect lagoon habitats – some saline lagoons will be lost to the sea by flooding or the landward movement of their seaward shingle barrier ridges. Conversely, new lagoons may be created by marine invasion of land through overtopping or the breaching of barriers. The upgrading of coastal defence works to prevent marine flooding may result in further threats to naturally formed lagoons, but could also create opportunities for new artificial sites, as will managed coastal retreat if low-lying areas are allowed to flood periodically.

Coastal saline ponds, although vulnerable to destruction by man as are natural lagoons, are more easily conserved through the maintenance of their containing barriers. They are also likely to be created as new habitats by civil engineering works on the coast, as noted above. These artificial sites are important refuges for natural lagoonal species, and are habitats which may, if suitably managed for the lagoon biota, be indistinguishable from the naturally formed lagoonal habitat.

Pye & French (1992) project a loss of 120 ha of saline lagoons (10% of the existing resource) within the next 20 years, primarily from coastal erosion due to sea level rise and increased frequency of stormy weather breaching barriers, but also from human activities.

SOURCES OF INFORMATION

The above mentioned reviews by Barnes (1989b) and Sheader & Sheader (1989), commissioned by the NCC, were based on surveys of lagoons associated with coastal habitats. Sites surveyed were larger than 0.1 ha in area (except where sites were considered of particular interest), and were predominantly in England and Wales. All lagoon data for England is summarised in Smith & Laffoley (1992), which provides details of the location and areas of all major sites around the coast. Bamber *et al.* (1992) examine the ecology of British saline lagoons, highlight areas warranting further study and offer guidelines for their management.

Scottish lagoons are not considered in the report by Sheader & Sheader (1989) on saline ponds, but Barnes (1989b) does include a few Scottish sites in his review. Information on distribution and flora and fauna of lagoon sites in Scotland is certainly lacking. Smith (1984) carried out a desk study of potential lagoon sites in Scotland, investigating sites including sea lochs and shallow bays, most of which were in western Scotland. A few lagoonal sites in Orkney were mentioned by Smith, but several others are mentioned in Bullard (1972). There was a Marine Nature Conservation Review (MNCR) survey of lagoons in Orkney in 1993. Two sites on the Scottish North Sea coast were considered to be interesting by McLusky (McLusky & Roddie 1984), but he did not find any of the rare or specialist lagoonal species. Surveys of brackish habitats (including houbs and vadills) in Shetland were carried out by the MNCR in 1993.

There is a lack of information on potential lagoon sites in Scotland and a lack of a complete overview of habitats where lagoonal species may be found. Brackish drainage ditches in coastal marshes often harbour some of the species mentioned above, but are not strictly lagoons. Equally, some sites in Scotland (particularly in Orkney) may be described as physical types of lagoon, but may well not harbour specialist lagoonal species. The species protected by the Wildlife and Countryside Act (1981) tend to have a southern distribution; it is not known whether these species are completely absent from the North, or if there is potentially suitable habitat available in northern brackish waters.

For the NCC-funded studies of coastal lagoons, emphasis was placed on identification of flora, specialist lagoonal invertebrates and invertebrates of marine origin. Both Barnes (1989b) and Sheader & Sheader (1989) recognised the lack of information on insect species (due to lack of surveyors' expertise in this subject). Selection of important sites by Barnes and Sheader was also biased towards sites with high salinity, species-rich, and generally with few insects. Many brackish drainage ditches, particularly in coastal grazing marshes, were not considered, although it is known that some of these contain typical lagoonal species (R. Mitchell pers. comm.). Coastal grazing marsh drainage ditch habitats are dealt with more fully in Section 4.7.

4.7 COASTAL GRAZING MARSHES

INTRODUCTION

Coastal grazing marshes are areas of flat, low-lying grassland which are drained by complex networks of brackish or freshwater drainage ditches. The water level in ditches is often poorly correlated with the water table in the field in clay areas. However, in some areas ditches provide supplies of drinking water for cattle and sheep and act as 'wet fences' to keep stock within the fields. Coastal grazing marshes generally originated through land reclamation of the upper vegetation zones of saltmarshes by construction of sea walls. They may also develop landward of natural barriers such as sand dunes or shingle storm beaches.

Coastal grazing marshes are important for a variety of nature conservation reasons. In particular, brackish marshes are valuable in that they represent a scarce national resource and support plant and animal species which in Britain show a distinct preference for this habitat type. Many of these species are nationally rare or scarce. Coastal grazing marshes are important for a wide range of breeding birds, including several protected under Schedule 1 of the Wildlife and Countryside Act 1981. They also provide winter feeding and roosting areas for sometimes nationally important numbers of waterfowl.

DISTRIBUTION

On the North Sea coast, grazing marshes are virtually absent from Scotland and northern England. They occur mainly on the south-east and south coasts of England where land is low lying and has been enclosed by sea walls.

DESCRIPTION OF RESOURCE

The coastal grazing marshes of the east coast of England contain few plant species in comparison with those of the south coast and inland unimproved pastures and hay meadows. Their vegetation consists of grassland flora (including that of the earth banks containing the marsh) and ditch flora. The faunal interest is predominantly in the networks of drainage ditches. Salinity is of overriding importance in determining species composition of both flora and fauna, but position in the hydrosphere and soil type are also significant (Leach 1991). Ditches are prevented from reverting to dry land by management by local drainage boards, land owners and the National Rivers Authority. This management creates a spectrum of ditch sizes ranging from broad, deep drains in which the vegetation is removed, usually annually, and re-profiling is undertaken regularly, to small field ditches which are irregularly managed, shallow, and may become quite overgrown.

Vegetation

Grasslands. Grazing marshes consist of two quite different types of vegetation; that of the grasslands, and that of the drainage ditches.

Grazing marsh grasslands are typically dominated by the more common grasses of neutral soils, for example meadow fox-tail *Alopecurus pratensis*, crested dog's-tail *Cynosurus cristatus*, rye grass *Lolium perenne* and meadow barley *Hordeum secalinum*. They do, however, support a number of nationally rare or scarce plants which, in Britain, are largely restricted to such habitats. Examples are:

divided sedge *Carex divisa*
slender hare's-ear *Bupleurum tenuissimum*
sea clover *Trifolium squamosum*
sea barley *Hordeum marinum*
least lettuce *Lactuca saligna*
curved hard-grass *Parapholis incurva* on
    embankments
pedunculate sea-purslane *Halimione
    pedunculata* (recently re-discovered in Britain).

Ditches. Ditches containing brackish water support quite different assemblages of plants to freshwater ditches further inland. In the most saline ditches the tasselweeds *Ruppia maritima* and *R. spiralis* can occur, and the fringing emergent vegetation resembles saltmarsh, with plants such as sea aster *Aster tripolium*, saltmarsh-grass *Puccinellia maritima* and cord-grass *Spartina anglica*. Less saline ditches typically have sea club-rush *Scirpus maritimus* as the dominant emergent, along with a restricted number of aquatic species such as fennel-leaved pondweed *Potamogeton pectinatus*, water-milfoil *Myriophyllum spicatum*, and two nationally scarce species, brackish water-crowfoot *Ranunculus baudotii* and soft hornwort *Ceratophyllum submersum*.

The transition to freshwater is either sharp or gradual, and is often marked by the abundance of common reed *Phragmites australis*. Inland from this transition are ditches supporting a varied and often very diverse assemblage of plant species, characterised by those more typically associated with freshwater swamps and fens, i.e. *Carex riparia* and *Glyceria maxima*.

Regional variation on the North Sea coast

In south-eastern England, where natural transitions between saltmarsh vegetation and other habitats have invariably been lost (see section 4.4), grazing marsh ditch vegetation often consists of upper saltmarsh communities that are either rare or absent from the adjoining saltmarsh proper. These communities are relict from before the containing sea walls were constructed to enclose the upper marsh areas, and can only exist along the wetter margins of drainage ditches.

The south coast grazing marshes tend to show a greater diversity of grassland flora and grassland community type. Here areas of typical wet grazing marsh grassland are interspersed with dry, acid grasslands dominated by mat grass *Nardus stricta* that have developed on old estuarine sand bars and areas of species-rich mesotrophic grassland characterised by the nationally scarce corky-fruited water-dropwort *Oenanthe pimpinelloides*.

There are several plants of grazing marshes which are restricted to the south-east of England. These include the re-discovered pedunculate sea-purslane *Halimione pedunculata*. These species give the south-eastern grazing marshes a distinctive appearance. Most plants of grazing marshes have a primarily 'continental' distribution, and are restricted on the North Sea coast of Britain to the south-east of England.

In oligohaline, or slightly brackish ditches, from Norfolk to Kent, a distinct assemblage of coastal species may be found, a large proportion of which are nationally scarce or rare as a consequence of the scarcity of the habitat. In this respect, the North Sea coast grazing marshes differ from the major sites in the west of Britain where the coastal element is poorly represented.

Invertebrates

The focus of interest in the invertebrate fauna of grazing marshes is in drainage ditches and their margins (Drake 1988, 1989). These systems may be species-rich and most sites support rare species. For some rare invertebrate species, coastal grazing marshes provide their national stronghold. The distributions of the great silver water beetle *Hydrophilus piceus*, three scarce beetles *Peltodytes caesus*, *Limnoxenus niger* and *Berosus affinis* and the soldier fly *Odontomyia ornata* closely follow that of the major grazing marshes.

The faunal composition and species-richness of ditches are strongly influenced by the cleaning cycle and by salinity. Grazing marshes with a high proportion of slightly brackish (oligohaline) ditches are characteristic of the coast from Kent to north Norfolk. Oligohaline ditches tend to be less species-rich than freshwater ditches but may be just as rich in terms of the numbers of rare species. Only in mesohaline ditches, such as those behind sea walls, does the number of rare species fall off, together with species-richness.

A feature of freshwater ditches, which may not be true of oligohaline marshes, is that the aquatic fauna of those that are moderately frequently maintained is richer, both in total numbers of species and in rare species, than those that are left to become overgrown. However, the reverse appears to be true for the terrestrial fauna of freshwater marshes and this may be related to the fact that the mown bank vegetation that often accompanies regularly cleared ditches is poor habitat for most invertebrates.

Frequently occurring species on the eastern marshes may be the amphipods *Gammarus duebeni* and *G. zaddachi*, the water boatman *Sigara stagnalis*, the caddis *Limnephilus affinis*, and the beetles *Agabus conspersus*, *Enochrus halophilus*, *Halipus apicalis*, *Limnoxenus niger* and *Berosus affinis*. Slightly brackish conditions may be essential to maintain healthy populations of some of these species, although some which are characteristic of oligohaline waters may be found in lower numbers in freshwater sites. This applies to species such as the water boatmen *Corixa affinis* and *Notonecta viridis*, the scarce emerald damselfly *Lestes dryas*, and the water beetles *Graptodytes bilineatus*, *Dytiscus circumflexus*, *Gyrinus caspius* and *Ochthebius punctatus*. Three species of beetle, *Limnoxenus niger*, *Berosus signaticollis* and *Helophorus alternans* are locally frequent in brackish grazing marsh ditches and saltmarshes, but are also occasionally found inland at peaty sites. In brackish ditches leeches are usually absent, and often only two species of snail *Lymnaea peregra* and *Potamopyrgus jenkinsi* are present. Apart from the localised presence of the scarce emerald damselfly *Lestes dryas*, the only frequently occurring dragonflies are the common damselfly *Ischnura elegans* and the darters *Sympetrum striolatum* and *Sympetrum sanguineum*. Common invertebrates which are intolerant of oligohaline conditions may nevertheless be found in ditches carrying freshwater from the hinterland across otherwise brackish marshes.

The dominant freshwater aquatic macro-invertebrates of drainage ditches with little or no saline influence are beetles (Coleoptera), bugs (Heteroptera), snails (Mollusca-Gastropoda) and fly larvae (Diptera). The first three of these groups form a substantial proportion of the British species on freshwater coastal grazing marshes. Other groups which may be found are crustaceans, leeches, flatworms, caddis and mayflies. These groups are generally represented by only a few, though sometimes abundant, species. Mites, worms and smaller crustaceans also occur, but there is little information on the distribution of these groups.

Grazing marshes are also undoubtedly important habitats for dragonflies. For example, 14 species out of a British total of 44 occur on the Essex marshes (Benton 1987). The terrestrial invertebrate fauna of grazing marshes appears to be dominated by two-winged flies, although this may reflect the expertise of the surveyors rather than the true fauna of these areas. These dipteral faunas can be very rich, with up to 270 species of flies being found in a survey of the north Kent grazing marshes (Stubbs *et al.* 1982). Several flies are strongly centred on the oligohaline marshes from Norfolk to Kent, often restricted to quite specific parts of these marshes, e.g. *Lejops vittata*, *Erioptera bivittata* and *Poecilobothrus ducalis*. The shore bug *Saldula opacula* is also frequent here but very scarce elsewhere.

IMPORTANT SITES

The grazing marshes of Essex and Kent are important floristically as they support several rare plant species of more continental distribution. The richest sites for invertebrates lie in the Thames estuary, both in north Kent and south Essex, notably Shorne to Cliffe and Elmley to Coldharbour in Kent, and Fobbing to Hadleigh in Essex. The grazing marshes of the Solent are of importance in supporting a greater diversity of grassland type and a richer flora than those on the east coast with those of the Beaulieu Estuary in Hampshire and Brading Marshes on the Isle of Wight providing good examples. Other valuable marshes are spread along the East Anglian coast and include Foulness Island, Langenhoe, Old Hall and Tollesbury Wick in Essex, Orfordness, Sizewell and Minsmere in Suffolk.

IMPACTS ON COASTAL GRAZING MARSHES

In recent years many coastal grazing marshes have been converted to arable land. In the Thames estuary, for example, nearly 70% of the grazing marsh has been lost in this way since the last war (Thornton and Kite 1990). This process not only destroys the grassland, but also results in a decline in the interest of the ditches as a consequence of the more intensive management of the 'improved' fields and the resulting eutrophication.

The main losses of grazing marsh occur as a result of agricultural intensification, notably to arable use. In the Thames Estuary, Kent, this has amounted to some 30% of the total resource since the 1930s (Thornton & Kite 1990). In Essex the loss has been even greater with an 82% decline in the last 50 years.

SOURCES OF INFORMATION

Most of the information contained within this section has been extracted from reports by the Nature Conservancy Council's England Field Unit. They have carried out floral and faunal surveys of grazing marshes in England over the past decade. Most of the major grazing marsh areas have been surveyed and reported on individually. However, the collation of information on coastal grazing marshes throughout Britain has not been carried out.

ACKNOWLEDGEMENTS

This chapter was compiled by Barbara Smith and Charlotte Johnston. The following people provided information or contributions: Fiona Burd, Martin Drake, Karen Goodwin, Roger Key, Dan Laffoley, Simon Leach, Roger Mitchell, Geoff Radley and Pippa Sneddon.

REFERENCES

BAMBER, R.N., BATTEN, S.D., & BRIDGWATER, N.D. 1992. On the ecology of brackish water lagoons in Great Britain. *Aquatic conservation: Marine and Freshwater Ecosystems: 2*, 65-94.

BARNES, R.S.K. 1989a. The coastal lagoons of Britain: An overview and conservation appraisal. *Biological Conservation, 49*: 295-313.

BARNES, R.S.K. 1989b. The coastal lagoons of Britain: An overview. (Contractor: Department of Zoology, University of Cambridge), *Nature Conservancy Council, CSD Report,* No. 933.

BEEFTINK, W.G. 1977. Salt-marshes. *In: The coastline*, ed. by R.S.K. Barnes. London, Wiley.

BENTON, E. 1987. *The dragonflies of Essex.* London, The Essex Field Club, Passmore Edwards Museum.

BRATTON, J.H., ed. 1991. *British Red Data Books: 3. Invertebrates other than insects.* Peterborough, Joint Nature Conservation Committee.

BULLARD, E.R. 1972. Lagoons and 'Oyces' in Orkney. *Orkney Field Club Bulletin, 3*: 7-8.

BURD, F. 1989. *The saltmarsh survey of Great Britain. An inventory of British saltmarshes.* Peterborough, Nature Conservancy Council. (Research and survey in nature conservation, No. 17.)

BURD, F. 1992. *Erosion and vegetation change in the*

saltmarshes of Essex and north Kent between 1973 and 1988. Peterborough, Nature Conservancy Council. (Research and survey in nature conservation, No. 42.)

CHAPMAN, V.J. 1964. *Coastal vegetation.* Oxford, Pergamon.

CHARMAN, K., FOJT, W., & PENNY, S. 1986. *Saltmarsh survey of Great Britain: Bibliography.* Peterborough, Nature Conservancy Council. (Research and survey in nature conservation, No. 3.)

COOPER, E.A. 1988. *Vegetation maps of British sea cliffs and cliff-tops.* Nature Conservancy Council & Lancaster University.

DARGIE, 1993. *Sand dune vegetation survey of Great Britain. Part 2, Scotland.* Peterborough, Joint Nature Conservation Committee.

DARGIE, in press. *Sand dune vegetation survey of Great Britain. Part 3, Wales.* Peterborough, Joint Nature Conservation Committee.

DAVIDSON, N.C., et al. 1991. *Nature conservation and estuaries in Great Britain.* Peterborough, Nature Conservancy Council.

DOODY, J.P. ed. 1984. *Spartina anglica in Great Britain.* Peterborough, Nature Conservancy Council (Research and survey in nature conservation, No. 5.)

DOODY, P. 1989a. Conservation and development of the coastal dunes in Great Britain. *In: Perspectives in coastal dune management*, ed. by F. van der Meulen, P.D. Jungerius and J.H. Visser. The Hague, Academic Publishing.

DOODY, P. 1989b. Dungeness - a national nature conservation perspective. *Botanical Journal of the Linnean Society, 101*: 163 -171.

DRAKE, C.M. 1988. *A survey of the aquatic invertebrates of the Essex grazing marshes.* Peterborough, Nature Conservancy Council. (England Field Unit Report, No. 50a.)

DRAKE, C.M. 1989. *A survey of the aquatic invertebrates of the Suffolk grazing marshes.* Peterborough, Nature Conservancy Council. (England Field Unit Report, No. 50b.)

FERRY, B., & WATERS, S. eds. 1985. *Dungeness ecology and conservation. Report of a meeting held at the Botany department, Royal Holloway and Bedford New College, on 16 April 1985.* Peterborough, Nature Conservancy Council. (Focus on nature conservation, No. 12.)

FRID C.L.J., & JAMES, R. 1989. The marine invertebrate fauna of a British coastal saltmarsh. *Holarctic Ecology, 12:* 9-15.

FULLER, R.M., & RANDALL, R.E. 1988. The Orford shingles, Suffolk, UK - classic conflict in coastline management. *Biological Conservation, 46*: 95-114.

GUILCHER, A. 1958. *Coastal and submarine morphology.* London, Methuen.

HUBBARD, J.C.E. & STEBBINGS, R.E. 1967. Distribution, dates of origin and acreage of *Spartina townsendii* (s.l.) marshes in Great Britain. *Proceedings of the Botanical Society of the British Isles.* Vol. 7, (1) pp. 1-7.

INSTITUTE OF TERRESTRIAL ECOLOGY. 1979. The invertebrate fauna of dunes and machair sites in Scotland. A report to the Nature Conservancy Council. *Nature Conservancy Council, CSD Report*, No. 255.

LEACH, S. 1991. Grazing marshes. *In*: Davidson, N. *et al.* 1991. *Nature conservation and estuaries in Great Britain.* Peterborough, Nature Conservancy Council.

MARSHALL, I.C., & GREEN, B.H. 1984. An appraisal of semi-natural ecosystems on a golf course in Kent. *Wye College Department of Environmental Studies and Countryside Planning Occasional Paper. No. 12.* University of London.

McLUSKY, D., & RODDIE, K. 1984. Coastal lagoon survey. (Contractor: Department of Biological Science, University of Stirling). *Nature Conservancy Council, CSD Report*, No. 554.

MITCHLEY, J. 1989. *A sea-cliff bibliography.* Peterborough, Nature Conservancy Council. (Research and survey in nature conservation, No. 18.)

MITCHLEY, J., & MALLOCH, A.J.C. 1991. *Sea cliff management handbook of Great Britain.* Lancaster, University of Lancaster.

NATURE CONSERVANCY COUNCIL. 1989. *Guidelines for selection of biological Sites of Special Scientific Interest.* Peterborough, Nature Conservancy Council.

PHILP, E.G., & McLEAN, I.F.G. 1985. The invertebrate fauna of Dungeness. *In*: *Dungeness, ecology and conservation,* ed. by B. Ferry and S. Waters. Peterborough, Nature Conservancy Council. (Focus on nature conservation, No. 12.)

PYE, K., & FRENCH, P.W. 1992. Targets for coastal habitat recreation. Report to English Nature from Cambridge Environmental Research Consultants Ltd.

RADLEY, G.P. In press. *Sand dune vegetation survey of Great Britain. Part 1, England.* Peterborough, Joint Nature Conservation Committee.

RADLEY, G.P., & WOOLVEN, S.C. 1989. National sand dune vegetation survey. Nature Conservancy Council's contract surveys 1988/1989. Peterborough, Nature Conservancy Council.

RANDALL, R. E. 1988. *A field survey of* Mertensia maritima *(L) Gray oyster plant in Britain during 1986 and 1987.* Peterborough, Nature Conservancy Council. (Contract survey report, No. 20.)

RANDALL, R.E. 1989. Shingle habitats in the British Isles. *Botanical Journal of the Linnean Society, 101*: 3-18.

RANDALL, R.E, SNEDDON, P., & DOODY, P. (1990). *Coastal shingle in Great Britain, a preliminary review.* Peterborough, Nature Conservancy Council. (Contract survey, No. 85.)

RANWELL, D.S. & BOAR, R. 1986. *Coast dune management guide.* Abbots Ripton, Institute of Terrestrial Ecology.

RATCLIFFE, D.A., *ed.* 1977. *A nature conservation review - The selection of biological sites of national importance to nature conservation in Britain.* Vols 1 & 2. Cambridge, Cambridge University Press.

RILEY, H. 1989. *Dungeness bibliography.* Peterborough, Nature Conservancy Council. (Research & survey in nature conservation, No. 21.)

RITCHIE, W., & MATHER, A. S. 1984. *The beaches of Scotland.* Perth, Countryside Commission for Scotland.

ROBERTS, M.J. 1985. *The spiders of Great Britain and Ireland.* Vol. 1. Colchester, Harley Books.

RODWELL. J. 1988. *National vegetation classification - maritime cliff communities.* University of Lancaster, unpublished report to Nature Conservancy Council.

RODWELL, J. 1989. *National vegetation classification - sand dune, strandline and shingle communities.* University of Lancaster.

RODWELL, J.S., *ed.* 1991. *British plant communities. Volume 2: mires and heaths.* Cambridge, Cambridge University Press.

RODWELL. J.S., *ed.* In press. *British plant communities. Volume 5: maritime and weed communities.* Cambridge, Cambridge University Press.

SCOTT, G.A.M. 1963. The ecology of shingle beach plants. *Journal of Ecology, 51*: 517-527.

SHAW, M.W., HEWETT, D.G., & PIZZY, J.M. 1983. Scottish coastal survey, main report. A report on selected soft coast sites in Scotland to the Nature Conservancy council by the Institute of Terrestrial Ecology. *Nature Conservancy Council, CSD Report*, No. 487.

SHEADER, M., & SHEADER, A. 1989. Coastal saline ponds of England and Wales: an overview. (Contractor: Department of Oceanography, University of Southampton.) *Nature Conservancy Council, CSD Report,* No. 1009.

SHIRT, D.B., *ed.* 1987. *British Red Data Books: 2. Insects.* Peterborough, Nature Conservancy Council.

SMITH, B.P., & LAFFOLEY, D. 1992. *Saline lagoons and lagoon-like habitats in England.* Peterborough, English Nature.

SMITH, S. 1984. Scottish saline lagoons with emphasis on the Mollusca. *Nature Conservancy Council, CSD Report*, No. 526.

SNEDDON, P. 1992. Variations in shingle vegetation around the British coastline. PhD thesis, Girton College, Cambridge.

SNEDDON, P., & RANDALL, R.E. 1989. *Vegetated shingle structures survey of Great Britain: Bibliography.* Peterborough, Nature Conservancy Council. (Research & survey in nature conservation, No. 20.)

SNEDDON, P., & RANDALL, R.E. 1993. *Coastal vegetated shingle structures of Great Britain: Main Report.* Joint

Nature Conservation Committee, Peterborough. [Appendix 1 - Wales, 1993. Appendix 2 (Scotland), Appendix 3 (England) in press.]

STUBBS, A.E., McLEAN, I.F.G., & SHEPPARD, D.A. 1982. The north Kent marshes: a report on the terrestrial invertebrates recorded in July and September 1980. *Nature Conservancy Council, CSD Report.*

THORNTON, D., & KITE, D.J. 1990. Changes in the extent of the Thames Estuary grazing marshes. London, Nature Conservancy Council, Internal Report.

TUBBS, C.R. 1984. *Spartina* on the south coast: an introduction. *In:* Spartina anglica *in Great Britain*, ed. by J.P. Doody, 3-4. Peterborough, Nature Conservancy Council. (Focus on Nature Conservation, No. 5.)

Chapter 5

MARINE HABITATS

5.1 INTRODUCTION

THE MARINE NATURE CONSERVATION REVIEW

The information presented here represents the data presently available to the Joint Nature Conservation Committee's Marine Nature Conservation Review (formerly part of the Nature Conservancy Council). This is a long-term project to describe and classify British marine ecosystems. The MNCR began in 1987 and aims to:

i) extend our knowledge of benthic marine habitats, communities and species in Great Britain, particularly through description of their characteristics, distribution and extent

ii) identify sites and species of nature conservation importance.

MNCR data also support more general measures opposing the adverse effects of development and pollution.

The MNCR is based on descriptions of habitats and the recorded abundance of conspicuous species for the whole of the coastal waters of England, Scotland and Wales, from the high water mark out to the limits of British territorial seas, extending into estuaries to the limits of maritime influence. In practice, most of the survey work is logistically limited to the shore and sublittoral areas within the 50 m depth contour.

Existing information has been reviewed and catalogued on a computer database, which allows access by author, geographical location to which the information relates, or by a series of keywords which describe the type of information. Additionally, a series of reports has been prepared which reviews the key information for each sector of coast, describing the dominant habitats and the available information. These reports deal with the Shetland Isles (Hiscock & Johnston 1990), the Orkneys, north-east Scotland, south-east Scotland and north-east England (Bennett 1991), eastern England and Eastern Channel (Covey 1991) and Western Channel (Davies 1991). A general introduction and review of offshore studies is given

in Hiscock (1991). Raw data from MNCR surveys and from other surveys are entered to the database to provide the basis for identifying the distribution of marine biological survey information. The descriptions of that information are being entered to a volume of the United Kingdom Digital Marine Atlas Project (UKDMAP, see Section 9.6).

Collection of new information by field survey initially concentrated on Shetland and the west coast of Scotland, with localised MNCR surveys of the Isle of May (Bennett 1989) and Berwick to Beadnell including the Farne Islands (Connor 1989). Recent MNCR work has been concentrated on North Sea coasts, with littoral and sublittoral surveys in 1992 carried out between Dunbar and Newcastle (Davies 1993; Holt 1993; Brazier & Murray 1993) and further work planned for 1993 between Newcastle and Flamborough Head. In addition to work on the north-east England–south-east Scotland coastline, MNCR surveys have been carried out on estuaries in south-eastern England during 1992 (Hill & Emblow in prep.) and these will be continued during 1993 and 1994. Other areas have been previously surveyed under contract to NCC, such as the Moray Firth (Bartrop *et al.* 1980), the sediment shores of Dorset, Hampshire and the Isle of Wight (Holme & Bishop 1980) and the shores of Devon and Cornwall (Powell *et al.* 1978) which were studied by the Intertidal Survey Unit of the Scottish Marine Biological Association and the Marine Biological Association as part of a survey of the littoral zone of the coast of Great Britain for the NCC. Chalk coast habitats and communities have been studied and a final report is currently in preparation. The marine inlets of southern Britain have also been surveyed by the Field Studies Council Oil Pollution Research Unit for the NCC and reports prepared on each area.

SURVEY COVERAGE

Maps showing areas for which we have adequate survey coverage are given in Figures 5.1.1 and 5.1.2. Detailed information for other areas is variable

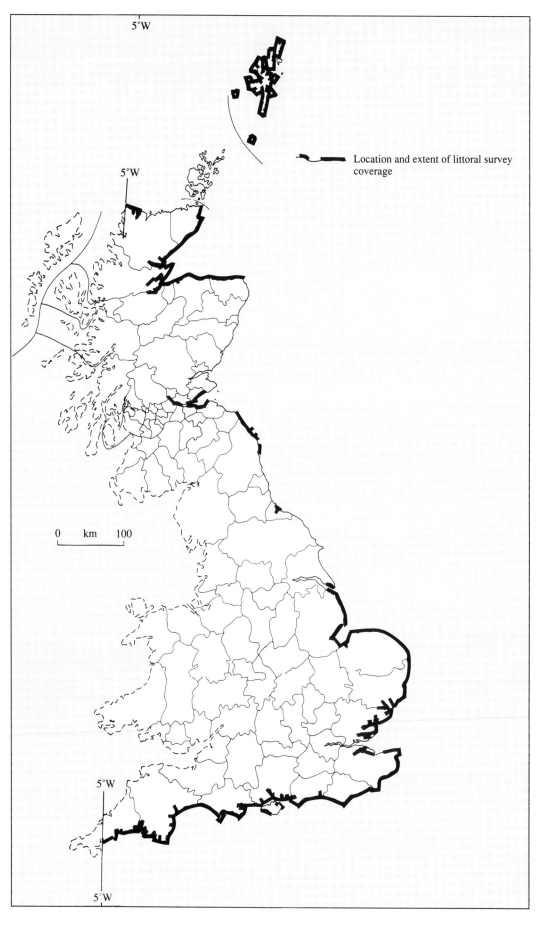

Figure 5.1.1
Littoral survey coverage by
NCC and JNCC of the North
Sea coast to the end of 1992.
Based upon the 1975 Ordnance Survey
1:1,250,000 map with the permission
of the Controller of Her Majesty's
Stationery Office © Crown Copyright.

Location and extent of littoral survey
coverage

0   km   100

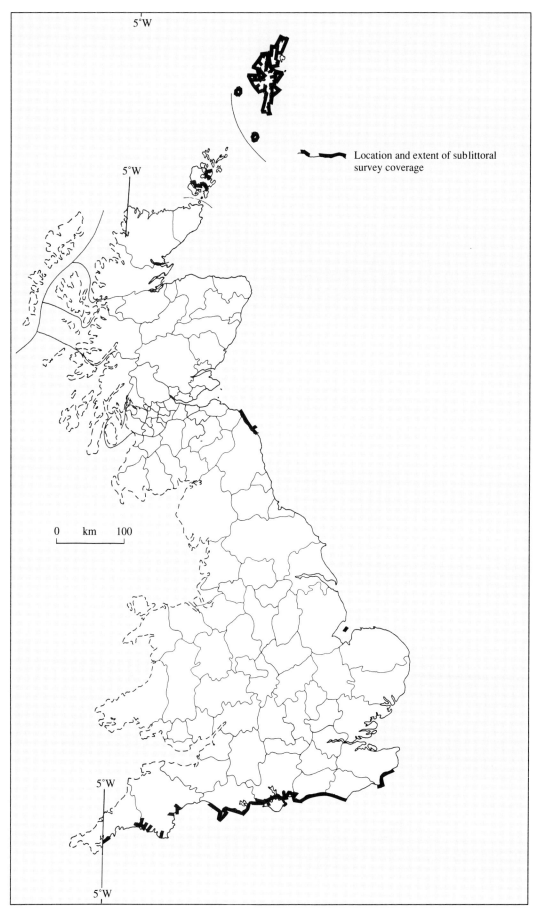

5°W

5°W

5°W

5°W

5°W

0   km   100

Location and extent of sublittoral
survey coverage

Figure 5.1.2
Sublittoral survey coverage
by NCC and JNCC of the
North Sea coast to the end of
1992.

Based upon the 1975 Ordnance Survey
1:1,250,000 map with the permission
of the Controller of Her Majesty's
Stationery Office © Crown Copyright.

83

in nature. Some areas have been studied in relation to fisheries interest or dumping and dredging grounds, while other areas near marine research institutes or universities have been the subject of field work and survey but available data is not readily interpreted into habitat or community descriptions. For other areas of the coast little or no reliable information is available and the generation of information by MNCR surveys will result in the known distribution of some habitats, communities and species changing. This is particularly the case for sublittoral habitats, which are difficult to map with any degree of certainty. For this reason, the information contained in the marine sections should be regarded as provisional and likely to be updated by the Marine Nature Conservation Review. Work is currently concentrated on the north-east England and south-east Scotland coast of the North Sea and on the estuaries of south-eastern England, and this work will continue during 1993.

MARINE BIOGEOGRAPHY

Great Britain lies in the centre of the Boreal (cold temperate) biogeographical province (Briggs 1970). However, the south-west of Britain is at the boundary of the Boreal-Lusitanean (warm temperate) province and the north at the boundary of a Boreal-Arctic province. The transition area between Boreal-Lusitanean and Boreal provinces lies between east Dorset and the Isle of Wight while a Boreal-Arctic flora and fauna is found in Shetland and parts of the north-east of mainland Britain. Thus, the North Sea area of this report effectively straddles three major biogeographical provinces. These discontinuities are transitions rather than abrupt changes, due to the seasonal mixing of water bodies and annual variation of temperature in these areas. This biogeographical influence, combined with local effects due to currents and differences in water quality in particular, gives rise to the presence of discrete areas with different environmental conditions and biological characteristics.

Within the North Sea, there are other features likely to cause biogeographical divisions. For instance, there is a marked boundary of water types in the summer months known as the Flamborough Front. This front, visible on satellite photographs, extends from Flamborough Head across the North Sea to the German Bight and is also associated with the separation of deep and shallow parts of the North Sea. A similar change in water quality and depth occurs in the English Channel. The south-east coast of England is therefore contained in a water mass in the area from just west of the Isle of

Wight to just south of Flamborough Head. Because physical water conditions outside these limits are slightly different, the marine flora and fauna reflects these conditions and differences will be described later in the text.

HISTORY OF STUDY

Studies of the marine biology along the North Sea coasts have a long history. In the late 18th century, for example, collectors such as John Ellis, a London merchant, sampled seaweeds and other 'corallines' (hydroids and bryozoans) in the south-east of England. Others, such as George Johnston of Berwick, also worked their nearby coastline with a following of fellow enthusiasts. Activity greatly increased in the early and mid-19th century with much collecting, resulting in the writing of authoritative monographs on the main species groups. Historical information sources describing assemblages of organisms rather than undertaking collections for taxonomy have, however, largely been confined to accessible areas of coast or clustered around research institutes such as the Marine Biological Association in Plymouth. Dredge studies of sublittoral communities were begun in the early part of the 19th century. In the North Sea, those undertaken in Shetland and reported by Jefferies in 1869 are particularly important for the comparison they provide of the fauna of Shetland with other parts of the British Isles. Edward Forbes brought together information obtained largely by dredging in the *Natural history of the European seas* (Forbes & Goodwin-Austin 1859). Species distribution related to geographical location together with patterns of zonation on the shore and underwater are given in this volume, thus laying the foundations for much of what we have refined today. The earliest marine station in the UK was established at St. Andrews in 1884, followed rapidly by many of the institutes which continue marine biological work today both on and offshore.

The thrust of marine work in the North Sea in the late 19th and early 20th century was towards fisheries research. The first systematic sampling and description of 'communities' was undertaken by the Danish zoologist Petersen (1914) initially based on assessing the food resources for fish. The concept of 'communities' plays a central role in describing marine benthic ecosystems and the naming of recurrent groupings of organisms according to characterising species is a shorthand that will be used throughout this chapter. Many other studies followed and much important work has been undertaken from the fisheries laboratories at Lowestoft and Aberdeen. In the mid-1970s, the focus of work shifted to investigating the effects of the oil industry in the North Sea, and many descriptive surveys have been undertaken in both littoral and sublittoral areas related to construction and operations in this industry. The invention of the aqualung and its application to scientific diving since the mid-1960s has resulted in more accurate *in situ* observations being possible, particularly in nearshore sublittoral hard-substratum areas.

All of these studies give us a basis for describing the marine biological resource of the North Sea, although it is only since the mid-1970s that surveys have been undertaken with the specific aim of describing and identifying the marine nature conservation importance of areas of the North Sea coast.

SEPARATION OF MAJOR HABITATS

In this chapter, descriptions are separated into:
5.2 Intertidal hard substrata
5.3 Intertidal sediment
5.4 Sublittoral hard substrata
5.5 Inshore sublittoral sediment
5.6 Offshore sediment.

'Inshore' areas are those which are considered to be under the local influence of the coastline, for instance through local shelter from wave action, acceleration or reduction of tidal stream strength as a result of coastal features, reduced or variable salinity or locally different water quality as a result of estuarine discharge. Inshore areas extend out to approximately 3 km where extensive level seabed is present.

INFORMATION COVERAGE

Survey coverage for marine biological information along most of the North Sea coast is patchy. Information is particularly sparse away from marine inlets and along largely unbroken coastlines. Offshore, there are extensive areas where little or no survey data is available. Also, the results of some surveys are presented in limited circulation, often confidential reports which would not have been located and incorporated into this review. The approach of naming sediment community types according to characterizing species, which has proved so valuable in summary reviews such as this, has been little undertaken by the studies related to industrial developments. The absence of such a system, for hard substratum habitats and communities (although currently being developed by the MNCR) makes summary and comparison difficult.

5.2 INTERTIDAL HARD SUBSTRATA

INTRODUCTION

This section describes those areas of hard substratum which occur between extreme high water of spring tides and extreme low water of spring tides. These include a wide range of types, varying from erosion-resistant granites to the soft chalk of the south-east coast. Shores of stable cobbles and boulders as well as artificial hard substrata such as jetty walls are included within this grouping because they form an essentially similar substratum to bedrock shores. The communities of plants and animals which occur on these shores are dependent predominantly on a combination of wave exposure, shore topography, geology and geographical location.

DISTRIBUTION

The distribution of predominantly rocky shores is limited to the northern and southern areas of the North Sea study area. The most extremely wave exposed shores are found in Orkney and Shetland. The north and north-east coast of Scotland face away from prevailing winds and are much less exposed. Rocky shores continue with a similar exposure and range of habitats south to the coast of Northumberland, where as well as bedrock shores, extensive areas of intertidal boulders occur. Areas of intertidal bedrock continue, interspersed with sandy bays, as far south as Flamborough Head where chalk bedrock is found. This is the southern limit of littoral hard substratum on the east coast, with the exception of Greensand exposures at Hunstanton and an outcrop of chalk bedrock at West Runton on the East Anglian coast. Hard substratum is noticeably absent between Bridlington and the North Kent coast, and communities associated with rock surfaces are limited to small areas of artificial substrata such as harbour walls, groynes, etc. These contain a very impoverished range of species in comparison with a true rocky shore.

From North Foreland on the Kent coast, chalk cliffs and shores continue intermittently to the Sussex coast at Beachy Head. From here, the coast is mainly sedimentary, with occasional outcropping headlands such as at Selsey Bill, and chalk exposures on the east and western tips of the Isle of Wight, with an extensive limestone ledge and lagoon system at Bembridge. From Swanage, steep limestone bedrock shores are found, interrupted by occasional sandy bays, such as Weymouth, and the more extensive stretch of shingle at Chesil Beach. The

Dorset coast consists of further rocky shores, interspersed with areas of sediment, a situation which continues along the south Devon and the south Cornish coasts.

DESCRIPTION OF RESOURCE

Habitats and communities

The basis for describing rocky shore ecosystems in Great Britain is in the textbook *The ecology of rocky shores* (Lewis 1964). The examples used by Lewis, mainly to illustrate zonation, are drawn mainly from the west of Scotland and Ireland but include shores in Sutherland and Caithness.

A system of classifying rocky shore habitats on the basis of physical characteristics such as wave exposure, tidal stream exposure and salinity, and identifying the communities found in different habitat types, is being developed by the MNCR. This was initially carried out for the Irish Sea and is being further refined to apply to all the coasts of Great Britain. The categories described in this volume are summarised according to wave exposure and habitats (Table 5.2.1), but a full list of community types is not given. There are currently 50 different communities defined for littoral hard substrata.

Rocky shore communities include a fairly restricted variety of species except on the lowest shore or in habitats such as rockpools or under boulders where the desiccating effects of exposure to air do not prevail. Limpets of the genus *Patella* together with barnacles (species of *Chthamalus*, *Balanus balanoides*) dominate shores particularly in wave exposed situations, while the immigrant barnacle *Elminius modestus* is now a major component of rocky shore communities mainly in shelter and not in the far north. Fucoid algae (species of *Fucus*, *Pelvetia canaliculata*, *Ascophyllum nodosum*) are prevalent in more sheltered situations. On the upper shore and in the splash zone above the intertidal area, encrusting lichens generally cover the rock, while on the lowest shore, red algae and the kelps (species of *Laminaria*, *Alaria esculenta*) are characteristic. Grazing gastropods (mainly species of *Littorina* with *Gibbula umbilicalis* except in the far north) occur mainly on sheltered fucoid-dominated shores while the predatory dogwhelk (*Nucella lapillus*) occurs throughout the exposure range. Mussels (*Mytilus edulis*) are a further important component of many rocky shore communities.

The vertical zonation of plants and animals as a result of varying degrees of immersion and emersion by the tide is the most conspicuous feature of the distribution of species on a rocky shore (Figure 5.2.1). Zones on the shore can be broadly divided into: a littoral fringe dominated by lichens, above the main barnacle population and below the orange and grey lichens of the supralittoral, with fucoid algae at the lowest level; a eulittoral generally within the rise-and-fall of all tides and where the populations of algae and animals characteristic of the shore are best developed; and a sublittoral fringe generally uncovered only by spring tides and with its own characteristic species. Further division of these bands is possible and the species which characterise them are different on shores with different physical attributes.

Exposure to wave energy (modified to some extent by rock slope) is the overriding environmental factor determining the type of plant and animal communities which occur on most shores. Several authors starting with Ballantine (1961) have attempted to introduce biologically defined exposure scales which are a form of classification of different shore community types named according to wave exposure. The approach by the MNCR has been to adopt a physical description of wave exposure but matched to community types (Hiscock 1990). This classification is used in Table 5.2.1.

The occurrence of rocky shore species is greatly affected by climate. Certain species such as the fucoids *Fucus distichus* and *Fucus spiralis* f. *nana* only occur in the far north, while the red algae *Callithamnion arbuscula*, *Odonthalia dentata* and *Ptilota plumosa* and the limpet *Tectura testudinalis* are prominent in appropriate habitats north of Flamborough Head. Overall, the northern flora and fauna is slightly less diverse than in the south, as the loss of 'southern' species is not compensated for by the addition of 'northern' forms.

The predominantly sedimentary coast from Flamborough Head to Kent, together with the tendency of the rocky coast in south-east England to erode, gives rise to high turbidity, which is likely to adversely affect algal growth. The rocky shore flora and fauna is reduced and consists mainly of typical boreal species which are present on most of the British coast. However, the presence of coastal chalk provides an unusual habitat for a range of species including boring bivalves and sponges, and a range of splash zone algae unique in Great Britain. The Isle of Wight is the eastern boundary for many 'western' and 'southern' species which penetrate the English Channel, such as the barnacle *Balanus perforatus* and the limpet *Patella depressa*, while some species such as the algae *Laminaria ochroleuca* and *Padina pavonica* also reach their northern limit in south-west England.

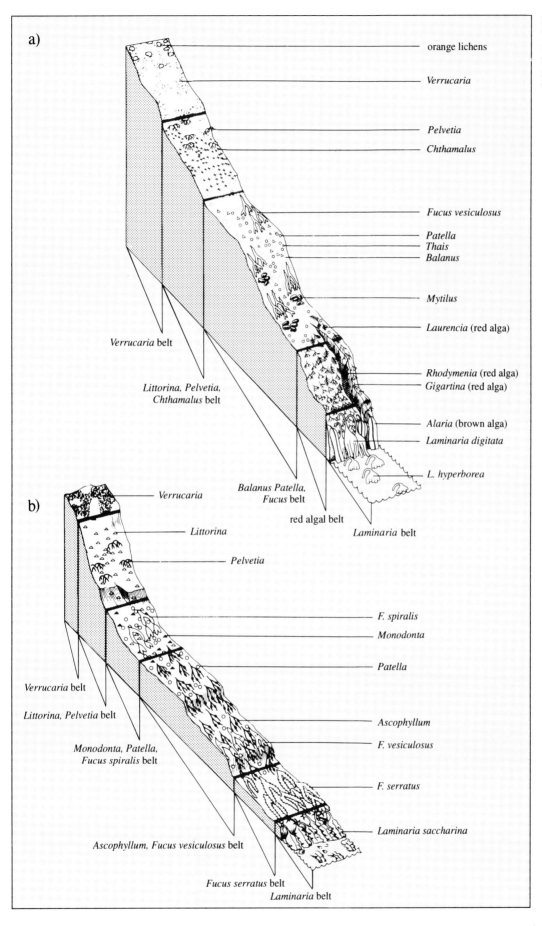

a)

orange lichens

Verrucaria

Pelvetia

Chthamalus

Fucus vesiculosus

Patella
Thais
Balanus

Mytilus

Laurencia (red alga)

Rhodymenia (red alga)
Gigartina (red alga)

Alaria (brown alga)
Laminaria digitata

L. hyperborea

Verrucaria belt

*Littorina, Pelvetia,
Chthamalus* belt

*Balanus Patella,
Fucus* belt

red algal belt

Laminaria belt

b)

Verrucaria

Littorina

Pelvetia

F. spiralis

Monodonta

Patella

Ascophyllum

F. vesiculosus

F. serratus

Laminaria saccharina

Verrucaria belt

Littorina, Pelvetia belt

*Monodonta, Patella,
Fucus spiralis* belt

Ascophyllum, Fucus vesiculosus belt

Fucus serratus belt
Laminaria belt

Figure 5.2.1
Typical zonation pattern on
a) an exposed rocky shore;
b) a sheltered rocky shore.
From Fincham 1984; illustration
© Milne Stebbing illustration 1984.

87

Table 5.2.1
MNCR habitat classification for littoral hard substratum communities (prepared for the Irish Sea and being used as a basis for a Great Britain classification).

Substratum	Wave exposure	Habitat	Species/groups characterising different communities
COMMUNITIES ON UPWARD-FACING HARD SUBSTRATUM			
1 Bedrock and very large boulders	Extremely exposed		Littoral fringe: *Verrucaria maura*; *Littorina neritoides*; *Porphyra* sp.; green and/or blue-green algae. Eulittoral zone: barnacles, limpets, predominantly *Patella ulyssiponensis* with *Patella vulgata*; *Mytilus edulis* with associated filamentous red algae; *Corallina officinalis*; foliose red algae including *Mastocarpus stellatus* and *Palmaria palmata*; *Lichena pygmaea*. Sublittoral fringe: *Alaria esculenta*; encrusting Corallinaceae.
2 Bedrock and very large boulders	Very exposed		Littoral fringe: *Verrucaria maura*; *Littorina neritoides*; *Porphyra* sp.; green and/or blue green algae. Eulittoral zone: barnacles, mainly *Chthamalus* spp. with some *Balanus balanoides*; limpets, mainly *Patella ulyssiponensis* with *Patella vulgata*; *Mytilus edulis* with associated filamentous red algae; *Corallina officinalis*; foliose red algae including *Mastocarpus stellatus* and *Palmaria palmata*; *Fucus vesiculosus* f. *linearis*; *Himanthalia elongata*; *Lichina pygmaea*. Sublittoral fringe: *Alaria esculenta*; scattered *Laminaria digitata*; encrusting Corallinaceae.
3 Bedrock and boulders	Exposed		Littoral fringe: *Verucaria maura*; *Littorina neritoides*; *Littorina saxatilis* agg.; *Porphyra* sp.; green and/or blue-green algae. Eulittoral zone: barnacles, *Chthamalus* spp. and *Balanus balanoides*; limpets, *Patella vulgata* and *Patella ulyssiponensis*; *Mytilus edulis* with associated filamentous red algae; *Nucella lapillus*; *Corallina officinalis*; foliose red algae including *Mastocarpus stellatus* and *Palmaria palmata*; *Fucus vesiculosus* f. *linearis*; *Himanthalia elongata*; *Lichina pygmaea*. Sublittoral fringe: *Alaria esculenta*; *Laminaria digitata*; encrusting Corallinaceae.
4 Bedrock and boulders	Moderately exposed		Littoral fringe: *Verrucaria maura*; *Littorina saxatilis* agg.; *Pelvetia canaliculata*; *Fucus spiralis*. Eulittoral zone: barnacles, predominantly *Balanus balanoides*; *Patella vulgata*; *Nucella lapillus*; *Fucus vesiculosus*; *Fucus serratus*; foliose red algae including *Laurencia* spp., *Lomentaria articulata*, *Mastocarpus stellatus* and *Palmaria palmata*; Chlorophycota; *Lichina pygmaea*. Sublittoral fringe: *Laminaria digitata*; encrusting Corallinaceae; foliose red algae.
5 Bedrock, boulders and cobbles	Sheltered		Littoral fringe: *Verrucaria maura*; *Littorina saxatilis* agg.; *Pelvetia canaliculata*; *Fucus spiralis*. Eulittoral zone: barnacles, *Balanus balanoides* with *Elminius modestus*; *Patella vulgata*; *Nucella lapillus*; *Littorina littorea*; *Littorina obtusata/mariae*; *Gibbula umbilicalis*; *Fucus vesiculosus*; *Fucus serratus*; *Ascophyllum nodosum*; Chlorophycota. Sublittoral fringe: *Laminaria digitata*; *Laminaria saccharina*.
6 Bedrock, boulders, cobbles and pebbles	Very sheltered		Littoral fringe: *Verrucaria maura*; *Littorina saxatilus* agg.; *Pelvetia canaliculata*; *Fucus spiralis*. Eulittoral zone: barnacles, mainly *Balanus balanoides* with *Elminius modestus*; *Patella vulgata*; *Mytilus edulis*; *Littorina littorea*; *Littorina obtusata/mariae*; *Gibbula umbilicalis*; *Fucus vesiculosus*; *Ascophyllum nodosum*; *Fucus serratus*; Chlorophycota. Sublittoral fringe: *Laminaria saccharina*; *Codium* spp.; *Anomia ephippium*; chitons.
7 Bedrock, boulders, cobbles and pebbles	Extremely sheltered		Littoral fringe: *Verrucaria maura*; *Pelvetia canaliculata*; *Fucus spiralis*. Eulittoral zone: *Patella vulgata*; *Mytilus edulis*; *Littorina littorea*; *Littorina obtusata/mariae*; *Littorina saxatilis* agg.; *Gibbula umbilicalis*; *Fucus vesiculosus*; *Ascophyllum nodosum*; *Fucus serratus*; Chlorophycota. Sublittoral fringe: *Laminaria saccharina*; *Laminaria digitata*; *Codium* spp.; *Anomia ephippium*; chitons.

Table 5.2.1 ...continued.

Substratum	Wave exposure	Habitat	Species/groups characterising different communities
COMMUNITIES ASSOCIATED WITH FEATURES OR MODIFIERS OF HARD SUBSTRATA			
8 Bedrock		Supralittoral rockpools	*Enteromorpha* spp.; *Ulva* spp.
9 Bedrock		Rockpools in the littoral fringe and eulittoral zone	Encrusting Corallinaceae; *Corallina* spp.; *Ceramium* spp.
10 Bedrock		Cave	*Hildenbrandia* spp.; encrusting sponges; bryozoans.
11 Bedrock and large boulders		Overhang	*Metridum senile*; Polyclinidae; *Plumaria elegans*.
12 Bedrock		Crevices	*Chthamalus* spp.; *Spirorbis borealis*; *Lasaea rubra*; *Cingula cingullus*; *Prasinelobus chevreuxi*; *Amphitritides gracilis*; *Cirratulus cirratus*.
13 Bedrock and boulders		Sandy/sand-covered	*Sabellaria alveolata*; *Polyides rotundus*; *Furcellaria lumbricalis*; *Audouinella* spp.
14 Boulders		Under boulders	*Porcellana platycheles*; encrusting sponges; bryozoans.
15 Boulders to pebbles	Extremely sheltered	Low salinity	*Fucus ceranoides*; *Cordylophora caspia*.

Extremely or very exposed bedrock and very large boulders

Extremely exposed shores are found only where deep water (over 50 m) occurs close inshore and where the prevailing wind and swell are onshore. Very exposed shores require only prevailing wind and swell.

Extremely or very exposed conditions favour animal-dominated communities with the major organisms present being limpets, barnacles and mussels. In the littoral fringe and supralittoral, there is an extensive zone of the black lichen *Verrucaria maura* often extending large distances up cliffs due to the continual moisture provided by spray. Small winkles, *Littorina neritoides* and *Littorina saxatilis* agg. occur in this area. Within the upper eulittoral zone characteristic algae include the *Porphyra* sp. and sometimes green and blue-green algae, *Fucus distichus* and *Fucus spiralis* f. *nana*, which have a very restricted distribution in Britain, occur on the most exposed shores in the far north. Mussels *Mytilus edulis* may be present over the midshore with attached red algae *Callithamnion arbuscula* and *Ceramium shuttleworthianum*. The lower eulittoral is dominated by red algae particularly *Corallina officinalis*, *Palmaria palmata* and *Mastocarpus stellatus*. The brown thongweed *Himanthalia elongata* is present on shores which are not extremely exposed. Communities on large, stable boulders are similar to those on solid bedrock, though smaller boulders tend to be too mobile to support any plant or animal growth other than ephemeral algae. The sublittoral fringe is dominated by crustose coralline algae and the kelp *Alaria esculenta*, although not on coasts east of Plymouth. The *Alaria* belt may be very broad on extremely exposed shores. The kelp *Laminaria digitata* will be present on very exposed shores and may dominate on the south coast.

Distribution and regional variation

Within the North Sea coastline extremely and very exposed bedrock and boulder shores are widespread in Shetland, Fair Isle and the Orkneys, while Powell *et al.* (1978) describe Start Point as open to the prevailing wind and Atlantic swell, and Bishop & Holme (1980) describe the western tip of Portland Bill as very exposed. Elsewhere on the North Sea, conditions fail to reach this degree of exposure. Figure 5.2.2 shows the distribution of these shores on the North Sea coastline.

Regional variations in communities present on extremely exposed and very exposed coasts occur

Figure 5.2.2
Distribution of extremely or
very exposed bedrock and
boulder shores on the North
Sea coastline.
Based upon the 1975 Ordnance Survey
1:1,250,000 map with the permission
of the Controller of Her Majesty's
Stationery Office © Crown Copyright.

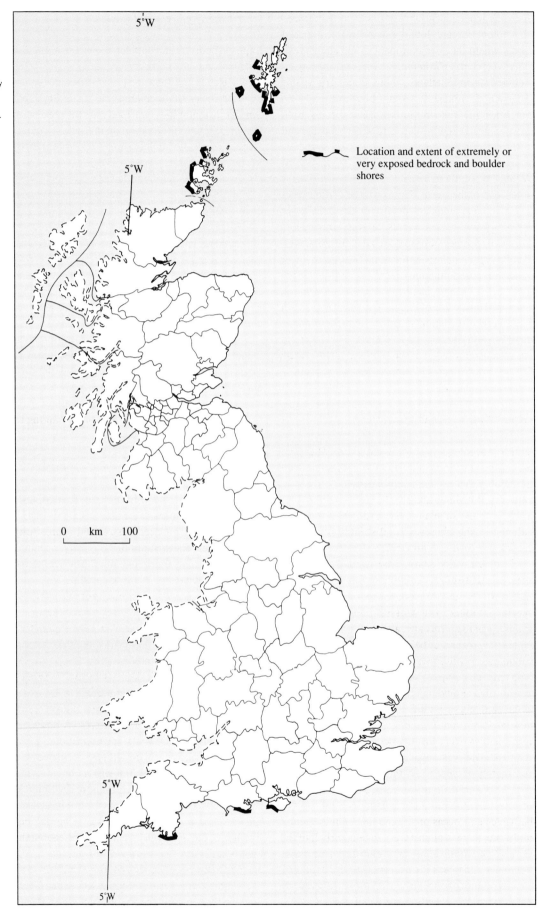

Location and extent of extremely or
very exposed bedrock and boulder
shores

due to the geographical range of some species. Species of *Chthamalus* are found especially on exposed coasts where they are dominant in the south-west. However, only *Chthamalus stellatus* has been recorded from Shetland where it is very sparse (Hiscock & Johnston 1990). Southward (1976) describes the distribution of this species both geographically and in relation to wave exposure and notes that both *Chthamalus* species extend eastwards along the Channel coast only as far as the Isle of Wight. The southern barnacle *Balanus perforatus* is absent east of the Isle of Wight on the south coast, but becomes most abundant in Britain along the outer reefs of wave-beaten shores in west Devon and Cornwall. Species of limpet are also different, with *Patella aspera* being dominant on the mid to lower shore in exposed situations but sparse or absent in the north. In the Channel, its eastward limit of distribution is reached on the Isle of Wight. Species of algae with a northern distribution include the fucoids *Fucus distichus* and *Fucus spiralis* f. *nana*. These species are present on wave-exposed shores in Shetland and Orkney but the latter is absent from the rest of the North Sea area.

Exposed bedrock and boulders

Within this category are included shores where the prevailing wind is onshore, but there is shelter from the direct effects of swell and no deep water directly adjacent. With increasing shelter from wave action, a wider range of plants and animals are able to colonise rocky shores. The distribution of these shores is shown in Figure 5.2.3.

Exposed rocky shores have a similar range of species to those of very exposed shores, though some zones are reduced in extent, and some additional species are found. The winkles *Littorina neritoides* and *Littorina saxatilis* agg. are abundant. The lichen *Lichina pygmaea* may be locally abundant, especially in the south. Midshore regions are dominated by barnacles and limpets with varying amounts of the fucoid alga *Fucus vesiculosus* f. *linearis*, with associated algae including *Spongomorpha arcta* and *Scytosiphon lomentaria*. Mussel/red alga communities occur locally, being most common in the north and west, especially on steep faces; this community is absent on midshore boulders. The dogwhelk *Nucella lapillus* may be common in groups of several hundred individuals feeding on the barnacles and occasionally mussels. On the lower midshore, there is often a well-developed belt of the algae *Himanthalia elongata* with foliose red algae. Some serrated wrack *Fucus serratus* may be present. The sublittoral fringe is generally dominated by *Alaria esculenta* together with *Laminaria digitata*.

Distribution and regional variation

Exposed bedrock and boulder shores are limited in distribution to the north and south of the North Sea area. Hiscock and Johnston (1989) describe typical exposed rocky shore communities from Shetland. Similar communities are likely to be present in Orkney, though information on this area is sparse. Exposed rock and boulder shores are present in the Moray Firth (Bartrop *et al.* 1980), the Isle of May (Bennett 1989), the Farne Islands (Connor 1989) and the coast of south Devon and Cornwall (Powell *et al.* 1978).

Bartrop *et al.* (1980) describe the distribution of 'southern' species which do not occur on the east coast south of Duncansby Head, or are only sparsely represented. These include the upper shore barnacle *Chthamalus montagui*, the gastropod *Littorina neritoides*, the mid to lower shore top-shell *Gibbula umbilicalis* and the limpet *Patella aspera*.

These species occur on south-western coasts, but do not occur eastwards of the Isle of Wight. The range of *Chthamalus montagui* extends to the west coast of Scotland, *Gibbula umbilicalis* which occurs as far north as Orkney but not in Shetland, and *Patella aspera* and *Littorina neritoides* ranging as far north as Shetland.

Moderately exposed bedrock and boulders

Moderately exposed shores are those where onshore winds are frequent but not prevalent, and where there is an absence of oceanic swell and no proximity to deep water. These conditions are likely to include most rocky shores on the mainland North Sea coast, except those which are sheltered by enclosure within inlets or estuaries. The distribution of this habitat is shown in Figure 5.2.4.

Moderately exposed rock has a reduced belt of the lichen *Verrucaria*, limited to a width of around 1–3 m, and partly within tidal limits. The gastropod *Littorina neritoides*, in contrast to more exposed shores, is scarce or absent, particularly in the north, while *Littorina saxatilis* is abundant in the lower part of the *Verrucaria* lichen zone. A zone of the fucoid *Pelvetia canaliculata* occurs on the upper shore, with some *Fucus spiralis* locally. Barnacles are predominantly species of *Chthamalus* in the south-west but *Balanus balanoides* in the north. The middle shore is dominated by a mixture of barnacles and limpets (*Patella vulgata*) and short *Fucus vesiculosus*. The lichen *Lichina pygmaea* may be present but the zone is indistinct. The gastropods *Monodonta lineata* and *Gibbula umbilicalis* may be common in the south and west, though *Monodonta* is absent on the North Sea coast eastwards of the Isle of Wight, and *Gibbula*

Figure 5.2.3
Distribution of exposed
bedrock and boulder shores
on the North Sea coastline.
Based upon the 1975 Ordnance Survey
1:1,250,000 map with the permission
of the Controller of Her Majesty's
Stationery Office © Crown Copyright.

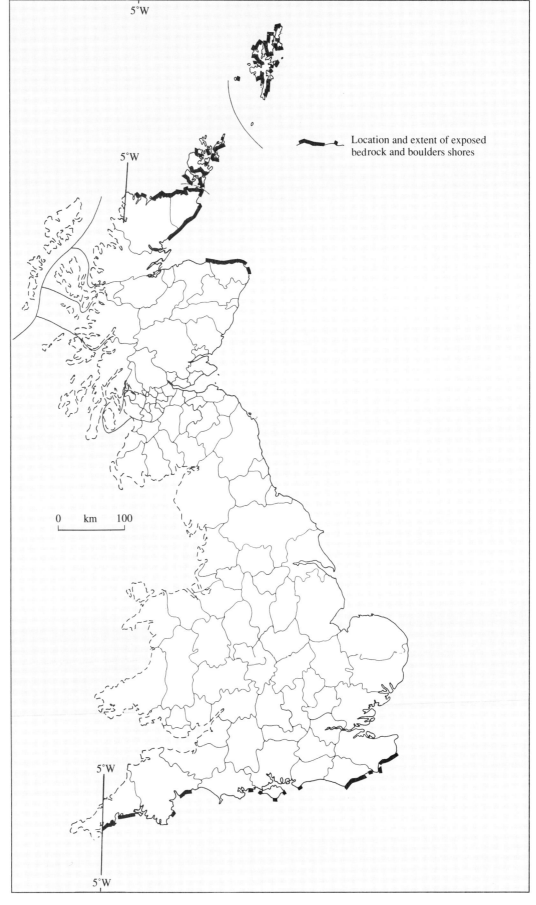

Location and extent of exposed
bedrock and boulders shores

5°W

5°W

0   km   100

5°W

5°W

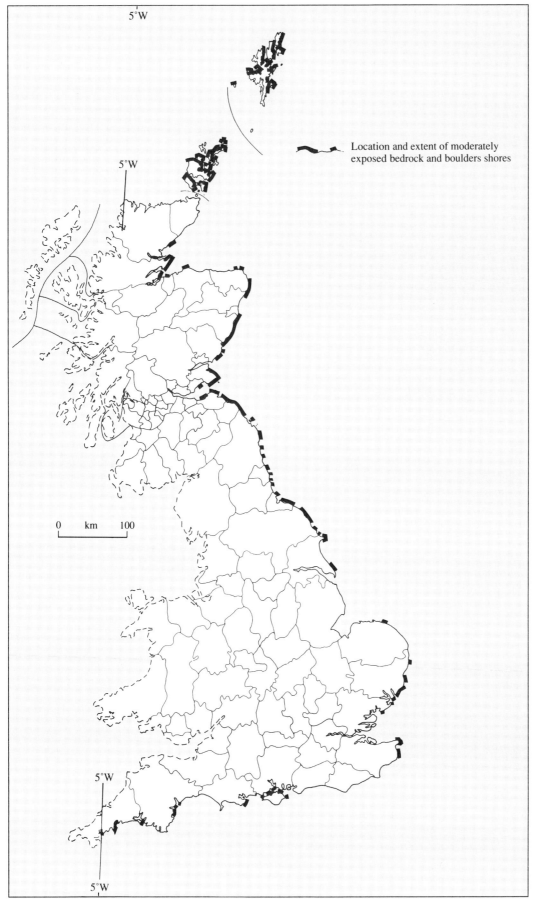

Figure 5.2.4
Distribution of moderately
exposed bedrock and boulder
shores on the North Sea
coastline.
Based upon the 1975 Ordnance Survey
1:1,250,000 map with the permission
of the Controller of Her Majesty's
Stationery Office © Crown Copyright.

Location and extent of moderately
exposed bedrock and boulders shores

umbilicalis fails to reach such high numbers in the north. On boulder shores where algal cover is low, abundant edible periwinkles *Littorina littorea* occur. On the lower shore a zone of the fucoid alga *Fucus serratus* is present, with associated red algae including *Laurencia* spp., *Mastocarpus stellata* and *Palmaria palmata* and thongweed *Himanthalia elongata*. Vertical faces and shaded areas which remain damp between tides are dominated by the algae *Plumaria elegans*, *Lomentaria articulata*, sponges and in the south-west the barnacle *Balanus perforatus*. *Patella aspera* occurs on the lower shore in the south-west. The sublittoral fringe is dominated by the kelp *Laminaria digitata* over a crust of crustose coralline algae. The sugar kelp *Saccorhiza polyschides* may be locally abundant in the south-west.

Distribution and regional variation

It is unlikely that many shores in the North Sea will contain the full range of species described above. However, moderately exposed rocky shores have been described from Shetland (Hiscock & Johnston 1990), the Moray Firth (Bartrop *et al.* 1980), the Isle of May (Bennett 1989), the Farne Islands (Connor 1989), Northumberland (Foster-Smith & Foster-Smith 1987), Bembridge Ledges on the Isle of Wight (Dixon & Moore 1987), the Dart estuary (Moore 1988b), Wembury Bay, Devon and Looe Bay in Cornwall (Powell *et al.* 1978).

Similar to other hard substratum shores, variation occurs in the range of some species over the North Sea area. Species such as the barnacle *Balanus perforatus*, the limpet *Patella depressa*, the alga *Bifurcaria bifurcata* and the gastropod *Monodonta lineata* have a south-westerly distribution and do not extend eastwards of the Isle of Wight. Other species such as the barnacle *Balanus balanoides* have a northerly distribution and become less dominant in the south-west.

Sheltered and very sheltered bedrock, boulders and cobbles

Sheltered shores are those where strong wind in an onshore direction is rare. For a shore to be very sheltered there must additionally be less than 20 km of open water offshore for wave development to take place.

Accompanying an increase in the degree of shelter from wave action on a shore is an increase in the dominance of algae, particularly fucoids.

Sheltered rocky shores have a very narrow zone of the lichen *Verrucaria maura*, which, in contrast to more exposed shores, is within the reach of most tides. Within this zone the rough periwinkle *Littorina*

saxatilis is abundant, particularly when the upper shore fucoids are scarce. *Littorina neritoides* is scarce or absent. A full zonation sequence of fucoids is present: *Pelvetia canaliculata*, *Fucus spiralis*, *Ascophyllum nodosum*, *Fucus vesiculosus* and *Fucus serratus*. The density of these algae is, however, insufficient to exclude populations of barnacles from the underlying rock surface. In the mid-littoral, barnacles are *Balanus balanoides* with *Elminius modestus* except in the far north, though thinly scattered and patchy, except on vertical surfaces where reduction in algal cover may allow them to become dominant. The periwinkles *Littorina littorea*, *Littorina mariae* and *Littorina obtusata* are abundant on all coasts, with *Monodonta lineata* and *Gibbula umbilicalis* abundant on south-western coasts. The limpet *Patella vulgata* is abundant, while *Patella aspera* is scarce or absent. Under lower shore boulders, large solitary ascidians such as *Ascidia mentula*, *Ascidia conchilega*, *Ascidiella aspersa* and *Ascidiella scabra* may occur. Under boulders resting on muddy sand, large numbers of terebellid polychaete worms such as *Eupolymnia nebulosa* may be found. In the sublittoral fringe the kelp *Laminaria digitata* is the dominant alga, with *Laminaria saccharina* and *Halidrys siliquosa* becoming common. *Chorda filum* and other algae may be attached to stones subtidally. Very rich faunas may be associated with boulders in tidal channels and rapids, though such features are rare in the North Sea area, occurring only in Shetland.

On rocky substrata in very sheltered areas the *Verrucaria* lichen zone is reduced to a narrow (less than 1 m) belt, which is almost entirely within the reach of spring tides. In shaded areas, especially in the south-west, there may be a well-developed belt of the algae *Catenella caespitosa* and *Bostrychia scorpioides*. There is a complete domination of all but steeply sloping or vertical shores by fucoids, especially *Ascophyllum nodosum*, with sheets of the alga *Pilayella littoralis* in summer; the associated fauna is often poor, particularly on boulder shores. Epiphytic hydroids, sponges, ascidians and bryozoans occur on the lower shore fucoids, particularly in areas of enhanced water movement. Barnacles are extremely scarce on bedrock, being confined to the vertical surfaces and rarely extending above mean high water of neap tides, especially in the north. The fauna of boulder shores is largely restricted to amphipods. On bedrock, occasional clumps of large mussels *Mytilus edulis* occur, frequently encrusted with the barnacles *Balanus balanoides* and *Elminius modestus*. In the sublittoral fringe the large 'cape' form of the kelps *Laminaria saccharina* and *Laminaria digitata* occur. The alga

Fucus ceranoides may occur on shores where streams flow over tidal flats.

Distribution and regional variation

Sheltered shores are largely limited to the enclosed coasts of marine inlets. Within the North Sea area sheltered fully saline rocky shores are primarily located in the north, in Shetland and northern Scotland, and in the rias of the south-west in Devon and Cornwall. On the eastern coast of England most sheltered areas are dominated by sedimentary substrata, and sheltered bedrock habitats may therefore be considered rare in a North Sea context. Because of the limited occurrence and extent of this habitat it is impossible to map on a whole North Sea scale.

Sheltered bedrock and boulder shores have been recorded from Shetland (Hiscock & Johnston 1990), Loch Eriboll (Jones 1975b), the Moray Firth (Bartrop *et al.* 1980) and most of the marine inlets of the south-west coast (for example Howard, Moore & Dixon 1988; Moore 1988a, b; Hiscock & Moore 1986).

Extremely sheltered bedrock, boulders, cobbles and pebbles

For a shore to be classified as extremely sheltered there must be less than 3 km of open water offshore for wave development and it must not face into the prevailing wind. These conditions rarely coincide with the existence of hard substratum, occurring more usually at the head of inlets and estuaries where conditions are usually sedimentary.

In extremely sheltered conditions even very small particles of hard substratum such as cobbles and pebbles may provide attachment surfaces for the algal dominated communities which are predominant. Species present are similar to those of very sheltered shores, with a complete dominance by algae, particularly fucoids such as *Ascophyllum nodosum.* On the upper shore, flowering plants may occur among the *Pelvetia,* particularly on shale substrata. Limpets and barnacles are sparse. Clumps of large mussels occur particularly on vertical surfaces.

Kelps such as *Laminaria saccharina* and *Laminaria digitata* are found growing in the 'cape' form in the sublittoral fringe.

Distribution and regional variation

Over the North Sea coastline rocky substrata and extremely sheltered conditions only coincide in the Shetland Isles, at the head of some of the larger voes, and in the rias of south-western England.

Chalk shores

Chalk shores are unusual in their softness. This provides a habitat for a range of rock-boring bivalves, polychaete worms and sponges, while limiting the availability of suitable hard substrata for attachment of larger algae.

The tendency of the substratum to erode ensures a continual availability of clear surfaces for colonisation, but limits the attachment of larger algae when they grow beyond a certain size. Particularly of note on chalk shores are the unique algal assemblages which occur in the splash zone on the backing cliffs. Many of these algae were described as new to science following descriptive surveys of chalk cliffs and some appear to be restricted to this habitat (see, for example, Tittley 1985, 1986, 1988 and Fowler & Tittley in prep.).

Distribution and regional variation

The distribution of coastal exposures of chalk bedrock is limited in a European context, with most of this unusual habitat occurring on the British North Sea coastline (shown in Figure 5.2.5). Much work has been carried out on this habitat by the Natural History Museum under contract to NCC. This work is presently being drawn together into a summary theme report to be produced for the MNCR.

Rockpool, cave, crevice and underboulder communities

All of these rocky shore habitats include particular communities, although they are generally poorly described in the literature and their distribution is difficult to map. Crevice communities include a range of characteristic species and a distinct zonation from entrance to end of the crevice. However, they occur only where suitable rock types are present in which crevices will develop. The classic study of crevice communities was undertaken at Wembury near Plymouth (Morton 1954). In rock pools, the communities present are often those further down the shore or the shallow sublittoral raised by protection from dessication (Lewis 1964). Rockpools are a feature of the open coast and are not generally found in inlets. Connor (1989) makes a special reference to rockpool communities at Lindisfarne where *Zostera* occurs in the pools. Underboulder communities are also protected from desiccation and, particularly where there is a flow of water under them, harbour rich species assemblages. These have been described for the Northumberland coast by Foster-Smith (1989). See Table 5.2.1 for a classification of these habitats.

Figure 5.2.5
Distribution of coastal chalk
exposures in Britain (MNCR
in prep.).
Based upon the 1975 Ordnance Survey
1:650,000 map with the permission of
the Controller of Her Majesty's
Stationery Office © Crown Copyright.

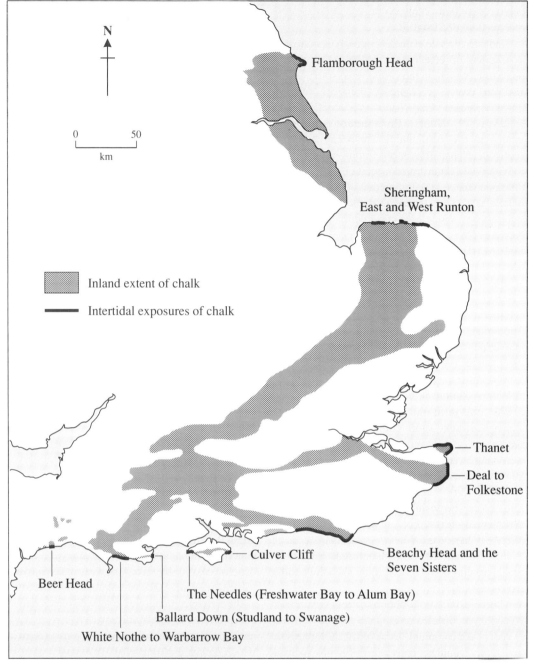

IMPACTS ON ROCKY SHORE HABITATS AND COMMUNITIES

Habitats on rocky substrata are generally robust, and not as susceptible to damage as sedimentary systems. However, cryptic communities on boulder shores which are subject to a large degree of boulder turning by fishermen searching for crabs or people looking at the marine life will be damaged if boulders are not replaced.

Some harvesting of algae for the alginate industry occurs on rocky shores in the Orkneys, but this is not widespread throughout the North Sea area. Harvesting of edible periwinkles *Littorina littorea* also occurs.

Land claim, dumping and coastal protection works can all result in smothering natural rocky shore communities or, in the case of coastal defences, may prevent salt spray critical to the maintenance of splash zone communities.

Due to their tendency to erode, many chalk shores are the subject of coastal protection work, such as concrete revetments, which removes the upper shore and splash zone habitats which are unique. This threat is specific among rocky shores to chalk bedrock, and is responsible for major habitat loss. Many chalk shores and cliffs are now protected by SSSI status.

Industrial waste effluent disposal may result in a gradient of effect away from point source discharges which, in the case of coal slurry on the Durham coast, is widespread. Chemicals entering the environment may have both localised and widespread effects. Enrichment and local modification of communities can occur near short sewage outfalls. Effects of chronic pollution are most widely demonstrated in relation to oil refinery effluents (for instance, see Dicks & Levell 1989) but coastal chemical works may also have a marked effect (the bromine extraction plant described by Hoare & Hiscock 1974 is a good example). More diffuse chronic pollution with effects on marine life occurs, but this is often difficult to demonstrate. However, in the case of tributyltin antifouling paint, a disastrous effect through the condition known as 'imposex' has occurred in populations of the dogwhelk *Nucella lapillus* leading to local extinctions in enclosed marine areas, particularly those which are popular yachting centres or ports (see Bryan *et al.* 1987).

Oil pollution and subsequent cleaning may cause long-term though usually recoverable damage to rocky shore communities. Effects are likely to be least severe and most transient on wave-exposed coasts but have long-lasting chronic effects in sheltered areas such as Shetland voes and other rocky marine inlets where subtle effects may be visible for as long as 25 years. Mechanical clean-up of oil will obviously cause damage where use of heavy machinery leads to changes to substrata and therefore to the biota. Steam cleaning of rocks may also have a potentially damaging effect.

The installation of offshore wave generators for electricity would effectively reduce wave exposure of shores and communities would change. Onshore generators would be likely to have minimal effects on shore communities.

5.3 INTERTIDAL SEDIMENT

INTRODUCTION

Soft (sedimentary) shores form a major component of the intertidal area of the North Sea coastline. This section describes shores of mobile substrata from pebbles through to mud and from the strandline at about mean high water of spring tides to the lowest part of the intertidal area. The softest and finest grained sediments are found within estuaries and embayments, and these form the most extensive

of the range of sediment sizes covered in this chapter. By contrast, sand and shingle shores are more restricted in distribution.

DISTRIBUTION

The species of plants and animals present on sedimentary shores is dependent on a range of variables, the most important of which is particle size. This is in turn largely dependent on the wave exposure of a particular site and the availability of sedimentary material. The distribution of some common species in relation to sediment grade is shown in Figure 5.3.1.

Maps of the distribution of muddy and sandy shores have been prepared based on inspection of a variety of published maps and to a very coarse scale. The results of the littoral and coastal habitat mapping which were undertaken by the project 'Coastwatch' (see Chapter 9) may provide more definitive mapping of substratum types.

DESCRIPTION OF RESOURCE

Habitats and communities

A system of classifying sediment shore habitats on the basis of physical characteristics such as wave exposure, tidal stream exposure, sediment grade and salinity and identifying the communities found in different habitat types is being developed by the MNCR. This was initially carried out for the Irish Sea and is being further refined to apply to all Great Britain coasts. The categories currently used are summarised in Table 5.3.1. The description of sedimentary communities in this chapter is largely based on the MNCR classification which particularly uses work by Bishop & Holme (1980) who described ten sediment shore communities.

Sedimentary shores form an important component of the coastal habitat because they are inhabited by a wide variety of specialist species. On the surface, seagrasses (mainly species of *Zostera*) grow while populations of the snail *Hydrobia ulvae* may form very dense aggregations. Below the surface, a wide range of burrowing species occur, consisting, among the macrofauna, chiefly of free-living (errant) and tube-dwelling (sedentary) polychaete worms, amphipod crustaceans and bivalve molluscs. The richest sediment shores are found in the shelter of marine inlets, notably in the south-west of England, where sheltered conditions allow the deposition of fine sediments, but the waters are fully saline.

Figure 5.3.1
Distribution of some sediment shore species in relation to sediment grade (redrawn from Holme 1949).

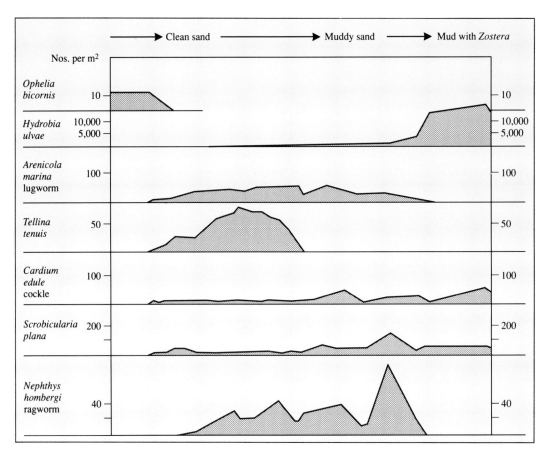

An increase in wave exposure results in an increase in the mean size of particles on a sediment shore, which in turn causes a decrease in the diversity of the infauna. At low levels of disturbance a mixed sediment of muddy sand may occur, which in some cases may be richer than pure mud. Such a sediment is likely to contain a greater range of bivalve and polychaete worm species. In general, however, an increase in wave exposure and an increase in particle size leads to a change in the invertebrate species present and a reduction in the biomass and diversity of the fauna. In the very disturbed environment of the shingle beach, no infaunal species occur except transient species living among strand line debris.

Muddy shores

Mud has a mean particle size of less than 0.062 mm. For sediments of this grade to be deposited, water conditions must be undisturbed, and there must be a readily available supply of fine sediment. These factors limit the distribution of this habitat to enclosed estuaries, inlets and embayments (see Figure 5.3.2). Within this category are included habitats such as pure mud, muddy sand and muddy gravel.

Pure mud substratum is limited in the littoral zone to areas which are very sheltered from wave action, for example the heads of estuaries and inlets or harbours. Typical inhabitants of this habitat include the ragworm *Hediste diversicolor*, the burrowing amphipod *Corophium volutator* and the bivalves *Scrobicularia plana* and *Mya arenaria*. The habitat of soft mud is widely distributed in estuaries of the North Sea which are sheltered from wave action. The habitat is not present to any large extent in the Orkney and Shetland due to the degree of wave exposure in most areas and the lack of a source of sedimentary material.

With increasing wave exposure a gradual transition to muddy sand occurs, commonly found in semi-sheltered areas around the mouths of some inlets and estuaries. Typically this habitat contains dense populations of the polychaete worm *Arenicola marina*, with the bivalves *Macoma balthica* and *Cerastoderma edule*. Other species include a range of polychaete worms *Cirriformia tentaculata*, *Nephtys cirrosa*, *Nephtys hombergi*, *Scoloplos armiger*, *Sigalion mathildae* and *Spiophanes bombyx*.

Intertidal muddy gravel occurs in areas which are sheltered from direct wave action and, due to the range of particle sizes, usually contains a rich community of bivalves, polychaetes and burrowing sea anemones. Typical bivalve species include *Venerupis senegalensis*, which is widely distributed

Substratum	Wave exposure	Salinity	Species/groups characterising different communities
SEDIMENT COMMUNITIES			
16 Coarse and medium sand, pebbles and gravel	Very exposed		Barren, devoid of all communities.
17 Medium sand	Exposed		Dominated by crustaceans and polychaete worms, hence classified as the crustacean/polychaete community by Bishop & Holme (1980) and Eleftheriou & McIntyre (1976). No bivalves present.
18 Medium sand	Moderately exposed		Referred to as the *Tellina* community by Bishop & Holme (1980), which is similar to the *Tellina tenuis* community of Sparck (1935). Occurs on clean, well-sorted sandy beaches partially sheltered from wave action. Other species in addition to *Angulus tenuis* include *Donax vittatus*, *Arenicola marina*, and other polychaete worms such as *Chaetozone setosa*, *Nephtys caeca*, and *Pygospio elegans*. This relates to Jones' (1950) boreal shallow sand community.
19 Medium sand	Moderately exposed		Bishop and Holme's *Lanice* community which may only be considered a distinct community at particularly high densities. Elsewhere *Lanice conchilega* occurs as a component of other sand communities.
20 Medium sand	Sheltered		Bishop and Holme's *Spisula* community occurring on offshore sand bars. Contains *Spisula solida*, *Nucula hanleyi*, *Glycymeris glycymeris*, *Circomphalus casina*, *Clausinella fasciata* and *Timoclea ovata*.
21 Sand/muddy sand	Sheltered		Agrees with Jones' (1950) boreal offshore sand community, with *Echinocardium cordatum*, *Chamelea gallina* and *Ensis siliqua*. Other species include *Cerianthus lloydi*, *Leptosynapta* and *Labidoplax* and *Ophiura texturata*. This community may also be associated with *Zostera marina*. In general, similar to the *Spatangus/ fasciata* community, this community is best considered a sublittoral one which occasionally reaches into the extreme lower shore.
22 Muddy gravel with pebbles	Sheltered		Bishop and Holme's *Pullastra* community, also defined by Holme (1966) as muddy gravel. *Venerupis senegalensis* need not necessarily be present, but sometimes occurs in large numbers in intertidal muddy gravel with the bivalves *Mya truncata* and *Ensis arcuatus*. Also present are *Amphitrite edwardsi* and *Neoamphitrite figulus*, *Megalomma vesiculosum*, *Myxicola infundibulum* and *Sabella pavonina*. Affixed to small stones and shells may also be *Cereus pedunculatus*. A variety of filamentous, filiform and flat red algae along with *Enteromorpha* and *Laminaria saccharina* may be found attached to pebbles.
23 Muddy sand (sometimes estuarine)	Sheltered	Often variable salinity	Classified as the *Arenicola* community by Bishop & Holme (1980) and in part agreeing with Petersen's (1914) *Macoma* and Jones' (1950) boreal shallow mud communities. Typical polychaete worm species include *Cirriformia tentaculata*, *Nephtys cirrosa*, *Nephtys hombergi*, *Scoloplos armiger* and the bivalves *Cerastoderma edule* and *Macoma balthica* along with the dominant species *Arenicola marina*. This community may also be associated with beds of *Zostera noltii*.
24 Mud	Very sheltered	Often variable or low salinity	Bishop & Holme's (1980) *Scrobicularia* community fitting in with part of Petersen's (1914) and Jones' (1950) boreal shallow mud communities. Contains *Scrobicularia plana* and *Mya arenaria*, *Ampharete grubei*, *Melinna palmata*, *Hediste diversicolor* and *Corophium volutator*. This community may also be associated with beds of *Zostera noltii*.

Table 5.3.1
MNCR habitat classification for littoral soft substrata (prepared for the Irish Sea and being used as a basis for a Great Britain classification).

Figure 5.3.2
Distribution of muddy
sediments on the North Sea
coastline.
Based upon the 1975 Ordnance Survey
1:1,250,000 map with the permission
of the Controller of Her Majesty's
Stationery Office © Crown Copyright.

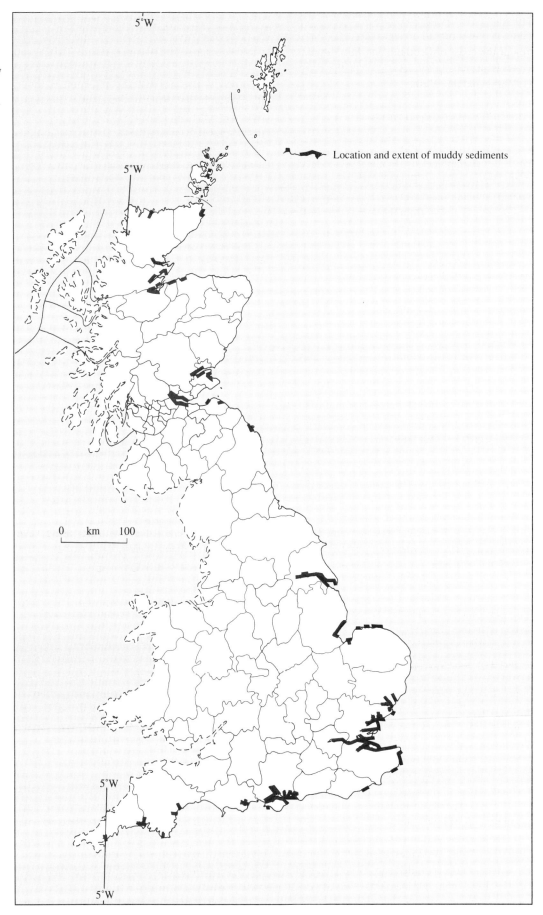

throughout the North Sea coasts, *Mya truncata*, which is present in all areas except the Aberdeen area of the coast of Scotland and *Ensis arcuatus*, which is present in all areas except the coast of Yorkshire and the Wash.

Distribution and regional variation

Variations in muddy littoral communities occur due to the geographical distribution of some species. In the south-west of England muddy substrata typically contain the bivalve *Scrobicularia plana*. This bivalve is absent from the south coast of Kent and Sussex as well as the north coast of Scotland, the Orkneys and Shetland Isles. However, the bivalve *Mya arenaria* is recorded throughout the area of the North Sea except south Devon, and this bivalve is likely to replace *Scrobicularia plana* in northern locations. Bishop and Holme recorded typical muddy communities with *Scrobicularia plana* in the Moray Firth, and point out that the limited recorded distribution of that bivalve may be due to its habitat of soft, glutinous mud which is difficult to sample. Typical muddy communities were recorded in Christchurch Harbour (Dixon 1988), Newtown and Bembridge Harbours (Howard, Moore & Dixon 1988), Poole Harbour (Howard & Moore 1989), The Dart estuary (Moore 1988b), the Exe estuary (Dixon 1986), the Teign estuary (Frid 1989) and Plymouth area (Hiscock & Moore 1986). Jones (1975a) describes muddy sediment from the Kyle of Durness on the north coast of Scotland, with the principal species present being *Hediste diversicolor*, *Nerine cirratulus* and the crustacean *Corophium volutator*.

Muddy sand communities occur throughout the North Sea area, with little difference between those of the north and south. They have been recorded by Bishop & Holme (1980) from the Moray Firth, and from numerous marine inlets along the south coast, for example Christchurch Harbour (Dixon 1988), Newtown and Bembridge Harbours (Howard, Moore & Dixon 1988), Poole Harbour (Howard & Moore 1989), Portland Harbour (Howard, Howson & Moore 1988) and the Exe estuary (Holme 1949; Dixon 1986). Probert (1981) also recorded the community from numerous sheltered sites around the East Anglian coast, including large expanses of the Wash. Many of these places are important sites for wading birds, which feed on infaunal species during periods of low water.

Although the occurrence of muddy gravel in the littoral zone may be widespread, its occurrence with a rich infauna is limited and the best examples are to be found in the marine inlets of the south and south-west coasts, where the presence of those

species which have a south-western distribution, such as *Venerupis decussata*, is important. This was demonstrated by Bishop & Holme (1980), who failed to find this habitat in the Moray Firth but recorded its presence in the Solent, Poole Harbour, the Salcombe and Kingsbridge estuary, Plymouth Sound and the Fal. Probert (1981) does not record this habitat as occurring on the coast of East Anglia. Species-poor examples of muddy gravel substrata are described from the Dart estuary (Moore 1988b).

Sandy shores

Sandy shores are those with a mean particle size of between 2 mm and 0.062 mm. This category encompasses the large majority of open coast sedimentary shores, with a wide distribution (Figure 5.3.3).

A broad range of communities may be present in sandy shores, depending on the range of particle sizes and the degree of exposure to waves and tides. The MNCR has divided sandy shores into five categories dependent on grain size and physical conditions (Table 5.3.1). The accurate distribution of these communities is poorly known, although the distribution of some of the constituent bivalves is better documented (Seaward 1982). Finer sand communities are limited to more sheltered enclosed areas such as the mouths of estuaries, while the wave-exposed coarse sand communities are to be found widely distributed on the open coast.

The richness of the community present in sandy sediments in general reduces with increasing wave exposure. In sheltered conditions in muddy sand a community characterised by the lugworm *Arenicola marina* is present; this habitat has been described in the section on muddy sediments. With increased wave exposure the lugworm becomes less dominant, and the community becomes characterised by a range of bivalves, predominant among which is *Angulus tenuis*, a bivalve which is absent from finer, more sheltered sediments. *Arenicola marina* is almost invariably still present and additional species include the polychaetes *Chaetozone setosa*, *Magelona papillicornis*, *Nephtys caeca*, *Pygospio elegans*, *Scololepis* spp., *Spio filicornis* and *Travisia forbesi*. This community is a feature of semi-sheltered open coasts.

In areas of fully saline fine sand occasionally with some silt content which are sheltered from strong wave action, a community may occur with the heart urchin *Echinocardium cordatum* and the bivalves *Chamelea gallina* and *Ensis siliqua*. *Chamelea gallina* is absent from Flamborough Head south to Sussex, while *Ensis siliqua* is absent from the Thames estuary. Suitable conditions for the

Figure 5.3.3
Distribution of sandy shores
on the North Sea coastline.
Based upon the 1975 Ordnance Survey
1:1,250,000 map with the permission
of the Controller of Her Majesty's
Stationery Office © Crown Copyright.

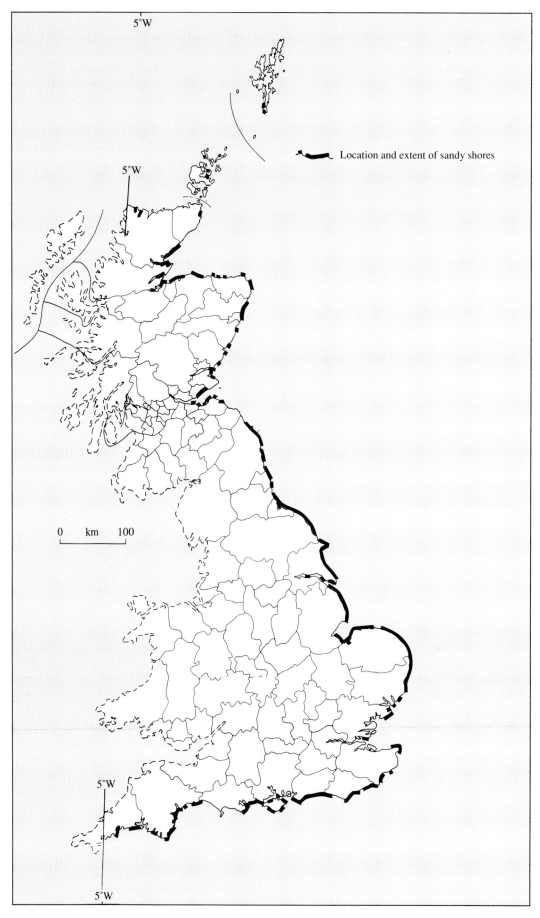

Location and extent of sandy shores

development of this community are likely to be infrequent.

In coarser sand which is exposed to moderately strong tidal streams, such as are found in the mouths of some of the larger estuaries and inlets, a community may occur which is dominated by a range of bivalves, principal of which is *Spisula solida*. Other bivalves which may be found in this habitat are *Nucula hanleyi*, the dog cockle *Glycymeris glycymeris*, *Circomphalus casina*, *Clausinella fasciata* and *Timoclea ovata*. Although the constituent organisms have a wide range it is unlikely that the habitat is also widely distributed, though accurate information is scarce.

A further increase in wave exposure encourages coarse, sandy shores. Here the sparse fauna is dominated by crustaceans and polychaetes. Of all sand habitats this is likely to be the most common and widespread on the open coast of the North Sea.

Distribution and regional variation

Differences in sandy substratum communities occur due to the distribution of some of their constituent species. For example *Angulus tenuis* and *Donax vittatus*, characteristic of clean fine sand in moderately exposed conditions, have a wide distribution over the whole North Sea coast, though *Donax vittatus* is absent from the Shetland Isles and the Wash area (Seaward 1982).

Many bivalves have a south-western distribution, and as such in the North Sea area are limited to the south coasts of Devon and Cornwall, rarely being found east of the Isle of Wight. The loss of southern species is not compensated by a corresponding gain in species with a northern distribution, and many communities are less rich in northern latitudes.

The geographical distribution of polychaete and amphipod crustacean species has not been mapped in the same way as for molluscs, so it is at present difficult to assess regional differences in the North Sea area.

Moderately exposed fine sand, characterised by the bivalve *Angulus tenuis*, has been recorded from the Moray Firth (Bishop & Holme 1980), Northumberland (Foster-Smith & Foster-Smith 1987; Connor 1989), north Norfolk (Probert 1981) and the Dorset, south Devon and south Cornwall coasts (Bishop & Holme 1980). Although primarily a community of open coasts it has also been recorded from the Exe estuary (Dixon 1986), where enhanced water movement by tidal current occurs.

Bishop and Holme did not record their *Echinocardium-siliqua* community in the Moray Firth, only from Poole westwards. Around the East Anglian coast Probert (1981) also found it to be absent. Detailed information on the distribution of this community is lacking.

The bivalve *Spisula solida*, which is characteristic of current swept coarse sands, has a wide distribution, being found in all coastal areas of the North Sea except the southern Kent and Sussex coasts. Other bivalves which may be found in this habitat are *Nucula hanleyi*, which has a distribution limited to the south coast; the dog cockle *Glycymeris glycymeris*, which is intermittently distributed down the eastern coast, though common elsewhere; *Circomphalus casina*, which is absent from the Isle of Wight to Flamborough Head; *Clausinella fasciata* which is present on all the North Sea coasts except around the Wash and Thames; and *Timoclea ovata*, which is again present over the whole North Sea coast except for the Thames estuary. Maps of these distributions are given in Figure 5.3.4. Although the constituent organisms have a wide range, it is unlikely that the habitat is also widely distributed, though accurate information is scarce. Bishop and Holme failed to find their *Spisula* community in the Moray Firth, though they describe its occurrence in Plymouth Sound and the Exe estuary on the south coast. Probert (1981) also fails to describe its occurrence on shores around East Anglia.

Bishop & Holme (1980) describe their crustacean/polychaete community on wave exposed mobile sand shores from beaches as widely separated as Wick, the Moray Firth, the Isle of Wight and south Cornwall. Probert (1981) also recorded exposed sand from most areas between the Humber and the Thames estuary. This habitat has also been recorded from the sandy beaches of the Northern Scottish coast (Eleftheriou & McIntyre 1976). This sediment type is likely to be widespread on most open coast sediment shores of the North Sea, and extends into the larger inlets of the south-west coast where tidal movement in addition to wave action leads to the presence of a coarse sediment. Dixon (1988) records the occurrence of a crustacean polychaete community in the Exe estuary. Records of this community also exist from the Dart estuary (Moore 1988b), the Teign estuary (Frid 1989) and Plymouth Sound (Hiscock & Moore 1986).

Shingle shores

True shingle shores have a limited distribution on the North Sea coastline, though they are more common out of the intertidal zone as maritime terrestrial habitat.

True shingle shores are composed of large, pebble-sized particles (between 4 and 64 mm in diameter). These particles are most likely to be deposited in the intertidal zone where the coastline

Figure 5.3.4
Distribution of some bivalve
species (from Seaward 1982).

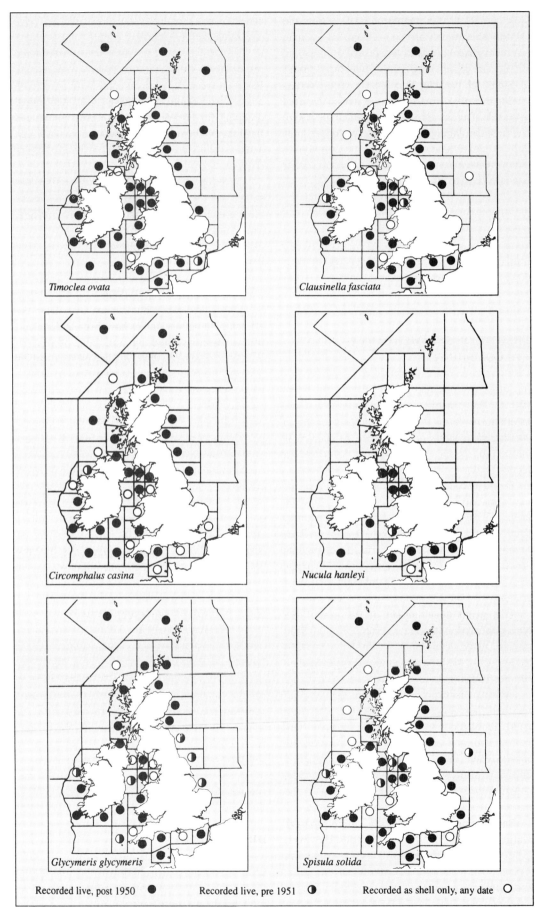

Timoclea ovata

Clausinella fasciata

Circomphalus casina

Nucula hanleyi

Glycymeris glycymeris

Spisula solida

Recorded live, post 1950 ●   Recorded live, pre 1951 ◐   Recorded as shell only, any date ○

is exposed to a high degree of wave action and where there is a supply of material from, for example, erosion of glacial deposits. Because of wave action, shingle beaches are very mobile, with large spaces between each particle. This leads to a low water-holding capacity at times when they are not covered by the tide. This, and the fact that the shingle is kept in almost constant motion by wave action, ensures that the habitat is generally barren, with the only animals present occurring in strandline debris rather than as a shingle infauna.

Distribution and regional variation

No geographical differences exist between intertidal shingle habitats in the North Sea. However, differences are present in the adjacent terrestrial habitats (see Section 4.5).

IMPACTS ON SEDIMENTARY HABITATS AND COMMUNITIES

The most obvious and direct impacts on inter-tidal sediment habitats are land claim (by the installation of barrages or by dumping on the shore) and dredging, both of which are of particular concern in estuaries and inlets (described in Section 2.12).

Sandy beaches in particular are popular for recreation and a degree of disturbance inevitably occurs, although usually to shores where natural disturbance from wave action is high anyway. Boat moorings, stranded boats and marina developments all result in some disturbance, and antifouling paints may adversely affect both planktonic stages of sediment species and the settled organisms.

The recent development of the use of the hydraulic suction dredge to fish for molluscan species is giving cause for concern. Fowler (1989) and Perkins (1988) report on the damage caused by commercial fishing operations and suction dredging, respectively. Fishing boats can suction dredge while intertidal flats are covered by the tide, removing populations of commercially valuable species such as *Cerastoderma edule*, *Mercenaria mercenaria* and *Ensis* spp. The disturbance caused results in a redistribution of the sediment, altering the intertidal habitat, and can cause the death of some of the associated non-commercial species.

Bait digging on a small scale is unlikely to have a large impact on intertidal sediments. However, some areas have become increasingly popular with collectors and have suffered from intensive digging. Apart from destructive effects on burrowing fauna which do not re-establish themselves, bait digging

can alter the character of shores by bringing long-covered substrata including cobbles and boulders to the surface and can also release pollutants (especially heavy metals) held in the sediments. Effects are recorded for areas of the Northumberland coast (Foster-Smith 1983; Olive 1984). Mechanical dredging for lugworms has also been introduced from the Netherlands to sediment shores in Essex and has similar effects to that of hand digging (Fowler 1992).

On the open coast specific threats to sedimentary shores are the sea defences which are prevalent along much of the south-east coast of the North Sea. The protection of soft earth cliffs from wave action halts the supply of new beach material, thus resulting in the gradual loss of the shore.

Pollution from point-source effluents commonly results in a gradient of effect on the biology of the shore with distance away from the effluent. Numerous studies have been undertaken, often commissioned by and confidential to industry. In general, there is a decrease in species diversity near to the source of effluents, with a high abundance of oligochaetes, opportunistic polychaetes and nematode worms, grading to the more diverse communities of bivalve molluscs, polychaetes and amphipods away from the effects of the effluent.

More widespread pollution such as that which occurs in enclosed industrialised areas or as a result of oil spills is uncommon. The chronic low-level pollution in enclosed areas has a more insidious effect than the single oil spill. However, where oil is spilt in sheltered areas, entrapment in sediments may itself be a source of chronic pollution.

5.4 SUBLITTORAL HARD SUBSTRATA

INTRODUCTION

This section describes the range of sublittoral hard substratum communities found in the North Sea and gives details of their present known distribution. Hard substratum includes a range of habitats, from solid bedrock and boulders to stable areas of cobbles, which are effectively colonised by a range of algae and sessile invertebrates.

DISTRIBUTION

Little survey work has been carried out by diving on the North Sea coast of Britain, and since this is the most practical way of describing hard substratum epibenthos, little information exists for these communities. Notable exceptions are the areas of chalk bedrock on the east and south-eastern coasts, associated areas of greensand reef, bedrock outcrops of the Farne Islands, the coasts of Shetland and the marine inlets of the south coast. Much of this work has been undertaken by the Nature Conservancy Council as part of the Marine Nature Conservation Review. Further survey work is currently being undertaken by the MNCR on the coastline between Dunbar and Flamborough Head. Work during 1992 concentrated on the coast between Dunbar and Newcastle (Davies 1993; Holt 1993; Brazier & Murray 1993) and will be continued south to Flamborough during 1993. Areas for which we have information at present are described in Section 5.1.

DESCRIPTION OF RESOURCE

Habitats and communities

The difficulty of classifying recurring assemblages of organisms on rocky sublittoral substrata has been recognised, due mainly to the range of habitat heterogeneity and environmental variability and consequently the often high species-diversity (Hiscock & Mitchell 1980).

A framework for the classification of epibenthic communities of rocky sublittoral habitats was suggested by Hiscock & Mitchell (1980), based on the prevailing physical environmental conditions. A classification prepared for the Irish Sea (Holt, Fisher & Graham 1990) is shown in Table 5.4.1.

Wave exposed bedrock and boulders

Wave-exposed bedrock and boulders are typically limited to the northern and southern limits of the North Sea area, Shetland and the south Devon and Cornwall coasts. In the shallower depths, where light penetration allows the growth of foliose algae (the infralittoral zone), the community present is largely algal-dominated with the kelps *Laminaria hyperborea* and *Alaria esculenta* (the latter particularly prevalent in the north), as well as a range of foliose red algae. The lower depth limit of the infralittoral zone varies between areas. In the clear waters of Shetland the lower limit may be up to 20–30 m below chart datum (bcd), see Hiscock & Johnston (1990), while Dipper, Irving & Fowler (1989) comment on the lack of an infralittoral zone in the Wash due to a combination of extremely high turbidity and a lack of suitable substratum.

Below the infralittoral zone communities become animal-dominated, and in suitable conditions where hard substratum is available a range of fauna occurs, including erect sponges such as *Polymastia* spp., *Axinella* spp., *Stelligera* spp. and *Raspailia* spp., anemones *Actinothoe* spp. and *Corynactis* spp., cup corals *Caryophyllia smithii*, and a range of erect bryozoans such as *Crisia* spp. and *Bugula* spp.

Distribution and regional variation

Wave-exposed bedrock is described from Shetland (Hiscock & Johnston 1990), the Isle of May (Bennett 1989), the Farne Islands (Connor 1989), St Abb's Head (Earll 1982), Flamborough Head (Wood 1988), south-east Kent (Wood & Wood 1986), Sussex (Wood & Jones 1986) and Plymouth Sound (Hiscock & Moore 1986).

Bedrock and boulders sheltered from wave action

Bedrock and boulder substratum which is sheltered from wave action is often covered with a thin layer of fine silt. In the infralittoral, plant-dominated zone, characteristic species include the sugar kelp *Laminaria saccharina*, a range of foliose and filamentous red and brown algae and brown crustose algae.

In the circalittoral zone under these conditions animal-dominated communities typically contain encrusting sponges such as *Plocomionida* spp., hydroids *Halecium halecinum*, *Kirchenpaueria* spp., *Nemertesia* spp. and *Obelia* spp., the calcareous tubeworm *Pomatoceros* spp., encrusting bryozoans, occasional holothurians, *Thyone* spp. and large solitary ascidians such as *Ascidia* spp. and *Ascidiella* spp.

Distribution and regional variation

This community is likely to be a feature of sheltered marine inlets, where bedrock occurs in the sublittoral zone. Where bedrock is limited to shallower depths, only the infralittoral component of the community will be found, the circalittoral component thus having a more restricted distribution.

This habitat has been recorded from Shetland (Hiscock & Johnston 1990), Portland and Weymouth Harbours (Howard, Howson & Moore 1988), Plymouth Sound (Hiscock & Moore 1986) and the Fal estuary (Rostron 1985).

Bedrock and boulders subject to tidal streams

Areas of bedrock and boulders which are subject to strong tidal streams are colonised by communities which are generally animal dominated even in shallow depths. Species present include the barnacle

Substratum	Wave exposure	Tidal streams	Species/groups characterising different communities
1 Bedrock; boulders	Exposed		Infralittoral: *Laminaria hyperborea*, foliose red algae.
2 Bedrock; boulders	Exposed		Circalittoral: Fauna incl. erect sponges (*Polymastia* spp., *Axinella* spp., *Stelligera* spp., *Raspailia* spp.), hydroids, *Actinothoe*, *Corynactis*, *Caryophyllia*, erect bryozoans (*Crisia*, *Bugula*).
3 Bedrock; boulders	Sheltered		Infralittoral: *Laminaria saccharina*, foliose/filamentous red and brown algae, brown crusts.
4 Bedrock; boulders	Sheltered		Circalittoral: Fauna incl. encrusting sponges (e.g. *Plocomionida*), hydroids (*Halecium halecinum*, *Kirchenpaueria*, *Nemertesia* spp., *Obelia* spp.), *Pomatoceros*, encrusting bryozoans, *Thyone* spp., large solitary ascidians (*Ascidia* spp., *Ascidiella* spp.).
5 Bedrock; boulders		Very strong	*Balanus crenatus, Tubularia indivisa, Sertularia argentia, Halichondria panicea, Mytilus edulis.*
6 Bedrock; boulders		Strong	*Alcyonium digitatum, Sertularia argentea, Actinothoe sphyrodeta, Sagartia elegans, Pachymatisma johnstonia.*
7 Bedrock; boulders – sand scoured		Moderately strong	*Sabellaria* reefs.
8 Bedrock – by/with sand			Infralittoral: *Halidrys siliquosa, Polyides/Furcellaria, Laminaria saccharina & Desmarestia* spp.
9 Bedrock – by/with sand			Circalittoral: *Ciocalypta, Polymastia* spp., *Urticina felina, Flustra.*
10 Bedrock – surge gulley	Surge		*Clathrina, Tubularia indivisa, Metridium, Sagartia elegans, Halichondria panicea*, polyclinids, *Dendrodoa, Pachymatisma, Mytilus.*
11 Bedrock – caves, overhangs			*Parazoanthus* spp., sponges (*Stryphnus, Stelleta, Dercitus, Thymosia*), *Parerythropodium.*
12 Boulder, cobble & coarse sediment		Moderately strong	Hydroid/bryozoan turf (*Flustra, Securiflustra, Alcyonidium diaphanum, Eucratia, Vesicularia, Abietinaria abietina, Hydrallmania*).
13 Cobble, pebble and coarse sediment		Moderately strong	*Ophiothrix/Ophiocomina* beds.
14 Cobble, pebble and gravel		Moderately strong	Ephemeral filamentous/foliose red algae (*Schmitzia, Scinaia, Naccaria, Dudresnaya, Actractophora*).

Table 5.4.1
A classification for sublittoral hard substrata for the Irish Sea (from Holt, Fisher & Graham 1990).

Balanus crenatus, the hydroids *Tubularia indivisa* and *Sertularia argentia*, the anemones *Actinothoe sphyrodeta* and *Sagartia elegans*, the sponges *Halichondria panicea* and *Pachymatisma johnstonia*, dead-man's fingers *Alcyonium digitatum* and the bivalve mollusc *Mytilus edulis*.

Distribution and regional variation

This community is described from Shetland (Hiscock & Johnston 1990), St Abb's Head (Earll 1981), the Farne Islands (Connor 1989), Plymouth Sound (Hiscock & Moore 1986), the Solent (Dixon & Moore 1987) and the Teign estuary (Frid 1989).

Sand-scoured bedrock

Localised communities may occur on bedrock which is adjacent to sand. The nature of the community which is found will vary with local conditions. In the infralittoral zone, where moderate wave exposure abrades the adjacent bedrock with medium and coarse sand, an algal-dominated infralittoral community develops, characterised by the algae *Halidrys siliquosa*, *Polyides rotundus*, *Furcellaria lumbricalis*, *Laminaria saccharina* and *Desmarestia* spp.

In the circalittoral, the community is dominated by animals such as the sponges *Ciocalypta penicillus* and *Polymastia* spp., the anemone *Urticina felina* and the bryozoan *Flustra foliacea*.

Distribution and regional variation

This community is likely to be widespread around the North Sea coastline and has been recorded from Shetland (Hiscock & Johnston 1990), St. Abb's Head (Earll 1981, 1982), the Farne Islands (Connor 1989), the Northumberland coast (Foster-Smith & Foster-Smith 1987), Flamborough Head (Wood 1988) and the Dart estuary (Moore 1988b). Little information exists on regional variations in the habitat and species present.

Bedrock surge gullies

The existence of surge gully communities is very localised. These occur where gullies in bedrock face into open seas with strong wave action. Water movement is amplified by the narrow sides of the gully such that organisms within the confined space experience a greatly increased rate of water movement compared with those on surrounding open bedrock surfaces. Typically, surge gully communities are dominated by sessile filter-feeding invertebrates, chief among which are the sea squirt *Dendrodoa grossularia* and the sponge *Clathrina coriacea*. Also typical are the sponges *Halichondria panicea* and *Pachymatisma johnstonia*; the anemones *Metridium senile* and *Sagartia elegans*; the hydroid *Tubularia indivisa* and the mussel *Mytilus edulis*.

Distribution and regional variation

In Shetland, Hiscock & Johnston (1990) describe surge gullies from wave exposed coasts. These typically were found in the infralittoral zone in geos, arches and caves. Within these, the kelp zone was generally compressed into the upper 1–4 m bcd followed by a band of foliose red algae, dominated by *Corallina officinalis*, *Cryptopleura ramosa*, *Delessaria sanguinea* and *Plocamium cartilagineum*. Below this the barnacle *Balanus crenatus* covered much of the rock along with dead-man's fingers *Alcyonium digitatum* and the plumose anemone *Metridium senile*. The rest of the gully walls were

colonised by a *Dendrodoa-Clathrina* community with other species including sponges *Grantia compressa* and *Scypha ciliata*, the hydroid *Tubularia indivisa*, sea anemones including the northern and characteristically exposed coast species *Phellia gausapata*, jewel anemones *Corynactis viridis*, the filigree tubeworm *Salmacina dysteri* and several low-growing ascidians.

Earll (1982) describes surge gullies from around St. Abb's Head. These were not as rich as sites described on Shetland. At one site the characteristic tunicate *Dendrodoa grossularia* appeared to be absent, though the second characterising species, the sponge *Clathrina coriacea,* was present in two colour morphs.

Large surge gullies are also described from the Farne Islands by Connor (1989), the Northumberland coast (Foster-Smith & Foster-Smith 1987) and adjacent to Plymouth Sound (Hiscock & Moore 1986).

Bedrock caves and large overhangs

Sublittoral marine caves are an unusual habitat in the North Sea, containing species and communities similar to those of surge gullies. Because of the lack of light, algal communities are much reduced and limited to crustose red algae near the cave entrance. Within the darker area of the cave, communities are animal-dominated, typically with sponges *Stryphnus fortis*, *Stellata grubii*, *Dercitus bucklandii* and *Thymosia guernii*, and anemone *Parazoanthus axinellae*. On western coasts the alcyonian *Parerythropodium corallinoides* is also found in this habitat, but its occurrence in the North Sea area is limited to the extreme south-west, around Cornwall and up the Channel to Plymouth (Hiscock & Moore 1986).

Distribution and regional variation

Cave communities are described from Shetland by Hiscock & Johnston (1990), who also describe the organic enrichment of caves from their use by seals. This organic enrichment is suggested as the cause of development of a polychaete/oligochaete turf on the rock surfaces.

Earll (1982) describes the presence of 'some caves' around St. Abb's Head, but gives no further details of their richness, however in an earlier report (Earll 1981) he records the occurrence of small (< 1 m diameter) caves with species such as *Ascidia conchilega*, *Ciona intestinalis* and the tubeworm *Pomatoceros* sp.

Bennett (1989) describes the presence of a surge cave on the Isle of May, in the Firth of Forth.

This feature, a cross between a surge gully and a cave, extended from the surface to 3 m bcd and appeared to have four main zones: an outer zone of *Laminaria saccharina* with encrusting coralline algae, foliose red algae, dead-man's fingers *Alcyonium digitatum*, the anemone *Urticina felina*, tubeworms *Pomatoceros* sp. and the urchin *Echinus esculentus*; a middle zone with a very rich faunal turf of sponges, hydroids, anthozoans, bryozoans, ascidians and very few foliose algae; an inner zone, dominated by foliose red algae with sponges and ascidians still present; and an upper zone characterised by barnacles and the mussel *Mytilus edulis* extending into the littoral zone.

Hiscock & Moore (1986) describe large overhangs in Plymouth Sound, particularly in bedrock around 30 m bcd, while Moore (1988b) describes tide-exposed cave walls from the Dart Estuary.

Tide-swept boulders and cobbles

Tide-swept boulders and cobbles occur in areas of enhanced water movement, typically in sounds, narrows and entrances to marine inlets. Communities on the substratum are generally animal-dominated, with a low turf of hydroids and bryozoans. Typical species include the bryozoans *Flustra foliacea*, *Securiflustra securifrons*, *Alcyonidium diaphanum*, *Eucrata loricata* and *Vesicularia spinosa*, and the hydroids *Abietinaria abietina* and *Hydrallmania falcata*.

Distribution and regional variation

Tide-swept boulders are found in Shetland, where fully saline water is constricted through sounds between islands (Hiscock & Johnston 1990). Elsewhere on the North Sea coastline they are a feature of the marine inlets, which are concentrated along the south and south-western coasts. Their occurrence offshore in the Channel is noted in Section 5.6.

The community is present in the Farne Islands, where Connor (1989) describes tide-swept cobbles colonised by a range of hydroid species including *Nemertesia antennina*, *Abietinaria abietina*, *Sertularia argentea*, and *Thuiaria thuia*. This latter species has a northerly distribution and is absent from similar habitats on the south coast.

Howard, Howson & Moore (1988) describe tide-swept cobbles at the entrance to the Fleet. This habitat contained a range of species including the ascidian *Ascidiella aspersa*, the hydroids *Plumularia setacea* and *Sertularia cupressina*. A variety of ascidians were present in smaller quantities, such as *Phallusia mammilata*, *Polyclinum aurantium* and the introduced species *Styela clava*. This species was introduced to the south coast and is not present in more northerly areas.

In the Narrows of Plymouth Sound, Hiscock & Moore (1986) describe bedrock and boulders subject to strong tidal streams. This substratum, to a depth of about 15 m bcd, was dominated by *Laminaria saccharina* with the bryozoan *Membranipora membranacea*, the hydroid *Obelia geniculata* and the ascidian *Dendrodoa grossularia*. Deeper than 15 m communities were dominated by *Dendrodoa grossularia* with frequent *Polycarpa rustica*. The hydroids *Nemertesia antennina* and *Plumularia setacea* were also present with the sponges *Hymeniacidon perleve*, *Halichondria panicea* and *Amphilectus fucorum*.

Frid (1989) describes tidally scoured boulders and cobbles from the Teign estuary in south Devon. Species present included the sponges *Hymeniacidon perleve* and *Halichondria* spp. and red algae. With increasing depth the algae were replaced with a turf of bryozoans and hydroids; *Cryptosula pallasiana*, *Sertularia argentea* and *Tubularia* spp.

Cobble, pebble, gravel and coarse sediment

This type of substratum is again a feature of tide-swept areas, since under still water conditions finer graded sediments tend to be deposited on top of coarser material, such that muddy gravel communities are formed as described in Section 5.5.

Distribution and regional variation

Bennett (1989) records a similar community of small boulders, cobbles and pebbles exposed to wave action in the circalittoral zone off the Isle of May. This habitat was characterised by the brittlestar *Ophiothrix fragilis* with a number of other species present in smaller numbers. These included the hydroids *Abietinaria abietina*, *Hydrallmania falcata*, and *Thuiaria thuia*, a hydroid which is absent from southern Britain.

Connor (1989) records tide-swept boulders, cobbles, coarse sand and gravel from the Farne Islands. This habitat was dominated by the brittlestar *Ophiothrix fragilis*, with the hydroid *Abietinaria abietina* present.

In the Solent, Dixon & Moore (1987) recorded current exposed pebbles and shells dominated by the introduced slipper limpet *Crepidula fornicata*, the empty shells of which provided much of the hard substratum. Cobbles and pebbles were colonised by the barnacle *Balanus crenatus*, the ascidian *Dendrodoa grossularia*, the hydroid

Nemertesia antennina and the bryozoan *Flustra foliacea*. These species are widespread in the North Sea with the exception of *Crepidula fornicata* which is only present on the east and southern coasts of England.

Hiscock & Moore (1986) record the occurrence of tide-swept infralittoral pebbles and cobbles in sand and gravel in Plymouth Sound. Here the substratum was colonised by an algal community characteristic of such situations, with *Dudresnaya verticillata, Gracilaria foliifera, Nacaria wiggii, Schmitzia hiscockiana, Schmitzia neopolitana* and *Cutleria multifida. Naccaria wiggii* is only present in the North Sea area around south-western coasts, only progressing up the Channel to the Dorset coast. *Cutleria multifida* has been recorded from suitable habitats from the south coast, Kent and the Firth of Forth (Norton 1985).

IMPACTS ON SUBLITTORAL HARD SUBSTRATA AND COMMUNITIES

Rock substrata are not generally subject to the range of damaging activities resulting from the use of mobile gear for fishing although areas of stable cobbles and pebbles together with associated comunities will be greatly disturbed and communities destroyed by dredging for scallops. Deployment of pots (creels) over areas of rocky seabed doubtless dislodges attached species and causes some damage to communities.

Dumping is not generally carried out over rocky substrata, although severe damage as a result of dumping has been recorded to hard substratum communities in Salcombe Harbour (Little 1987).

Some shallow sublittoral areas are harvested for algae for the alginate industry although this is a very localised activity and not yet on the large scale seen for kelps on the coast of Brittany.

Industrial waste effluent disposal may result in a gradient of effect away from point source discharges. Although none are known to be documented for the North Sea coast, Hoare & Hiscock (1974) describe the impact of a chemical effluent on rocky sublittoral communities on the Anglesey coast.

More broad-scale effects may occur as a result of reduced water quality and the studies of kelp holdfast faunas indicate possible effects of pollution. These studies have been undertaken separately by D. Jones and by P.G. Moore and published in series of papers, most recently Jones (1973), who suggests the pollution theory and Moore (1973), who suggests natural turbidity gradients.

Oil pollution and subsequent cleaning may cause damage to shallow, rocky sublittoral communities

though this is usually recoverable. Effects are likely to be least severe and most transient on wave-exposed coasts, but long-lasting chronic effects in sheltered areas such as Shetland voes and other rocky marine inlets may occur.

The installation of offshore wave generators for electricity would effectively reduce wave exposure of the shallow sublittoral and communities would change.

5.5 INSHORE SUBLITTORAL SEDIMENT

INTRODUCTION

This section reviews the available information on the inshore sublittoral soft substrata of the North Sea coastline. Some overlap between the information included in this section and the offshore section is inevitable as there is some similarity between the habitats.

DISTRIBUTION

Inshore areas are considered to be those under the direct influence of the coast because of the presence of coastal topographical features, accelerated tidal flow around headlands, embayment effects, etc. On the open coast, this is likely be for about 3 km offshore and generally within the 50 m depth contour but including all of the large bays. The area falls largely, but not entirely, within the 'infralittoral étage' of Glémarec (1973). (Classification is described in Section 5.6.)

Typically around the coast of Britain as a whole, bedrock fringes the coast, continuing into the shallow sublittoral to be replaced at depth by sedimentary substrata. Deep bedrock habitats are localised and unusual. On much of the North Sea coast, even shallow bedrock is lacking and the sediment beaches grade into sublittoral sediments.

DESCRIPTION OF RESOURCE

Habitats and communities

The key works for separation of distinctive habitats and communities are the studies of Petersen (1914, 1915, 1918), which described communities on the seabed named by conspicuous characteristic species, and the work of Jones (1950), which separated communities on the basis of depth and substratum type. These works, together with a wide range of other studies, are being used by the MNCR to prepare a classification of habitats and communities for sublittoral sediments. A classification prepared for the Irish Sea (Holt, Fisher & Graham) is shown in Table 5.5.1.

Detailed specific information on inshore sedimentary habitats and communities is sparse. Some areas, such as the larger marine inlets (for example, the Firth of Forth, the Humber, the Thames, and the Solent and Plymouth Sound) have been well studied, while open coast areas remain little studied except in areas of dumping grounds or of fishery importance. An exception is the Channel coast of England where Holme (1961) undertook extensive dredge surveys. The results of those studies together with work further offshore are described most usefully in Holme (1966) where associations are named according to the approach of Jones (1950) and their distribution mapped (Figure 5.5.1). An example of a more detailed

survey and mapping undertaken in the Firth of Forth is illustrated in Figure 5.5.2.

Inshore sublittoral soft substrata range from the soft, estuarine muds of many shallow estuaries and the deep, muddy substrata of some of the Shetland voes to the tide-swept sands and gravels of the English Channel. Within these differing substrata a wide range of animal-dominated communities occur. The development of rich infaunal and epifaunal communities in sublittoral sediments depends on the degree of wave and tidal stream exposure, which in turn affects the grade of sediment present and its mobility; the richest communities developing in sheltered and therefore stable but fully saline sediments.

Muddy gravel with cobbles

This community and variations of it is probably the most widespread in the nearshore sublittoral zone of the North Sea. Typical species include the

Substratum	Wave exposure	Tidal streams	Species/groups characterising different communities
15 Gravel/ shell gravel			Maerl beds
16 Gravel/ shell gravel			*Neopentadactyla, Glycymeris*; *Spatangus* (= infaunal community 1 and 6)
17 Gravel – muddy, with cobble and boulder			*Chaetopterus/Lanice/Pecten* (= infaunal community 5)
18 Sand – coarse, gravelly			*Ensis arcuatus/Mya truncata* (= infaunal community 8)
19 Sand – clean, mobile			Barren; *Ammodytes/Pagurus bernhardus* (= infaunal community 2 and 3)
20 Sand			*Zostera marina* bed
21 Sand			*Laminaria saccharina/Chorda*; filamentous algae (*Audouinella/Trailliella*)
22 Sand – fine			*Echinocardium cordatum, Amphiura brachiata & Labidoplax digitata* (= infaunal community 7)
23 Sand – muddy			*Virgularia/Amphiura* spp. with *Corymorpha, Thecocarpus, Molgula occulta, Arctica, Cerianthus, Ophiura* spp., *Turritella, Aporrhais, Astropecten* (= infaunal community 10)
24 Mud with shell			*Modiolus* beds
25 Mud with shell			*Ascidiella aspersa/Sabella pavonina*
26 Mud			*Virgularia/Amphiura* spp. with *Philine aperta*
27 Mud			Megafaunal burrowers (*Nephrops, Goneplax*) (= infaunal community 12 and 13)

Table 5.5.1
A classification for sublittoral soft substrata for the Irish Sea (from Holt, Fisher & Graham 1990).

Figure 5.5.1
The distribution of different 'boreal offshore associations' in the Channel redrawn from Holme (1966).
Titles of associations according to Holme are keyed. Equivalent or near equivalent habitat/community types from the MNCR classification are given in brackets [ ].

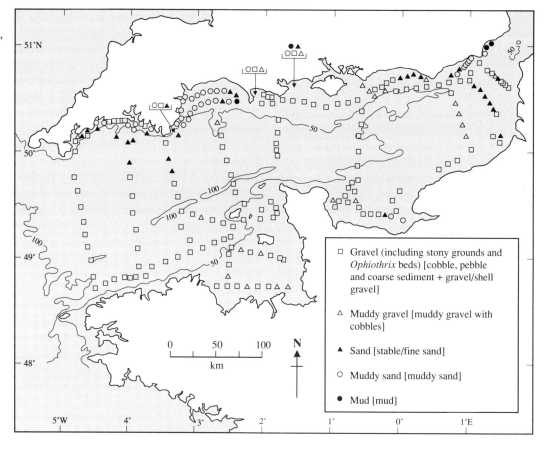

☐ Gravel (including stony grounds and *Ophiothrix* beds) [cobble, pebble and coarse sediment + gravel/shell gravel]

△ Muddy gravel [muddy gravel with cobbles]

▲ Sand [stable/fine sand]

○ Muddy sand [muddy sand]

● Mud [mud]

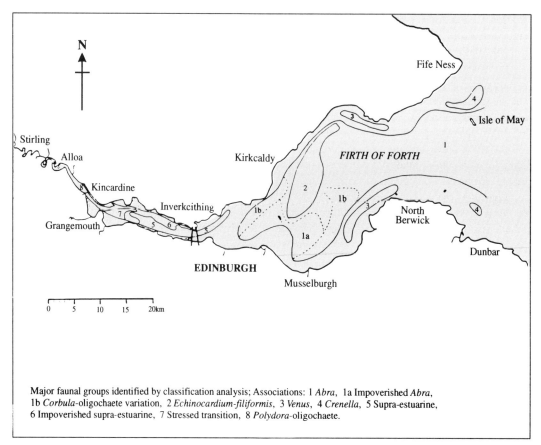

Figure 5.5.2
Map of benthic habitats in Firth of Forth.

Major faunal groups identified by classification analysis; Associations: 1 *Abra*, 1a Impoverished *Abra*, 1b *Corbula*-oligochaete variation, 2 *Echinocardium-filiformis*, 3 *Venus*, 4 *Crenella*, 5 Supra-estuarine, 6 Impoverished supra-estuarine, 7 Stressed transition, 8 *Polydora*-oligochaete.

sandmason worm *Lanice conchilega* and the tube-dwelling polychaete *Chaetopterus variopedatus*, though within the North Sea a wide range of species may be present. Hiscock & Johnston (1989) in a review of marine biological information for Shetland record the occurrence of a coarse, muddy gravel seabed at the sides of some voes. This sediment contained a diverse range of species including many bivalves and polychaetes as well as less abundant but widely distributed epifauna such as the pelican's foot shell *Aporrhais pespelecani*, the decapod *Munida rugosa* and the starfish *Astropecten irregularis*. Holme's (1966) 'Boreal offshore muddy gravel association', recorded from the channel, probably falls into this type.

Distribution and regional variation

Jones *et al.* (1979) describe a coarse gravel with a high silt/clay content from the eastern side of Scapa Flow in the Orkneys. This sediment was dominated by polychaetes, with some molluscs and chitons attached to shell debris and the brittlestar *Ophiothrix fragilis* among empty shells and worm tubes. The bivalve species *Mysella bidentata*, *Thyasira flexuosa* and *Abra* spp. also occurred.

In the mouth of the Humber, Murray *et al.* (1980) give details of a muddy gravel community characterised by beds of the horse mussel *Modiolus modiolus*, the brittlestar *Ophiothrix fragilis* and the erect bryozoan *Flustra* sp. This was considered to be typical of the seabed in this area.

Further south, off the Norfolk coast at Cromer, a muddy gravel characterised by infaunal polychaetes and the epifaunal ascidian *Molgula manhattensisis* is found. In another survey, Anglian Water studied the effects of the sewage outfall at Caister (Anglian Water 1984), describing the benthic communities. They found a similar muddy gravel community to that off Cromer.

In a survey around Dover and Folkestone, Wood & Wood (1986) describe mixed sediment ground found offshore from the chalk exposures. This was predominantly muddy sand and gravel, dominated by the brittlestar *Ophiura albida*, with numerous surface dwellers such as the necklace shell *Lunatia* sp., the starfish *Asterias rubens*, hermit crabs *Pagurus* spp. and infaunal species such as the anemone *Cerianthus lloydi*, and the polychaetes *Lanice conchilega* and *Lagis koreni* and the cockle *Cerastoderma edule*.

In the central area of the west Solent the bottom consists of angular pebbles with whole shells overlying mud and muddy sand (Dixon & Moore 1987). The introduced slipper limpet *Crepidula fornicata* dominated this habitat in a community

which consisted mostly of mobile crustaceans with encrusting bryozoans, ascidians, sponges, polychaetes and barnacles on pebbles and cobbles. A very similar community of shells (live and dead) of *Crepidula fornicata* and pebbles on mud was recorded from Portland Harbour by Howard, Howson & Moore (1988). This is also one of the very few areas where native oysters *Ostrea edulis* occur naturally in sufficient abundance to support commercial exploitation.

Spooner & Holme (1961) record the presence of a muddy gravel community off Lulworth on the Dorset coast. This substratum contained two species of burrowing prawn *Upogebia deltaura* and *Upogebia stellata* as well as epifauna such as tower shells *Turritella communis* and the pelican's foot shell *Aporrhais pespelecani*. Similar communities were present mainly off Plymouth described in Holme (1966). These included the topshell *Gibbula magus* and the burrowing anemone *Mesacmaea mitchelli* which are likely to occur only in the south-west. Off Looe Island, large burrows noted by Holme may have been of the red band fish *Cepola rubescens*.

The Dart estuary contains a range of mixed sediments including pebbles, cobbles and shells overlying silty sediment (Moore 1988). Red algal assemblages attached to hard substrata were fairly rich, particularly in the lower reaches of the estuary. Fauna attached to the hard substratum was of low diversity and included *Clavelina lepadiformis*, *Pomatoceros* sp., *Balanus crenatus*, *Dendrodoa grossularia* and a variety of sponges, hydroids and bryozoans in low abundances in the upper estuary, but becoming dominant in the circalittoral zone of the lower estuary.

In Plymouth Sound Hiscock & Moore (1986) describe a mixed muddy sediment from Jennycliffe Bay. A range of epiphytic species were recorded.

Coarse, gravelly sand

This type of substratum is likely to occur in areas of relatively strong wave action or enhanced water movement by tidal action. The habitat is dominated by bivalves, the numbers of individuals and species depending on the conditions. Typically they include bivalves such as *Ensis arcuatus*, *Mya truncata* and *Glycymeris glycymeris*, the urchin *Spatangus purpureus* and the holothurian *Neopentadactyla mixta*. This community is closest to the 'boreal offshore gravel association' of Holme (1966), which he equates to the *Spatangus purpureus-Venus fasciata* community of Ford (1923), and is grouped by Thorson (1957) as the '*Branchiostoma*' bottom type of the *Venus fasciata-Spisula elliptica-Branchiostoma* community.

Distribution and regional variation

In Shetland coarse sediments including shell gravel supported a fauna characterised by bivalve molluscs such as the burrowing species *Ensis arcuatus*, *Lutraria* sp., *Fabulina fabula*, *Angulus tenuis*, *Mya truncata*, *Dosinia exoleta*, *Venus striatula*, *Venerupis pullastra* and *Arctica islandica* (Hiscock & Johnston 1990). They also describe similar habitats in clean gravel and maerl (unattached calcified seaweed), with *Ensis* sp. being common along with *Mya truncata* and the burrowing sea cucumber *Neopentadactyla mixta*. Epifauna is limited to hydroids and bryozoans attached to stones and shells, with the gastropod molluscs *Tectura virginea*, *Gibbula tumida*, *Gibbula cineraria* and *Gibbula magus* often frequent, together with crabs *Ebalia tuberosa* and *Atelecyclus rotundatus*, and the brittlestars *Ophiothrix fragilis*, *Ophiocomina nigra*, *Ophiopholis aculeata* and *Ophiura* spp. The rarely recorded burrowing urchin *Spatangus purpureus* is also found in this habitat.

Pearson and Eleftheriou (1981), in a long-term study of Sullom Voe in Shetland, describe patches of coarse sand and gravel in the outer voe area where the urchin *Echinus esculentus* was the dominant epifaunal organism. The infauna was dominated by surface deposit-feeding terebellid and spionid polychaetes and the filter-feeding bivalve *Cochlodesma* with low numbers of *Phoronis*, *Thyasira* and *Turritella* which were more common in more silty sediments further towards the head of the voe.

In Orkney Jones *et al.* (1988) present records of coarse sand and gravel from the north-western side of Scapa Flow. These contained an impoverished fauna dominated by polychaetes, with few molluscs, mostly juveniles. The small bivalve *Semierycina nitida* was present, which is indicative of gravelly and stony sand.

Khayrallah & Jones (1975) review information on the sublittoral substrata of the Firth of Tay on the east coast of Scotland. Coarse sand was present in the middle reaches of the firth, though no information is given on the benthos specific to this sediment type.

Shell gravel communities in the vicinity of St. Abb's Head are described by Earll (1982). Coarse sediments of stone and shell gravel contained an assortment of robust bivalve species (*Venus verrucosa*, *Tellina crassa*, *Venerupis rhomboides* and *Spisula solida*) as well as the infaunal holothurian *Neopentadactyla mixta*, the solitary hydroid *Corymorpha nutans*, the infaunal solitary ascidian *Molgula occulta* and its associated predator *Okenia pulchella*. This type of habitat is further described by Pagett (1983) who recorded its presence

extensively offshore from the Lumsdaine shore north of St. Abb's Head.

Connor (1989) also describes the occurrence of coarse sand and shell gravel to the south-east of the Farne Islands.

Bamber and Coughlan record the presence of coarse, impoverished sand in the vicinity of Sizewell (Bamber & Coughlan 1980). This sediment had no characterising species, but contained the amphipod *Urothoe elegans* and polychaete *Nerinides cantabra*.

The area of the Barrow Deep, in the Thames estuary, was surveyed by Norton *et al.* (1981). They describe a range of coarse sediments based on gravel with varying admixtures of sand. Sediments became coarser further out of the estuary, forming part of the extensive submarine gravel deposits which occur between the English and Belgian coasts.

Along the Channel coast, the offshore gravel association of Holme (1966) is widespread and is noted as often associated with dense beds of the brittle stars *Ophiothrix fragilis* and *Ophiocomina nigra* which fall within the MNCR category of 'cobble, pebble and coarse sediment swept by moderately strong tidal streams'.

Coarse sands are recorded from the edges of the deeper water channels in Poole Harbour (Howard & Moore 1989). This substratum supported one of the most species-poor communities in the harbour, with the sand eel *Ammodytes tobianus* as the only common species.

The tide-swept entrance to the Exe estuary has a substratum of mixed sediments, ranging from fine sand with shells and stones to flat beds of cobbles and pebbles over coarse sand (Dixon 1986). The predominant epifauna were *Carcinus maenas* and *Crangon crangon*, with sparse infaunal populations of *Nephtys cirrosa*, *Bathyporeia sarsi* and *Urothoe brevicornis*.

In the Teign estuary, sublittoral gravel, cobbles and coarse sand are described by Frid (1989). Stones and cobbles were colonised by algae *Ceramium* spp., *Gracilaria verrucosa*, the barnacle *Balanus crenatus* and Anthozoa. The sediment contained the spat of the mussel *Mytilus edulis* and the bivalve *Gari fervensis* with the polychaetes *Lanice conchilega*, *Eteone flava* and *Nephtys hombergi*.

Offshore from the breakwater in Plymouth Sound Hiscock & Moore (1986) give details of a coarse shell sand dominated by the bivalve *Spisula elliptica*, with other bivalves *Dosinia lupinus*, *Gari tellinella* and the polychaete *Glycera lapidum*.

Clean mobile sand

As with the previous habitat, this substratum is likely to be a feature of areas with strong wave action or tides. Fauna is impoverished, dominated by crustaceans, polychaetes and hermit crabs such as *Pagurus bernhardus*. This substratum is likely to be widespread along much of the shallow east coast, where it is likely to occur as an extension of exposed sandy shores.

Thorson (1957) describes these as *Tellina* communities, which typically occur in exposed areas rarely deeper than 10 m.

Distribution and regional variation

Clean sand is recorded from Shetland (Hiscock & Johnston 1989). From Orkney, Jones (1975c) describes areas where the bottom is largely sandy and tidal streams are pronounced. Here ophiuroids *Ophiocomina nigra* and *Ophiura albida* are the dominant forms.

Clean mobile sand is recorded from Loch Eriboll (Moss 1986) in the outer area of the loch. The sediment was poor in fauna apart from the occasional sandmason worms *Lanice conchilega* and crabs.

Earll (1983) reviews the benthos of the Moray Firth and describes much of the area to be dominated by mobile sands which are species-poor.

In a review of the benthos of the Tay estuary Khayrallah & Jones (1975) describe the presence of medium and fine sands in the central regions of the firth. No specific information is given on the benthos of these sediments, but in view of the tidal movement described they are likely to be very mobile and impoverished.

Connor (1989) describes mobile rippled sand from around the Farne Islands. This had a poor infauna, with the predominant species being the polychaete *Chaetozone setosa* and the amphipod *Bathyporeia guilliamsoniana*. Also recorded were the sandmason worm *Lanice conchilega*, the sand eel *Ammodytes* sp. and the burrowing anemone *Cerianthus* sp. in low numbers.

On the Northumbrian coast exposed bays have impoverished coarse sands in the sublittoral zone. These sediments are characterised by the crabs *Eupagurus bernhardus* and *Liocarcinus depurator*, with no apparent infauna (Foster-Smith & Foster-Smith 1987).

Within the Humber estuary, sublittoral sands influenced by current action contain an impoverished community of the catworm *Nephtys* spp., *Spiophanes bombyx* and *Spio filicornis* (Rees, Barnet & Urquhart 1982).

Dipper, Irving & Fowler (1989) in a survey of the Wash found areas of current-swept sand community with little epifauna.

Offshore from Caister and Great Yarmouth Anglian Water (1984) describe mobile sands at the edges of the main tidal channels of Caister and Yarmouth Roads.

Mobile sand is a feature of the outer Thames estuary surveyed by Norton *et al.* (1981). They describe coarse sand populations occurring only as localised deposits in the central bed of the 'Deeps', while fine sands were ubiquitous over most of the outer Thames survey area. Boreholes showed that these sediments formed almost the entire thickness of the sandbanks in the estuary. The fact that these clean sands are very mobile was shown by the widespread occurrence of sand waves and megaripples. Fauna within these deposits was predominantly composed of amphipods and polychaete worms.

Wood & Wood (1986) deal with some inshore sublittoral sediments in the Dover and Folkestone area of Kent. Clean sands were found off East Wear Bay, with few species including *Arenicola marina*, *Lanice conchilega* and *Hinia reticulata*.

Most areas of the sublittoral zone of Kent and Sussex consist of mobile sand and fine silt. These sediments are frequently deposited over flatter areas of bedrock and are typically impoverished due to their mobility (Wood 1984, 1986, 1990).

The closest association to this, noted by Holme (1966) for the English Channel, is the 'shallow-sand association' which was characterised by *Arenicola marina*, *Nepthys* sp., *Angulus tenuis* and *Donax vittatus* and occurred intertidally and in very shallow water.

Dixon & Moore (1987) describe current swept clean sand from the central area of the Solent. Conspicuous species in this habitat were sparsely distributed or absent, typically including the crab *Pagurus bernhardus* and the sedentary species *Lanice conchilega* and *Urticina felina*. A similar habitat occurs offshore from Christchurch Harbour (Dixon 1988).

In Poole Harbour Howard & Moore (1989) record medium and fine sands around some of the main channels. Characteristic species included the polychaete *Lanice conchilega*, with localised beds of the peacock fanworm *Sabella pavonina*, the introduced slipper limpet *Crepidula fornicata* and the immigrant 'Japweed' *Sargassum muticum*.

Frid (1989) describes mobile sublittoral sand banks in the mouth of the Teign estuary. Here the substratum was of coarse sand and gravel, species-poor containing only *Scololepis squamata*, *Eteone longa*, *Aonides oxycephala*, Nemertea indet. and occasionally small *Mytilus edulis*.

Stable fine sand

Stable sublittoral sands are a feature of semi-sheltered areas including deep areas where wave action is reduced by depth and which are not subject to the deposition of finer silts and muds. Communities which are found in this habitat are variable, according to local conditions. Areas which are slightly exposed to wave action or are tide-swept may develop an infaunal community characterised by the heart urchin *Echinocardium cordatum*, the brittlestar *Amphiura brachiata*, and occasionally the burrowing sea cucumber *Labidoplax digitata*. In slightly more sheltered and shallow areas beds of the marine angiosperm *Zostera marina* may occur, which in turn stabilise the sediment and provide shelter, attachment and a food source for a range of invertebrate species. In very sheltered areas larger algae may occur attached to small stones and pebbles. Such algae include the sugar kelp *Laminaria saccharina*, the bootlace weed *Chorda filum*, and a range of other filamentous red algae.

Holme (1966) identifies his 'offshore sand association' with Petersen's (1914) '*Venus*' community and with a subgroup of Ford's (1923) *Echinocardium cordatum-Venus striatula* community.

Distribution and regional variation

Hiscock & Johnston (1989) describe shallow, stable sediments from Shetland. In a few locations these sediments are colonised by eelgrass *Zostera marina*, or where salinity is reduced by freshwater, including some basins almost fully enclosed, the eelgrass *Ruppia cirrhosa* may occur. Also recorded are a range of algae from sediment surfaces in shallow waters. These include the kelp *Laminaria saccharina*, the bootlace weed *Chorda filum*, together with *Cystoclonium purpureum*, *Asperococcus compressus*, *Asperococcus turneri* and *Enteromorpha* spp.

Within Scapa Flow in Orkney, Jones (1975c) describes sandy areas with frequent dense beds of *Ensis siliqua* together with *Echinocardium cordatum*. Jones also comments that considerable populations of scallops *Pecten maximus* and queens *Chlamys opercularis* are scattered round the island sounds, firths and in Scapa Flow, many of these beds being commercially exploited.

In the Moray Firth, Earll (1983) records the occurrence of more stable sands at depths which are sheltered from wave action. The fauna of these sediments consists of the bivalves *Fabulina fabula*, *Donax* spp., *Ensis arcuatus* and *Ensis siliqua*, the heart urchin *Echinocardium cordatum* and the tube worm *Branchiomma vesiculosum*.

In the St. Abb's Head area, Earll (1982) gives details of a sand community at a depth of 25 m containing a range of species including *Echinocardium cordatum, Ensis siliqua* and other bivalves.

Connor (1989) describes mobile, rippled sand with a rich infauna from the mouth of Budle Bay on the Northumbrian coast. This sediment supported a rich infauna, including the heart urchin *Echinocardium cordatum* and the bivalves *Angulus tenuis* and *Ensis arcuatus,* which were common or abundant, and the bivalves *Donax vittatus*, *Chamelea gallina* and *Tellimya ferruginosa* were common.

Off the Northumbrian coast, sand plains at around 17 m depth are typically inhabited by the heart urchin *Echinocardium cordatum* and *Ensis* spp.

In the vicinity of Sizewell power station Bamber & Coughlan (1980) describe a sandy sediment community which is largely stabilised by the dense aggregations of the tubeworm *Phoronis muelleri*. Also present in the community were dense hydroids which assisted in anchoring the sediment. Other species were predominantly epifaunal and included bryozoans and five species of pycnogonid.

Holme (1966) notes that his 'offshore-sand association' tends to occur either very close inshore or much further offshore.

Muddy sand

In areas which are sheltered from wave action and subjected to the deposition of fine material, a substratum of muddy sand may be present. This substratum contains a range of species including brittlestars *Amphiura* spp. and *Ophiura* spp., bivalve molluscs *Artica islandica*, the hydroid *Corymorpha nutans*, gastropod molluscs *Turritella communis* and *Aporrhais pespelecani*, the starfish *Astropecten irregularis*, and the burrowing anemone *Cerianthus lloydii*. This is the 'offshore muddy sand association' of Holme (1966) which he equates to Petersen's (1914) '*Echinocardium cordatum-Amphiura filiformis* community' and Ford's (1923) 'deep and shallow water silty-sand communities'.

Distribution and regional variation

Jones *et al.* (1988) describe a fine sediment from Scapa Flow in the Orkneys, which was polychaete-dominated, with a high number of the bivalve *Mysella bidentata* and the brittlestar *Amphiura filiformis*.

Muddy sand is the dominant substratum in the central sublittoral section of Loch Eriboll (Moss 1986). This was characterised by the presence of the lugworm *Arenicola marina*, a range of bivalve molluscs and the burrowing anemone *Cerianthus lloydi*. Patches of tower shells *Turritella communis*, scallops *Pecten maximus*, queens *Chlamys opercularis* and hermit crabs were recorded.

Studies by the Ministry of Agriculture, Fisheries and Food (Eagle *et al.* 1979) show the change in sediment characteristics off the Northumbrian coast due to the dumping of solid wastes from collieries and coal-fired power stations. Studies by Buchanan (1963) before the commencement of dumping showed sediments to be fine sand, with around 20% silt and clay content. These sediments contained a typical *Amphiura filiformis* community, with patches of the tower shell *Turritella communis*. By the time Eagle *et al.* carried out their survey, the dumping of waste had resulted in a much finer sediment being present (up to 50% silt and clay) and a community dominated by the polychaetes *Paraonis gracilis* and *Lumbriconereis gracilis* and the bivalve *Mysella bidentata*. The previously characteristic brittlestar *Amphiura filiformis* was uncommon.

Rees, Barnett & Urquhart (1982) described a muddy sand substratum in the Humber estuary. This contained a variable range of organisms with occasional polychaetes, but was dominated by mysids and gammarids.

Dipper, Irving & Fowler (1989) describe a fine silty sand community in the Wash which was dominated by the brittlestar *Ophiura albida*.

The sediments in the vicinity of Sizewell power station were surveyed by Bamber & Coughlan (1980) who described six infaunal communities. Of these, two communities were found on muddy sands, a *Nucula* community and a *Polymnia* community. The former was typically in the deeper central channel and consisted of a dense fauna typical of sandy muds. Species included *Nucula turgida, Nephtys hombergi, Spiophanes bombyx, Mysella bidentata, Macoma balthica* and *Abra nitida*. Adjacent to the central channel, muddy sands supported the polychaete-dominated *Polymnia* community, in which the dominant species were *Polymnia nebulosa, Magelona papillicornis, Perioculoides longimanus, Nephtys* spp. and *Spiophanes bombyx*.

Spooner & Holme (1961) record the ocurrence of a silty sand off the Dorset coast. This was inhabited by a range of crustacea. Lamellibranch molluscs were abundant, including *Abra alba, Spisula subtruncata, Nucula turgida* and *Pandora albida*. Also found were a number of tower shells *Turritella communis*.

Howard & Moore (1989) record a range of communities transitional between sand and mud in Poole Harbour. Typical species included the burrowing anemones *Cereus pedunculatus* and *Sagartia troglodytes*, the ascidian *Styela clava*, occasional brittlestar *Ophiothrix fragilis* beds along with occasional oysters *Ostrea edulis*.

A muddy sand habitat offshore from Plymouth breakwater is described by Hiscock & Moore (1986). This sediment was characterised by frequent starfish *Asterias rubens* and casts of the lugworm *Arenicola marina*. Other muddy sands were recorded in numerous locations around Plymouth Sound, many of them rich in species. A particularly rich site was Cawsand Bay, which contained a diverse community of very small polychaetes, dominated by *Scoloplos armiger* and *Chaetozone setosa*. Bivalves were represented by *Venus striatula, Nucula turgida* and *Cultellus pellucidus*.

Mud with shells

This community is largely a feature of enclosed water bodies in the North Sea area. The shells often provide an attachment for species such as the sea squirt *Ascidiella aspersa,* and beds of horse mussel, a bivalve mollusc *Modiolus* spp., may occur in Shetland at least. The peacock fanworm *Sabella pavonina* is also frequent. This community falls largely into Thorson's (1957) *Turritella* group of communities, though *in situ* observation has lent greater weight to epifauna which Thorson generally fails to describe.

Distribution and regional variation

Pearson & Eleftheriou (1981) describe extensive areas of *Modiolus*-dominated poorly sorted sediment from Sullom Voe in Shetland. On a substratum of mud with admixtures of coarser material and dead shells *Modiolus* formed the dominant component of the epifaunal community with the queen scallop *Chlamys opercularis* in locally dense aggregations. Live and dead *Modiolus* shells formed a solid substratum for attachment of the red algae *Phyllophora* and numerous small hydroids, bryozoans and serpulid polychaetes. The poorly sorted sediments and empty shells encouraged the settlement of a wide variety of epiphytic organisms. The ascidian *Ascidiella aspersa* was abundant, along with the boring sponge *Cliona celata*. Three species of brittlestar *Ophiothrix fragilis, Ophiocomina nigra* and *Ophiopholis aculeata* were common, forming locally dense aggregations.

In a sublittoral survey of the Wash, Dipper, Irving & Fowler (1989) describe a *Sabella pavonina* community on fine mud overlaying clay.

This type of community is found in many of the rias of south-west England.

This habitat is likely to be more widespread than records suggest and further work is required to provide a full picture of its distribution.

Mud

Pure mud is usually a feature of calm conditions on the sea bed. These can be due to the sheltered nature of the water body (such as within marine inlets) or may be due to the depth of the seabed below the surface, where disturbance by wave and tidal action is minimal. Species present may include a range of organisms from the seapen *Virgularia mirabilis*, brittlestars *Amphiura* spp., the sea slug *Philine aperta* and the scampi *Nephrops norvegicus*. This is closest to Holme's (1966) 'offshore mud association', although the characteristic species he mentions for surveys in the Channel is *Maxmulleria lankesteri* and the main characterising feature is the scarcity or absence of molluscs and echinoderms. Ford (1923), however, identified an *Echinocardium cordatum-Venus gallina* community of soft mud, which Holme equates to his offshore mud association, though Ford describes the sediment as composed of 60% very fine sand and only 20% silt and clay.

Distribution and regional variation

The relatively calm conditions at the head of Sullom Voe in Shetland have led to the development of organic silt sediments (Pearson & Eleftheriou 1981). This substratum had very few epifaunal species other than some large specimens of the brittlestar *Ophiura texturata* with the occasional dab (*Limanda* and *Hippoglossoides*). Infauna of these deoxygenated sediments was composed almost entirely of small deposit feeding polychaetes such as *Capitella*, *Pectinaria* and *Scalibregma*. These small tube-dwelling species rarely penetrated below 4 cm depth in these sediments where the oxygenated layer was at most only a few millimetres below the sediment water interface.

Studies by Moss (1986) in Loch Eriboll (Sutherland) describe a deep mud habitat in the central part of the Loch. This sediment was characterised by the seapen *Virgularia mirabilis* and the scampi *Nephrops norvegicus*. Within the mud was also the brittlestar *Amphiura filiformis*.

Rees, Barnett & Urquhart (1982) report the occurrence of a rich mud fauna from the Humber estuary, dominated by polychaetes such as *Polydora* sp. and *Pygospio elegans*.

A soft mud community, dominated by small polychaete tubeworms, has been recorded from the Wash by Dipper, Irving & Fowler (1989).

In the central area of Portland Harbour, Howard, Howson & Moore (1988) describe a soft mud plain dominated by the sea pen *Virgularia mirabilis*. Additional characterising species included *Philine aperta*, the anemones *Sagartigeton undatus* and

Edwardsia claparedii and the gastropod mollusc *Aporrhais pespelecani*. Although the red band fish *Cepola rubescens* was not found by Howard, Howson & Moore they state that it is known to be present.

Spooner & Holme (1961) describe a soft mud substratum from Weymouth Bay with characteristic species including the bivalve molluscs *Abra alba* and *Spisula subtruncata* and the brittlestar *Amphiura filiformis*.

Extensive tracts of soft anoxic mud are present in the upper parts of Poole Harbour (Howard & Moore 1988). These areas have few infauna, though firmer areas support patches of the phoronid *Phoronis psammophila* and burrows of the eel *Anguilla anguilla*. Other species *Melinna palmata*, *Nephtys hombergi* and *Corophium volutator* were widely distributed and locally abundant.

In the Exe estuary Dixon (1986) describes mud from the main channel in the upper regions of the estuary. The infauna was very sparse with a limited range of species. The epifauna consisted of *Carcinus maenas* and *Crangon crangon* common or abundant, with young *Pleuronectes platessa*, *Anguilla anguilla* and *Pomatoschistus minutus*.

From the Cattewater area of Plymouth Sound Hiscock and Moore (1986) describe a black, sulphurous mud with sparse fauna, dominated by a few large *Cirratulus cirratus* and *Nephtys hombergi*. The most abundant species were *Capitella capitata* and *Tharyx* sp.

Studies by Holme & Probert (1978) on the deposition of china clay waste in St. Austell Bay describe the unnatural soft mud substratum which is present over much of the Bay. Although this is an artificially created substratum (historical evidence suggests the bottom was once of muddy gravel deposits) the bay supports a comparatively rich bottom fauna.

IMPACTS ON INSHORE SEDIMENT HABITATS AND COMMUNITIES

A range of impacts specific to sublittoral sediment habitats are found. Dredging, both for marine aggregates and as part of harbour or marina works has a substantial impact on sedimentary benthos. MAFF is carrying out research into the former activity. Removal of large quantities of sedimentary material and the subsequent dumping of dredge spoil can have a deleterious effect on the marine communities present and the nature of the sediment remaining on the sea bed (Little 1987).

The impacts of aggregate dredging vary from minimal to severe, depending on the sensitivity of the areas involved, and the degree to which the type of substrate left after the dredging operations is similar to that which existed beforehand. If the surface substrate left is different, the benthic community which colonises it will be different (de Groot 1979, 1986; Cressard 1975). All dredging activities will obviously have fairly dramatic short-term, localised effects, such as the physical removal of material and organisms, but long-term effects on, for instance, fish stocks or geomorphology are much more difficult to assess due to the difficulties of isolating the effects of dredging from many other factors.

A number of the sites at which sewage sludge disposal takes place at sea under licences issued by DAFS and MAFF are in areas of sedimentary substrata. In most of the areas the rate of input of the sewage sludge is roughly in equilibrium with the rates of output by decomposition and physical removal processes. Local organic enrichment is detectable in a few instances, causing minor changes to the benthos structure. Litter introduced via unscreened or inadequately screened sludges has also caused local problems, mainly of an aesthetic nature. A recent study of disposal of Lothian Region sewage sludge showed that it had little effect on the benthic environment and that the macrobenthos showed no signs of stress (Moore & Davies 1987).

Some sublittoral hydraulic dredging for bivalves such as *Ensis* has taken place to a limited extent in Orkney. A recent study of a western sea loch (Hall *et al.* 1990) indicated that the faunal community recovered in a relatively short period from this activity.

Dredging for shellfish such as scallops *Pecten maximus* and queens *Chlamys opercularis* in nearshore sublittoral sediments causes damage to benthic communities (Bullimore 1985). Heavy, toothed dredges effectively 'plough' the seabed, with the result that much of the epifauna is removed while the infauna is redistributed, often either on the surface or buried too deep. Some areas are so intensively dredged that before original communities can become re-established they are disturbed again, so a typical pristine benthos is never present. Instead, a modified community, capable of surviving such disturbance, develops.

Trawling for fish also has an effect on seabed habitats and communities inshore, as noted in Section 5.6.

5.6   OFFSHORE SEDIMENT

INTRODUCTION

This section reviews available information on the offshore benthic habitats and communities of the North Sea, and is based largely on the review of Mitchell (1987), with additional information from studies in the English Channel (for instance Holme 1966; Cabioch *et al.* 1977) and recent studies from the North Sea (for example, Eleftheriou & Basford 1989; Basford *et al.* 1989). Although concentrating on studies undertaken in British offshore waters, the whole of the North Sea has to be considered to obtain a view of the range of habitats and associated communities there.

The basis of our present knowledge of benthic ecosystems in the North Sea proper comes from studies by workers in the early part of this century (for example, Petersen 1914, 1915, 1918), expanded especially by studies into particular areas of fisheries or oil exploration and production interest. In the Channel, the early inshore work based around the Marine Biological Asssociation laboratory at Plymouth was extended all along the Channel coast and offshore by Holme (1961, 1966) and by French workers (Cabioch *et al.* 1977) working up to the English coast. Several hundred surveys of the North Sea oil and gas fields have been carried out as a requirement of the Department of Energy and coordinated by MAFF or SOAFD. Faunistic studies naturally focus on sediment communities in the North Sea proper, as hard substrata are very infrequent offshore. However, the strong tidal streams of the Channel create extensive areas of hard substratum offshore, colonised by epifaunal species. Recent interest has also been shown in 'pockmarks' on the seabed of the North Sea. Studies have shown them to be caused by seepages of natural gases and hydrocarbons. These areas have an unexpectedly rich fauna (Hovland & Judd 1988).

PHYSICAL CONDITIONS

The offshore area of the North Sea shows a range of differing physical conditions, most obviously depth which grades from deep (40–150 m) in the north and west, to shallow (20–40 m) in the south and south-east (Figure 3.6.1. in Section 3.6). The water budget of the North Sea proper is dominated by inflow and outflow between Shetland and Norway. Two oceanic inflows occur between Scotland and Norway, one around 19,000 km^3 per annum east of Shetland, and one of 22,000 km^3 per annum along the western edge of the Norwegian Trench (ICES 1983). A third inflow occurs betwen Orkney and Shetland of around 9,500 km^3 per annum. In contrast, input to the southern North Sea from the English Channel is estimated at 4,700 km^3 annually. Other minor inputs total around 1,500 km^3 per annum, mostly from Scottish coastal water entering around the north of Scotland, and freshwater inflow from the Baltic. Total freshwater run-off to the North Sea amounts to around 361–373 km³ per annum, with the greatest amount coming from the Norwegian west coast. The final freshwater input to the water budget is the excess of precipitation over evaporation, amounting to some 86 km³ per annum. This precipitation shows marked regional variation, with higher values in the north. The major outflow from the North Sea is by the Norwegian coastal current, an estimated 57,000 km³ per annum (Mitchell 1987).

Data on water temperature and salinity in the North Sea are summarised by Lee & Ramster (1981), see Figure 5.6.1. Winter mean bottom temperatures are around 5°C in the central southern North Sea, increasing to 7–7.5°C between Shetland and the

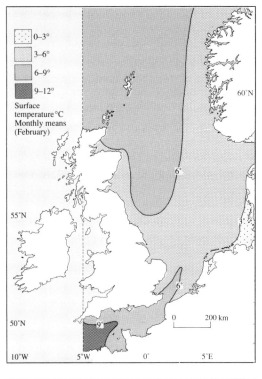
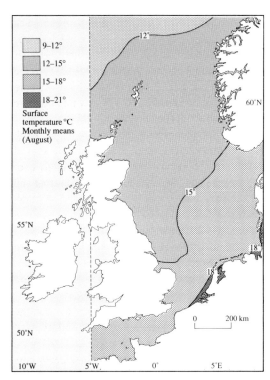
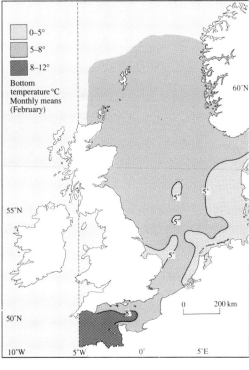
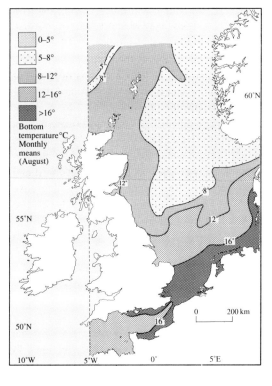

Figure 5.6.1
Top left: Mean winter surface temperature.
Top right: Mean summer surface temperature.
Bottom left: Mean winter bottom temperature.
Bottom right: Mean summer bottom temperature.
© Crown Copyright, 1981.
Reproduced from Lee & Ramster 1981.

west coast of Norway. In summer a large difference occurs in the mean bottom temperatures between northern and southern parts of the North Sea. These are 11–12°C off the coast of eastern Scotland but 16–17°C off the southernmost part of the North Sea proper and off the coasts of south-east England. These large differences in the bottom temperatures in summer and winter in the northern and southern parts of the North Sea arise from the depth of overlying water. The deeper northern waters show a greater thermal stability than the shallow southern North Sea and eastern Channel waters which are quick to heat up in summer and quickly chilled in winter. Deeper water extending into the western approaches to the Channel causes greater thermal stability in offshore waters, which extends eastwards to a line offshore from Portland Bill (Lee & Ramster 1981).

The vertical temperature structure of the North Sea exhibits substantial temporal and spatial variability. A seasonal thermocline develops over much of the area, depending on surface heating and the redistribution of this heating by wind and tide. Stratification is normal in the northern regions of the North Sea and in the western Channel where tides are weaker and depths greater. However, in the southern area of the North Sea proper and the eastern Channel, depths are shallower, tides are stronger and consequently the water mass is well mixed. The boundary between the vertically mixed and the stratified regimes is marked by a well-defined front with a sharp change in sea surface temperature. On the eastern coast of Britain, this transitional area occurs between the Humber and Flamborough Head and extends eastwards approximately following the 40 m depth contour from Flamborough head to the German Bight and is known as the Flamborough Front. In the Channel, a front occurs in the region of Start Point, although almost all of the Channel is of mixed or transitional between stratified and mixed water (Pingree & Griffiths 1978).

Little difference exists between the mean bottom salinity in the North Sea in winter and summer. The highest values occur in the northern North Sea, where salinity reaches 35.25‰ between Shetland and Norway. Salinities gradually decrease southwards and inshore to values of 34.55‰ to 34‰ off most of the east coast of England.

DIVISIONS OF THE NORTH SEA – WATER COLUMN, FISHERIES AND PLANKTON

The International Council for the Exploration of the Sea (ICES) statistical rectangles (see Section 5.7) reflect, to a certain extent, the different zones of the

North Sea for fisheries. As a result of recent studies on the water column of the offshore North Sea undertaken during research into fisheries and plankton, Jones (1972) proposed the division of the North Sea into areas for the purposes of demersal fish research. In spite of the fact that such boundaries were recognised at the time as being far from conclusive and likely to vary annnually and seasonally, the divisions were accepted as the basis for the areas adopted by ICES in 1978 for the grouping of demersal fish biological data. More recently Adams (1987) suggested finer subdivisions of the North Sea based largely on depth contours, which Adams cites as the major underlying factor for differing physical conditions in distinct areas. This map of subdivisions (shown in Figure 5.6.2) is then used by Adams to provide a summary of the salient features of their plankton communities, with each subdivision being described in terms of its physical characteristics and hydrography, its phytoplankton and its zooplankton. Planktonic species can be referred to as neritic, intermediate or oceanic. Neritic species are those which are most abundant in the shallower waters of the continental shelf. Oceanic species are those which are more abundant in waters beyond the continental shelf, while intermediate species are those which are equally abundant in both areas.

In the Offshore Northern area depths range from 100 to 200 m. Oceanic North Atlantic water is

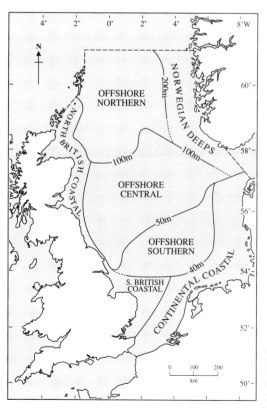

Figure 5.6.2
Subdivisions of the North Sea used by Adams (1987) for plankton studies.

directly and indirectly introduced to the area by currents flowing along the northern and eastern boundaries, and by the Fair Isle current flowing across the western and southern parts of the area. The water column is thermally stratified in the summer months. Neritic plankton species are relatively scarce, while intermediate species are abundant. In autumn a considerable number of oceanic species may be carried into the area; however, individual oceanic species are rarely found in large numbers.

The Offshore Central area is bounded by the general line of the 100 m and 50 m depth contours

in the north and south respectively, while in the west the boundary depth varies from 50 to 80 m. As for the Offshore Northern area, the water is of north Atlantic origin, although during the summer a marked thermocline develops and there is a modification by low salinity water. The plankton community is similar to that in the Offshore Northern area but neritic species are more numerous, particularly towards the east.

The Offshore Southern area can be considered as that lying between the 40 and 50 m depth contours, though the depth is considerably less than 40 m on the Dogger Bank and in excess of 50 m in parts of

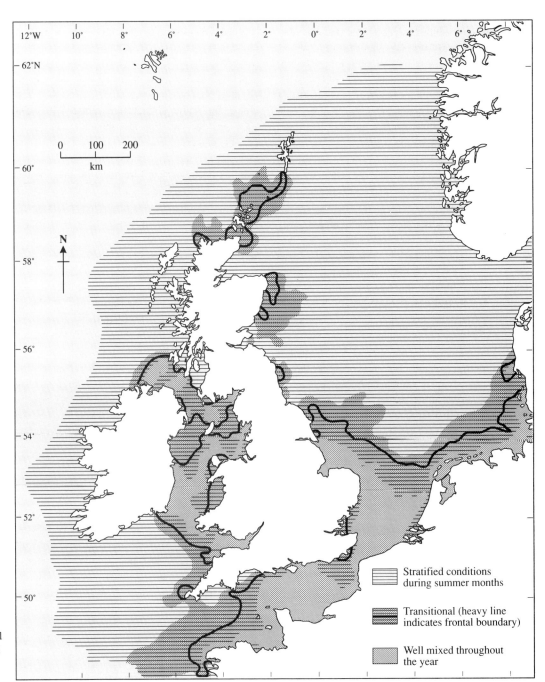

Figure 5.6.3
Predicted positions of frontal boundaries from a numerical model (from Pingree & Griffiths 1978).

Stratified conditions during summer months

Transitional (heavy line indicates frontal boundary)

Well mixed throughout the year

the southern and north-eastern regions. The north Atlantic water mass is a minor component of the mixed waters of the area and consequently the mean salinity is less than 35‰ throughout the year. Except over the Dogger Bank the water body is stratified during the summer, but this may be temporarily destroyed by summer storms. The plankton is characterised by southern intermediate and neritic species, and the northern boundary of the area has been shown to coincide with a line of demarcation between separate populations of the diatom *Rhizosolenia styliformis* (Lucas & Stubbings 1948; Robinson & Waller 1966).

The North British Coastal area is bounded by the 100 m depth contour north of 57°30'N. South of this latitude the boundary depth varies from 80 m to 50 m. Vertical stratification of the water column develops during the summer in areas where tidal currents are weakest, such as the middle of the Moray Firth and off the Firth of Forth, while off the north-east coasts of England and Scotland and east of Orkney fronts develop between vertically mixed and vertically stratified water bodies. This area is generally characterised by neritic plankton communities, but intermediate species are also abundant. Oceanic species arrive in the area in the autumn of some years.

Extending to a depth of 40 m, though generally less than 30 m, the South British Coastal area is well mixed throughout the year, though towards the boundary with the Offshore Southern area there occurs a transitional zone where waters may become stratified at neap tides or during periods of calm weather (Pingree & Griffiths 1978). The plankton is typically neritic although southern intermediate species are also present. In the autumn, a number of species more characteristic of the admixture of coastal and oceanic waters in the north-western North Sea arrive in the area.

In the English Channel, much less work has been undertaken to establish the different water masses present. However, it has been suggested that a body of well mixed water occurs in the central Channel, while a small area of the Channel west of the Straits of Dover and much of the western approaches are transitional between mixed and stratified (Pingree & Griffiths 1978). The position of fronts, stratified, transitional and mixed water bodies is shown in Figure 5.6.3.

DIVISIONS OF THE NORTH SEA – SEABED AND BENTHIC COMMUNITIES

The separation of the offshore areas of the North Sea into regions which are meaningful in relation to the distribution of physical conditions and communities of species associated with those conditions has been undertaken by several authors recently (Glémarec 1973; Dyer *et al.* 1983; Basford *et al.* 1989, 1990; Eleftheriou & Basford 1989; Künitzer 1990).

Maps illustrating the divisions in the North Sea proper according to these studies are shown in Figures 5.6.4, 5.6.5 and 5.6.6.

The definition of étages by Glémarec, based on water depth and thermal stability, is described below.
❖ **i Infralittoral étage.** In the infralittoral étage, variations in temperature exceed 10°C. This zone extends to a water depth of about 40 m north of the Dogger Bank, although to 60 m to the south of this bank. In the Channel, this étage is probably limited mainly to embayed areas or very close to the coast.
❖ **ii Coastal étage.** In the North Sea proper, Glémarec's coastal étage corresponds to a zone where the water temperature remains less than 12°C and the variation less than 5°C. This étage encompasses the greater part of the central North Sea north of the Dogger Bank to about 58°N, and extends north-west to circumscribe the Shetland Isles all within about the 100 m depth contour. In the Channel, the demarcation between this and the next étage lies along about the 70–80 m isobath which extends no further east than off Start Point.
❖ **iii Open sea étage.** In the North Sea proper this corresponds to areas where the water temperature is less than 10°C and is relatively constant. This roughly coincides with the region north of the 100 m isobath (and therefore with the offshore northern area of Adams 1987). In the Channel, this étage is south and west of the 70–80 m isobath.

The different types of benthic communities which have been recorded for these regions of the North Sea are described below. The text refers to non-British examples where it is likely that these communities occur in Britain, but no reference to their presence has been identified.
❖ **iv Infralittoral étage.** This étage is the shallow inshore area described in the previous section. However, it extends far offshore in the southern North Sea proper including areas off all of the coast of Europe. The *Abra alba* community occurs extensively in the southern and south-eastern North Sea. With an increased sand content of the sediment the *Abra alba* community gives way via transitional communities to species of the bivalve *Venus* communities. These have been widely recorded from the southern North Sea, particularly mainland Europe, occurring at depths of about 10–30 m. In the shallow water, sandy sediments of the western North Sea *Venus striatula* communities (usually

also *Fabulina fabula*-dominated) have been recorded off north-east England (Buchanan 1963; Atkins 1983; Rees 1983) and off the east coast of Scotland (Stephen 1933; McIntyre 1958; Hartley 1978). The Dogger Bank also mainly supports a form of *Venus striatula* community (Davis 1923, 1925; Ursin 1960). Here the community is commonly dominated by the bivalve *Spisula elliptica*. This variant of the community is associated with loose sand whereas the *Fabulina fabula*-dominated form is characteristic of hard sand bottoms (Thorson 1957).

In the infralittoral étage at water depths greater than about 15–20 m, and where there is a transition from sands to muddy sands, *Venus* communities give way to the brittle star *Amphiura filiformis* communities. *Amphiura* communities have been recorded from numerous locations off the coast of continental Europe and are very widespread. They have been described from the north-eastern coast of England by Buchanan (1963). *Amphiura filiformis* communities mainly occur on silty sands at depths of 30–70 m, and give way to *Amphiura chiajei*

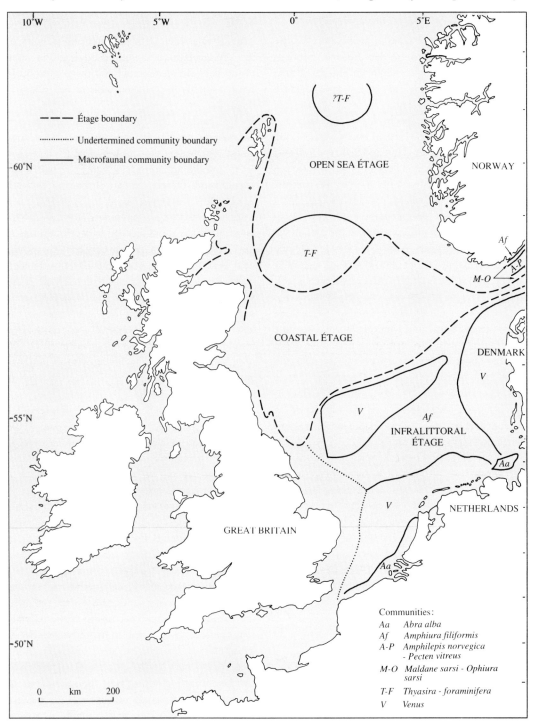

Figure 5.6.4
Subdivisions of the North Sea defined by Glémarec (1973).

communities on muds at 60–100 m. Off the north-east coast of England a *Haploops tubicola* community overlaps the *Amphiura filiformis* and *Amphiura chiajei* communities of the infralittoral and coastal étages (Buchanan 1963; Glémarec 1973).

Dyer *et al.* (1983) analysed the distribution of macrobenthic invertebrates taken during ground fish surveys of the North Sea. Grouping of southern species corresponded to Glémarec's (1973) infralittoral étage. Many of the species common in the south were also trawled in the north, though at much lower numbers (for example, the starfish *Asterias rubens* and *Astropecten irregularis*; the heart urchin *Echinocardium cordatum*, the sea mouse *Aphrodita aculeata* and the crab *Corystes cassivelaunus*). Only a few species were confined to the southern region (for example the sea urchin *Psammechinus miliaris;* see also Cranmer 1985) or concentrated in certain areas of the south (for example, *Ophiothrix fragilis* and *Alcyonidium gelatinosum,* which were common on the northern Dogger Bank).

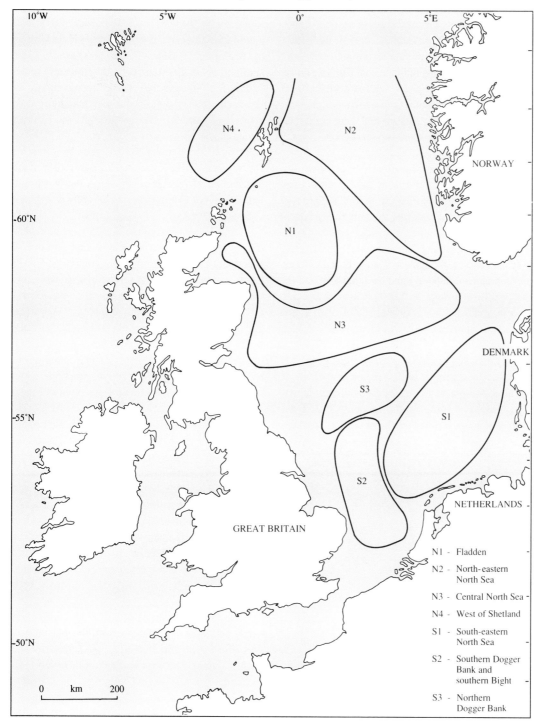

N1 - Fladden

N2 - North-eastern North Sea

N3 - Central North Sea

N4 - West of Shetland

S1 - South-eastern North Sea

S2 - Southern Dogger Bank and southern Bight

S3 - Northern Dogger Bank

Figure 5.6.5
Subdivisions of the North Sea defined by Dyer *et al.* 1983.

❖ **v Coastal étage**. This is the central North Sea where Kingston & Rachor (1982) point out that detailed benthic studies have been undertaken only in the vicinity of the Ekofisk oilfield. They suggest that the fauna of this region may be a variation of an *Amphiura filiformis* community. Glémarec (1973), however, regards this community as belonging to the infralittoral étage. Hartley (1982) also questions the widespread designation of the *Amphiura filiformis* communities by Kingston & Rachor (1982).

The *Amphiura chiajei* community (for example, as described by Buchanan 1963) does, however, clearly belong to the coastal étage (also identifiable as an offshore grouping from the work of Buchanan *et al.* 1978). Long-term studies around the north-east coast of England indicate that the *Amphiura chiajei* community occurs with a well-defined offshore mud meiofauna community which may prove to be a widely distributed community of muddy shelf sediments around northern Britain (Warwick & Buchanan 1970).

The work of Basford *et al.* (1989) describes the results of epifaunal surveys in an area extending from off the Firth of Forth north to off Shetland and therefore including samples in depths shallower than 100 m. Their groups which appear to fall within this étage are: 1 (characterised by Porifera), 2 (characterised by tunicates and the crustacean *Spirontocaris lilljeborgi*) and 3a (characterised by the hermit crab *Pagurus bernhardus* with species from the main group 3: the shrimp *Crangon allmani*, the urchin *Spatangus purpureus* and the mollusc *Colus gracilis*).

❖ **vi Open sea étage**. Kingston & Rachor (1982) have discussed benthic studies in this area which, at the time, comprised mainly localised surveys at two main groups of oilfields: the Magnus, Murchison Hutton and Brent fields north-east of the Shetland

Isles and the more southerly group of the Buchan, Forties and Maureen fields. Hartley (1982) concluded that there was then insufficient information available on the benthos of the northern North Sea to allow confident definitions of the different communities inhabiting different sediment types within the open sea étage. One community that has been identified is the boreal foraminifera community of Thorson (1957), described originally by Stephen (1923, 1933, 1934) from the deepest part of the North Sea. Hartley (1982) made a detailed study of this community (his *Thyasira-foraminifera* community) occurring on sandy mud in the vicinity of the Forties oilfield, and a similar fauna was recorded from the Fladden Ground by McIntyre (1961). The fauna shows a basic similarity from the Magnus field in the north to the Forties field in the south. The epifaunal survey by Dyer *et al.* (1983) suggests the open sea étage can be divided into at least two sub-groups: the Fladden Group and the north-east region. Observations on the epifauna of the Fladden Ground are also given by Hartwig *et al.* (1983). Cranmer's (1985) study of the distribution of regular echinoids in the North Sea indicates that *Echinus acutus* is a widely distributed species of this étage.

The work of Basford *et al.* (1989) includes areas deeper than 100 m in their epifaunal surveys. It seems that groups occuring within this étage are: 3b (characterised by the hermit crab *Pagurus pubescens* with species from the main group 3: the shrimp *Crangon allmani*, the urchin *Spatangus purpureus* and the mollusc *Colus gracilis*) and 4 (characterised by the sea pen *Pennatula phosphorea*).

The most recent studies of infaunal communities by Eleftheriou & Basford (1989) were undertaken in an area which coincides with the open sea étage of Glémarec and the 'zone deeper than 100 m to the north of 58°N' of Stephen (1933). The first paper (Basford *et al.* 1989) describes the results of epifaunal surveys in an area extending from off the Firth of Forth north to off Shetland. Indicator species analysis suggested five faunistic groupings and their distribution is illustrated in Figure 5.6.6.

❖ Group I. Occupies the Ling Bank at depths of less than 80 m with fine sand sediments characterised by the polychaetes *Ophelina neglecta* and *Travisia forbesii*, the crustaceans *Bathyporeia elegans* and *Eudorellopsis deformis* and the mollusc *Abra prismatica*.

❖ Group IIa. Found at 100–120 m with coarse sandy sediments characterised by the polychaetes *Hesionura elongata*, *Protodorvillea kefersteini* and *Protomystides bidentata* and the mollusc *Moerella pygmaea*.

❖ Group IIb. Found at 100–120 m with medium to very fine sand sediments characterised by the

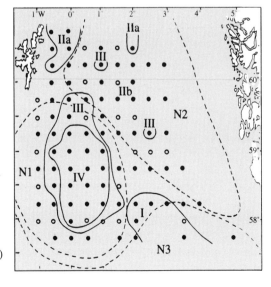

Figure 5.6.6
Four subgroupings (I-IV) of benthic infauna related to sediment type and depth for the northern North Sea, including subgroups (N1, N2 and N3 - broken lines) from Dyer *et al.* 1983 defined by Eleftheriou & Basford 1989. (The sampling stations analysed for macrofauna are indicated with a filled circle.)
© Crown Copyright.

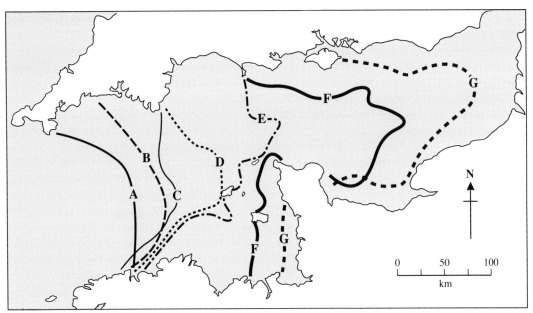

Figure 5.6.7
The eastern limits of selected
epifaunal species along the
Channel coast.
A: *Porella compressa.*
B: *Diphasia pinaster.*
C: *Thuiaria articulata.*
D: *Lafoea dumosa.*
E: *Caryophyllia smithii.*
F: *Sertularella gayi.*
G: *Rhynchozoon bispinosum.*
Redrawn from Cabioch *et al.* 1977.
Copyright Pergamon Press PLC.

polychaetes *Spiophanes kroyeri, Amphictene auricoma, Myriochele* sp. and *Aricidea wassi* and the amphipod *Harpinia antennaria.*

❖ Group III. Found at 120–140 m with very fine sandy sediment characterised by the ophiuroids *Amphiura filiformis* and *Amphiura chiajei*, the mollusc *Antalis entalis* and the cumacean *Brachydiastylis resima.*

❖ Group IV. The deepest stations at depths in excess of 140 m with mainly silty sediments characterised by the polychaetes *Lumbrineris fragilis* and *Levinsenia gracilis* and the amphipod *Eriopisa elongata.*

THE CHANNEL

Studies in the North Sea proper have centred around distributions of sediment communities perceived to be associated mainly with depth and thermal stability. In the Channel, the studies of Holme (1961, 1966) and Cabioch *et al.* (1977) have been interpreted mainly in a biogeographical context with limits of distribution plotted. Holme (1966) indicates several distribution patterns but concludes an eastern boundary for many species off Dorset. Eastern limits of distribution for epifaunal species shown by Cabioch *et al.* (1977) are illustrated in Figure 5.6.7. A major feature of offshore habitats in the Channel is the presence of areas of tide-swept hard substratum, usually cobbles and pebbles sometimes 'concreted' together by the tube worm *Sabellaria spinulosa*, and sometimes outcrops of bedrock. Holme & Wilson (1985) described the faunas of such areas at depths of 50–55 m 37 km off Dorset. Three types of epifauna are described:

Type A. Stable faunal assemblages with diverse sponge cover. The bryozoan *Pentapora foliacea* is also characteristic and a variety of coelenterates and ascidians are noted.

Type B. Present on hard surfaces of rock, cobbles or pebbles subject to sand scour/cover. A well-developed assemblage characterised by *Polycarpa violacea* but with two 'impoverished' assemblages; *Polycarpa violacea-Flustra foliacea*, and *Balanus-Pomatoceros triqueter.* Similar to assemblages in the western Channel described by Cabioch (1968) and known from depths of about 20 m off Selsey Bill to the east (K. Hiscock pers. comm.).

Type C. Cobble floor covered by sand. This includes species able to withstand the sand cover notably *Tealia felina, Flustra foliacea* and *Sabellaria spinulosa.*

Further work on offshore hard substrata is required and the conclusions of Cabioch (1968) for the seabed communities off Brittany provide a basis for comparison and classification of community types.

IMPACTS ON OFFSHORE HABITATS AND COMMUNITIES

This large water mass is subject to a wide variety of uses such as extraction of oil and gas, fishing, waste disposal and aggregate and maintenance dredging. All of these activities have some effect on the surrounding habitats and communities, though the effect may be localised or widespread.

The effect of beam trawling gear on the seabed has been studied by the Netherlands Institute for Sea Research (1990) and by Lindeboom (pers.

comm.). These studies show that in some of the more intensively fished areas the seabed may be trawled as many as five times per year, while most areas of the Dutch part of the North Sea are trawled at least once a year. Where heavy beam trawl gear is used this can have a major effect on the benthic communities. The impact of beam trawling has been examined experimentally (Hak & Blom 1990). This suggested that after trawling up to 50% of the heart urchins, starfish and certain polychaete worms disappeared, while 20% of the small crustaceans and molluscan shellfish were killed. Of the other animals actually caught in the net, between 80 and 100% of the starfish and hermit crabs survived; however 90% of the large bivalve *Arctica islandica*, a species which may live up to 120 years, were killed. For every kilogram of commercial fish landed, it has been estimated that between 2 and 4 kg of other dead fish are thrown overboard.

The changes caused to the receiving benthic community by sewage sludge dumping have been extensively studied by the Ministry of Agriculture, Fisheries and Food (for example, Norton & Rolfe 1978; Eagle *et al.* 1978; Eagle *et al.* 1978; Murray *et al.* 1980; Talbot *et al.* 1982). No evidence for gross effects on the receiving benthos has been found, though it is postulated (Talbot *et al.* 1982) that in the Thames estuary faunal density, diversity and probably production rates were elevated in areas where the organic content of the sediment was above average.

Oil spills from offshore exploration and production and longer term routine pollution from drilling activities can have a significant impact on the biology of the North Sea, although effects have been shown to decrease rapidly with distance from a point source of discharge. The effects of the oil and gas industry on the environment of the North Sea have been extensively dealt with in literature, and numerous reviews exist (for example Newman & Agg 1988; Royal Society 1987).

ACKNOWLEDGEMENTS

This chapter was written by Roger Covey and Keith Hiscock, Joint Nature Conservation Committee Marine Nature Conservation Review, with comments by Dr S. J. May, Field Studies Council Research Centre.

REFERENCES

ADAMS, J.A. 1987. The primary ecological divisions of the North Sea: some aspects of their plankton communities. *In: Developments in fisheries research in Scotland*, ed. by R.S. Bailey & B.B. Parrish. Farnham, Fishing News Books.

ANGLIAN WATER. 1984. *Preliminary survey of the inshore marine benthos in the vicinity of Great Yarmouth*. Norwich, Anglian Water.

ATKINS, S.M. 1983. Contrasts in benthic community structure off the North Yorkshire coast. *Oceanologica Acta, Proceedings 17th European Marine Biology Symposium, Brest, France, 27 September - 1 October 1982:* 7-10.

BALLANTINE, W.J. 1961. A biologically-defined exposure scale for the comparative description of rocky shores. *Field Studies, 1* (3): 1-19.

BAMBER, R.N., & COUGHLAN, J. 1980. *A survey of the marine benthos in the vicinity of Sizewell Power Station, June 1976*. Central Electricity Research Laboratories (report no. RD/L/N 40/80).

BARTROP, J., BISHOP, G., HARVEY, R., HOLME, N.A., KNIGHT, S.J.T., & POWELL, H.T. 1980. Survey of the littoral zone of the coast of Great Britain, 7. Report on the shores of the Moray Firth. Contractor: Scottish Marine Biological Association/Marine Biological Association, Intertidal Survey Unit. *Nature Conservancy Council, CSD Report*, No. 308.

BASFORD, D.J., ELEFTHERIOU, A., & RAFFAELLI, D. 1989. The epifauna of the northern North Sea (56°-61°N). *Journal of the Marine Biological Association of the United Kingdom, 69*: 387-408.

BASFORD, D.J., ELEFTHERIOU, A., & RAFFAELLI, D. 1990. The infauna of the northern North Sea. *Netherlands Journal of Sea Research, 25*: 165-173.

BENNETT, T.L. 1989. Littoral and sublittoral survey of the Isle of May, Fife. *Nature Conservancy Council (Marine Nature Conservation Review, Report MNCR/SR/002/89), CSD Report*, No. 907.

BENNETT, T.L. 1991. Benthic marine ecosystems in Great Britain: a review of current knowledge. Orkney, north Scotland, east Scotland and north-east England (MNCR coastal sectors 2 to 5). *Nature Conservancy Council, Marine Conservation Review, Report MNCR/OR/007), CSD Report*, No. 1171.

BISHOP, G.M., & HOLME, N.A. 1980. Survey of the littoral zone of the coast of Great Britain. Final report part 1: The sediment shores - an assessment of their conservation value. Contractor: Scottish Marine Biological Association/Marine Biological Association, Intertidal survey Unit. *Nature Conservancy Council, CSD Report*, No. 326.

BRAZIER, P., & MURRAY, E. 1993. A littoral survey of the estuaries of north-east England and south-east Scotland. *Joint Nature Conservation Committee, JNCC Report. Marine Nature Conservation Review*.

BRIGGS, J.C. 1970. Faunal history of the North Atlantic Ocean. *Systematic Zoology, 19*: 19-34.

BRYAN, G.W., GIBBS, P.E., HUMMERSTONE, L.G., & BURT, G.R. 1987. Copper, zinc and organotin as long term factors governing the distribution of organisms in the Fal Estuary, south-west England. *Estuaries 10*: 208-219.

BUCHANAN, J.B. 1963. The bottom fauna communities and their sediment relationships off the coast of Northumberland. *Oikos, 14*: 154-175.

BUCHANAN, J.B., SHEADER, M., & KINGSTON, P.F. 1978. Sources of variability in the benthic macrofauna off the south Northumberland coast. *Journal of the Marine Biological Association of the United Kingdom, 58*: 191-210.

BULLIMORE, B. 1985. *An investigation into the effects of scallop dredging within the Skomer marine reserve.* A report to the Nature Conservancy Council by the Skomer Marine Reserve Subtidal Monitoring Project. Peterborough, Nature Conservancy Council.

CABIOCH, L. 1968. Contribution à la connaissance des peuplements benthiques de la Mancheoccidentale. *Cahiers de Biologie Marine, 9*: 493-720.

CABIOCH, L., GENTIL, F., GLACON, R., & RETIERE, C. 1977. Le macrobenthos des fonds meubles de la Manche: distribution générale et écologie. *In: Biology of Benthic Organisms*, ed. by B.F. Keegan, P.O Céidigh & P.J.S.Boaden, 115-128. Oxford, Pergamon Press.

CONNOR, D.W. 1989. Marine biological survey of Berwick to Beadnell including the Farne Islands. *Nature Conservancy Council, Marine Nature Conservation Review, Report No. MNCR/SR/001/89), CSD Report*, No. 902.

COOK, W. 1990. Studies on the effects of hydraulic suction dredging on cockle and macrobenthic populations at Traeth Lafan. First Summary report, May 1990. North Western and North Wales Sea Fisheries Committee, Lancaster.

COVEY, R. 1991. Benthic marine ecosystems in Great Britain: a review of current knowledge. Eastern England and Eastern Channel (MNCR coastal sectors 6 and 7). *Nature Conservancy Council (Marine Nature Conservation Review, Report MNCR/OR/008), CSD Report*, No. 1172.

CRANMER, G.J. 1985. Recent investigations into the distribution of regular echinoids in the North Sea. *Journal of the Marine Biological Association of the United Kingdom, 65*: 351-357.

CRESSARD, A. 1975. The effect of offshore sand and gravel mining on the marine environment. *Terra et Aqua, 8/9*, 24-33.

DAVIES, J. 1991. Benthic marine ecosystems in Great Britain: a review of current knowledge. Western Channel and Bristol Channel and approaches (MNCR coastal sectors 8 and 9). *Nature Conservancy Council (Marine Nature Conservation Review, Report MNCR/OR/009), CSD Report*, No. 1173.

DAVIES, J. 1993. Littoral and sublittoral survey of the south-east Scotland coastline from Dunbar to Burnmouth. *Joint Nature Conservation Committee, JNCC Report. Marine Nature Conservation Review.*

DAVIS, F.M. 1923. Quantitative studies on the fauna of the sea bottom: I. Preliminary investigations of the Dogger Bank. *Ministry of Agriculture and Fisheries, Fish Investigations, Series II,* vol. vi, No. 2, London.

DAVIS, F.M. 1925. Quantitative studies on the fauna of the sea bottom: II. Results of quantitative investigations in the southern North Sea, 1921-24. *Ministry of Agriculture, and Fisheries, Fish investigations, Series II,* vol. viii, No. 4, London.

DE GROOT, S.J. 1979. The potential environmental impact of marine gravel extraction in the North Sea. *Ocean Management, 5*, 233-249.

DE GROOT, S.J. 1986. Marine sand and gravel extraction in the North Atlantic and its potential environmental impact, with emphasis on the North Sea. *Ocean Management, 10*, 21-36.

DICKS, B., & LEVELL, D. 1989. Refinery-effluent discharges into Milford Haven and Southampton Water. *In: Ecological impacts of the oil industry*, ed. by B. Dicks, 287-316. Chichester, John Wiley & Sons.

DIPPER, F.A., IRVING, R.A., & FOWLER, S.L. 1989. Sublittoral survey of the Wash by diving and dredging. *Nature Conservancy Council, CSD Report*, No. 976.

DIXON, I.M.T. 1986. Surveys of harbours, rias and estuaries in southern Britain. The Exe. Contractor: Oil Pollution Research Unit, Pembroke, Dyfed. *Nature Conservancy Council, CSD Report*, No. 670.

DIXON, I.M.T. 1988. Surveys of harbours, rias and estuaries in southern Britain, Christchurch Harbour. Contractor: Oil Pollution Research Unit, Pembroke, Dyfed. *Nature Conservancy Council, CSD Report*, No. 815.

DIXON, I.M.T., & MOORE, J. 1987. Surveys of harbours, rias and estuaries in southern Britain: The Solent System. Contractor: Oil Pollution Research Unit, Pembroke, Dyfed. *Nature Conservancy Council, CSD Report*, No. 723.

DYER, M.F., FRY, W.G., FRY, P.D., & CRANMER G.J. 1983. Benthic regions within the North Sea. *Journal of the Marine Biological Association of the United Kingdom, 63*: 683-693.

EAGLE, R.A., HARDIMAN, P.A., NORTON, M.G., & NUNNY, R.S. 1978. The field assessment of dumping wastes at sea: 3. A survey of the sewage sludge disposal area in Lyme Bay. *Ministry of Agriculture, Fisheries and Food, Directorate of Fisheries Research Technical Report*, No. 49.

EAGLE, R.A., HARDIMAN, P.A., NORTON, M.G., NUNNY, R.S., & ROLFE, M.S. 1979. The field assessment of effects of dumping wastes at sea. 5. Disposal of solid wastes off the North East coast of England. *Ministry of Agriculture, Fisheries and Food Directorate of Fisheries Research, Lowestoft. Fisheries Research Technical Report*, No. 51.

EAGLE, R.A., NORTON, M.G., NUNNY, R.S., & ROLFE, M.S. 1978. The field assessment of effects of dumping waste at sea: 2. Methods. *Ministry of Agriculture,*

Fisheries and Food, Directorate of Fisheries Research, Fisheries Research Technical Report, No. 47.

EARLL, R.C. 1981. The sublittoral ecology of the St Abb's area, Berwickshire. Contractor: Underwater Conservation Society. Nature Conservancy Council, CSD Report, No. 411.

EARLL, R.C. 1982. The sublittoral ecology of the St Abb's area, Berwickshire. Contractor: Underwater Conservation Society. Nature Conservancy Council, CSD Report, No. 468.

EARLL, R.C. 1983. Shallow sublittoral ecosystems in the Moray Firth. Contractor: Underwater Conservation Society. Nature Conservancy Council.

ELEFTHERIOU, A., & BASFORD, D.J. 1989. The macrobenthic infauna of the offshore Northern North Sea. Journal of the Marine Biological Association of the United Kingdom, 69: 123-143.

ELEFTHERIOU, A., & MCINTYRE, A.D. 1976. The intertidal fauna of sandy beaches - a survey of the Scottish coast. Department of Agriculture and Fisheries for Scotland. (Scottish Fisheries research report, No. 6.).

ELLIOTT, M., & KINGSTON, P.F. 1987. The sublittoral benthic fauna of the Firth of Forth, Scotland. In: The natural environment of the estuary and Firth of Forth, ed. by D.S. McLusky. Proceedings of the Royal Society of Edinburgh. Series B: Biological sciences, 93 (3/4): 449-466.

FORBES, E., & GOODWIN-AUSTIN, R. 1859. The natural history of the European Seas. London, Van Voorst.

FORD, E. 1923. Animal communities of the level sea bottom in the waters adjacent to Plymouth. Journal of the Marine Biological Association of the United Kingdom, 13: 164-224.

FOSTER-SMITH, J. 1983. A preliminary marine survey of The Haven at Newtown-by-the-sea, Northumberland. London, British Ecological Society.

FOSTER-SMITH, R.L. 1989. A survey of boulder habitats on the Northumberland coast, with a discussion on survey methods for boulder habitats. Contractor: R.L. Foster-Smith. Nature Conservancy Council, CSD Report, No. 921.

FOSTER-SMITH, R.L., & FOSTER-SMITH, J. 1987. A marine biological survey of Beadnell to Dunstanburgh Castle, Northumberland. Contractor: R.L. Foster-Smith & J.L. Foster-Smith. Nature Conservancy Council, CSD Report, No. 798.

FOWLER, S.L. 1989. Nature conservation implications of damage to the seabed and benthic organisms by commercial fishing operations. Nature Conservancy Council, CSD Contract Report, No. 79. Peterborough.

FOWLER, S.L. 1992. Survey of bait collection in Britain. Joint Nature Conservation Committee Report, No. 107. Peterborough.

FOWLER, S.L., & TITTLEY, I. in prep. The marine nature conservation interest of British coastal chalk cliff habitats. English Nature Research Series.

FRID, C. 1989. Surveys of harbours, rias and estuaries in southern Britain: the Teign Estuary. Contractor: Field Studies Council Research Centre. Nature Conservancy Council, CSD Report, No. 920.

GLÉMAREC, M. 1973. The benthic communities of the European North Atlantic continental shelf. Oceanography and Marine Biology, Annual Review, 11: 263-289.

HAK, W. VAN DER, & BLOM, W.C. 1990. Cruise reports experiments on the interaction fishing gear (beamtrawl) - benthos with a commercial beam trawler, 21 August - 1 September 1989. Beleidsgericht Ecologisch Onderzoek Rapport, 8: 23-31.

HALL, S., BASFORD, D.J., & ROBERTSON, M.R. 1990. The impact of hydraulic dredging for razor clams Ensis sp. on an infaunal community. Neth. J. Sea Res. 27.

HARTLEY, J. 1978. Survey of the macrobenthos of the Beatrice field in the Moray Firth. In: Annual Report 1977-78. Field Studies Council, Oil Pollution Research Unit, Pembroke, Dyfed, 27-29.

HARTLEY, J. 1982. Benthic studies in two North Sea oilfields. PhD Thesis. University College of Wales, Swansea.

HARTWIG, E., FAUBEL, A., & THIEL, H. 1983. On the ecology of the benthos of sublittoral sediments, Fladen Ground, North Sea II. Quantitative studies on macrobenthic assemblages. Meteor Forschungsergebnisse, D 36: 49-64.

HILL, T.O., & EMBLOW, C.S. in prep. Marine biological surveys of estuaries in south-east England. Joint Nature Conservation Committee Report, No. 149 (Marine Nature Conservation Review Report, No. MNCR/SR/23).

HISCOCK, K. 1990. Marine Nature Conservation Review: Methods. Marine Nature Conservation Review, Report (MNCR/OR/05). Nature Conservancy Council, CSD Report, No. 1072.

HISCOCK, K. 1991. Benthic marine ecosystems in Great Britain: a review of current knowledge. Introduction and Atlantic - European perspective. Nature Conservancy Council (Marine Nature Conservation Review, Report MNCR/OR/006), CSD Report, No. 1170.

HISCOCK, K., & JOHNSTON, C.M. 1990. Review of marine biological information for Shetland. Nature Conservancy Council (Marine Nature Conservation Review, Report MNCR/OR/001/89), CSD Report, No. 1000.

HISCOCK, K., & MITCHELL, R. 1980. The description and classification of sublittoral epibenthic ecosystems. In: The Shore environment, Vol. 2: Ecosystems, ed. by J.H. Price, D.E.G. Irvine & W.F. Farnham, 323-370. London, Academic Press.

HISCOCK, K., & MOORE, J. 1986. Surveys of harbours, rias and estuaries in southern Britain: Plymouth area including the Yealm. Contractor: Oil Pollution Research Unit, Pembroke, Dyfed. Nature Conservancy Council, CSD Report, No. 752.

HOARE, R., & HISCOCK, K. 1974. An ecological survey of the rocky coast adjacent to a bromine extraction works. *Estuarine & Coastal Marine Science,* *2*: 329-348.

HOLME, N.A. 1949. The fauna of sand and mud banks near the mouth of the Exe estuary. *Journal of the Marine Biological Association of the United Kingdom,* *28*: 189-237.

HOLME, N.A. 1961. The bottom fauna of the English Channel. *Journal of the Marine Biological Association of the United Kingdom, 41*: 397-461.

HOLME, N.A. 1966. The bottom fauna of the English Channel. II. *Journal of the Marine Biological Association of the United Kingdom, 41*: 401-493.

HOLME, N.A., & BISHOP, G.M. 1980. Survey of the littoral zone of the coast of Great Britain, 5. Report of the sediment shores of Dorset, Hampshire and the Isle of Wight. Contractor: Scottish Marine Biological Association/ Marine Biological Association, Intertidal Survey Unit. *Nature Conservancy Council. CSD Report*, No. 280.

HOLME, N.A., & PROBERT, P.K. 1978. Disposal of solid waste in the marine environment with particular reference to the china clay industry. *In: Environmental management of mineral wastes*, ed. by Goodman, G.T., & Chadwick, M.J., Netherlands, Alphen aan den Rijn, Sijthoff and Noordhoff.

HOLME, N.A., & WILSON, J.B. 1985. Faunas associated with longitudinal furrows and sand ribbons in a tide-swept area in the English Channel. *Journal of the Marine Biological Association of the United Kingdom, 65*: 1051-1972.

HOLT, R.H.L. 1993. Littoral and sublittoral survey of the Northumberland coast: Berwick on Tweed to Craster. *Joint Nature Conservation Committee, JNCC Report. Marine Nature Conservation Review.*

HOLT, R., FISHER, E., & GRAHAM, C. 1990. Coastal resources of the Irish Sea. 2.1. Coastal classification and description. *In: The Irish Sea – an environmental review. Part 1: Nature Conservation,* ed. by Irish Sea Study Group, 5-37. Liverpool, Liverpool University Press for Irish Sea Study Group.

HOVLAND, M., & JUDD, A.G. 1988. *Seabed Pockmarks and seepages.* London, Graham & Trotman.

HOWARD, S., & MOORE, J. 1989. Surveys of harbours, rias and estuaries in southern Britain, Poole Harbour. Contractor: Oil Pollution Research Unit, Pembroke, Dyfed. *Nature Conservancy Council, CSD Report,* No. 896.

HOWARD, S., HOWSON, C., & MOORE, J. 1988. Surveys of harbours, rias and estuaries in southern Britain: Portland and Weymouth Harbours. Contractor: Oil Pollution Research Unit, Pembroke, Dyfed. *Nature Conservancy Council, CSD Report,* No. 851.

HOWARD, S., MOORE, J., & DIXON, I.M.T. 1988. Surveys of harbours, rias and estuaries in southern Britain: Newtown and Bembridge Harbours. Contractor: Oil Pollution Research Unit, Pembroke, Dyfed. *Nature Conservancy Council, CSD Report,* No. 852.

ICES. 1983. Flushing times of the North Sea. *Cooperative Research Report (International Council for the Exploration of the Sea) 123*: 1-759.

JEFFREYS, J.G. 1869. Last report on dredging among the Shetland Isles. *British Association, Report for 1868,* 232-247.

JONES, A.M. 1975a. *A littoral survey of the Kyles of Durness, Sutherland.* Dundee, The University of Dundee, Department of Biological Sciences.

JONES, A.M. 1975b. *A littoral survey of the Loch Eriboll Area, Sutherland.* Dundee, The University of Dundee, Department of Biological Sciences.

JONES, A.M. 1975c. The Marine environment of Orkney. *In: The natural environment of Orkney,* ed. by R. Goodier, 85-94. Edinburgh, Nature Conservancy Council.

JONES, A.M., PAYNE, C., SIMPSON, J.A., ATKINS, S.M., & NOBLE, S. 1988. A survey of the infaunal benthos of Scapa Flow. (Contractor: University of Dundee, Environmental Advisory Unit.) *Nature Conservancy Council, CSD Report,* No. 855.

JONES, A.M., SIMPSON, J.A., JONES, Y.M., & BAXTER, J.M. 1979. Fourth report of the Orkney Marine Biology Unit (December 1977 to December 1978). A report by the Orkney Marine Biology Unit to the Orkney Islands Council.

JONES, D.J. 1973. Variation in the trophic structure and species composition of some invertebrate communities in polluted kelp forests in the North Sea. *Marine Biology, 20*: 351-365.

JONES, N.S. 1950. Marine bottom communities. *Biological Reviews, 25*: 283-313.

JONES, R. 1972. The subdivisions of demersal stocks within the North Sea. *International Council for the Exploration of the Sea. CM 1972/F:13,* 7.

KHAYRALLAH, N., & JONES, A.M. 1975. A survey of the benthos of the Tay estuary. *Proceedings of the Royal Society of Edinburgh, 75B*: 113-135.

KINGSTON, P.F., & RACHOR, E. 1982. North Sea level bottom communities. *International Council for the Exploration of the Sea, C.M.1982/L:41,* Biological Oceanography Committee.

KÜNITZER, A. 1990. The benthic infauna of the North Sea: species distribution and assemblages. *International Council for the exploration of the sea. C.M. 1990/ Mini:2.*

LEE, A.J., & RAMSTER, W.J. 1981. *Atlas of the seas around the British Isles.* Ministry of Agriculture, Fisheries and Food, Directorate of Fisheries Research. Fisheries Research Technical Report, No. 20. Lowestoft, MAFF.

LEWIS, J.R. 1964. *The ecology of rocky shores.* London, The English Universities Press.

LITTLE, A.E. 1987. Salcombe and Kingsbridge Estuary. Assessment of extent and effects of spoil dumping. Contractor: Oil Pollution Research Unit, Pembroke, Dyfed. *Nature Conservancy Council, CSD Report,* No. 819.

LOCKWOOD, S.J. 1989. *Mackerel: its biology, assessment and the management of a fishery.* Farnham, Fishing News Books.

LUCAS, C.E., & STUBBINGS, H.G. 1948. Continuous plankton records: size variations in diatoms and their ecological significance. *Hull Bulletins of Marine Ecology, 2*: 133-171.

MACER, C.T., & EASEY, M.W. 1988. *The North Sea cod and the English fishery.* Ministry of Agriculture, Fisheries and Food. Directorate of Fisheries Research. Laboratory Leaflet 61. Lowestoft, MAFF.

MCINTYRE, A.D. 1958. The ecology of Scottish inshore fishing grounds. 1. The bottom fauna of east coast grounds. *Marine Research,* No. 1.

MCINTYRE, A.D. 1961. Quantitative differences in the fauna of boreal mud associations. *Journal of the Marine Biological Association of the United Kingdom, 41*: 599-616.

MILLS, D. 1989. *Ecology and management of Atlantic salmon.* London, Chapman & Hall.

MITCHELL, R. 1987. *Conservation of marine benthic biocenoses in the North Sea and Baltic.* Council of Europe. (*Nature and Environment series No. 37,* Strasbourg).

MOORE, D. C., & DAVIES, I.M. 1987. Monitoring the effects of the disposal at sea of Lothian Region sewage sludge. *Proceedings of the Royal Society of Edinburgh, 93B*: 467-477.

MOORE, J. 1988a. Surveys of harbours, rias and estuaries in southern Britain: Avon and Erme estuaries. Contractor: Oil Pollution Research Unit, Pembroke, Dyfed. *Nature Conservancy Council, CSD Report,* No. 854.

MOORE, J. 1988b. Surveys of harbours, rias and estuaries in southern Britain: Dart estuary including the Range. Contractor: Oil Pollution Research Unit, Pembroke, Dyfed. *Nature Conservancy Council, CSD Report,* No. 818.

MOORE, J. 1991. Studies on the impacts of hydraulic suction dredging on intertidal sediment flat communities, final report to the Nature Conservancy Council from the Field Studies Council.

MOORE, P.G. 1973. The kelp fauna of north-east Britain. II. Multivariate classification: turbidity as an ecological factor. *Journal of Experimental Marine Biology and Ecology, 13*: 127-163.

MORTON, J.E. 1954. The crevice faunas of the upper intertidal zone at Wembury. *Journal of the Marine Biological Association of the United Kingdom, 33*: 187-224.

MOSS, D. 1986. Report of a sublittoral survey of Loch Eriboll (Sutherland). Contractor: Mathematics Department, University of Manchester. *Nature Conservancy Council, CSD Report,* No. 697.

MURRAY, L.A., NORTON, M.G., NUNNY,R.S., & ROLFE, M.S. 1980. The field assessment of dumping wastes at sea: 6. The disposal of sewage sludge and industrial waste off the River Humber. *Ministry of Agriculture, Fisheries and Food, Directorate of Fisheries Research, Fisheries Research Technical Report,* No. 55.

NETHERLANDS INSTITUTE FOR SEA RESEARCH 1990. *Effects of Beamtrawl fishery on the bottom fauna in the North Sea.* Gravenhage, Policy Linked ecological research North Sea and Wadden Sea (BEON).

NEWMAN, P.J., & AGG, A.R. *eds.* 1988. *Environmental protection of the North Sea.* Oxford, Heinemann Professional Publishing.

NICHOLS, J.H., & BRANDER, K.M. 1989. Herring larval studies in the west-central North Sea. *Rapp. P.-v. Reun. Cons. int. Explor. Mer. 191*: 160-168.

NICHOLS, J.H., & THOMPSON, B.M. 1988. Quantitative sampling of crustacean larvae and its use in stock size estimation of commercially exploited species. *Symposium of the Zoological Society of London, 59*: 157-175.

NORTON, M.G., EAGLE, R.A., NUNNY, R.S., ROLFE, M.S., HARDIMAN, P.A., & HAMPSON, B.L. 1981. The field assessment of effects of dumping wastes at sea: 8. Sewage sludge dumping in the outer Thames estuary. *Ministry of Agriculture, Fisheries and Food, Directorate of Fisheries Research, Fisheries Research Technical Report,* No. 62.

NORTON, M.G., & ROLFE, M.S. 1978. The field assessment of effects of dumping wastes at sea: 1. An introduction. *Ministry of Agriculture, Fisheries and Food, Directorate of Fisheries Research, Fisheries Research Technical Report,* No. 45.

NORTON, T.A. *ed.* 1985. *Provisional atlas of the marine algae of Britain and Ireland.* Huntingdon, Institute of Terrestrial Ecology and Peterborough, Nature Conservancy Council.

OLIVE, P. 1984. A survey of the littoral infauna at Newtown-on-sea: its scientific and educational value and the likely effect of unrestricted bait-digging. Contractor: Dove Marine Laboratory. *Nature Conservancy Council, CSD Report,* No. 533.

PAGETT, R. 1983. The sublittoral ecology of the St Abb's area, Berwickshire (III). Contractor: Marine Conservation Society. *Nature Conservancy Council, CSD Report,* No. 512.

PEARSON, T.H., & ELEFTHERIOU, A. 1981. The benthic ecology of Sullom Voe. *Proceedings of the Royal Society of Edinburgh, 80B*: 241-270.

PERKINS, E.J. 1988. The impact of suction dredging upon the population of cockles in Auchencairn Bay. *Report to NCC South-west Scotland Region.* Edinburgh, Nature Conservancy Council.

PETERSEN, C.G. 1914. Valuation of the sea. II. The animal communities of the sea bottom and their importance for marine zoogeography. *Danish Biological Station Report, 21,* and Appendix.

PETERSEN, C.G. 1915. On the animal communities of the sea bottom in the Skagerrack, the Christiania Fjord and the Danish waters. *Danish Biological Station Report, 23*: 3-28.

PETERSEN, C.G. 1918. The sea bottom and its production of fish food. A survey of work done in connection with the valuation of the Danish Waters from 1883-1917. *Danish Biological Station Report*, 25.

PINGREE, R.D., & GRIFFITHS, D.K. 1978. Tidal fronts on the shelf areas around the British Isles. *Journal of Geophysical Research, 83*: 4615-4622.

POWELL, H.T., HOLME, N.A., KNIGHT, S.J.T., & HARVEY, R. 1978. Survey of the littoral zone of the coast of Great Britain: report of the shores of Devon and Cornwall. Contractor: Scottish Marine Biological Association/Marine Biological Association, Intertidal Survey Unit. *Nature Conservancy Council, CSD Report*, No. 209.

PROBERT, P.K. 1981. Report on the shores of Lincolnshire and East Anglia. A biological survey of the littoral zone. Peterborough, *Nature Conservancy Council*.

RANKINE, P.W. 1986. Herring spawning grounds around the Scottish coast. *International Council for the exploration of the sea. Pelagic Fish Committee paper CM 1986/H:15*.

REES, H.L. 1983. Pollution investigations off the north-east coast of England: community structure, growth and production of benthic macrofauna. *Marine Environmental Research. 9*: 61-110.

REES, H.L., BARNET, B.E., & URQUHART, C. 1982. Chapter 5. Biological surveillance. *In: The quality of the Humber estuary, 1961-1981*, ed. by A.L.H. Gameson, 34-50. Yorkshire Water Authority for the Humber Estuary Committee.

ROBINSON, G.A., & WALLER, D.R. 1966. The distribution of *Rhizosolenia styliformis* Brightwell and its varieties. *In: Some contemporary studies in marine science*, ed. by H. Barnes. London, Allen and Unwin, 645-633.

ROSTRON, D. 1985. Surveys of harbours, rias and estuaries in southern Britain: Falmouth. Contractor: Oil Pollution Research Unit, Pembroke, Dyfed. *Nature Conservancy Council, CSD Report*, No. 623.

ROYAL SOCIETY. 1987. *Environmental effects of North Sea oil and gas developments*. London, The Royal Society.

SEAWARD, D.R. ed. 1982. Sea area atlas for the Marine Molluscs of Britain and Ireland. *Nature Conservancy Council for the British Conchological Society. CSD Report*, No. 412.

SOUTHWARD, A.J. 1976. On the taxonomic status and distribution of *Chthamalus stellatus* (Cirripedia) in the north-east Atlantic region: with a key to common intertidal barnacles of Britain. *Journal of the Marine Biological Association of the United Kingdom, 56*: 1007-1028.

SPOONER, G.M., & HOLME, N.A. 1961. Bottom fauna off the Dorset coast. *Proceedings of the Dorset Natural History and Archaeological Society, 82*: 77-82.

STEPHEN, A.C. 1923. *Preliminary survey of the Scottish Waters of the North Sea by the Petersen Grab*. Edinburgh, Fisheries Board for Scotland, Scientific Investigations, 1922, No. 3, 1-21.

STEPHEN, A.C. 1933. Studies on the Scottish marine fauna: quantitative distribution of the echinoderms and the natural faunistic divisions of the North Sea. *Royal Society of Edinburgh. Transactions, 57* (3): 777-787.

TALBOT, J.W., HARVEY, B.R., EAGLE, R.A., & ROLFE, M.S. 1982. The field assessment of dumping wastes at sea: 9. Dispersal and effects of sewage sludge dumped into the Thames estuary. *Ministry of Agriculture, Fisheries and Food, Directorate of Fisheries Research, Fisheries Research Technical Report*, No. 63.

THORSON, G. 1957. Bottom communities (sublittoral or shallow shelf). *Memoirs of the Geological Society of America, 67* (1): 461-534.

TITTLEY, I. 1985. *Chalk cliff algal communities of Kent and Sussex, South-east England*. Contractor: Department of Botany, British Museum (Natural History). Peterborough, Nature Conservancy Council (South-east Region).

TITTLEY, I. 1986. *A preliminary survey of the intertidal benthic marine algal communities between Shakespeare Cliff and Abbot's Cliff, Dover, Kent*. Contractor: Department of Botany, British Museum (Natural History). Peterborough, Nature Conservancy Council (South-east Region).

TITTLEY, I. 1988. Chalk cliff algal communities: 2. Outside south-eastern England. Contractor: Department of Botany, British Museum (Natural History). *Nature Conservancy Council, CSD report*, No. 878.

URSIN, E. 1960. A quantitative investigation of the echinoderm fauna of the central North Sea. *Meddelelser Fra Kommission for Danmarks Fiskeri- og Havundersogelser. New Scientist 2*(23): 1-204.

WARWICK, R.M., & BUCHANAN, J.B. 1970. The meiofauna off the coast of Northumberland. I. The structure of the nematode population. *Journal of the Marine Biological Association of the United Kingdom, 50*: 129-146.

WOOD, C. 1984. Sussex sublittoral survey. Selsey Bill to Beachy Head. Contractor: Marine Conservation Society. *Nature Conservancy Council, CSD Report*, No. 527.

WOOD, C. 1986. *Hastings sublittoral survey*. Contract report to Hastings Borough Council from the Marine Conservation Society.

WOOD, C. 1990. Seasearch survey of sandstone reefs off Eastbourne, East Sussex, June–July 1989. (Contractor: Marine Biological Consultants Ltd., Ross-on-Wye.) *Nature Conservancy Council, CSD Report*, No. 1145.

WOOD, C., & JONES, E. 1986. Seven Sisters marine surveys. Contractor: Marine Conservation Society. *Nature Conservancy Council, CSD Report*, No. 684.

WOOD, E. 1988. Flamborough Headland; sublittoral survey. Contractor: E. Wood. *Nature Conservancy Council and the Flamborough Headland Heritage Coast Project. CSD Report*, No. 832.

WOOD, E. 1989. Channel Tunnel site: sublittoral monitoring. Nature Conservancy Council, Chief Scientist Directorate report, No. 1001.

WOOD, E., & WOOD, C. 1986. Channel tunnel sublittoral survey. Contractor: Marine Conservation Society. *Nature Conservancy Council, CSD Report*, No. 674.

Chapter 6

FISHERIES IN THE NORTH SEA

6.1 FISHERIES MANAGEMENT

The North Sea is an important area for populations of a number of commercial fish species, providing spawning grounds and nursery and feeding areas for the fish. Consequently it is an area of considerable importance to the fishing fleets of all countries bordering the North Sea.

For the purpose of stock management, the North Sea, as defined by the International Council for the Exploration of the Sea (ICES), extends from 4°W to the north of Scotland to 51°N at the Straits of Dover. Elsewhere in this directory the limit of 5°W is used as defining the extent of the North Sea both in the north and the south. The relevant area under discussion in this section is ICES subarea IV; this is shown along with other ICES areas on Figure 6.1.1.

Management responsibility for North Sea fisheries is undertaken either by the European Community (EC) and Norway, acting jointly on shared stocks, or by the EC acting alone on exclusive stocks. This extends from the low water mark. The Common Fisheries Policy, which controls fishing within the EC zone, came into effect in 1983. It was subject to a limited mid-term review of access arrangements in 1992 and a thorough review is planned for 2002. Under this policy, Britain has declared an area up to 12 nautical miles from the coast within which fishing is restricted to British boats and, in some areas, vessels from other EC countries with traditional rights (Territorial Sea Act 1987). This is to protect the interests of local fishermen. Outside the coastal margin, all EC member countries in general have equal access to the Exclusive Fishing Zone (EFZ), whereas non-member countries are only allowed to fish by agreement. Certain areas along the British coastline are also subject to restrictions on the types of fishing allowed, normally to protect important spawning or nursery areas, and there are general rules on the amount of fish that can be landed and the minimum size of nets.

The International Council for Exploration of the Sea is the body that provides scientific advice on the management of all the important commercial species of fin fish and some shellfish in the North Sea. Each year working groups report to ICES on the state of stocks in all areas of the north-east Atlantic. This work is summarised in the annual report of the Advisory Committee on Fishery Management (ACFM) which is responsible for providing advice on total allowable catches (TACs) and other conservation measures. The TACs and catch quotas themselves are decided by the Council of Ministers on the basis of this advice after negotiation with Norway on shared stocks; the ACFM advise.

In Britain, the Scottish Office Agriculture and Fisheries Department (SOAFD, formerly Department of Agriculture and Fisheries for Scotland, DAFS) and the Ministry of Agriculture, Fisheries and Food (MAFF) are responsible for collecting and collating information on North Sea fish stocks. The work involves three approaches:

i)   Routine monitoring of commercial landings at the main ports, in order to estimate the total number, weight and size composition of fish and shellfish caught each year. This is supported in some cases by estimates of discarding.

ii) Regular surveys of various kinds (see below).

iii) Stock assessments and research investigations carried out using data from i and ii in order to provide the basis for management advice, nationally and through ICES.

Examples of important surveys are given below.

❖ Routine groundfish surveys, which cover a large part of the North Sea, have been carried out by SOAFD and MAFF in August during the last decade (DAFS started in 1982) and provide an annual index of abundance and information on the distribution of all species and size groups of demersal fish.

❖ The International Young Fish Surveys commenced in 1970 and were carried out in February under the coordination of ICES. From 1991 onwards this same survey is carried out within the International Bottom Trawl Survey. In addition, IBTS surveys are carried out at other times of the year. This provides information on the distribution

Figure 6.1.1
The North Sea as defined by the International Council for Exploration of the Sea (ICES). (Note that this lies within the 5°W boundary used in this directory and for the rest of the fishery sections.)

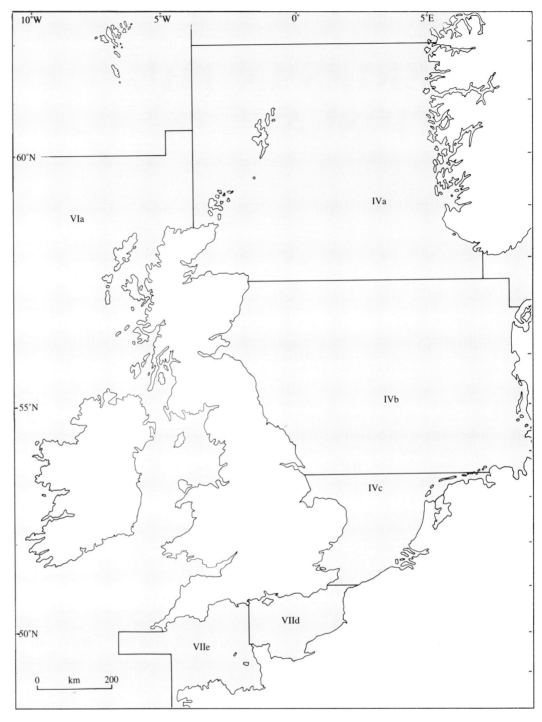

and abundance of all species in the North Sea, with particular reference to immature fish not caught in the commercial fisheries.

❖ An international acoustic survey for herring, started in 1972, is carried out annually around July.

❖ An international plankton survey is carried out between September/October and December/January to obtain an index of abundance of herring larvae over spawning grounds adjacent to the British coast.

Other surveys are carried out as required for specific purposes (e.g. sandeel surveys,

flatfish surveys, surveys of eggs and larvae, etc.).

In addition to the surveys, MAFF, SOAFD and other countries fishing the North Sea take regular samples of commercial landings, and in some cases of fish discarded at sea, to estimate the total number and weight of fish caught each year in the North Sea.

A review of fish species which use estuaries has been undertaken by the Nature Conservancy Council and this is detailed in the Estuaries Review (Davidson *et al.* 1991).

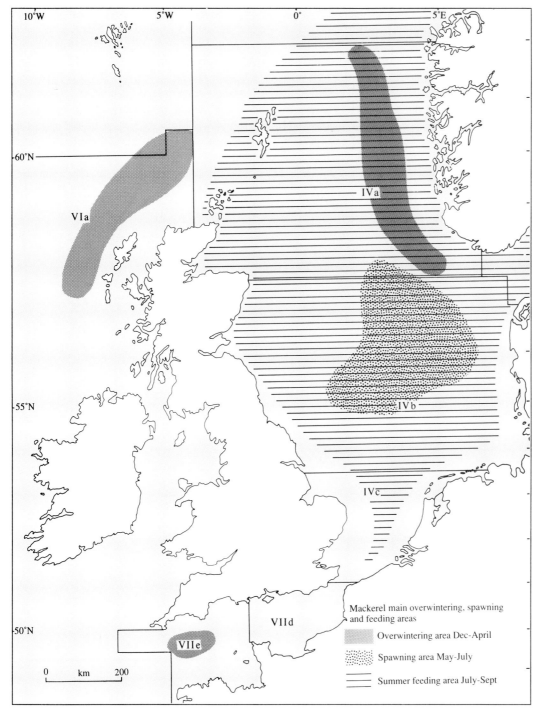

Figure 6.2.1
Distribution of mackerel *Scomber scombrus* spawning grounds and the main summer and winter fishing areas in the North Sea. (The latter two concentrate on the summer feeding and overwintering areas.)

Mackerel main overwintering, spawning and feeding areas

▨ Overwintering area Dec-April

⬚ Spawning area May-July

≡ Summer feeding area July-Sept

6.2   PELAGIC FISH SPECIES

The most important shoaling pelagic fish in the North Sea are mackerel, herring and sprats.

MACKEREL

Mackerel *Scomber scombrus,* a pelagic species that can reach up to 60 cm in body length, is widely distributed around Britain. The largest numbers are found offshore but at some times of year, particularly summer, they can be caught close inshore. Mackerel feed on small fish as well as on plankton, and feeding intensity is greatest in summer after spawning.

Two stocks of mackerel are found in north-west European waters, the western stock which spawns along the shelf edge west of Britain and the North Sea stock which spawns in the central North Sea. Seasonal immigrants from the western stock also occur in the North Sea. Spawning in the North Sea occurs from May to July, peaking in June. The females lay eggs directly into the upper part of the water column and the eggs hatch after about seven days, depending on the temperature. Spawning grounds are located by identifying the presence of mackerel eggs in the plankton and fish with ripe gonads in the trawl catches. The distribution of spawning grounds in the North Sea is shown in Figure 6.2.1. The size of the stock of mackerel spawning in the North Sea is very low at present (less than 50,000 tonnes), and has shown little sign of recovery since it declined in the 1970s.

The western stock of mackerel, which spawns along the shelf edge from west of Ireland to southern Biscay, migrates up the west coast of Britain to the northern North Sea and Norwegian Sea after spawning. The return migration west of Scotland has become progressively later in recent years, now occurring mainly in January–March (Walsh & Martin 1986). Whilst the reasons for this change in migration pattern are not certain, it may be associated with the change in flow of the North Atlantic drift at the continental shelf edge. Some migration from

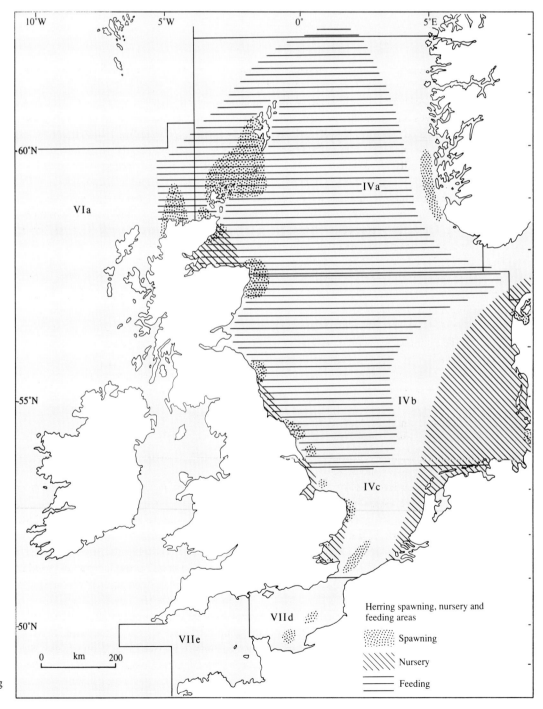

Figure 6.2.2
Distribution of herring *Clupea harengus* spawning grounds, nursery and feeding areas in the North Sea.

the west also takes place through the channel to the southern North Sea area and here too it has been noted that the return movement now occurs later in the season. The western spawning stock is very large, approximately 2 million tonnes in 1989, and it is this stock that sustains the bulk of the international fishery which takes place from late summer to early spring. The main summer and winter fishing areas of the western mackerel stock are given in Figure 6.2.1 (this figure refers only to the position in the northern North Sea). (See Lockwood 1989 for further information.)

HERRING

Herring *Clupea harengus* reach a maximum size of 40 cm and are abundant and widely distributed in the seas of the north-eastern Atlantic shelf. This species typically lives in large shoals and the population can be divided into a number of distinct breeding stocks. It is an important commercial fish which declined drastically in abundance in the North Sea from the 1950s up until 1977 as a result of overfishing of both adults and immature fish on their nursery grounds, and as a result of poor survival of young herring. From 1978 to 1982 all directed catches of North Sea herring were banned to allow stocks to recover. Recovery was first noted in the southern North Sea in 1982, while that of the northern and central North Sea stocks started later and has continued in recent years.

Spawning of herring in the North Sea mainly takes place in the autumn to winter, exact timing depending on locality. In addition, there are local stocks that spawn in spring in inshore areas such as the Thames and Blackwater estuaries. Herring which spawn in autumn or winter tend to do so a little further offshore on the edge of sediment banks. Egg laying takes place where there is coarse shell, grit, gravel or marl for attachment of the eggs, and the distribution of spawning grounds in the North Sea can be very roughly equated with the distribution of known gravel deposits (Figure 6.2.2). Most of the known areas of gravel beds have supported spawning grounds in the past, even if spawning has not been recorded on all of them in recent years.

A high proportion of the herring larvae from the North Sea and west coast spawning grounds drift a considerable distance to nursery grounds in the shallow central and southern North Sea (Heath & Richardson 1989). Along the British coastline there are also nursery areas in the inner Moray Firth, Firth of Forth and along parts of the English coast.

Larval herring are pelagic and drift in the currents until they reach a length of 5 cm when they begin to form shoals and move into shallow water. Up to a year may be spent in inshore feeding areas. Herring feed on a variety of planktonic animals including larvae and small crustaceans. The distribution of herring during summer and autumn is given in Figure 6.2.2 (see Lee & Ramster 1981, sheet 3.14). This species also migrates considerable distances between its spawning and overwintering grounds. (See Nichols & Brander 1989 and Rankine 1986 for further information.)

SPRATS

Sprats *Sprattus sprattus* are relatively shallow water pelagic fish which spawn offshore and migrate inshore to overwinter. The sprat stock in the North Sea is currently at a very low level and its present distribution is largely confined to the south-eastern North Sea and the southern Bight of the North Sea. Small concentrations are also found in coastal inlets – the firths along the east coast of Scotland, the Wash and the Thames estuary. There is also a very small sprat stock in Lyme Bay. Sprat spawning and fishing areas are given in Lee & Ramster (1981), sheets 3.100 and 3.101.

6.3 DEMERSAL FISH SPECIES

The abundant demersal fish species in the North Sea include all the important commercially exploited roundfish and flatfish species together with a number of smaller species, most important of which are Norway pout *Trisopterus luscus* and sandeels *Ammodytidae* sp., which are also exploited.

COD

Cod *Gadus morhua* have a wide distribution around Britain. The North Sea population is self-contained and largely independent of the other populations of the North Atlantic. In general, mature cod migrate south in winter to the spawning areas. Growth rates are variable, with North Sea cod growing up to 130 cm in length.

Cod spawn between February and April on established spawning grounds inside 200 m. The distribution of spawning grounds north of $55°30'N$ is given in Figure 6.3.1 (see Lee & Ramster 1981, sheet 3.06). Both eggs and larvae drift in the plankton. After two months the young fish become demersal where they feed initially on copepods, and later on a

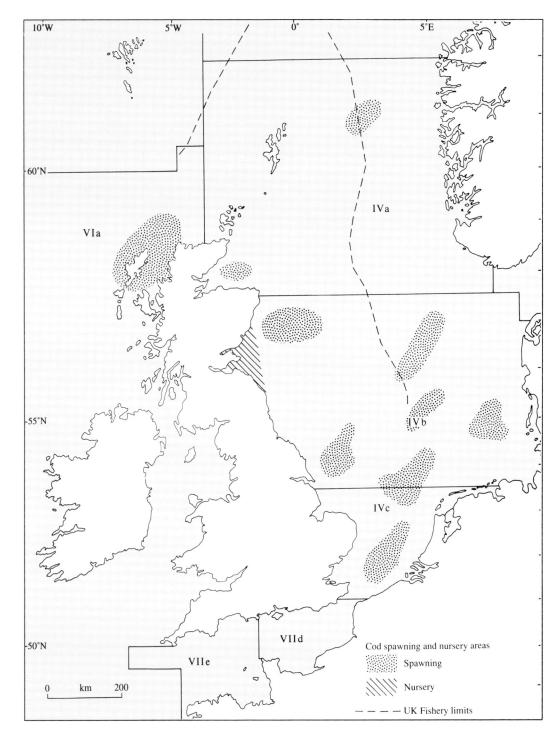

variety of other invertebrates and small fish. Cod reach maturity between three and five years of age.

In the North Sea there has been a reduction in the number of cod which reach spawning age and stocks are presently at their lowest levels since the early 1960s (SOAFD unpublished data 1989). Exploitation and poor recruitment have been responsible for the recent decline in catches. Quotas were set for 1989 and 1990 to allow more young fish to reach maturity. (See Macer & Easey 1988 for further information.)

HADDOCK

Haddock *Melanogrammus aeglefinus* is an important commercial fish in the north-east Atlantic. The species is widely distributed around Britain and Ireland and is most abundant in the northern parts of the North Sea. These fish feed close to the sea bed, taking invertebrates and small fish. Their body length reaches a maximum of about 80 cm.

Spawning takes place between February and June in depths of 100–150 m. The main spawning area in

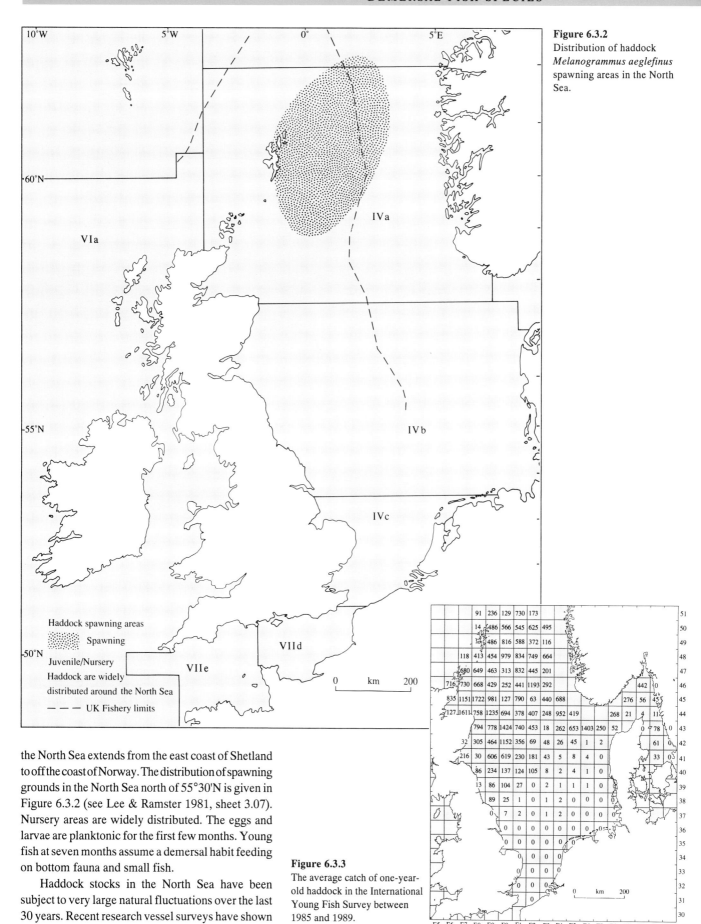

Figure 6.3.2
Distribution of haddock *Melanogrammus aeglefinus* spawning areas in the North Sea.

Haddock spawning areas

    Spawning

Juvenile/Nursery
Haddock are widely
distributed around the North Sea

— — — UK Fishery limits

Figure 6.3.3
The average catch of one-year-old haddock in the International Young Fish Survey between 1985 and 1989.

the North Sea extends from the east coast of Shetland to off the coast of Norway. The distribution of spawning grounds in the North Sea north of 55°30'N is given in Figure 6.3.2 (see Lee & Ramster 1981, sheet 3.07). Nursery areas are widely distributed. The eggs and larvae are planktonic for the first few months. Young fish at seven months assume a demersal habit feeding on bottom fauna and small fish.

Haddock stocks in the North Sea have been subject to very large natural fluctuations over the last 30 years. Recent research vessel surveys have shown

141

Figure 6.3.4
Distribution of the spawning areas of whiting *Merlangius merlangus* in the North Sea.

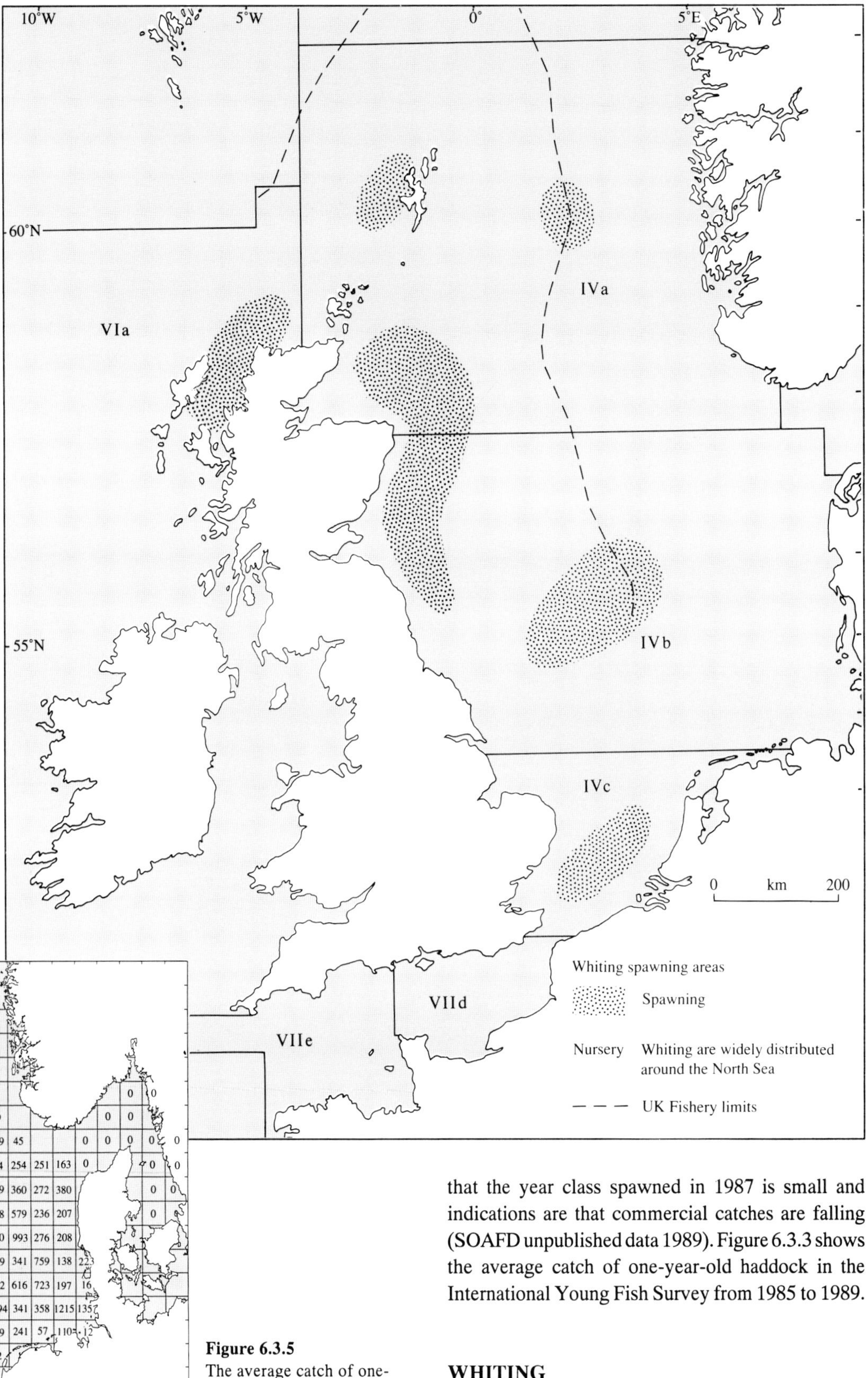

Whiting spawning areas

Spawning

Nursery   Whiting are widely distributed around the North Sea

– – –   UK Fishery limits

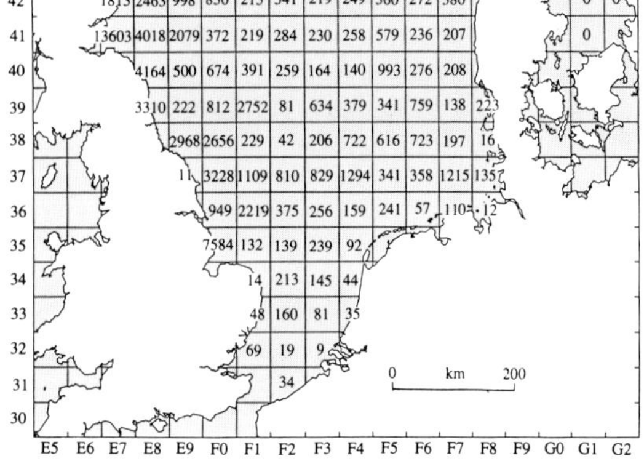

Figure 6.3.5
The average catch of one-year-old whiting on the International Young Fish Survey between 1985 and 1989 (data from DAFS and MAFF).

that the year class spawned in 1987 is small and indications are that commercial catches are falling (SOAFD unpublished data 1989). Figure 6.3.3 shows the average catch of one-year-old haddock in the International Young Fish Survey from 1985 to 1989.

WHITING

The whiting *Merlangius merlangus* is widely distributed around Britain and is extremely common in the North Sea. It is very common in inshore

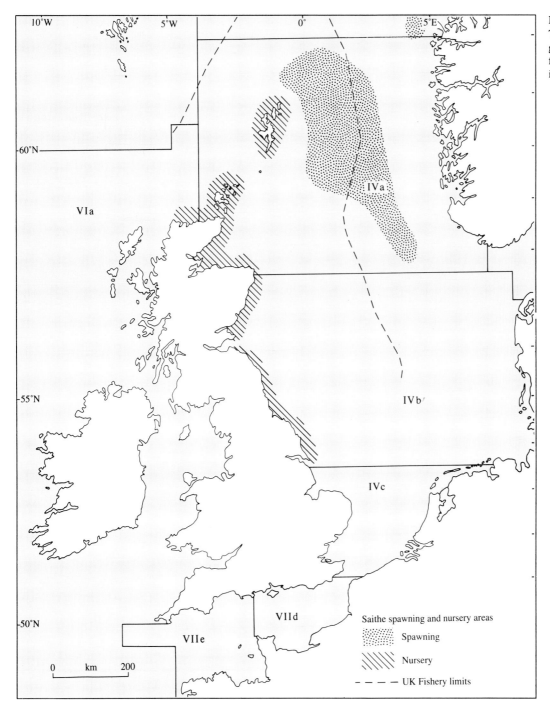

Figure 6.3.6
The distribution of spawning grounds and nursery areas for saithe *Pollachius virens* in the North Sea.

waters and at depths between 30 and 100 m. It is an important commercial fish for inshore fisheries as well as being an important prey species for larger fish. Maximum body length is about 50 cm.

Spawning takes place from January to July. The distribution of spawning grounds is given in Figure 6.3.4 (see Lee & Ramster 1981, sheet 3.09). Nursery areas are widely distributed in the North Sea. After hatching, young fish drift in the plankton for several months and are often found associated with jellyfish. Young fish feed on crustaceans and on small fish of other fish species.

North Sea stocks have remained fairly constant over a long period. An indication of the distribution of whiting in the North Sea is given in Figure 6.3.5. This shows the average catch of one-year-old whiting on the International Young Fish Survey between 1985 and 1989 (data from SOAFD).

SAITHE

The saithe (coley), *Pollachius virens*, is an important commercial fish and is heavily exploited in northern waters during its migration to the spawning grounds. This species can reach 120 cm in body length.

Spawning takes place between January and April in deep water. Both eggs and larvae are planktonic, drifting towards shallower waters. The distribution of spawning grounds and nursery areas in the North Sea is given in Figure 6.3.6. (see Lee & Ramster 1981, sheet 3.08). Young fish are particularly abundant in inshore waters, especially from Scotland northwards, where they feed on

small crustaceans and small fish. Adults feed almost entirely on a variety of fish species.

PLAICE

Plaice *Pleuronectes platessa* are bottom-living fish which are most often found on sandy substrate down to depths of 120 m, but this species also occurs on muddy bottoms and gravel. Growth rates vary between males and females. Females grow

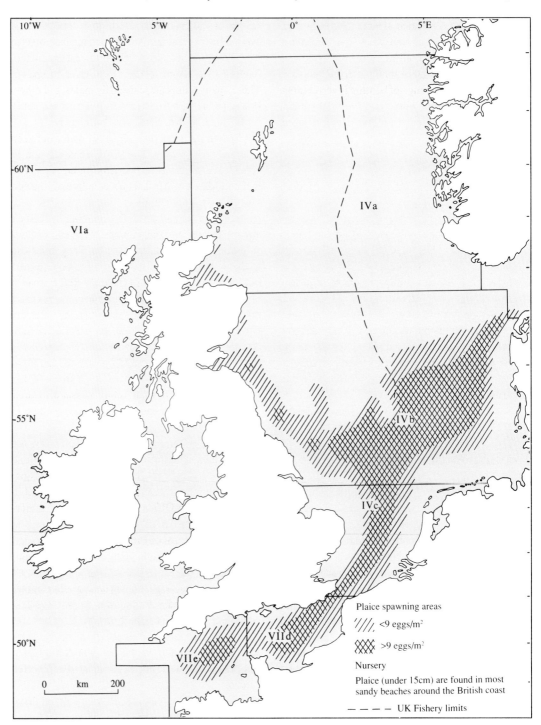

Figure 6.3.7
Distribution of plaice *Pleuronectes platessa* spawning areas in the North Sea.

faster and live longer reaching a maximum length of about 60 cm.

Plaice are long-lived fish which reach maturity after three years. Spawning takes place on well-defined spawning grounds in early spring at depths of between 20 and 40 m. The distribution of spawning grounds in the North Sea is given in Figure 6.3.7 (see Lee & Ramster 1981, sheet 3.041). The eggs and larvae live in the plankton for six weeks where they drift towards the coast to metamorphose into bottom-living flatfish. Most sandy beaches are potential nursery grounds. Some nursery grounds for plaice are not presently used but may recover in time and be used in the future. Young plaice live in shallow water for up to two years and may be found in sandy intertidal pools.

Plaice eat a wide range of benthic invertebrates, and the adult fish may come into the tidal zone at high tide to feed on the invertebrates which live in sand and mud flats.

SANDEELS

One species of lesser sandeel *Ammodytes marinus* is estimated to be one of the most abundant fish in the North Sea. This species supports a large international fishery, particularly in the central and north-eastern North Sea, with a small isolated fishery close inshore at Shetland. Sandeels form an important prey for many other species of fish, seabirds and sea mammals and a SOAFD/Glasgow University research programme is underway in the waters around Shetland to examine the ecology of the species in relation to its importance for feeding seabirds.

Sandeel distribution is given in Lee & Ramster (1981) sheet 3.13. The biology of sandeels in the vicinity of the Shetland Isles sea bird colonies is described in Wright & Bailey (1992).

SOLE

The sole *Solea solea* is an important commercial species in the southern North Sea. It is at the northern limit of its north-east Atlantic distribution in the North Sea. This species is particularly abundant in areas of muddy sand and fine sand where the polychaetes that it feeds on are also abundant.

Spawning takes place in the North Sea in coastal waters and at the mouth of estuaries. Egg laying occurs from April until June, hatching after five to eleven days. The first two weeks are spent in the plankton before metamorphosis into flatfish which are found on the seabed in inshore areas such as the Thames estuary. After two or three years adult sole move to deeper waters. Distribution is given in Lee & Ramster (1981) sheets 3.050 and 3.051.

SALMONIDS

Atlantic salmon *Salmo salar* are anadromous, which means that they are born in fresh water where they feed and grow for one to four years before heading downstream to the sea. At sea they may feed for a further one to four years. During this time Atlantic salmon travel great distances to rich feeding areas in the Norwegian Sea and in waters off west Greenland. Salmon then return to their natal river to spawn. There, many adults die, especially males, but others (known as kelts) return to sea and may subsequently return again to their home rivers to spawn.

Spawning takes place in fresh water between October and January. The yolky eggs are laid in coarse, clean gravel in fast-flowing streams, and hatch in March or April. The alevin live off the egg sac at first, and remain within the gravel bed, emerging as fry and actively beginning to feed on aquatic insects by midsummer. By the end of their first year the fish are known as parr. They live close to the bed of the stream, often among cobbles and boulders, as sit-and-wait feeders. Each year a proportion of the large male parr become sexually mature. After one to four years in fresh water the parr is transformed into a more slender, silvery fish, the smolt, which moves downstream and enters the sea. Feeding salmon from UK rivers are caught at west Greenland and north of the Faroes in the Norwegian Sea. On their return passage to their natal rivers they are caught along the coast and in the rivers themselves.

Along the North Sea margin salmon rivers are concentrated in the north and north-east of Scotland and on the border between England and Scotland. The distribution of rivers is given in Figure 6.3.8.

The Scottish Office Agriculture and Fisheries Department and MAFF collate and publish the number and weight of salmon, grilse (salmon that return to freshwater after only one winter at sea) and sea trout reported as caught in their respective jurisdictions. In Scotland the annual figures are based on notified returns from proprietors and occupiers of salmon fish farms. In England and Wales, they are based on catch returns provided by anglers and netsmen to the regional NRA Units. The published data do not take account of unreported catches.

In some areas catches of wild salmon have declined in recent years and this has been attributed

Figure 6.3.8
Distribution of the major salmon rivers which feed into the North Sea.

Salmon present
Salmon probably present
Salmon rehabilitation programme

to various factors: closure of coastal salmon fisheries and subsequent reduction in fishing effort, obstructions on natal rivers and pollution. Rehabilitation schemes have been undertaken on a number of rivers where physical obstructions to upstream movement, long-term water quality problems or lack of suitable habitats have reduced capacity for production of juvenile fish. Restocking may involve the planting out of artificially spawned eggs, or the introduction of hatchery-reared fry, parr or smolts. (See Mills 1989 for more information.)

6.4 SHELLFISH (EXPLOITED SPECIES)

CRUSTACEANS

Nephrops

Off the east coast of Scotland, the major crustacean fishery is that for *Nephrops norvegicus* (Dublin Bay prawn, Norway lobster). This species is widely distributed in areas of soft, grey mud, sandy mud and

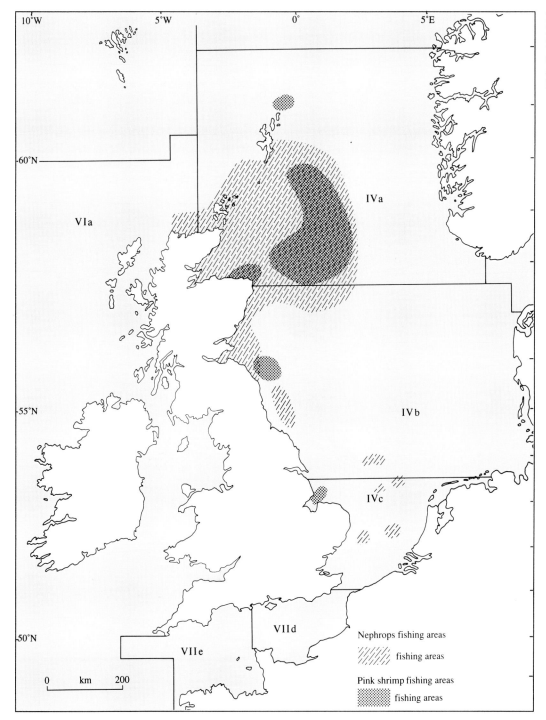

Figure 6.4.1
Main fishing areas for Dublin Bay prawn *Nephrops norvegicus* and pink shrimp *Pandalus montagui* in the North Sea.

muddy sand. The main fisheries take place in the Firth of Forth, the Moray Firth, off Arbroath, west of Orkney, and north-east of Peterhead in areas known as the Fladen and Witch grounds. The fisheries in these offshore areas have become increasingly important as *Nephrops* have been more intensively exploited elsewhere. *Pandalus borealis* (pink shrimp, deep water shrimp) has a contiguous distribution with *Nephrops* in the offshore areas, and is similarly exploited. Fisheries for both species are undertaken by trawl and there

is no significant creel fishery for them on the east coast. An indication of the extent of the fishery for these species in the northern North Sea is given in Figure 6.4.1.

There is a significant trawl fishery for *Nephrops* in the Farne Deeps off the north-east coast of England (see sheet 3.06 of Lee & Ramster 1981). Landings from this fishery have increased over the last 10 years to 2,633 tonnes in 1989. In the southern North Sea there is a smaller *Nephrops* fishery (556 tonnes in 1989) exploited by Belgian trawlers in the

Botney Gut and Silver Pit. As in Scotland *Nephrops* are associated with the muddy sand substrates found at these locations.

Shrimps

The main east coast shrimp fisheries occur in the Wash, where a range of vessel sizes use traditional single shrimp trawls or double beam trawls with shrimp mesh. The main fishery is now for *Crangon crangon* which settle as juveniles very close inshore on the estuarine flats and channel edges in spring and summer before migrating seaward in autumn to overwinter outside the estuary and along the north Norfolk coast. Landings, formerly below 500 tonnes per annum, increased to a peak of 1,500 tonnes in 1987 when market opportunity encouraged new effort, but have since fallen back somewhat. Fishing for the pink shrimp *Pandalus montagui* also occurs in the Wash, mainly during the summer incursion into the area by shrimps which overwinter offshore between the Lynn Deeps and the Silver Pit.

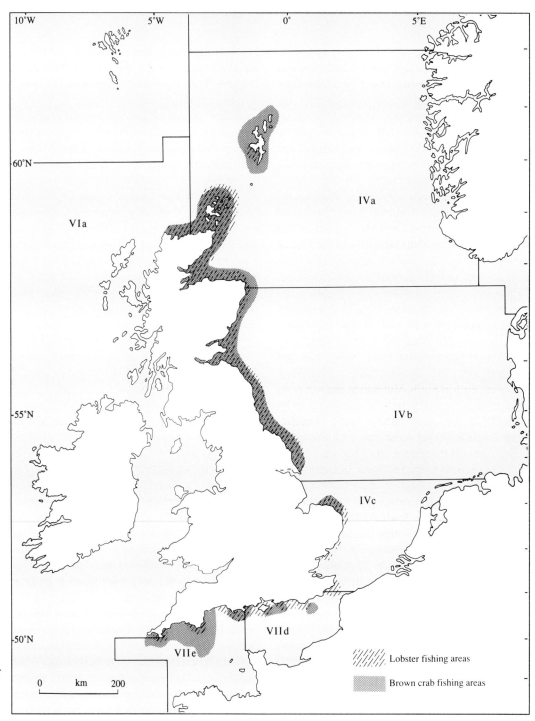

Figure 6.4.2
Main fishing areas for lobster *Homarus gammarus* and brown crab *Cancer pagurus* in the North Sea.

Elsewhere fishing for *Crangon* occurs near Yarmouth and Lowestoft, and in the Humber and the Thames, but on a smaller scale than in the Wash. *Pandalus montagui* also occur in the Thames in summer, but again on a smaller scale. The Humber and Thames fisheries, formerly significant but in recent years rather defunct, have shown signs of picking up in the last year or two. *Crangon* is primarily associated with sandy-muddy substrates, but *Pandalus* is also popularly believed to show preference for coarser substrate, including colonies of *Sabellaria*.

Lobster and crab

The two decapod species, the lobster *Homarus gammarus* and the brown crab *Cancer pagurus,* have a similar distribution in inshore waters and are generally fished together, although seasonal migrations of the brown crab off Scotland cause some spatial separation of the species and the fisheries. There is a discontinuous distribution of the species on the east coast from the Scottish border northwards, with the main fisheries occurring from Berwick to St. Andrews, along the Angus coast, between Peterhead and Macduff, and along the north-west coast of the Moray Firth. The species are also heavily exploited around the Orkney and Shetland Isles, and off the north coast of the mainland. Figure 6.4.2 shows the distribution of lobsters and brown crabs in the North Sea (SOAFD, unpublished data). In recent years the exploitation of two other crab species has occurred – the velvet crab *Liocarcinus puber* is taken in the Orkney Isles and the green crab *Carcinus maenas* is taken in Orkney and in the Firth of Forth. Monitoring and sampling of lobsters, brown and velvet crabs is carried out by SOAFD in the main fishing areas. Tagging experiments are being carried out on lobsters and velvet crabs off the west coast of Scotland.

While brown crab and lobster fisheries occur along much of the English coast bordering the North Sea, the main fisheries are in Northumberland, Yorkshire, and Norfolk. Traditionally, fishing using creels (traps) occurred within 6 nautical miles of the coast, but recently fishing off Norfolk and Yorkshire has extended out to 12 nautical miles, and a new crab fishery has developed some 40 nautical miles east of the Humber. Landings of lobsters along the English North Sea coast now (1988–89) exceed 200 tonnes per annum. Crab landings from the traditional grounds have averaged just over 1,600 tonnes per annum over the last 10 years. The adjacent eastern and western English Channel also support major lobster and especially crab fisheries.

The distribution of lobster and crab is preferentially associated with shelter in the form of bedrock, outcrops, boulders, pits, wrecks, etc. English east coast populations are subject to periodic research investigations, including, at present, an experiment on lobster stock enhancement in Bridlington Bay. This has involved the release of microtagged hatchery reared stock in the three mile belt and associated recapture investigations to measure survival.

MOLLUSCA

In Scotland, mussels *Mytilus edulis* are gathered in the Montrose basin (for bait) and at Tain in the Dornoch Firth (for human consumption). Small quantities of mussels are cultivated in Orkney and Shetland. Scallops *Pecten maximus*, queens *Aequipecten opercularis* and Pacific oysters *Crassostrea gigas* are all cultivated in the Orkney Isles. A dredge fishery for scallops takes place on the sandy-gravel sediments of the north-west coast of the Moray Firth, and around Orkney and Shetland. An indication of the distribution of scallops and queens is given in Figure 6.4.3. The winkle *Littorina littorea* is gathered from the littoral zone. In many areas the exploitation pattern is similar to that of the lobster. Whelks *Buccinum undatum* are fished for by pot in Shetland and along with the spindle shell (whelk) *Neptunea antigua* are both landed as by-catch by some North Sea trawlers.

The distribution of areas in which various species of shellfish are cultivated in England, Wales and Scotland is given in Figure 6.4.4 (MAFF unpublished data 1990).

Squids *Loligo forbesi* and *Alloteuthis subulata* have a wide distribution in the North Sea, and are taken as a by-catch in white fish catches. Concentrations of these species may occur in the Moray Firth and Firth of Forth in late summer and autumn. When this happens, directed fisheries take place on an opportunistic basis. Squids are short-lived species, having a life span of 12–16 months, and stock sizes fluctuate considerably from year to year. The octopus *Eledone cirrhosa* is frequently caught by trawl and in creels. Landings of this species are made at some ports, the bulk of landings being made at Fraserburgh.

In north-east England, there are small fisheries for mussels at Holy Island and for scallops in the deep water east of the Farne Islands. An intermittent queen fishery is located east of Flamborough Head. Further south, the intertidal flats of the Wash support major dredge fisheries for mussels and cockles. Along the adjoining north Norfolk coast mussels

Figure 6.4.3
Main fishing areas for scallops *Pecten maximus* and queens *Aequipecten opercularis* in the North Sea.

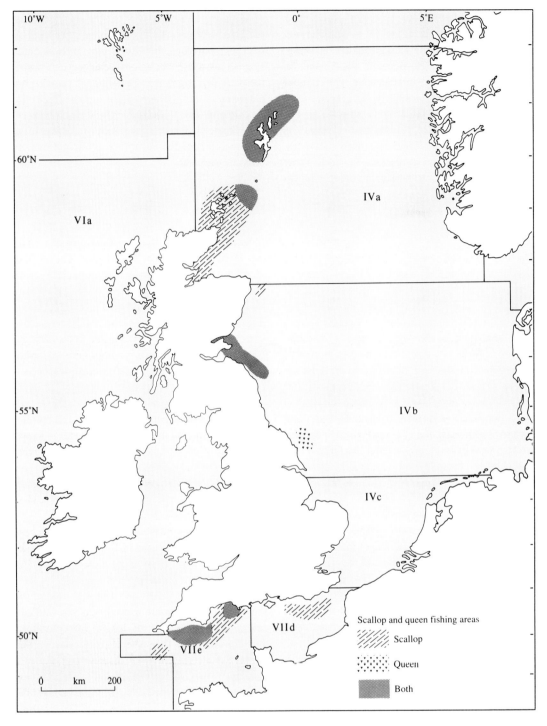

are cultivated and cockles gathered in several inlets while whelks are fished offshore. A few Pacific oysters are also cultivated here in some creeks and harbours. In the Thames Estuary, native oysters *Ostrea edulis* are fished from natural stocks and these and Pacific oysters are also cultivated in various estuaries along the south Suffolk, Essex and north Kent coasts (Figure 6.4.4). A large cockle fishery is based on the flats and shallow sublittoral zone off the Essex coast. There is a small whelk fishery in north Kent.

In the eastern Channel (ICES area VIId) there are important fisheries for native oysters, and in the Solent and nearby Hampshire and Poole Harbours for the American hard-shell clam *Mercenaria mercenaria* (introduced accidentally). Offshore, whelks are fished from Kent to the Isle of Wight, and scallop grounds are scattered out to mid-Channel on gravels off Sussex. Further west (ICES area VIIe), a major fishery for scallops extends from Lyme Bay to the Lizard and far out to mid-Channel. In several estuaries and rias from the Exe to the Fal

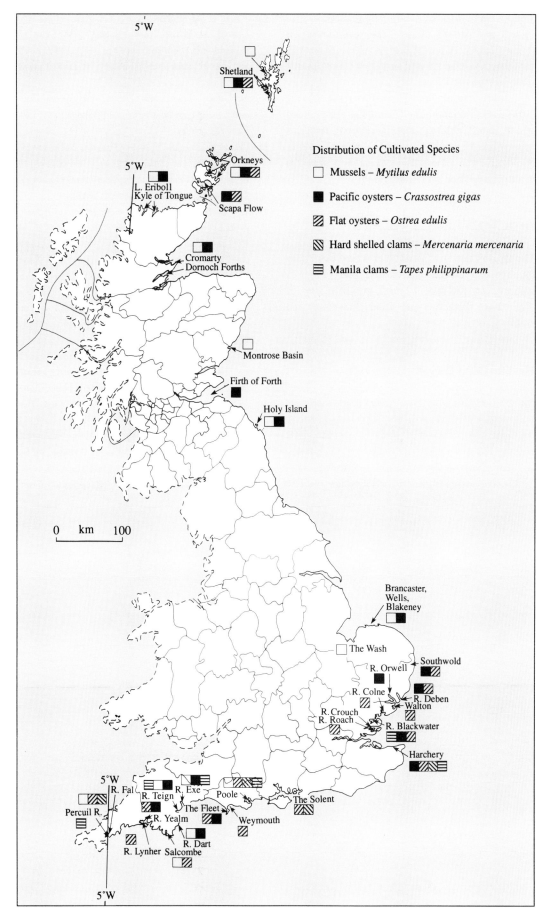

Figure 6.4.4
Distribution of cultivated bivalve species (1990).
Based upon the 1975 Ordnance Survey 1:1,250,000 map with the permission of the Controller of Her Majesty's Stationery Office © Crown Copyright.

Distribution of Cultivated Species

☐ Mussels – *Mytilus edulis*

■ Pacific oysters – *Crassostrea gigas*

▨ Flat oysters – *Ostrea edulis*

▧ Hard shelled clams – *Mercenaria mercenaria*

▤ Manila clams – *Tapes philippinarum*

there are small-scale cultivations of mussels, Pacific oysters and Manila clams *Tapes philippinarum* (Figure 6.4.4). A wild stock of native oysters is fished in the Fal estuary and cultivated in the adjacent Helford River.

Squids, mainly *Loligo forbesi*, are widely distributed throughout the Channel and are landed as a by-catch, although directed autumn fisheries may occur off South Cornwall. Cuttlefish *Sepia officinalis* form an important by-catch of trawlers in autumn west of the Isle of Wight.

ACKNOWLEDGEMENTS

The information for this chapter was provided by the Scottish Office Agriculture and Fisheries Department (Aberdeen) and the Ministry of Agriculture, Fisheries and Food (Lowestoft and Conwy).

REFERENCES

DAVIDSON, N.C. *et al.* 1991. *Nature conservation and estuaries in Great Britain*. Peterborough, Nature Conservancy Council.

HEATH, M., & RICHARDSON, K. 1989. Comparative study of early life survival variability of herring *Clupea harengus* in the north-eastern Atlantic. *Journal of Fish Biology, 35* (supplement A): 49-57.

LEE, A.J., & RAMSTER, W.J. 1981. *Atlas of the seas around the British Isles*. Ministry of Agriculture, Fisheries and Food, Directorate of Fisheries Research. Fisheries Research Technical Report, No. 20. Lowestoft, MAFF.

LOCKWOOD, S.J. 1989. *Mackerel: its biology, assessment and the management of a fishery*. Fishing News Books, Farnham, Surrey.

MACER, C.T., & EASEY, M.W. 1988. The North Sea cod and the English fishery. *Ministry of Agriculture, Fisheries and Food. Directorate of Fisheries Research, Laboratory Leaflet 61*. Lowestoft, MAFF.

MILLS, D. 1989. *Ecology and management of Atlantic salmon*. London, Chapman and Hall.

NICHOLS, J.H., & BRANDER, K.M. 1989. Herring larval studies in the west-central North Sea. *Rapp. P.-v. Reun. Cons. int. Explor. Mer., 191*: 160-168.

RANKINE, P.W. 1986. Herring spawning grounds around the Scottish coast. *International Council for the Exploration of the sea. Pelagic Fish Committee paper CM 1986/H:15*.

WALSH, M., & MARTIN, J.K.A. 1986. Recent changes in the distribution and migration of the western mackerel stock in relation to hydrographic changes. *International Council for the Exploration of the Sea. Pelagic Fish Committee. CM 1986/H:17*.

WRIGHT, P.J., & BAILEY, M.C. 1992. Biology of sandeels in the vicinity of seabird colonies in Shetland. *Second Annual Report-June 1992. Fisheries Research Services Report No.19/92. Scottish Office Agricultural and Fisheries Department*.

Chapter 7

RARE AND PROTECTED SPECIES

7.1 INTRODUCTION

This chapter describes those plant and animal species which live along the North Sea coastal margin or in inshore waters at some stage in their life cycle and which are protected under the Wildlife and Countryside Act (1981) or by other international legislation. Rare and protected species of invertebrate and lower plants have not been included here, although many are recorded from or restricted to coastal habitats. Some information on coastal invertebrates is presented in Chapter 4.

Each animal and plant group is considered separately. The distribution of the species or group is shown together with a brief description of lifestyle and protected status. Geographical variation in distribution and factors affecting populations are also given.

Animal and plant groups included in this chapter are listed below.
7.2 Birds
7.3 Seals
7.4 Otters
7.5 Cetaceans
7.6 Amphibians and reptiles
7.7 Rare fishes
7.8 Rare vascular plants.

7.2 BIRDS

INTRODUCTION

The coast of northern Britain is the most important area within the North Sea in terms of both numbers and diversity of seabirds.

Internationally important numbers of several species of seabird – gannet *Morus bassanus* (17% of world population), razorbill *Alca torda* (14%) and great skua *Catharacta skua* (55%) – breed on the North Sea coasts of Britain. These species and others using the North Sea as feeding grounds may be divided into three main groups depending on their foraging behaviour – offshore and inshore seabirds and coastal waterfowl. There are also some other bird species for which the North Sea coast provides important habitat.

Seabirds rely on the sea for their food. Different species forage at various distances from land – those which commonly feed out of sight of land (offshore species) and those which feed in shallower coastal waters nearer to the land (inshore species). The third group feed primarily in the intertidal and terrestrial parts of the coastal zone (coastal waterfowl – chiefly waders and wildfowl). Each group is described separately within this section.

Twenty-eight species of seabird (*c.* 4.25 million birds) breed around the North Sea, with a further six species also feeding in the waters during some part of the year at least. The composition of species in any one area varies seasonally and during autumn many species leave the North Sea but are replaced by visitors from the north and west. The United Kingdom has a particular responsibility for the conservation of birds in the North Sea since the coastal margin forms a large part of the boundary.

Wintering and breeding coastal bird surveys have shown the great importance of the North Sea coast for waders and wildfowl, both nationally and internationally. Many species which breed in arctic regions use the coastal habitats of Britain as wintering grounds or as migration stopovers *en route* to countries in southern Europe and western Africa. Britain has an important role in the life of migratory birds because it is situated along several migration routes and benefits from a mild winter climate which allows continuous access to feeding areas.

Migration patterns and the use of individual coastal sites are complex and the loss of one feeding/roosting site may have severe implications for the huge numbers of birds which use the estuary or coastal habitat. Two international measures provide for the protection of areas of importance to bird species. These measures, the Convention on Wetlands of International Importance especially as a Waterfowl Habitat (Ramsar Convention) and the EC Directive on Conservation of Wild Birds (Directive 79/409), which requires the designation

Figure 7.2.1

Distribution of seabird
breeding colonies within the
North Sea coastal margin.

Based upon the 1975 Ordnance Survey
1:1,250,000 map with the permission
of the Controller of Her Majesty's
Stationery Office © Crown Copyright.

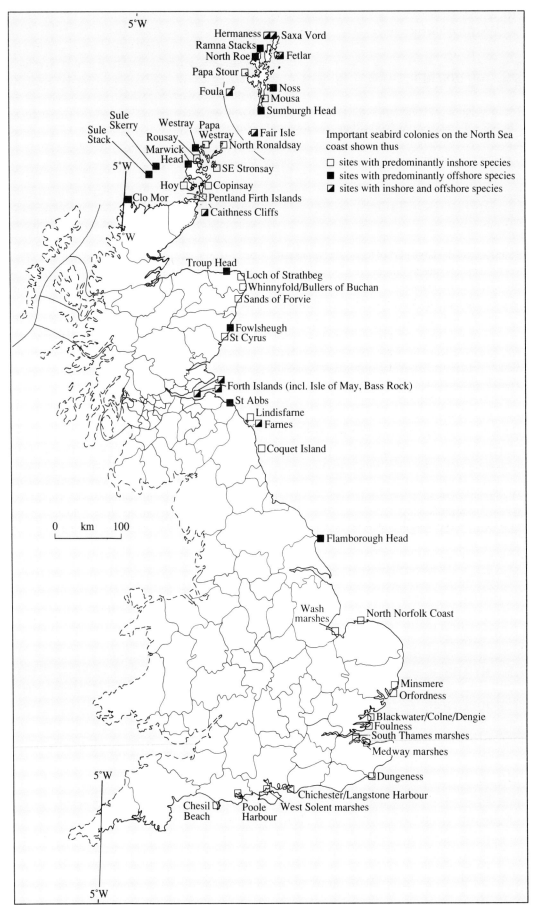

154

of Special Protection Areas, are described elsewhere in this directory (Section 10.2).

SEABIRD DISTRIBUTION

The distribution of most seabird species in the North Sea is centred off Scotland but the inshore areas of the southern North Sea are also used for feeding. The distribution of major seabird breeding colonies which lie within the North Sea coastal margin is given in Figure 7.2.1.

Offshore species

Seabirds spend a large part of their lives at sea and oceanic species such as fulmar *Fulmarus glacialis*, storm petrel *Hydrobates pelagicus* and Leach's petrel *Oceanodroma leucorhoa* may frequently be found far from land even during the breeding season. Several species dive and pursue their prey (small shoaling fish) below the water surface; others feed mainly on the surface with large numbers often feeding on discarded offal from fishing vessels. The distribution of each species in the North Sea is described further in Tasker *et al.* (1987) and to the north-west of Scotland by Webb *et al.* (1990).

Breeding distribution

More than one-tenth of the world's population of gannets, razorbills and great skuas breed on the North Sea coastal margin with more than 1% of the

world's total of storm petrel, Arctic skua *Stercorarius parasiticus*, fulmar, kittiwake *Rissa tridactyla*, guillemot *Uria aalge* and puffin *Fratercula arctica* also using this area. The main breeding area for offshore species in the North Sea is the north-west. Most colonies are situated in the northern North Sea, the exception being east Yorkshire. Birds breed on cliffs or on rocky islands which are free from mammalian ground-predators.

The numbers of seabirds (offshore species) in any one area during the breeding season (April to July) is outlined in Table 7.2.1 (based on Tasker *et al.* 1987). This table gives the number of pairs (number of individuals for auks) of breeding birds in 11 sectors of the North Sea. Lloyd *et al.* (1991), describe numbers of all seabirds breeding in Britain and Ireland, and put these numbers in a wider context.

The most commonly observed species in the North Sea are fulmar, guillemot, kittiwake and gannet. Shetland is one of the most important seabird breeding areas with high numbers of individuals and high species diversity. The greatest numbers of guillemot, razorbill and kittiwake breed on Orkney and north Caithness.

Fulmars breed along the North Sea coastal margin wherever there is suitable nesting habitat but the highest concentrations are to be found in Orkney and Shetland which support 88% of the estimated North Sea population (Tasker *et al.* 1987). Breeding adults return to their colonies during winter to defend their nest sites, leaving for a short

Species	Area										
	1	2	3	4	5	6	7	8	9	10	11
Fulmar	208,314	63,358	22,456	7,303	1,572	1,782	1,939	368	329	453	2,708
Manx shearwater	150	100	0	0	0	0	0	0	0	0	0
Storm petrel	<1,000	0	0	0	0	0	0	0	0	0	0
Leach's petrel	<100	0	0	0	0	0	0	0	0	0	0
Gannet	21,648	0	0	0	21,600	0	530	0	0	0	0
Arctic skua	1,912	1,034	42	0	0	0	0	0	0	0	0
Great skua	5,647	1,652	0	0	0	0	0	0	0	0	0
Kittiwake	39,960	117,117	49,529	74,891	8,953	32,615	83,490	0	2,571	3,665	517
Guillemot	167,864	214,846	124,777	72,708	24,308	43,647	26,946	0	0	300	5,254
Razorbill	17,152	22,116	15,269	8,347	2,146	2,123	5,644	0	0	1,930	
Puffin	101,748	22,271	270	1,816	25,428	48,197	4,532	0	0	0	113

Area	1 Shetland	4 NE Scotland	7 Flamborough	10 East Channel
	2 Orkney	5 Firth of Forth	8 Humber/Wash	11 South Channel
	3 Moray Firth	6 NE England	9 Thames	

Table 7.2.1
Number of pairs of breeding birds (offshore species) in the North Sea (based on Tasker *et al.* 1987, from surveys in the mid-1980s).

period prior to egg laying then remaining near the colony from May until August.

Kittiwakes are the commonest birds within the North Sea and breed throughout the area. Breeding birds return to their colonies between January and March. Both breeding and non-breeding birds leave the vicinity of the colony by September.

There are eight colonies of gannets on the British North Sea coast (about 17% of the world population), the largest being at Bass Rock in the Firth of Forth. Nearly all adult gannets feed within 120 km of breeding colonies during the breeding season.

The majority of guillemots nest in Orkney, Shetland and the Moray Firth, with other concentrations further south on the east coast of Scotland and north-east England. During the breeding season, densities in the eastern and southern North Sea are extremely low. Recent surveys show that most breeding guillemots in the North Sea do not feed further than 30 km from their breeding sites in June.

Razorbills have a similar breeding distribution within the North Sea to that of the guillemot. Over 10% of the world's population of razorbills is thought to breed in the North Sea. During the breeding season most birds stay near their colonies in the north western North Sea, feeding generally closer to the shore than guillemots.

At sea

During winter, offshore species may range over considerable distances in search of food. A description of the movements during the non-breeding season of the most common offshore species is given here. Further details are given in Tasker *et al.* (1987).

Fulmars disperse away from breeding colonies in September and October. The number of birds in central and southern North Sea reaches a peak in September. Non-breeding birds disperse widely, whilst breeding adults move out to sea to moult, returning to the vicinity of the colony from November onwards.

Kittiwakes are found in high densities near the colonies from February until August. In winter many birds leave the North Sea with birds from north Scotland moving out into the Atlantic, although those from eastern Scotland remain in the North Sea. Those that remain are widely scattered throughout this area.

Large numbers of gannets leave the North Sea in autumn to spend the winter further south. Adults return first in spring with the highest numbers of gannets occurring at sea prior to, and immediately

after, the breeding season. Non-breeding birds further increase the density of gannets at sea between March and September.

Guillemots disperse in July from their breeding colonies with numbers peaking in the North Sea in August. Densities remain high around Orkney and north-east Scotland with many birds found also in the central North Sea. During the moult guillemots concentrate in rafts off eastern Scotland and north-east England before moving south later in autumn. The southern North Sea is also important for guillemots during most winters.

By July razorbills begin to disperse to the north with subsequent movement east and south, again concentrating during the moult in similar areas to guillemots. The Moray Firth area remains important during the winter with birds dispersed throughout the southern central North Sea.

Inshore species

Seabirds which are considered within the 'inshore' category feed within sight of land but may be found further offshore over shallow water with sandy sediments. In many cases these species feed by diving from the surface of the water to find prey on or near the sea-bed. Tern species *Sternidae* and gulls *Laridae* plunge dive and take food near the surface of the water.

Breeding distribution

The North Sea coast is important as a breeding area for many inshore seabirds with more than one-tenth of the world's population of lesser and great black-backed gulls (*Larus fuscus* and *Larus marinus*) and 1% of the world total of Sandwich tern *Sterna sandvicensis*, red-throated diver *Gavia stellata* and herring gull *Larus argentatus*. The main breeding areas for inshore seabirds in the North Sea are in the Northern Isles, northern Moray Firth and the outer Firth of Forth although black-headed gulls *Larus ridibundus* and little terns *Sterna albifrons* show a preference for low-lying islands in the southern North Sea.

The distribution of inshore species during the breeding season is outlined in Table 7.2.2 which gives the number of pairs of breeding birds for each species in the North Sea. The distribution of breeding colonies for inshore species is shown on Figure 7.2.1.

Large colonies of lesser black-backed gull are found on low coastal islands with most birds breeding on the eastern side of the North Sea. Adult birds return to their breeding locations by mid-March.

Species	Area										
	1	2	3	4	5	6	7	8	9	10	11
Red-throated diver	700	93	0	0	0	0	0	0	0	0	0
Cormorant	428	442	613	7	237	398	61	0	18	180	678
Shag	8,366	2,553	2,567	666	2,399	1,413	85	0	0	18	1,044
Black-headed gull	441	2,849	165	2,267	9,000	4,713	0	5,920	13,352	25,584	2,800
Common gull	852	14,282	636	50	0	30	0	203	0	0	8
Lesser black-backed	308	1,924	351	100	2,062	18	0	15	5,063	6	195
Herring gull	4,351	9,597	27,879	25,489	7,777	3,045	4,134	0	3,405	2,300	5,479
Great black-backed	2,738	5,745	1,396	25	6	0	0	0	0	1	496
Roseate tern	0	0	0	0	0	31	0	0	0	0	0
Common tern	20	200*	937*	257	671	801	1	534	364	1,424	122
Arctic tern	31,792	23,417*	742*	149	486	4,714	0	13	0	0	0
Little tern	0	0	31	143	88	44	44	280	490	474	22
Black guillemot	12,008	7,102	1,737	3	0	0	0	0	0	0	0

Area	1 Shetland	4 NE Scotland	7 Flamborough	10 east Channel
	2 Orkney	5 Firth of Forth	8 Humber/Wash	11 south Channel
	3 Moray Firth	6 NE England	9 Thames	

* These are minimum figures for populations of common and Arctic terns. The total number for each of these species included a small number of birds which were not accurately identified as either of the above.

Table 7.2.2
Numbers of pairs of breeding birds (inshore species) in the North Sea (based on Tasker *et al.* 1987, from surveys in the mid-1980s).

Great black-backed gulls breed around the northern coasts of the North Sea with substantial numbers breeding on the Orkney and Shetland islands. The most southerly breeding colonies on the British North Sea Coast are found in the Firth of Forth. During the breeding season (May to August) this species is present mainly in the north-western area.

Red-throated divers breed on freshwater lochs but make use of sheltered inshore areas near their nesting sites. They feed on marine fish supplemented occasionally by freshwater fish and invertebrates at Shetland breeding sites. There are approximately 800 pairs breeding within the North Sea and most of these are on the Shetland Isles.

Eiders *Somateria molissima* are the only seaduck that breed in large but so far uncounted numbers along the coast of the North Sea. The main breeding colonies are in Shetland, Orkney, Grampian, Firths of Tay and Forth and the Farne Islands. Very few scoter breed along the coastal margin so numbers have not been included in the above table.

All tern species are summer visitors to the North Sea, spending the winter in southern latitudes. Sandwich terns breed mainly on low sandy coasts in the southern North Sea, as do little terns. Common terns *Sterna hirundo* breed on offshore islands along the North Sea coastal margin whilst Arctic terns *Sterna paradisaea* are recorded in highest numbers in Orkney and Shetland. All roseate terns *Sterna dougallii* found in the North Sea (36 pairs) breed at a few sites in north-eastern England and south-eastern Scotland. This species is internationally rare having declined in numbers, possibly as a result of persecution at wintering sites in Ghana.

At sea

During winter numbers of birds are increased by immigration from northern latitudes to the North Sea, particularly seaduck species. The southern North Sea holds the largest populations of many inshore birds.

The lesser black-backed gull is principally a summer visitor to the North Sea. Numbers at sea increase during spring and autumn migration.

The highest densities of great black-backed gulls are present in the North Sea between September and April. Shetland and Fair Isle are important areas for this species during the winter as is the north-eastern coast of England.

About 14,500 divers of three species (red throated-diver, black-throated diver *Gavia arctica* and great northern diver *Gavia immer*) have been estimated to winter on British North Sea coasts. Red-throated divers, in general, are found in the

Figure 7.2.2a
The distribution of seabirds in the North Sea in June (after Carter *et al.* 1993).

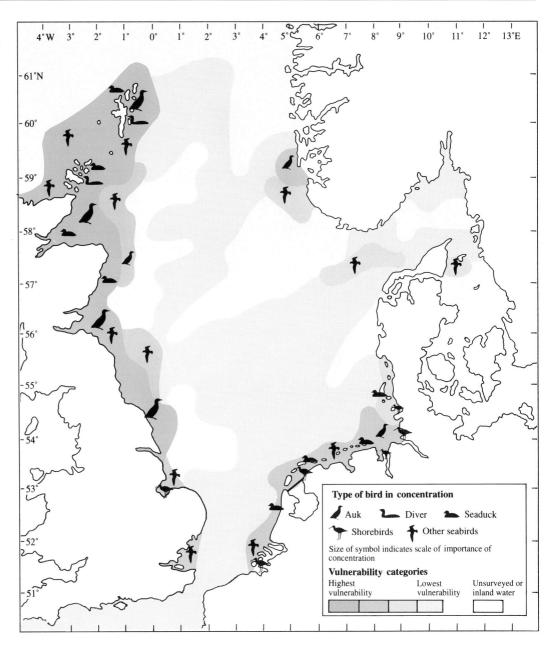

British part of the North Sea within 4 km of the coastline. Red-throated divers move south in the autumn and birds are frequently recorded on migration past major headlands in the North Sea.

Red-throated and great-northern divers are completely flightless during moult which takes place in early October to late November. During winter (Tasker *et al.* 1987) birds have been recorded principally south of Caithness with additional numbers thought to have come into the North Sea from Scandinavia, the Faroes, Iceland and Greenland. The areas which are important for divers during this time are inner and southern Moray Firth, Firth of Forth, Tay Bay, outer Wash and the Thames Estuary.

Eiders move short distances from breeding sites to moulting and wintering sites on the British coast. It is estimated that 53,500 eiders overwinter in the western North Sea (Tasker *et al.* 1987). The outer Firth of Tay, eastern Grampian, Firth of Forth, Lindisfarne and Golspie all hold large numbers, but due to the presence of very large numbers off Denmark, only the first two areas ever approach international importance.

An indication of the movements of seabirds and waterfowl species in the North Sea can be derived from Figures 7.2.2 a, b and c which outline the vulnerability of bird concentrations to surface pollution in the North Sea at different times of the year. An assessment of vulnerability is based on the amount of time the species spends on the water and

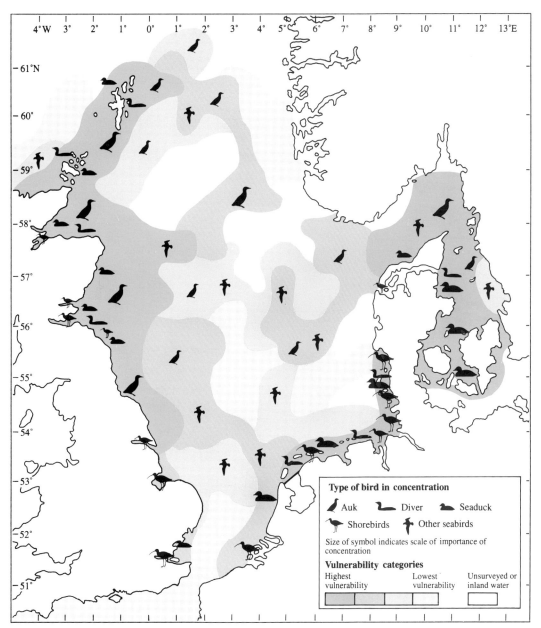

Figure 7.2.2b
The distribution of seabirds
in the North Sea in
September (after Carter *et al.*
1993).

the importance of the area to the world population of that species. Information is taken from Carter *et al.* (1993) and shows bird concentration for the months of June (breeding), September and December (non-breeding).

Trends

The seabird populations in the North Sea have, in general, increased in recent decades. However, there have been some recent declines associated with the breeding failure of certain species in Shetland (kittiwake, Arctic tern, Arctic skua and puffin). There has also been a decline in the number of herring gulls *Larus argentatus* throughout Britain. Recent trends in populations are presented in Lloyd *et al.* (1991) and examples are given in Figure 7.2.3 for populations of cormorant, razorbill and kittiwake.

WATERFOWL DISTRIBUTION

Waders and wildfowl (collectively known as waterfowl) use the coastal habitats of the Britain as winter feeding sites, as staging posts during migration and as breeding sites. The abundance of invertebrate animals living in the soft sediments of many coastal habitats provides food for many of the large numbers of birds which visit Britain at different times of the year. Other species feed on vegetation of tidal flats, saltmarshes and coastal grasslands.

Figure 7.2.2c
The distribution of seabirds in the North Sea in December (after Carter *et al.* 1993).

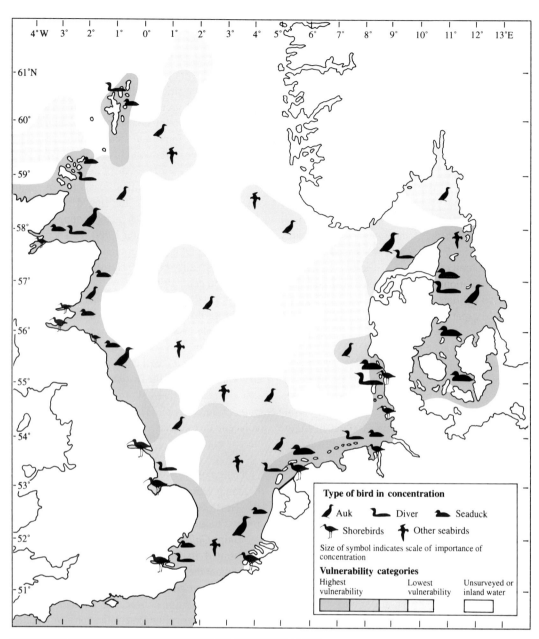

Type of bird in concentration

Auk   Diver   Seaduck

Shorebirds   Other seabirds

Size of symbol indicates scale of importance of concentration

Vulnerability categories

| Highest vulnerability | | | Lowest vulnerability | Unsurveyed or inland water |

Figure 7.2.3
Changes in populations of cormorants, razorbills and kittiwakes, 1969/70–1985/87.

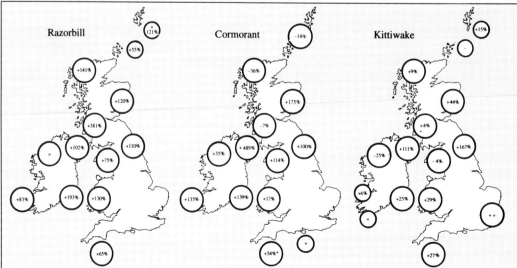

Breeding distribution

Several surveys of breeding waders have been made covering particular habitats and species, for example Prater (1989) and Smith (1988), with the British population of breeding waders being estimated by Reed (1985) and updated by Stroud, Mudge & Pienkowski (1990). A comparison of this data with European populations (Piersma 1986; Stroud, Mudge & Pienkowski 1990) illustrates the importance of British estuaries as a habitat for breeding waders.

The major breeding habitats are shingle structures and beaches, sand dunes and saltmarshes. Coastal grazing marshes and wet grasslands close to the tidal limit of estuaries also support important wader populations. Twelve species of wader breed in coastal habitats in Britain; several of these are described separately below. Along the North Sea coastal margin three estuaries support an assemblage of eight of these species (Dornoch Firth, the Wash, and the north Norfolk coast). Other estuaries in Orkney, East Anglia and south-east England also support important breeding wader assemblages. The number of species using each estuary along the North Sea coastal margin is given in Figure 7.2.4. Further details are given in Davidson *et al.* (1991).

Lapwing *Vanellus vanellus* are the most abundant breeding wader in Europe, with Britain supporting the largest breeding population. Lapwing breed widely along the North Sea coast, especially where there are areas of wet grassland and farmland. The highest densities of wet grassland nesting lapwing occur in parts of East Anglia and Kent. Lapwings also breed in some saltmarshes in east Scotland (Allport, O'Brien & Cadbury 1986).

Redshank *Tringa totanus* are one of the most common coastal breeding waders with many breeding in eastern Britain on marshes where grazing pressure is low. On the coast, redshank breed particularly in saltmarsh and wet grassland habitats. High densities occur in Orkney, East Anglia and Kent. Large numbers are found on the Wash, Norfolk Broads and the North Kent marshes (446 pairs). A decline in the numbers of redshank which breed on inland sites (Smith 1983) and on wet grassland (Smith 1988) has increased the importance of remaining saltmarsh habitats as breeding sites.

Oystercatchers *Haematopus ostralegus* are predominantly coastal birds, usually nesting on rocky, shingle or sandy shores, saltmarshes and grasslands. In Scotland and northern England this species commonly nests inland as well. The absence of breeding sites in the south and east of England has been attributed to disturbance and a lack of suitable feeding habitat (Sharrock 1976).

Britain supports 64% of the European population of ringed plover *Charadrius hiaticula* which breed in temperate locations. Other populations breed in sub-arctic and arctic regions. The main coastal breeding habitats for this species are shingle and sandy beaches. Important areas for this species on the North Sea coast are found in Orkney and Shetland, the Humber estuary, the Wash and the north Norfolk coast. British coasts are of major international importance for ringed plover. The British North Sea coastal margin supports over 4,000 breeding pairs (Prater 1989). This represents 47% of the total British population, and 30% of the north-west and central European population (Davidson *et al.* 1991).

Avocets *Recurvirostra avosetta* nested in Britain until the late 1800s but were then absent until the late 1940s when they began to recolonise the East Anglian coast. Now breeding in 18 localities along the east coast of England between the Wash and Kent, the British population stands at 2% of the north-west and central European population. Most birds breed on brackish lagoons, adjacent to estuaries, and feeding takes place on nearby mudflats.

Dunlin *Calidris alpina* breed widely in arctic and subarctic regions with less than 10,000 pairs breeding in Britain, mainly in upland areas. Along the North Sea coastal margin breeding sites are limited to the Dornoch and Cromarty Firths.

Snipe *Gallinago gallinago* are widely but thinly distributed in Britain with about 30,000 pairs throughout the country. In lowland areas snipe nest mostly on wet grasslands, bogs and fen. Extensive losses of traditional breeding habitats through drainage and agricultural intensification have resulted in population decline of this species particularly in southern England (Smith 1988). Important sites for breeding snipe are the Ouse and Nene Washes.

About 35,500 pairs of curlew *Numenius arquata* breed in Britain, typically in upland areas, especially poorly drained moors and heaths. This species does not often breed on the coast but has been recorded on estuarine saltmarsh in eastern Scotland and on Orkney on small wetlands adjacent to the coast.

Few wildfowl breed on the coast of Britain. Most species breed further north and then migrate south to overwinter. Many species of goose breed in the arctic and subarctic regions between eastern Canada and western Siberia, and only resident feral populations of two species, Canada goose *Branta canadensis* and greylag goose *Anser anser*, occasionally breed on coastal habitats in Britain.

Figure 7.2.4
The number of species of breeding waders on estuaries along the North Sea coastal margin (after Davidson *et al.* 1991).

Based upon the 1975 Ordnance Survey 1:1,250,000 map with the permission of the Controller of Her Majesty's Stationery Office © Crown Copyright.

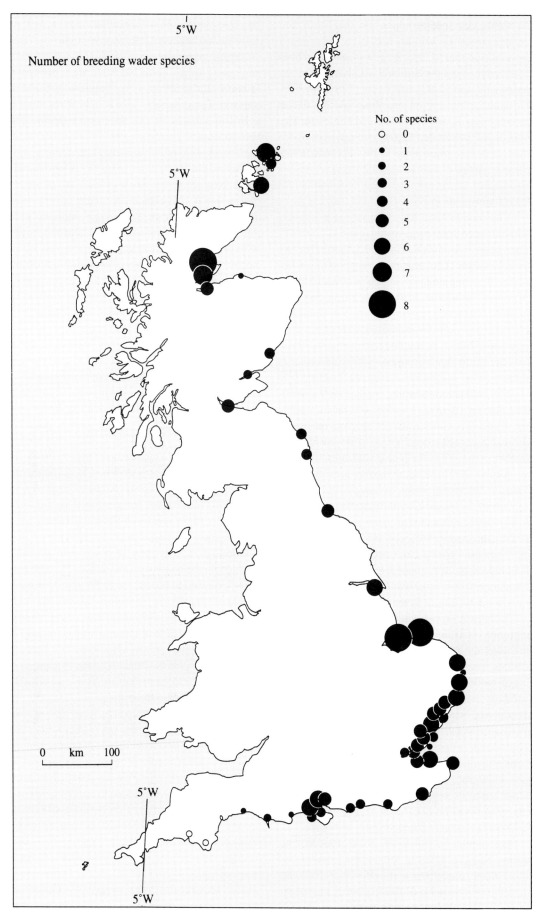

Most duck species which use the North Sea coastal areas in winter breed in freshwater habitats. However, shelduck *Tadorna tadorna* breed extensively round the British coast, wherever there are suitable sandy or muddy shores close to sand dunes and grazing marshes. Shelduck depend on estuarine ecosystems for their entire life cycle. The British population (*c.* 15,000) is internationally important and represents at least 11% of the European total.

Non-breeding distribution

Approximately 60% of the waders which overwinter on the coast of Britain (1.3 million) use the North Sea coastal margin. This represents some 40% of the waders wintering along the Atlantic shores of Europe (Moser & Prys-Jones 1990). The North Sea also provides important staging areas and moulting grounds during spring and autumn and the figure given above is a minimum estimate of the total number of individuals using habitats on the east coast of Britain.

The most common wader species on the North Sea coast outside of the breeding season are dunlin, knot *Calidris canutus*, oystercatcher and redshank. The importance of coastal habitats for waders using the British margin of the North Sea varies between species in a European context. Details are given in Figure 7.2.5.

Differences in the distribution of wader species between estuarine and non estuarine habitats have been established by Moser & Summers (1987) and are shown in Figure 7.2.6. Certain species such as black-tailed godwit *Limosa limosa* use estuaries exclusively whilst other waders, e.g. curlew, have a more even distribution between coastal habitats. Others, such as purple sandpiper *Calidris maritima* and turnstone *Arenaria interpres,* overwinter chiefly on non-estuarine shores.

The main influx of waders to the North Sea begins in August. Migration to and from arctic breeding areas requires that birds stop at staging areas to feed. Many birds stop to moult on the North sea coastal sites. Wing moult takes two or three months and having completed this, some species move to wintering grounds elsewhere in Britain or western Europe where an individual bird may move between several sites over winter. Other birds remain on the same estuaries throughout the winter months.

The number of birds using estuaries on the North Sea coast peaks in September and October when birds move from the Wadden Sea and elsewhere in mainland Europe after moulting. The influx of birds from the continent continues

into November and December. Some further movement of waders (and wildfowl) into North Sea estuaries from the east, and some westward movement from North Sea estuaries, occurs in January and February in response to severe weather. The relatively mild weather experienced in British estuaries gives them added importance in such times.

The midwinter (January) numbers and distribution of waterfowl (waders and wildfowl) using British North Sea estuaries is shown in Figure 7.2.7. Large numbers occur on estuaries throughout the North Sea coastal margin, with particularly large midwinter concentrations in the Moray Basin, the Humber, the Wash and north Norfolk coast, the complex of estuaries in Suffolk, Essex and Kent, and around the Solent. In January

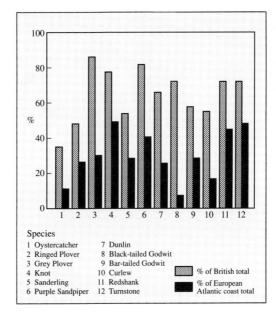

Figure 7.2.5
The percentage of some European and British wader populations on the British North Sea coast (based on Moser & Prys-Jones 1990).

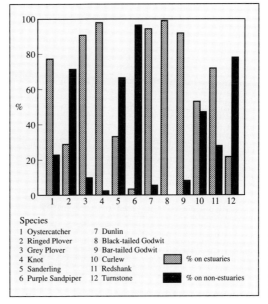

Figure 7.2.6
Distribution of waders on estuarine and non-estuarine habitats (after Moser & Summers 1987).

Figure 7.2.7
The number of waterfowl
(waders and wildfowl) which
use estuarine sites along the
North Sea coastal margin in
January, based on five-year
January mean between 1983
and 1987. (After Davidson
et al. 1991.)

Based upon the 1975 Ordnance Survey
1:1,250,000 map with the permission
of the Controller of Her Majesty's
Stationery Office © Crown Copyright.

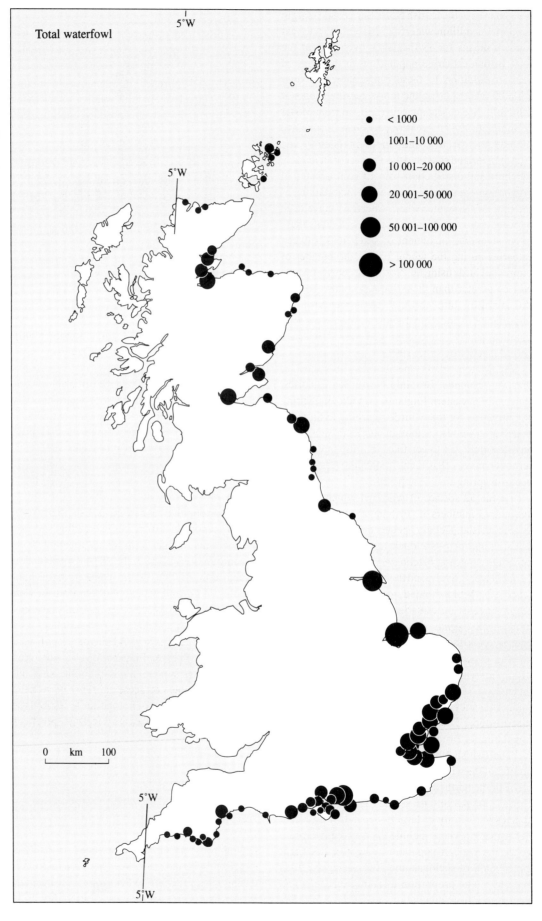

the estuaries of the British North Sea coastal margin support 1.1 million waterfowl (based on five-year January means for 1983–1987), over 60% of the total British estuarine populations at that time of year. In addition to these birds, there are over 130,000 waders using the non-estuarine shores of this North Sea coastal margin (derived from Moser & Summers 1987). Areas of particular importance include the Orkney and Shetland Islands, the Northumberland coast and the Thanet coast. January numbers and distributions permit comparisons of population size with international populations at the time of the winter when waterfowl move least between estuaries. Note, however, that since there is considerable movement of waterfowl between estuaries during the winter period the number of individual birds using the North Sea coastal margin will be greater than these January totals. To take this mobility into account, assessments of the importance of individual sites are based on peak monthly winter counts averaged over a five-year period (see Kirby *et al.* 1991).

By March, many species start to return to breeding grounds. Britain's North Sea estuaries, especially in eastern England, provide vital spring staging areas for many birds returning to northern breeding grounds. Although numbers present at any one time are lower than in midwinter, rapid turnover means that many more individual birds occur in spring than is apparent.

Of the 32 species of wildfowl which occur in substantial numbers in Britain, 25 are wholly or largely coastal. Certain species depend entirely on estuaries in winter – shelduck, light-bellied and dark-bellied Brent geese, *Branta bernicla* sspp. *hrota* and *bernicla* respectively, and the barnacle goose *Branta leucopsis*. White-fronted geese *Anser albifrons albifrons* roost on estuaries and large numbers of mute swan *Cygnus olor*, whooper swan *Cygnus cygnus*, pink-footed goose *Anser brachrhynchus*, greylag goose, wigeon, teal *Anas crecca*, mallard *Anas platyrynchos*, and pintail *Anas acuta* also use this habitat. Many species of goose depend on a few traditional sites whereas shelduck are more widely distributed. The largest wintering wildfowl population in Britain is in the Wash.

The British North Sea coast supports about a quarter of the wildfowl which overwinter in Britain (16% of the north-west European population). The British populations of several species and sub-species are wholly or largely dependent on North Sea estuaries. These include the dark-bellied brent goose, the Svalbard population of light-bellied Brent goose, 60% of shelduck and 50% of wigeon *Anas penelope*. The proportion of some European and British wildfowl populations using the North Sea

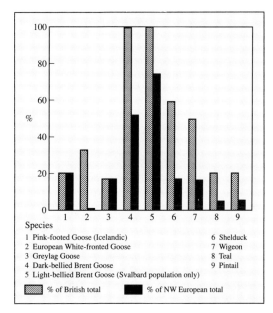

Figure 7.2.8
The percentage of some British and European wildfowl populations found on the British North Sea coast (after Salmon 1990).

coast is given in Figure 7.2.8. (after Salmon 1990). Further details are also given in Davidson *et al.* (1991).

At least 29 estuaries along the British North Sea coast contribute to the network of internationally important sites under the Ramsar Convention and/ or the EC Directive on the Conservation of Wild Birds. Sites are shown in Figure 7.2.9.

Trends

Waterfowl populations can vary substantially from year to year due to differences in breeding success. There are also longer term trends apparent. Poor breeding seasons in the early 1970s contributed to a long-term decline in the population of knot breeding in Greenland and northern Canada with proportional increases occurring again only recently. Increases in populations of oystercatcher, grey plover, bar-tailed godwit and ringed plover were identified by Smit & Piersma (1989), who also noted decreases in populations of dunlin, knot and redshank. Numbers of geese are reported to have increased in some parts of Europe due to restrictions on shooting and to changes in agricultural practices (Ebbinge 1985).

OTHER SPECIES

Breeding distribution

Several other species of bird breed in habitats associated with the coast. Reed beds are important nesting sites for bearded tits *Panurus biarmicus*, marsh harrier *Circus aeruginosus*, bittern *Botaurus*

Figure 7.2.9
Estuaries along the North Sea coastal margin which are internationally important for overwintering wildfowl populations.
Based upon the 1975 Ordnance Survey 1:1,250,000 map with the permission of the Controller of Her Majesty's Stationery Office © Crown Copyright.

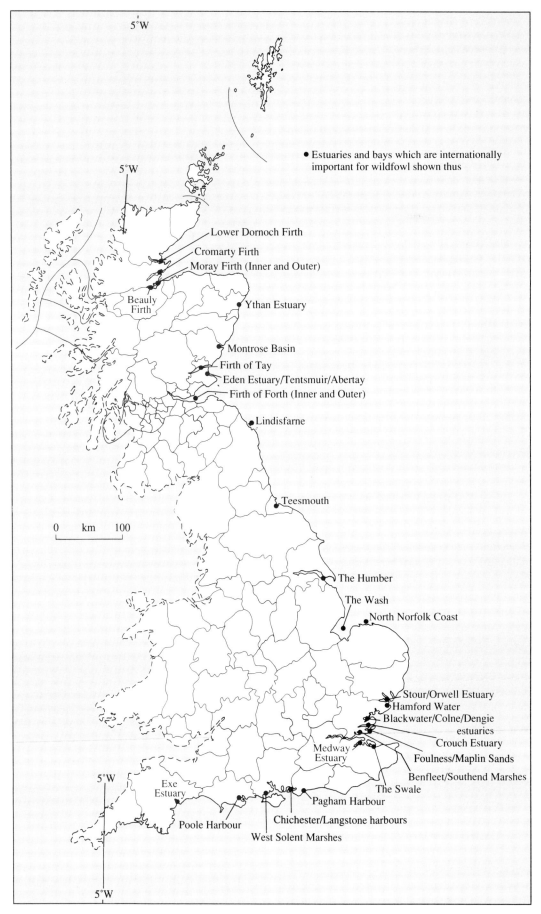

● Estuaries and bays which are internationally important for wildfowl shown thus

Lower Dornoch Firth
Cromarty Firth
Moray Firth (Inner and Outer)
Beauly Firth
Ythan Estuary
Montrose Basin
Firth of Tay
Eden Estuary/Tentsmuir/Abertay
Firth of Forth (Inner and Outer)
Lindisfarne
Teesmouth
The Humber
The Wash
North Norfolk Coast
Stour/Orwell Estuary
Hamford Water
Blackwater/Colne/Dengie estuaries
Crouch Estuary
Medway Estuary
Foulness/Maplin Sands
Benfleet/Southend Marshes
The Swale
Pagham Harbour
Exe Estuary
Chichester/Langstone harbours
Poole Harbour
West Solent Marshes

stellaris, reed warbler *Acrocephalus scirpaceus* and sedge warbler *Acrocephalus schoenobaenus.* Reed beds also provide an important habitat for many species of insectivorous migratory birds during the autumn. The most extensive area of reed bed in Scotland is on the Tay estuary. Other extensive reed beds occur on the east coast of England with numerous smaller reed beds occurring on the south coast.

Wintering distribution

Saltmarshes and coastal grazing marshes are used by several species of bird of prey – short-eared owls *Asio flammeus,* merlin *Falco columbarius,* peregrine *Falco peregrinus* and sparrowhawk *Accipiter nisus.* More specifically on the east coast, hen harriers *Circus cyaneus* overwinter in the reed beds and marshes of the Wash and north Norfolk coast as well as using other coastal areas between the Humber and Kent.

During the winter various passerine species feed on seeds in the saltmarshes and along strandlines. Three species which are largely restricted to the east coast are lapland bunting *Calcarius lapponicus,* shorelark *Eremophla alpestris* and twite *Caruelis flavirostris.* In Britain the twite winters principally in the Wash and on the Essex estuaries.

IMPACTS ON BIRDS

Natural changes in the marine environment include long-term changes in water temperature and circulation and associated changes in abundance and distribution of marine species; and changes in area of intertidal mudflat and saltmarsh as a result of changing sea levels, *Spartina* die back and increased erosion. These in their turn affect the bird populations, and superimposed on this are changes brought about as a result of man's activities such as intertidal infilling and land claim for industrial use, recreation and agriculture.

Fisheries

Most bird populations are regulated by the availability and abundance of their food. There is at present insufficient information on the interactions between fish species and their avian predators, although depletion of larger individuals of predatory, commercially exploited fish or pelagic fish stock collapses in the late seventies may have allowed populations of smaller fish to increase. This in turn may have allowed birds that feed on these smaller fish to increase their populations.

Some fish stocks in the North Sea have declined in recent years and there may also have been changes in the availability of certain fish species to seabirds (NCC 1989). Small fish such as sandeels Ammodytidae, young herring *Clupea harengus,* sprat *Sprattus sprattus* and young gadoids Gadidae are the most important species taken by seabirds. Changes in stock size and availability of sandeels around Shetland have in recent years been implicated in the unsuccessful breeding of some species of seabird (Monaghan *et al.* 1992). Little is known about how small fish behaviour affects their availability to seabirds or how this might be altered by fisheries practices.

Concern has been expressed at the level of mortalities of birds caused by fishing gear. Monofilament gill nets and tangle nets, which are now illegal in Scotland, pose a particular problem to diving seabirds which fail to see the nets in the water. There have been reports of mortalities of auks in bag and fly nets which are set along shorelines to intercept salmon off the north-east coast of Scotland. In north-east England drift net fishing for salmon may cause a similar problem (Dunnet *et al.* 1990).

The exploitation of intertidal shellfish stocks, particularly in relation to the harvesting of cockle *Cerastoderma edule* stocks, is also of concern to conservationists. Certain species of coastal birds feed directly on cockles and are therefore dependent on the maintenance of shellfish stocks. Human disturbance of feeding waders on the flats can be a problem during harvesting of any commercial shellfish species. Digging for bait worms such as lugworms *Arenicola marina* and ragworms *Hediste diversicolor* also causes disturbance and commercial farming of bivalves on tidal flats may further disrupt feeding time for birds using these areas (Rees & Tasker 1990).

Land claim

Land claim has been responsible for major losses of coastal habitat over the last century and further piecemeal enclosure continues the destruction of the intertidal zone, putting further pressure on the estuarine ecosystem and the birds which it supports. Birds displaced from traditional feeding sites become concentrated into smaller areas or are forced to move to less good areas where mortality may be greater (Goss-Custard 1985). Studies from the infill of the Tees estuary (Evans & Pienkowski 1983) show that the pattern of displacement varies for different species of wader. The birds most seriously affected tend to be juveniles and those species which need to feed for a high proportion of the tidal cycle to meet their energy requirements. (For a description of land-claim impacts see Davidson *et al.* 1991.)

Oil pollution

Major incidents which involve single large oil spills (acute pollution) are fairly well documented. Chronic oil pollution incidents are caused by operational discharge from a variety of sources and often go undetected until oil contaminated birds are found on beaches. Species which are vulnerable to oil pollution are those which spend most of their time on the surface of the sea. In particular, species which are flightless during moult (divers, auks and seaduck), or those with juveniles which leave the nest before they can fly, are most at risk from oil spills. These species are present in summer in high densities off Shetland, Orkney, Moray Firth, eastern Scotland and north-east England. The time and location of oil spills is crucial in assessing the potential threat to seabirds.

Oil pollution causes seabird mortality principally during winter when birds may be in a weaker condition. Oil soaks into plumage and destroys insulation and waterproofing properties. Birds may ingest toxic substances from oil as they try to clean their feathers, leading to organ failure and death.

Inshore areas hold vulnerable populations of divers, shags, cormorants, black guillemots and seaduck. The vulnerability of seabirds in the North Sea is categorised by Tasker & Pienkowski (1987) on the basis of the amount of time spent on the water and the importance of the area to the world population of the species. The enclosed and narrow nature of estuaries means that oil spillage there can have a major impact on the waterfowl using the area (Salmon 1990). See also Section 9.3.

Chemical pollution

Causes of mortality are not always obvious since it may take days for the dead birds to be washed up on shore. Polychlorinated biphenyl (PCB), which is very slow to degrade in the environment, may have contributed to the death of seabirds in the past. High levels of contaminants have been found in seabirds which have an inshore distribution around the more heavily industrialised regions of the North Sea. In the 1970s egg-shell thinning was correlated with contamination by chlorinated hydrocarbon pesticides with effects most marked in guillemots and gannets. Organochlorine levels in puffins on the Isle of May are currently being monitored. Continued monitoring of levels of chemical residues

in seabirds has shown a decline in dieldrin in recent years. However, there are regional differences in the levels of chemicals found in bird tissue.

The levels of heavy metals is known to be high in some estuaries, e.g. the Tees, and these become concentrated in invertebrates which in turn are the food source of many waterfowl species. Enrichment from sewage effluent and agricultural run-off has affected the ecology of certain coastal ecosystems, for instance the Ythan estuary (Raffaelli *et al.* 1989).

Introduced predators

The introduction by man of predatory mammals (cats *Felis domesticus*, rats *Rattus norvegicus*, hedgehogs *Erinaceus europeaus* and American mink *Mustela vison*) to sites previously free of these animals can extirpate breeding seabird colonies. Ground-nesting birds such as terns and gulls and burrow-nesting petrels, shearwaters and puffins are all particularly at risk.

Litter

Birds may become entangled or may try to eat discarded plastic materials. Small beads, polythene packaging and discarded/lost fishing nets are the principle cause of mortality. Gannets, in particular, get tangled in pieces of netting which they use as nesting material. Species most at risk from ingesting plastic beads are pelagic feeders such as shearwaters, storm petrels and fulmars.

Disturbance

Disturbance from human activities may adversely affect the success of cliff-nesting seabird colonies. For instance, low flying aircraft can cause considerable damage. Terns and beach-nesting waders are becoming increasingly restricted in choice of nesting sites as recreational pressure increases on coastal habitats. Most successful nesting now takes place in nature reserves and other protected areas. Tern colonies are particularly vulnerable and some are actively patrolled by wardens to prevent disturbance. In winter the number of undisturbed roosting places may be limited. On estuaries waders are particularly vulnerable to disturbance at high tide roosts as well as on their feeding grounds. During severe weather, when energy demands are particularly high, disturbance to feeding waterfowl may lead to increased risk of mortality through reducing the time for which birds can feed.

Wildfowl can be disturbed by water-based recreational activities which have increased enormously in recent years. This problem is particularly acute on the south-east and south coasts (Salmon 1990).

SOURCES OF INFORMATION

The development of the offshore oil industry raised fears that oil pollution might increase and have an adverse effect on birds in the North Sea. After an initial examination of the feasibility of surveying the distribution of seabirds in the North Sea the Nature Conservancy Council (NCC) set up the Seabirds at Sea Team (SAST) in 1979. Most of the data were collected during passages on ships in the North Sea and the results of this work are described in Tasker *et al.* (1987) and Tasker & Pienkowski (1987). For the north of Scotland information is described by Webb *et al.* (1990) and Tasker *et al.* (1990). Over the winter of 1989/90 a special survey of the coastal birds in Poole Bay was undertaken by Aspinall & Tasker (1990). A similar survey of the birds of the Solent was undertaken the following year (Aspinal & Tasker 1992).

The diets of seabirds in the North Sea are not well understood. Limited studies concentrate on particular groups (Blake *et al.* 1985; Harris & Wanless 1990) or on diet during the breeding season (Furness & Hislop 1981; Galbraith 1983). An outline of populations of prey species and a summary of knowledge of diets is given in Tasker *et al.* (1987).

The Seabird Monitoring Programme (JNCC) coordinates and encourages seabird monitoring throughout Britain and Ireland by both amateur and professional researchers. Seabird breeding performance is being monitored, with numbers and breeding success recorded annually for kittiwakes and other species. This cooperative programme provides a cost-effective mechanism of monitoring the quality of offshore waters for seabirds. It also summarises data gathered independently by Shetland Oil Terminal Environmental Advisory Group (SOTEAG) and RSPB.

The Seabird Colony Register is a joint JNCC/Seabird Group project collating data for colonies throughout Britain and Ireland. Results from a 1985–1988 seabird census of cliff-nesting birds have been published (Lloyd *et al.* 1991).

The movements of waders and wildfowl have been studied by extensive catching, ringing and colour marking programmes since the mid-1960s. In 1947 The Wildfowl & Wetlands Trust (WWT) started coordinating wildfowl counting through the 'National Wildfowl Count' scheme, and in 1969 the British Trust for Ornithology was responsible for organising the 'Birds of Estuaries Enquiry'

programme. In October 1993 these two schemes were integrated to form the new Wetland Bird Survey (WeBS). WeBS is a new partnership between BTO, WWT, the Royal Society for the Protection of Birds and the JNCC to count non-breeding waders and wildfowl at wetland sites throughout the UK. The programme involves a series of monthly counts, by over 3,000 dedicated volunteers, of waterfowl at key wetland sites, both inland and coastal. An International Waterfowl Census was also initiated in 1967 to count waterfowl in the Western Palearctic region in January of each year.

A survey of the numbers of waders using non-estuarine shores was undertaken during the winter of 1984/1985 by the BTO and the Wader Study Group (WSG). This covered almost all the non-estuarine shores of the UK, permitting the wader populations in estuaries to be set in context.

Further BOEE and WSG data allowed a revision of population estimates for waders wintering on the coastline of Britain (Moser 1987). The wintering populations of wildfowl and waders on estuarine and non-estuarine habitats in Britain are described in Prater (1981), Moser & Summers (1987) and Lack (1986).

Waterfowl species which breed in coastal habitats have been less well studied. Complete quantitative surveys of all coastal breeding waterfowl have not yet been achieved. The breeding distribution of all bird species in the British Isles has been mapped (Sharrock 1976) and a more recent national survey is soon to be published.

A comprehensive review of the wildlife and nature conservation of estuaries in Britain has been published by the NCC (Davidson *et al.* 1981). This includes an assessment of all North Sea estuaries in Britain for overwintering, breeding and migrating waterfowl.

Single species surveys such as for ringed plover (Prater 1989) provide comprehensive national distributions; other surveys have used a sampling approach for some habitats (e.g. Allport *et al.* 1986), or have surveyed single localities.

7.3 SEALS

INTRODUCTION

Two species of seal breed in British waters – the common or harbour seal *Phoca vitulina* and the grey seal, *Halichoerus grypus*. Both are members of the Phocidae, or true seals, which are characterised by their fur-covered flippers, the absence of external ear pinnae, and hind flippers which cannot be turned forwards.

Figure 7.3.1
Distribution of common seals *Phoca vitulina* in the North Atlantic (after Bonner 1972 with modifications by J. Harwood)

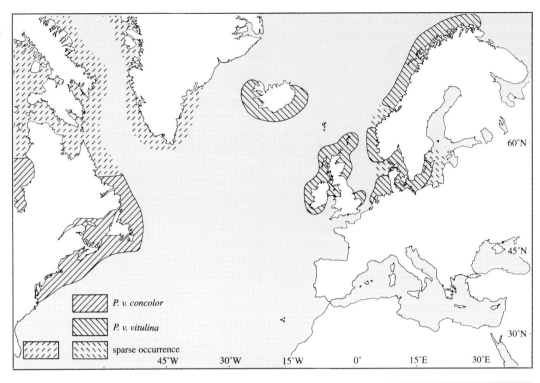

Figure 7.3.2
Worldwide distribution of grey seals *Halichoerus grypus* (after Bonner 1972 with modifications by J. Harwood)

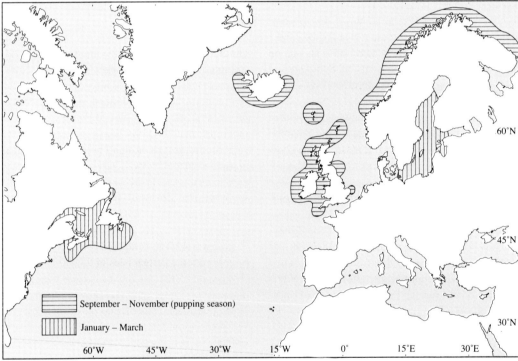

The common seal is one of the most widely distributed seal species, occurring along the temperate sub-arctic and arctic coasts of the north Pacific and north Atlantic oceans (Figure 7.3.1). There are five sub-species divided by distribution. The British population of *Phoca vitulina* ssp. *vitulina* was estimated to be a minimum of 24,640 in 1991 (Hiby *et al.* 1993). This represents around 5% of a total world population of *Phoca*

vitulina of around 500,000 individuals (Anderson 1988).

The grey seal has a much more limited worldwide distribution than the common seal. It occurs in the east Atlantic around the British Isles, the Baltic sea, northern Scandinavia and Iceland; and around Newfoundland in the west Atlantic ocean (Figure 7.3.2). The worldwide population is estimated to be around 200,000–250,000. The population in Great Britain in 1991 was estimated to be around 93,500, i.e. around 40% of the world population (Anderson 1988).

Grey seals, although less numerous worldwide, are more numerous in the British Isles than common seals. For the last 30 years up until 1988 there has been little evidence of any significant change in the number of common seals in British waters. The number of grey seals increased steadily over this period, due largely to increased availability of undisturbed offshore island habitats for breeding. This occurred largely as a result of the decline in human population of remote offshore islands, particularly in the outer Hebrides (Northridge 1990).

DISTRIBUTION OF SEALS IN THE NORTH SEA

Common seals

Common seals breed around the west coast of Scotland, northern and western Ireland, Shetland and Orkney, the Moray and Tay firths, Donna Nook in Lincolnshire, the Wash, the north Norfolk coast and some of the Essex estuaries. See Figure 7.3.4.

In Shetland and Orkney common seals pup on rocky shores; on the east coast of Scotland and England they tend to pup on intertidal sandbanks or in creeks in saltmarshes. On the North Sea coast of Britain, prior to the phocine distemper epidemic in 1988, the largest breeding populations of common seals were in Orkney and in the Wash. Orkney now holds many more common seals than the Wash.

The Blackwater and Crouch estuaries in Essex also have small breeding populations. Common seals do not breed and are rarely seen south of Essex on the North Sea coast. Their absence extends right round the Channel and Welsh coasts to the Irish sea and southern Scotland. It is not known why common seals are rarely seen within this area, as suitable habitat does exist, for example in Poole Harbour where common seals are occasionally seen.

The following are maximum counts (which represent a minimum number of seals in the population) from surveys in 1986-91 (Hiby *et al.* 1993):

Shetland	4,700	(1984)
Shetland	4,784	(1991)
Orkney	7,100	(1989)
Moray & Tay Firths	1,663	(1991)
The Wash	1,551	(1991)

The common seal count for the North Sea coast is 15,000, compared to the total for the British Isles count of 25,000 individuals.

Year	Orkney	Shetland	Isle of May	Farne Islands
1977	3,700	700	-	1,200
1979	4,300	-	300	1,300
1983	-	1,000	300	900
1984	5,000	-	500	800
1988	6,200	-	700	800
1989	7,100	-	900	900
1990	7,300	-	1,200	1,000
1991	8,400	-	1,200	900

Table 7.3.1
Pup production for North Sea grey seal populations (from Sea Mammal Research Unit unpublished data).

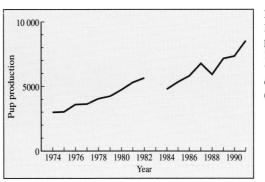

Figure 7.3.3
Estimates of grey seal pup production in Orkney from 1974 to 1991, based on the 'revised' method for estimating pup production (Harwood pers. comm.)

Grey seals

The outer Hebrides, the Orkney and Shetland Islands and south west Wales are the main breeding centres for grey seals in Britain. Small populations breed on the north coast of Scotland and outer Moray Firth, and on sandbanks at Donna Nook in Lincolnshire and Scroby Sands in Norfolk. There are scattered groups on small beaches and in caves in south western Cornwall. Grey seals do not breed and are rarely seen in the area between Norfolk and south western Cornwall, probably due to lack of suitable habitat.

The grey seal population breeding on the North Sea coast is 40,700, compared to a total population estimate for the British Isles of 93,500 individuals (Hiby *et al.* 1993). See Figure 7.3.5. It is estimated that 44% of British grey seal pups are born on the North Sea coast. Data on pup production for grey seal populations are presented in Table 7.3.1, with estimates of pup production in Orkney also presented in Figure 7.3.3 (SMRU unpublished data).

DESCRIPTION OF RESOURCE

Common seals

Large aggregations of common seals can be found at suitable sites throughout the year in both rocky and sandy habitats. Within breeding groups there is segregation of male and female, breeding and non-

Figure 7.3.4
Distribution of common seal
breeding colonies on the
North Sea coast (Harwood
pers. comm.).
Based upon the 1975 Ordnance Survey
1:1,250,000 map with the permission
of the Controller of Her Majesty's
Stationery Office © Crown Copyright.

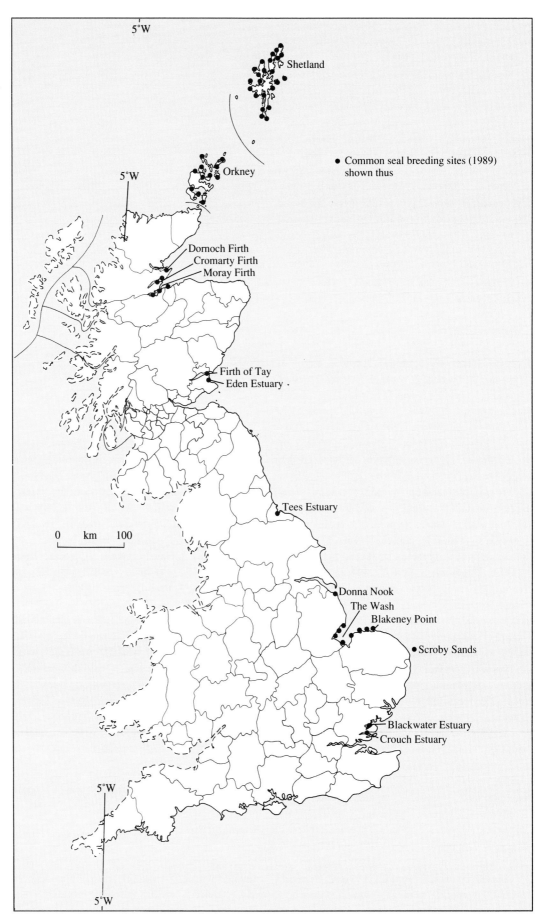

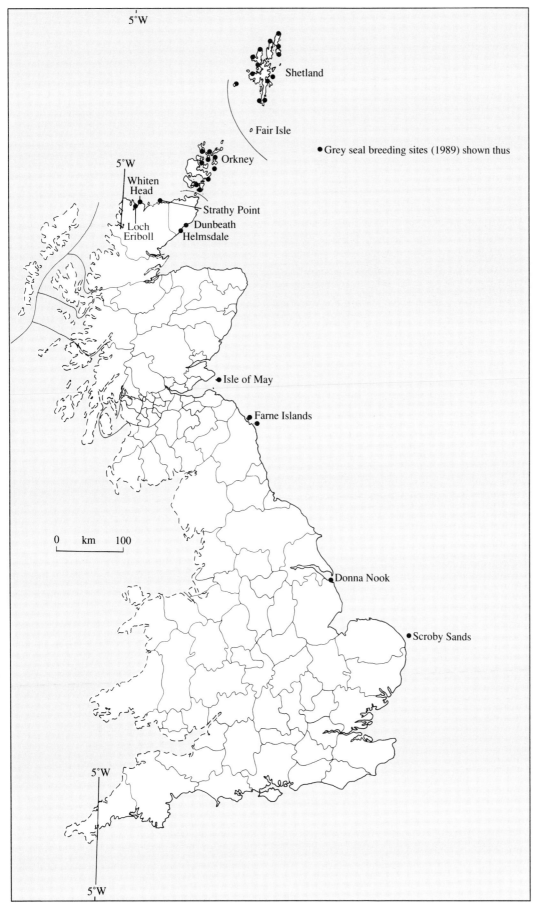

Figure 7.3.5
Distribution of grey seal
breeding colonies on the
North Sea coast (Harwood
pers. comm.).
Based upon the 1975 Ordnance Survey
1:1,250,000 map with the permission
of the Controller of Her Majesty's
Stationery Office © Crown Copyright.

5°W

Shetland

Fair Isle

● Grey seal breeding sites (1989) shown thus

Orkney

5°W

Whiten
Head

Strathy Point

Loch
Eriboll

Dunbeath
Helmsdale

● Isle of May

● Farne Islands

0   km   100

● Donna Nook

● Scroby Sands

5°W

5°W

173

breeding animals during the pupping season (Thompson 1989). Yearling animals are less often seen with the main group after about the middle of June (Bonner 1972). Common seals pup in early June and July. Common seals do not show the same degree of aggregation during the breeding season as do grey seals, so the pups are spread out over a much larger area. However, recent research has shown that aerial photographic counts of hauled out common seals during the moult in August gave the highest and most consistent minimum counts for the Orkney common seal population (Thompson & Harwood 1990). To what extent this method may apply to other populations which tend to haul out on intertidal sandbanks is not yet known. For the Orkney population rocky shore haul out sites are always available, and tidal state made no significant difference to counts made during the middle of the day (Thompson & Harwood 1990). For estuarine populations haul out behaviour is likely to be much more variable according to time of the tidal cycle at which the count is made.

Other than the above recent estimates for Orkney, population estimates for common seals are probably of a lower degree of accuracy than those for grey seals. Estimates are made using total numbers of hauled-out animals, and these will always be lower than the total population size. An indication of this inaccuracy is that the number of dead common seals found in the Wadden Sea during the epidemic of phocine distemper virus in 1988 exceeded the best estimate for total population size in that area (Harwood 1990).

The breeding season is followed by the moulting period in late July and early August, with some animals moulting as early as June and as late as mid-September. Yearlings moult first, followed by older seals, females before males, and immature males before mature males (Thompson & Rothery 1987). The first moult of common seal pups occurs in the womb (Gubbay 1988).

Grey seals

Grey seals are confined to rocky coasts and a limited number of estuaries. The grey seal breeding season begins in early September in south-west England and October in the northern Scottish islands, but does not commence until November or December on the east coast at the Isle of May, Donna Nook and Farne Island sites. Neither male nor female feeds during their stay at the breeding site, which is 2.5 weeks for females (the length of lactation), and up to six weeks for males.

Moult occurs after breeding, in January to March for females, and March to May for males.

Average life span of male grey seals is around 25 years, with the oldest recorded male being 29 years old. Average life span of females is greater, usually 30–35 years, with the oldest recorded animal in Britain being a 46-year old female recorded from Shetland.

There is overlap in habitat preference between the two species, and they sometimes occur in mixed groups. There is a growing body of information on the movements of grey and common seals based on results obtained using various forms of telemetry (e.g. Hammond *et al.* in press; McConnell *et al.* 1992; Thompson *et al.* 1991).

Information on feeding behaviour is also sparse, especially for common seals, and, as for other UK mammals, that which does exist is based on indirect methods such as faecal and stomach analysis. The existing data from both faecal and stomach analysis indicate that grey seals tend to be opportunistic feeders, taking advantage of prey which are locally abundant. Most prey items appear to be fish, although some squid, crustacean and mollusc remains are found. Prey species include gadoids such as cod *Gadus morhua*, clupeoids such as herring *Clupea harengus*, pleuronectids such as plaice *Pleuronectes platessa*, salmonids such as salmon *Salmo salar*, and sand eels Ammodytideae (Hammond & Prime 1990; Prime & Hammond 1990). The diet of seals is likely to vary considerably from year to year depending on the composition and size of fish stocks, as well as with location. Radio tracking studies show that both species of seal appear to go on feeding forays that may take them a considerable distance from their haul-out sites (McConnell *et al.* 1992; Thompson *et al.* 1989). Common seals are known to feed near their haul-out sites as well (Thompson 1989). Long trips occur more often out of the breeding season, and may last several days or a few weeks before the seal returns. Due to difficulties in tracking seals at sea, it is not known exactly where the seals go on these forays. However, studies in the Moray Firth have indicated that adult common seals will travel up to 50 km from haul out sites on feeding trips of up to five days (Thompson & Miller 1990).

PROTECTED STATUS

Grey seals were first afforded statutory protection by the 1914 Grey Seal Protection Act, which prohibited culling during the breeding season. At that time the number of grey seals in Britain was thought to be around 500, reduced to such low numbers as a result of hunting by man. Protection did not extend to common seals, and only protected grey seals during the breeding season in autumn and winter. A second Grey Seal Protection Act extended the length of the close season, but killing of seals was still permitted in areas where seals were thought to cause serious damage to fisheries.

Common seals were not afforded statutory protection until the 1970 Conservation of Seals Act introduced a close season for both species during their breeding seasons; from 1 September to 31 December for grey seals, and from 1 June to 31 August for common seals. Humane killing of animals damaging or threatening fishing gear, or fish caught in such gear, was exempt provided that the animals were killed by an approved method. The fine for illegally killing a seal was £50, but offenders were rarely caught, and those caught were not always prosecuted (Ross 1988). In addition, the Act allowed for the management of seal stocks by permitting culling under licence for fishery protection, commercial purposes and research. Licences are issued by the relevant Secretary of State for the Home Office and the Scottish Office, after consultation with the Natural Environment Research Council.

The Conservation of Seals (Scotland) Order in 1973 gave protection to common seals in Shetland throughout the year. Killing of animals to prevent damage to fish or fishing gear was exempt, as for the 1970 Act. This order was, however, withdrawn as a consequence of the 1988 Order (see below).

Schedule 7 of the Wildlife and Countryside Act 1981 allows licences to be granted for the protection of flora and fauna in National Parks, Sites of Special Scientific Interest (SSSI) and Marine Nature Reserves, which may apply to the killing of seals.

Numbers of animals killed under licence are reported to the Home Office or Scottish Office. It is not known accurately, however, how many seals are killed legally to prevent damage to fisheries, since operators are only required to report seals killed under licence.

As a result of the phocine distemper virus in 1988, which led to the death of large numbers of seals (especially common seals) in European waters, a decision was taken to extend the protection of seals. The Conservation of Seals (England and Wales) Order 1988, and the Conservation of Seals (Common Seals) Order 1988 were introduced. Both of these Orders had the effect of extending the close season to the whole year for both species in England and Wales and for common seals only in Scotland. This protection was extended for a further three years on the east coast of England from December 1990 for both species of seals (the Conservation of Seals (England) Order 1990) while in Scotland protection was continued indefinitely for common seals in the Shetland area through the Conservation of Seals (Common Seals) (Shetland Islands Area) Orders of

1990 and 1991. Licences can still be issued for predator control and research purposes during the close season, while shooting of seals damaging fishing gear may still be carried out without the need for a licence.

IMPACTS ON SEALS

Disease

In 1988 more than 3,000 seals were found dead around the UK coast (NERC 1989), and many more on some European coasts. In addition seals were found at various stages of illness. Most of the animals were common seals, but a very few grey seals were also affected. Mortality for common seals in the Wadden Sea, Kattegat/Skagerrak and the Wash was estimated at 60%. The Moray Firth common seal population was found to be down by around 10–20% between summer 1988 and summer 1989 (Thompson pers. comm.), and in general Scottish populations appear to have been much less affected than English and Continental ones. At the time there was great concern that populations would be wiped out, and many investigations were carried out in Britain and abroad in order to determine the reason for the deaths, and try to reduce loss of animals. Although in many cases the cause of death could not be established, it is generally believed that the primary agent was a previously undescribed morbillivirus called phocine distemper virus, similar to canine distemper virus (NERC 1989).

In 1988 the number of grey seal pups born in Britain was 12% lower than expected, and many grey seals were found to have antibodies to morbillivirus, compared to none with antibodies prior to 1988 (Harwood 1990; Harwood *et al.* 1991). It has not yet been determined whether the observed reduction in pup production was as a result of infection with the phocine distemper virus.

Since August 1990, the Institute of Zoology, in collaboration with the Natural History Museum, the Sea Mammal Research Unit, and other institutes, and funded in part by DoE, has been investigating diseases in dead stranded seals found on the British coast.

Pollution

There has been considerable debate about the possible role of pollution in seal susceptibility to the virus. Research is being carried out under contract to the Department of the Environment by the Sea Mammal Research Unit (SMRU), to try to determine whether the effectiveness of the immune response of common seals around the UK is related to their burden of organochlorines and other contaminants. This work is being carried out in collaboration with Liverpool University, St. Thomas' Hospital and fisheries departments in England, Wales and Scotland (Hall *et al.* 1992, Hall, Pomeroy & Harwood 1992; Kendall *et al.* 1992). Organochlorines have also been implicated in changes in the fertility of seals (Reijnders 1984).

Destruction

There is also considerable debate as to whether killing of seals by fishermen and fish farmers is a threat to seal populations. Both groups are allowed to shoot seals with approved firearms if the seals are damaging or threatening their fish, nets or other gear. Damage to fish farms involves both species, damage to salmon nets mostly involves grey seals. The majority of fish farms are located on the west coast of Scotland. Of those in the North Sea, most are in Shetland, with a few in Orkney and in the lochs in Sutherland and the Moray Firth. Salmon netting is carried out at river and burn mouths all along the east coast of Scotland, and also of England – particularly in the north. It is not known whether the killing of seals by fishermen or fish farmers is either damaging the seal population or effective in reducing damage by seals to fish and fishing gear.

Competition for fish resources is also thought to occur between seals and large-scale commercial fisheries in the North Sea, leading to pressure to introduce seal culls when populations appear to be increasing. Grey seals are perceived as the greater problem where competition with fishermen for resources is considered. This is due to their larger population in Britain compared with common seals, their larger body size and food consumption. There is strong public opposition to the re-introduction of seal culling for any reason. A further problem is that the British population represents a large proportion of the world population of grey seals. However, seals have been culled on the Farne Islands in order to protect seabird breeding sites.

SOURCES OF INFORMATION

Information concerning distribution and population size of indigenous seal species for the North Sea coast is not yet available in a collated form, although results of surveys are regularly published in the NERC News. Summary information from the annual surveys carried out by the Sea Mammal Research Unit (SMRU) at Cambridge is available in the UK Digital Marine Atlas (see Section 9.6). Work is being carried out at Glasgow and Aberdeen Universities

on particular aspects of local seal populations, and the SMRU is continuing research on various aspects of seal ecology, principally of grey seals.

In August 1990, a long-term project to study strandings and by-catches of marine mammals in the UK was initiated, funded in part by the Department of the Environment as a contribution to its coordinated programme of research on the North Sea. It is being coordinated by the Institute of Zoology, and is carried out in collaboration with a large number of individuals and institutes, including the Natural History Museum, the Sea Mammal Research Unit, the MAFF Fisheries Laboratory, the University of Liverpool, and various Veterinary Investigation Centres. The work mainly consists of carrying out postmortems on marine mammals found dead on the coast, and taking samples for further studies. These include examining lesions histologically, isolating bacteria and viruses, identifying parasites, measuring contaminant levels, establishing the immune and reproductive status, identifying stomach contents, and ageing the animals.

Published information on grey seals concerning their breeding biology and distribution, population size and possible impact on commercial fisheries, is reasonably comprehensive. There is limited data on their distribution out of the breeding season.

Information on breeding biology of common seals is more limited than for grey seals. The lack of information is partly due to the fact that estimates of population size are much more difficult to obtain for common seals than grey seals. Common seals are less numerous than grey seals in British waters, although the difference may not be as great as previous estimates suggest (Thompson pers. comm.). Common seals therefore appear to present less of a potential problem to fishermen and fish farmers in terms of competition for resources and damage to fishing gear than do grey seals. Consequently, their ecology has not been studied as much as that of grey seals. However, the relative abundance of each species differs regionally, so that common seals may present more of a problem to fishermen or fish farmers in some areas. The problem is exacerbated by the fact that many people are not able to distinguish between the two species.

7.4 OTTERS

INTRODUCTION

Otters *Lutra lutra* are large members of the weasel family Mustelidae, average adult length of males being 110 cm and of females 102 cm. Otters are opportunistic carnivores adapted to live in water, having webbed feet and thick waterproof fur. Though primarily found in freshwater habitats they also make extensive use of the sea and coastal areas. Reviews of otter biology are found in Chanin (1985) and Mason & Macdonald (1986).

The otter population in Great Britain (especially Scotland for the North Sea coast) is of particular importance in a European context since much of the rest of western Europe has suffered an even greater decrease in numbers than here (Foster-Turley, Macdonald & Mason, 1990; Macdonald & Mason, in press).

DISTRIBUTION

It is difficult to count accurately the number of otters within a population. Otter spraints are widely used to indicate the positive presence of animals in an area and the standard survey technique is considered to be very efficient at detecting otters and enables broad comparisons to be made between and within catchments (Mason & Macdonald 1987). However, Kruuk & Conroy (1987) suggest that further comparisons between known otter populations and their spraint distributions are needed to test the validity of assessing populations in this way. There is a good estimate of the population of otters in Shetland (based on counts of otters and holts) where there are 700–900 adults along 1400 km of coast (Kruuk *et al.* 1989).

The distribution of otters along the North Sea coastal margin, derived from national surveys carried out between 1980 and 1990, is summarised in Figure 7.4.1. Data for this map are taken from Green & Green (1980, 1987), Andrews & Crawford (1986) and Strachan, Birks, Chanin & Jeffries (1990).

In Scotland otters using coastal habitats are mainly found in sheltered, undisturbed sea lochs where there is extensive seaweed cover on rocks and boulders. This habitat is more common on the west coast and in Shetland, but there are a few in Orkney and along the east coast of Scotland. Otters formerly used estuarine habitats over much of England and are likely to do so again if populations recover.

DESCRIPTION OF RESOURCE

Otters are largely nocturnal inland, but forage extensively by day on the coast and where there is little disturbance by man. This is thought to be connected with the behaviour of available prey species (Kruuk 1989).

Diet, in general, is dictated by what is abundant and most easily caught. Coastal waters provide an important habitat for otters because they are very productive. Populations on the Shetland Islands forage almost entirely in the sea with adjacent freshwater habitats being used in conjunction with coastal areas. Most information for otters using coastal areas comes from studies on the Shetland Islands. Prey consists of small bottom living fish (eelpout *Zoarces viviparus*, butterfish *Pholis gunnellus* and Yarrel's blenny *Chirolophis ascannii*) eels *Anguilla anguilla* and crustacea, crabs and squat lobsters (Kruuk *et al.* 1989; Kruuk & Moorhouse 1990; Kruuk, Wansink & Moorhouse 1989). Larger prey items are also eaten where available and occasionally birds such as puffin are taken from their burrows. Foraging behaviour depends on age, with young otters taking easier prey (Watson 1978).

The availability of prey items at specific times of year appears to influence the size of the otter population in that area (Kruuk 1989). Although otters can breed at any time of the year, in Shetland breeding takes place in midsummer when fish populations are highest. Fish trapping experiments have verified that if high numbers of eelpout are caught in July and August this is reflected in an increase in the number of litters in the following winter (Kruuk, Conroy & Moorhouse 1991).

Over winter, coastal habitats and estuaries may become more important as ice-free refuges where feeding can continue during severe weather.

Otters are highly dependent on a supply of freshwater within or near their holt as this is necessary for washing salt out of their fur and appears to maintain its insulation value (Kruuk & Balharry 1990; Kruuk *et al.* 1989). Observations of behaviour on Shetland have identified a preference for holts to be formed in peaty soils, thereby providing a source of freshwater (Kruuk 1989). The requirement for freshwater washing facilities may explain the reason for fewer otters being present on Orkney and on the east coast where agricultural practices have drained coastal land.

On the coast, holts are found among rocks, in caves or in peat banks. Otters also find shelter within the root systems of mature trees and in 'couches' or nests of reeds and grass. Otters, particularly males, can cover considerable distances. A home range may be up to 10 km in size on the coast (a smaller range than those otters living on a river). Observations have shown up to five females able to occupy the same area with their cubs, without aggression, each merely avoiding the feeding areas of the other (Kruuk 1989).

Figure 7.4.1
Distribution of otters in
Great Britain. Data from
Green & Green (1980),
Andrews & Crawford (1986),
Green & Green (1987) and
Strachan *et al.* (1990).
Based upon the 1975 Ordnance Survey
1:1,250,000 map with the permission
of the Controller of Her Majesty's
Stationery Office © Crown Copyright.

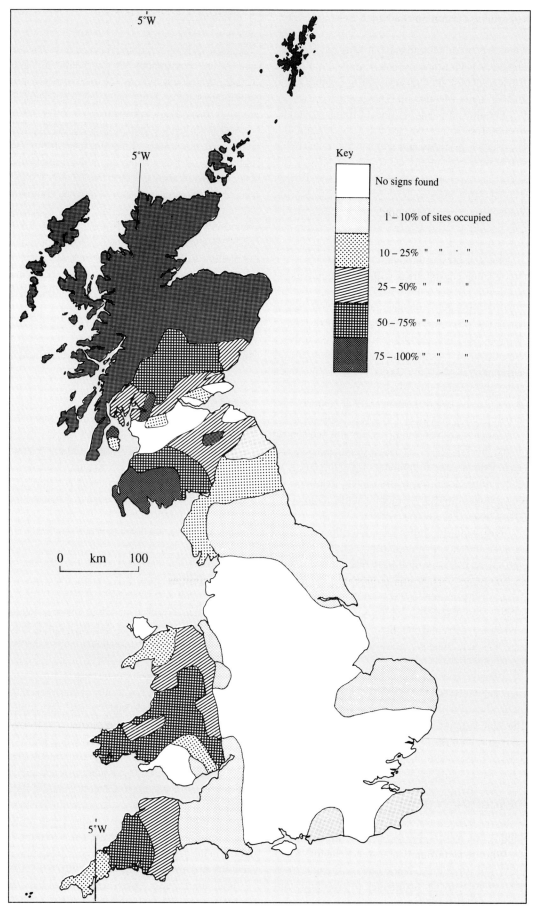

Regional variation on the North Sea coast

Otters are more widespread in Scotland than in England. Results of surveys carried out in 1984–1986 indicate 65% of sites re-surveyed in Scotland had positive signs of otter presence with increase in distribution in Tayside, Central, Fife and Lothian regions. Despite increases in these areas, the number of animals is probably still restricted.

Otters are frequently seen on the Northern Isles where they are active during daylight hours. It is estimated that there were 700–900 individuals in Shetland in 1988. This population in Shetland is isolated and individuals are characterised by throat patterns.

Otters are present throughout the highland region and on some coastal areas with fewer numbers in the eastern and central lowlands. In Grampian and Tayside regions coastal records are largely associated with estuaries, bays (Montrose Basin, Findhorn Bay) and coastal lochs (Loch of Strathbeg, Loch Loy). It would appear that the coastal distribution in Montrose Basin, inner Firth of Tay, the Eden estuary and possibly the Tyne estuary (Forth) is more extensive than previously suggested by the national survey (J. Green pers. comm.).

Survey work carried out in England from 1984 to 1986 showed that of 3,188 sites examined only 284 (8.9%) showed positive signs of otters (Strachan *et al.* 1990). These results show a slight increase in populations from the first national otter survey in 1979 (when 6% of the sites were recorded as positive). Along the North Sea coastal margin otters are restricted to Northumberland and Yorkshire, with a few still surviving in Norfolk. The natural population in East Anglia is probably extirpated (Mason & Macdonald in press, b). Re-introduction to Norfolk and Suffolk is taking place from captive-bred sources to try and establish breeding populations in areas where there are presently no otters.

PROTECTED STATUS

The European otter *Lutra lutra* is listed under the Convention on International Trade in Endangered Species (Cites 1986, Appendix 1) and is officially classified as being vulnerable to extinction (IUCN Red Data Book 1982). Legal protection of otters and their holts was introduced in England and Wales in 1978 (Conservation of Wild Creatures and Wild Plants Act 1975) and in Scotland in 1981 by the Wildlife and Countryside Act (Schedule 5 and 6). This act prohibits intentional killing, injuring or taking of otters and disturbance of their holts and places of shelter.

IMPACTS ON OTTERS

The sharp decline in otter numbers in Britain in the late 1950s, most marked in the south and east (Chanin & Jeffries 1978), has been attributed to both hunting pressure and a change in agricultural practices which saw increased use of chemicals and an increase in land reclamation. In the past, otters were hunted in this country because they were regarded as an exciting quarry and it was believed that they competed with anglers for fish, in particular trout and salmon. In other parts of Europe they have been exploited for their skins. Mason (pers. comm.) considers that only the introduction of toxic chemicals can explain the widespread and sudden decline in numbers in the late 1950s and 1960s.

Various factors still appear to restrict otter populations in certain areas, including those which directly affect the otter itself and those which indirectly affect its habitat or food supply.

Habitat destruction and disturbance

Otters require shelter and undisturbed access to food (particularly females with cubs). Extensive drainage of coastal marshes to improve farmland has removed much of the dense scrub and reed beds which provided cover for otters, although borrow dykes still provide suitable habitat. Low-level disturbance may not be a problem since otters will avoid the source. However, if the level of disturbance is constantly high the animals may retreat from the area, which effectively reduces the habitat available to them.

Road mortalities

In coastal areas a significant number of otter deaths occur on roads which separate coastal habitats from freshwater habitats (Green 1991).

Eel fyke nets and crustacean traps

Mortality has been caused by the accidental capturing and drowning of otters in underwater fish and crustacean traps. The death of otters in eel fyke nets and crustacean traps is considered by Jeffries, Green & Green (1984). This study concentrated on identifying methods to prevent otters entering fyke nets. Fyke nets are used to catch eels in freshwater, estuaries and coastal waters and otters are attracted to fyke nets because of the unnaturally high density of prey in the net. The only access is by entering the series of funnels and escape is difficult.

In Scotland, where rivers tend to be acidic, eels are of poorer quality. However, two large eel fisheries have developed on the estuaries of the rivers Spey and Tay. In England much of this fishery takes place on the east coast. In Dorset, Hampshire and the Isle of Wight the eel fishery is entirely marine and less likely to impact on otters.

Otters are also attracted to the bait and catch in creels. Creels set in shallow water among seaweed appear to trap more otters than those set on sandy bottoms. Once an otter has entered the crustacean trap or fyke net it has a maximum of three or four minutes to escape before it will drown.

Toxic pollution

There was a rapid increase in the use of agricultural pesticides from the 1950s and, at the same time, increased industrialisation led to growing discharges of pollutants. A sharp decline in otter numbers occurred during this period. Available data concerning UK inputs to the North Sea show considerable loadings of chemicals such as polychlorinated biphenyl (PCB, used in a wide range of industrial processes) and heavy metals (mercury, cadmium and lead), from rivers, sewage and dumping of sewage sludge. It is not known if these present a threat to otters using the coastal environment. Because otters were not analysed at the time of this major decline it is difficult to be sure of the precise reason for the sudden fall in their numbers, but those more recently analysed have contained a suite of pesticides, PCBs and heavy metals.

The use of organochlorine-based pesticides and herbicides in the 1950s could therefore be consistent with the sharp decline in the otter population and widespread destruction of suitable habitat, and removal of vegetation cover may have exacerbated the destructive effect of these chemicals. Otter populations at that time had already suffered considerably from hunting. Available data concerning persistence and toxicity indicate that organochlorine and organomercury compounds have had a serious impact on otters. Otters ingest pollutants through their food since fish and other biota concentrate chemicals in their tissues. The use of organochlorine is now restricted, and dieldrin has been totally withdrawn.

Another likely cause of the falling population is PCBs, which are more toxic to the closely related mink than dieldrin. Experiments have shown that PCBs, at levels which occur naturally in fish tissues, have severely reduced reproductive output in mink and seals. PCBs are currently the most significant contaminant in otter tissues, in some areas at levels likely to be a threat to populations (Mason 1989; Mason & Macdonald in press a, b; Macdonald &

Mason in press); although the high levels of PCBs in Shetland otters do not appear to be having any effect on the fecundity of that population (Kruuk, pers. comm.). In Shetland, otter mortality is caused mainly by a combination of food shortage and high levels of mercury (which appears to occur naturally there). Otters in Shetland have an average life-span of three to four years (Kruuk & Conroy 1991).

Oil pollution

The vulnerability of otters to oil spills has been demonstrated by Baker *et al.* (1981). Beached oil or slicks floating close to shore will clog otter fur and cause smothering, hypothermia or may induce toxic effects following grooming when the oil is ingested. Oil may also be ingested if an otter eats oiled corpses of seabirds.

An oil spill at Sullom Voe Terminal, Shetland in 1978 resulted in the deaths of at least 13 otters. It was concluded that the otters died of haemorrhagic gastroenteropathy after ingesting large amounts of oil. Only a few otters died as a result of the 1993 Braer spill (the numbers were particularly low because of the very bad weather and swift dispersal of the oil on the open coast). The small isolated population of otters in Shetland, which is dependent entirely on coastal waters, is very vulnerable to oil spills in the islands.

SOURCES OF INFORMATION

Hunt records were the only means of establishing the size of otter populations until 1971, during which time populations became fragmented and in certain areas totally disappeared (Chanin & Jeffries 1978). In 1976, as a result of mounting concern over the rapid decline in numbers, a Joint Otter Group was set up to assess available information and to consider the status of the otter further.

The first national otter surveys were initiated in 1977 by the Joint Otter Group of the Nature Conservancy Council and the Society for the Promotion of Nature Conservation (Wood 1979). Those surveys which concern the North Sea coastal margin were carried out in England under research contract between Exeter University and the Nature Conservancy Council (Lenton, Chanin & Jeffries, 1979) and in Scotland by Green & Green (1980) funded by Vincent Wildlife Trust (VWT). Most of the sites in England were resurveyed between 1984 and 1986 (Strachan *et al.* 1990) but in Scotland only those regions which showed evidence of a sub-optimal distribution during the first survey were repeated (Green & Green 1987). These surveys provided information on the changing distribution of the otter population in Britain.

Individual population studies include those by the Institute of Terrestrial Ecology, Banchory on the ecology and distribution of otters on Shetland (Kruuk *et al.* 1989). In north Norfolk, otters were looked at in detail by Vincent Weir between 1969 and 1980 (Weir 1988). Studies on the relationship between otters and habitat, and the role of toxic chemicals and other pollutants in influencing current otter distribution, are being carried out at the University of Essex.

The distribution of otters in estuaries in Britain was recently reviewed by the Estuaries Review Team (Davidson *et al.* 1991).

7.5 CETACEANS

INTRODUCTION

Cetaceans form a group of top predators in the marine environment about which relatively little is known. Those species which occur in the North Sea include large and small cetaceans and are divided into two suborders – the whalebone or baleen whales (Mysticeti) and the toothed whales (Odontoceti). The Odontoceti have teeth and include dolphin and porpoise species, whereas whalebone whales use plates of baleen (keratin) to filter out food from the water column. Only two species of Mysticeti are found regularly in the North Sea, these being the minke whale *Balaenoptera acutorostrata* and the fin whale *Balaenoptera physalus*.

DISTRIBUTION

Of the 25 species of cetacean which have been recorded in the North Sea, eleven species occur more regularly than the others. However, individuals or small groups of several other species occur occasionally throughout the North Sea. Cetaceans are more common in northern areas, with many species entering from the Atlantic Ocean. Since most distribution information is based on unstructured surveys it is difficult to produce accurate distribution maps for cetacean species which are not biased by the effort and distribution of observers. An example of the distribution of white-beaked dolphin based on sightings from shore and ship is given in Figure 7.5.1 (after Evans 1990a). White-beaked dolphins are the most common dolphin species in the North Sea.

DESCRIPTION OF RESOURCE

Most cetaceans are social animals which live together in groups. Group size varies but tends to be small for species of baleen whales and larger for the toothed species which regularly form schools or pods. An indication of average group size is given by Evans (1987).

Baleen whales (fin whale and minke whale) tend to feed individually or in small dispersed groups but toothed whales, particularly dolphins, may often join together to herd fish into a tight shoal. Some cetaceans cover large areas in search of food whilst resident populations are more localised in their habits. Some species of baleen whale annually migrate thousands of miles from food-rich cold waters in summer to tropical waters where they give birth in winter.

Baleen whales feed on planktonic crustaceans and small fish which they extract from water filtered through keratin plates. Toothed whales feed on larger items. Pilot whales, Risso's dolphin and sperm whales feed mainly on squid and consequently are generally found in deep offshore waters. Killer whales are known to have catholic diets, feeding on various fish species, squid and marine mammals.

Dolphin species of the genus *Lagenorynchus* feed on fish such as mackerel *Scomber scombrus*, cod *Gadus morhua*, herring *Clupea harengus* and whiting *Merlangius merlangus*. Harbour porpoises also take sprat *Sprattus sprattus* and sandeels, Ammodytidae, although, as with other species, diet probably varies seasonally and geographically.

Regional variation in the North Sea

Those species which most regularly occur in the North Sea are listed below. For a description of each species see Evans (1987).

The minke whale *Balaenoptera acutorostrata* is moderately common, particularly in the northern North Sea (Flamborough northwards) in late summer/early autumn. This species is rarely seen in the North Sea before May and most sightings are made within 100 km of the coastline.

The fin whale *Balaenoptera physalus* is rare in the North Sea and occurs mostly in the deep waters to the north and west of Shetland. Only occasionally do individuals come further south in the North Sea.

The harbour porpoise *Phocoena phocoena* is the most frequently sighted species of cetacean in the North Sea. It is commonest in the north and west North Sea, particularly in late summer/autumn. Harbour porpoises are often found in the same areas as large numbers of feeding seabirds. It is the only species which is seen regularly in the southern

North Sea. Numbers of harbour porpoises in the North Sea may have declined over the last 50 years, particularly in the southern North Sea and English Channel. Since 1982 there has also been some evidence of a decline at several coastal sites in the northern North Sea (P.G.M. Evans pers. comm.).

The common dolphin *Delphinus delphis* occurs irregularly in the North Sea, being mainly an Atlantic species occurring off south-west Britain and Ireland. When present it is often in relatively large groups.

The Moray Firth contains one of the best known resident groups of bottle-nosed dolphins *Tursiops truncatus* in UK waters. A minimum population of at least 62 dolphins, including seven calves, was counted in the area in August 1989 (Hammond & Thompson 1991). Most animals are observed in the inner part of the firth, particularly in the narrow mouths of the Cromarty, Beauly and Inverness Firths, although the species may also be seen regularly along the coast north to Wick and east to

Banff. Elsewhere in the North Sea the species appears to be rare.

The Atlantic white-sided dolphin *Lagenorynchus acutus* is uncommon in the region except in the northernmost North Sea. Occasionally large schools are seen in the north and west.

The white-beaked dolphin *Lagenorynchus albirostris* is the commonest dolphin species in the North Sea. Although found in greatest numbers in the north and west, it is also recorded regularly in the central North Sea south towards the coast of Norfolk. It can be seen throughout the year but is more often observed in late summer/autumn (Figure 7.5.1).

Killer whales *Orcinus orca* are uncommon in the North Sea. This species occurs throughout the year often feeding close inshore, sometimes on seals. Most occurrences are in the northern North Sea as far south as the Farne Islands.

Long finned pilot whales *Globicephala melaena* occur commonly in the northern North Sea, particularly in deep water north of 57° N. This

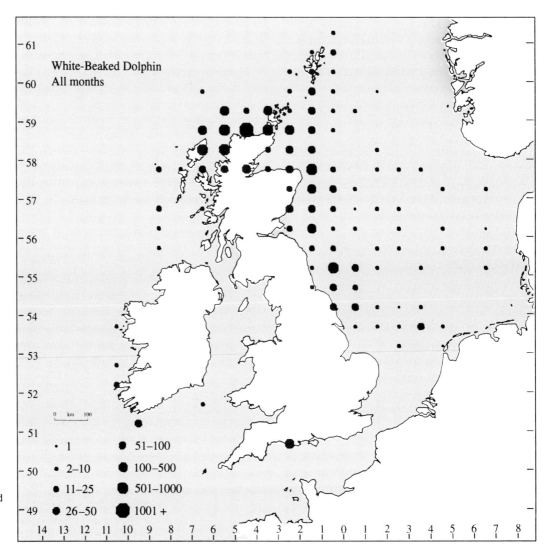

Figure 7.5.1
Distribution of white-beaked dolphin *Lagenorhynchus albirostris* around Great Britain (after Evans 1990a).

species is seen throughout the year, although in the North Sea numbers are highest in autumn. Pilot whales also occur in the English Channel.

Risso's dolphin *Grampus griseus* is generally a deep water species but in the northern North Sea individuals occur regularly in coastal waters during the summer months.

Most cetacean species that are regularly recorded in the North Sea have their main distributions in the Atlantic in deeper waters.

IMPORTANT SITES

Northern Isles (Shetland and Orkney)

In the North Sea, the major coastal concentrations of cetaceans occur in Shetland and Orkney, providing the highest number of sightings of harbour porpoise and of other species such as white-beaked and Risso's dolphin, minke whales, killer whales and pilot whales, all regularly observed in coastal waters. The Northern Isles are the only coastal region in the UK where sperm whales have been sighted regularly.

Deep water to the north and west of the Shetland Islands provides feeding grounds for the larger baleen whales such as fin whale, and the squid eaters – sperm and pilot whales.

Moray Firth

The sheltered waters of the inner Moray Firth support a resident population of bottlenose dolphin. Resident or semi-resident groups of bottlenose dolphins are known to occur in only a few areas around the British Isles. These include populations in the Moray Firth, Cardigan Bay in west Wales and along the Atlantic coast of Ireland. Harbour porpoises, white-beaked dolphin and Risso's dolphin are also seen fairly regularly within the Moray Firth.

PROTECTED STATUS

All cetaceans are protected in British waters as a result of the Quinquennial Review in 1986 of the Wildlife and Countryside Act (1981, schedule 5) and the Whaling Industry (Regulation) Act (1934, as amended 1981). Prior to this only the harbour porpoise, common dolphin and the bottlenose dolphin were protected. Most cetaceans move through the territorial waters of many countries and certain species found in waters around Britain are also protected under international agreements to which the United Kingdom is a signatory. These

agreements are the Convention on International Trade in Endangered Species (CITES 1986), the Convention on the Conservation of Migratory Species and Wild Animals (Bonn Convention 1980) and the Convention on the Conservation of European Wildlife and Natural Habitats (Berne Convention 1979). Cetacean species which are protected by both international legislation and the Wildlife and Countryside Act (1981) which have been recorded in the North Sea are given in Inskipp & Barzdo (1987).

IMPACTS ON CETACEANS

Whaling

Whaling has reduced the populations of many species of larger cetaceans. Populations of species such as the northern right whale and humpback whale were reduced substantially in number. The grey whale was hunted to extinction in the North Atlantic by the 17th century. Commercial whaling is no longer carried out by Britain and cetaceans are protected in British waters under the Wildlife and Countryside Act (1981, reviewed 1986) and the Whaling Industry (Regulation) Act (1934, as amended 1981).

Interaction with fisheries

Incidental entanglement of cetaceans in fishing gear may have contributed to the decline in numbers of some species. Northridge (1988) has reviewed the incidence of accidental catches in fishing gear although there is a lack of detailed knowledge. Those species of cetacean which feed in deeper water (sperm whale, Risso's dolphin and long-finned pilot whale) rarely become entangled in fishing nets. Porpoises appear to be most at risk, although common and white-beaked dolphins have also been caught regularly.

The increase in use of monofilament gill nets is of concern, with static gill nets thought to present a greater hazard than demersal trawls and purse seines. Dr M. Klinowska (Cambridge) and D. Goodson (Loughborough) are looking at ways to deter cetaceans from entering fishing gear.

A national voluntary scheme to monitor the incidental catches of marine mammals (cetaceans and seals) by fishermen came into operation on 1 January 1992. Fishermen are being requested to report incidental catches of marine mammals from any waters they have fished, including outside UK waters. This puts into effect one of the initiatives agreed at the Third North Sea Conference in 1990 (see Sources of Information, below). The scheme should lead to more information about the status of marine mammals around the UK and their interaction with fisheries.

Diseases

In 1988 a morbillivirus infection was detected in six harbour porpoises *Phocoena phocoena* stranded on the coast of Northern Ireland. In 1990, morbillivirus was detected in a harbour porpoise stranded on the east coast of England, and one stranded on the east coast of Scotland (T. Kuiken, pers. comm.).

Since August 1990, the Institute of Zoology, in collaboration with the Natural History Museum, the Sea Mammal Research Unit, and other institutes, and funded in part by the DoE, has been investigating diseases in dead stranded cetaceans found on the British coast.

Pollution

Until very recently there was no systematic scheme for monitoring the level of pollutants accumulated by cetaceans in British waters. Some analyses have been carried out on stranded cetaceans and results from these show that some small cetaceans have had high levels of polychlorinated biphenyls (PCBs), and the organochlorines DDT and dieldrin in their tissues (Evans 1990; Kayes 1985). Heavy metals are also known to be present. Organochlorines have been implicated in changes in the reproductive activity of both male and female marine mammals (Reijnders 1984; Subramanian *et al.* 1987).

Since August 1990, the MAFF Fisheries Laboratory in Burnham-on-Crouch, under contract to the Sea Mammal Research Unit, and funded in part by the DoE, is measuring the levels of organochlorines and heavy metals in tissue samples of dead stranded cetaceans found on the British coast.

Changes in food supply

Over the last 50 years major changes have taken place in the stocks and distribution of several fish species. These changes in food stocks may have affected numbers of porpoises in some coastal waters.

Disturbance

The large amount of shipping traffic using the North Sea and the Channel presents a potential hazard to cetaceans. Disturbance could be a serious problem in the southern North Sea where shipping traffic is particularly concentrated. This might also be a problem in inshore areas further north where populations of small cetaceans are more frequent. The sounds generated by speedboats may interfere with communication and echolocation used for feeding or overlap with the hearing and vocal range of dolphins and porpoises. Some cetaceans have been found dead with injuries caused by ship's propellers.

Individuals wishing to photograph and watch local populations of cetaceans may cause disturbance by repeatedly pursuing the animals by boat.

SOURCES OF INFORMATION

Information on the distribution of cetacean populations in the North Sea is limited.

In England and Wales cetaceans are considered to be 'Royal Fish' and as property of the Crown all incidents of stranding must be reported. In Scotland only cetaceans of a length greater than 8 m are considered to be 'Royal Fish'. Stranded cetaceans are officially classed as wrecks and these incidents are reported to the coastguard service and the Receiver of Wrecks who then pass information to the Natural History Museum in London for inclusion within their cetacean sightings database. The museum has recorded strandings since 1913, although stranding records only form 5–10% of the sightings database.

In August 1990, a long-term project to study strandings and by-catches of marine mammals in the UK was initiated, funded in part by the DoE as a contribution to its coordinated programme of research on the North Sea. It is being coordinated by the Institute of Zoology in England and Wales and the Scottish Agricultural College in Scotland and is carried out in collaboration with a large number of individuals and institutions, including the Natural History Museum, the Sea Mammal Research Unit, the MAFF and SOAFD Fisheries Laboratory, the University of Liverpool, Veterinary Research Laboratories, Belfast and the various Veterinary Investigation Centres. The work mainly consists of carrying out postmortems on marine mammals found dead on the coast, and taking samples for further studies. These include examining lesions histologically, isolating bacteria and viruses, identifying parasites, measuring contaminant levels, establishing the immune and reproductive status, identifying stomach contents, and ageing the animals.

The Mammal Society's Cetacean Group, set up in 1973, collects information on sightings from observers throughout the UK. This information has been analysed and current knowledge of the distribution of cetaceans in British and Irish waters is given by Evans *et al.* (1986) and Evans (1991).

Other regular observers include the Seabirds at Sea Team (JNCC), Ministry for Agriculture, Fisheries and Food, Department of Agriculture and Fisheries for Scotland, NERC vessels, Dutch Mammal Group and the Danish Ornithological Society not to mention land-based observers recording on a regular basis.

The International Whaling Commission (IWC) holds estimated population figures based on information collected during historic whaling operations and more recently, dedicated sightings surveys. These mainly cover the larger whales, though data is also available on the small cetaceans. The IWC was set up in 1946 to decide on quotas for countries which operated whaling fleets. A moratorium on commercial whaling was introduced in 1985. This excludes whales taken for scientific research, or under the special arrangements that exist for aboriginal subsistence hunting. However, all members are currently observing the moratorium, including the two who have formally objected to the decision.

At the third North Sea Conference in March 1990, concern was expressed about populations of small cetaceans in the North Sea which may be affected by marine pollution, by-catches and habitat deterioration. A Memorandum of Understanding was signed to the effect that various management measures would be undertaken to provide better protection for all *Odontoceti* except the sperm whale *Physeter macrocephalus* (Annex 1, Memorandum of Understanding on Small Cetaceans in the North Sea, Third International Conference on the Protection of the North Sea 1990). Sperm whales are currently dealt with by the International Whaling Commission.

There is little background information on the status of populations of most species, their birth and death rates or the common causes of mortality. The Sea Mammal Research Unit (SMRU) in Cambridge carries out some research on cetaceans and is currently collecting biological material from strandings and accidental catches in fishing nets of harbour porpoises. Samples taken from stranded cetaceans will be used in studies of pathology, reproduction and diet. SMRU also hope to monitor movements of individuals using radio telemetry.

Research on bottle-nose dolphins in the Moray Firth is being carried out in collaboration with Aberdeen and Oxford Universities. The JNCC's Seabirds at Sea Team (SAST) and the Mammal Society's Cetacean Group both have databases which hold information on observations of cetaceans made in the North Sea during the 1980s.

7.6 AMPHIBIANS AND REPTILES

INTRODUCTION

There are twelve species of freshwater and terrestrial amphibian and reptile in Britain. Three of these have restricted distributions and are found primarily in heath and dune habitats. Species found along the North Sea coastal margin are the natterjack toad *Bufo calamita*, the sand lizard *Lacerta agilis* and the smooth snake *Coronella austriaca*. All three species have a restricted distribution in Britain. In addition five species of marine turtle have been sighted or accidentally caught in British waters, or have been identified from specimens washed up on the shore.

The natterjack toad, the sand lizard and the smooth snake, and all species of turtle are fully protected under Schedule 5 of the Wildlife and Countryside Act 1981.

AMPHIBIANS

Natterjack toad *Bufo calamita*

The natterjack toad is one of three bufonids indigenous to Europe. It is listed by the International Union for the Conservation of Nature and Natural Resources (IUCN) as 'vulnerable' within the EEC, i.e. is not yet in danger of extinction, but likely to become so if trends continue as they are.

In Europe the natterjack is not found exclusively in coastal habitats. However, in Britain it is now almost confined to coastal habitats. It occurs on dunes and a few heaths with a source of alkaline or neutral freshwater. It shows a preference for loose, sandy soils into which it can burrow easily. Natterjacks inhabit virtually all stages of dune development from littoral zones through to the most mature fixed structure, but prefer to breed in incipient slacks close to high water (see Section 4.3). They may also occupy flat, marshy areas, especially where there are small patches of open sand which facilitate burrowing, and nearby shallow freshwater or slightly brackish pools.

Natterjacks emerge from hibernation and assemble around areas of standing water to breed from late March to June. The water is shallow and often transient. The tadpoles hatch from the egg strings in five to eight days and metamorphose in six to eight weeks (Frazer 1983). The adults burrow by day and search for food by night in the summer. They feed on a variety of invertebrates which they may search for in strand line debris and vegetation seawards of sand dunes. Natterjack toads hibernate,

Figure 7.6.1
Distribution of natterjack toad *Bufo calamita*, sand lizard *Lacerta agilis* and smooth snake *Coronella austriaca* on the North Sea coast.

Based upon the 1975 Ordnance Survey 1:1,250,000 map with the permission of the Controller of Her Majesty's Stationery Office © Crown Copyright.

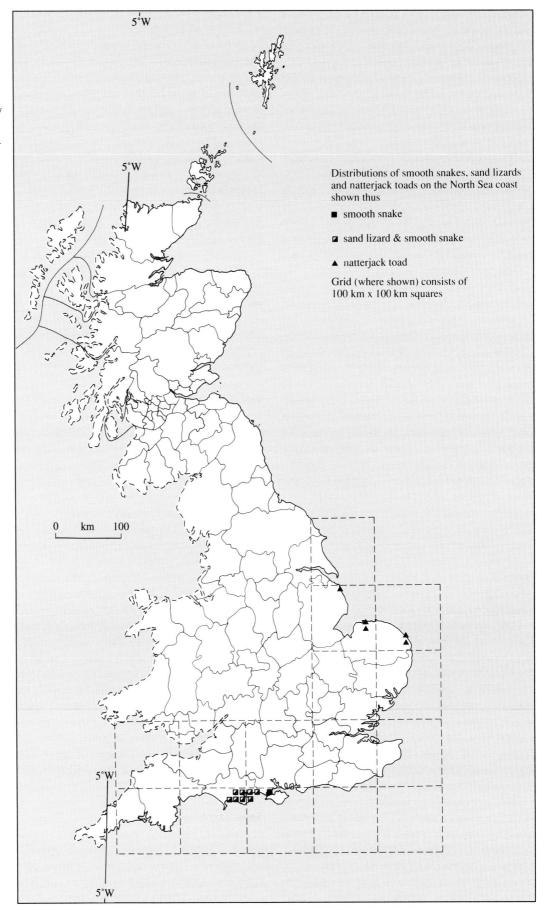

Distributions of smooth snakes, sand lizards and natterjack toads on the North Sea coast shown thus

■ smooth snake

▣ sand lizard & smooth snake

▲ natterjack toad

Grid (where shown) consists of 100 km x 100 km squares

buried 25 to 50 cm under the ground or in sand martin, rabbit or rodent burrows. Their life span may be 5 to 6 years, with the oldest recorded individual being 15 years old.

The total number of natterjack toads in Britain was thought to be around 20,000, distributed amongst 32 populations in 1980 (Nature Conservancy Council 1983). Before 1960 there were 17 known colonies on the North Sea coast; since then, these have progressively disappeared. Natural distribution on the North Sea coast is now limited to four colonies in eastern and southern England (see Figure 7.6.1). In addition the species has been introduced to Holme dunes in north Norfolk. No populations on the North Sea coast occur outside dune habitat. Estimated population size for the four areas were (Nature Conservancy Council 1983):

Saltfleetby dunes (Lincolnshire)   10
Holkham dunes (Norfolk)   100
Winterton dunes (Norfolk)   100s
Syderstone (Norfolk)   10(<100)

In the late 1980s the Saltfleetby and Holkham populations increased somewhat but the Syderstone population may have become extinct (A. Cooke pers. comm.)

Threats to natterjack populations are largely from habitat damage. Long-term drying out of dune slacks and other shallow breeding pools resulted in widespread breeding failure in the 1970s. Other threats to their habitats include holiday development, house building and recreational pressure, and afforestation on dunes (Nature Conservancy Council 1983).

REPTILES

Being ectothermic ('cold blooded'), coastal reptile species require warm temperatures to enable them to move about, catch and digest food, and to incubate eggs or embryos. This factor probably limits the habitat types they can use, and their distribution, more than any other. They need a mixture of exposure to the sun, dense vegetation for cover, a supply of insects, moths, and flies (or amphibians, mammals and other reptiles for snakes), and a well drained underground retreat for hibernation. Sand lizards and smooth snakes are virtually confined to lowland heathland, and coastal dunes and marshes (Nature Conservancy Council 1983). Other species of reptile may, however, occur on rough grassland, low-level moorland, overgrown dry stone walls or banks – none of these necessarily coastal. Golf courses, whether coastal or not, may also be good sites for reptiles as they provide a variety of habitats from sandy banks to ponds, with areas of open and dense vegetation (Frazer 1983).

Marine turtles

Marine turtles are occasionally recorded from British waters. Their preference for warm sea temperatures and requirement for warm and undisturbed sandy beaches for laying their eggs means that these reptiles tend to have a primarily tropical distribution. There have been over 100 records of turtles which allowed identification up to 1984, and at least a further twenty unidentified specimens have been recorded. Although no species breeds in Britain, southern British North Sea waters are regarded as being within the natural range of the leathery turtle *Dermochelys coriacea* (A. Gent pers. comm.).

The leathery turtle (leatherback or luth turtle) is the most frequently recorded species. It is the largest of the turtle species and believed to be the widest ranging as it moves with warm currents in search of its main food of jellyfish. This behaviour accounts for its seasonal occurrence in British waters primarily in summer and autumn.

The loggerhead *Caretta caretta* is the next most frequently recorded turtle in British waters. Sightings are most common in winter months.

Kemp's ridley (or Atlantic ridley) *Lepidochelys kempi* has also been recorded in British waters. These records, usually as young specimens, all occurred in the winter months.

Up to 1984 there were only 107 confirmed sightings of turtles in British waters, of which 54 were leathery turtles, 31 loggerheads and 14 Kemp's ridley. The remaining observations are hawksbills *Eretmochelys imbricata* (6) and green turtles *Chelonia mydas* (2) (A. Gent pers. comm.). The majority of sightings occur off south west and western coastlines, with further sightings off Ireland. At least 17 sightings of leathery turtles have been made in the English Channel and North Sea, these occurring off Shetland, the Firth of Forth, Humberside, Norfolk, Suffolk, Kent, Essex, the Solent, Dorset, and south Devon. Nine loggerheads have been found in the North Sea region, being observed along the coasts of Shetland, Grampian, North Yorkshire, West Sussex, the Solent and Dorset. One Kemp's ridley has been found dead in West Sussex (A. Gent pers. comm.). Records of marine turtle sightings are kept by the Natural History Museum in London.

Sand lizard *Lacerta agilis*

The distribution of the sand lizard extends from Scandinavia in the north to central Asia in the south. It is at its north-western distribution limit in Britain. In Europe it occurs in a wide range of habitats, but in

Britain it is now restricted mainly to lowland heathland, soft rock sea cliffs and sand dunes (Frazer 1983). Two main types of dune habitat are used by sand lizards: frontal dunes and fixed dune. The areas of loose sand in the form of patches, paths and general inter-plant sand are important to sand lizards as warm areas for basking and laying of eggs, with cover from predators nearby.

Sand lizards feed on invertebrates mainly from the following orders: Araneae, Coleoptera, winged Hymenoptera, Diptera, and Lepidoptera. Breeding occurs in May and occasionally early June. Initially females incubate the developing eggs by basking and, in June or July, usually between 6 and 13 eggs are laid in a gently sloping hole excavated in open sand. These sites are selected to maximise the amount of radiation to warm the eggs and to avoid shading. Eggs hatch around August or early September (depending on temperature). Hatchlings are vulnerable to predation from a variety of vertebrate species. Indeed if there is not sufficient area for the young to disperse after hatching, the adults may eat their own young. Both adults and young hibernate, with adults entering hibernation between late August and October, and some juveniles remaining active until November. Sand lizards emerge from hibernation between mid-March and early April.

Distribution of the sand lizard is given in Figure 7.6.1. On the North Sea coast the most important coastal site for sand lizards is Studland National Nature Reserve in Dorset – an extensive system of dune with acid heath vegetation on the Channel coast (see Section 3.2.3). Some 5% of the British population was estimated to occur on the Bournemouth cliffs in 1982 (Frazer 1983). In 1976 the British population was estimated to be between 7,000 and 8,000 adults. 4,700 were estimated to be present on inland and coastal heaths between Poole and Dorchester, and at Purbeck in Dorset; and 2,400 on the inland and coastal heaths of the New Forest, Avon valley and Bournemouth in Hampshire and Dorset. The rest of the population was inland or on the west coast. Since 1976 local declines have taken place due largely to habitat loss, and the total population was estimated to be down to 5,000 adults in 1980 (Nature Conservancy Council 1983).

The main impact on sand lizard populations in Britain is destruction and fragmentation of heathland and dune habitat. This may be caused by afforestation, urbanisation, land reclamation, military activity and mineral extraction. Heathland loss may also occur due to natural succession to woodland. Fire on dry heaths is also a problem. The sand lizard's main predators are birds of prey, domestic cats and snakes.

Smooth snake *Coronella austriaca*

The smooth snake is listed by the IUCN as 'vulnerable' in Europe. Smooth snakes feed on lizards, snakes and small mammals. In Britain they are on the edge of their European range in southern England, and are mainly confined to areas of lowland heath associated with tertiary sands and lower Greensand geology. These areas, on the Channel coast, are in Hampshire and Dorset, and inland in Surrey. It occupies the same habitat and has a similar but less widespread distribution to the sand lizard, but is restricted to southern Britain (Figure 7.6.1).

Smooth snakes give birth to between four and fifteen live young, between August and the end of October. The snakes hibernate, possibly communally, from mid-October to mid-March. Smooth snakes are relatively long-lived compared to other reptiles, living up to 10 years (Frazer 1983). Smooth snakes forage both above and below ground. Their diet is thought to be about 70% other reptiles and 30% small mammals, the proportions varying depending on the availability of prey within the habitat (Prestt, Cooke & Corbett 1974). They may also eat slugs, crickets and grasshoppers, and when young, caterpillars, spiders and larval tipulids. Prey is constricted by enveloping in the coils before being swallowed. They are thought not to be cannibalistic.

Its rarity, secretive nature, and burrowing habit prevents accurate estimates of population size and distribution. However, it is thought that the British population may be of the order of 2,000 adults. Densities of one or two adults per hectare in lowland heath areas are thought to be usual. The most important coastal site for smooth snakes is Studland National Nature Reserve in Dorset.

7.7 RARE FISHES

The North Sea is historically important for its commercial fish stocks, which have influenced the economic development of many countries within Europe. While there is management of the commercial species by the Ministry of Agriculture, Fisheries and Food (MAFF), Scottish Office Agriculture and Fisheries Department (SOAFD), International Council for the Exploration of the Sea (ICES) and European fisheries organisations (see Chapter 6), often the importance of non-commercial species has been overlooked. The abundance of commercial fish stocks is controlled by fishing pressure, but the remaining 150 or more non-commercial fishes are not directly subjected to such pressure and their numbers provide a better

Species	EC Directive Annex(es)	Bern Convention Appendix	CITES Appendix	Wildlife and Countryside Act Schedule
Natural Range GB				
Lampetra fluviatilis (river lamprey)	IIa, Va	III	-	-
Petromyzon marinus (sea lamprey)	IIa	III	-	-
Alosa alosa (allis shad)	IIa, Va	III	-	5 (killing, injuring, taking)
Alosa fallax (twaite shad)	IIa, Va	III	-	-
Salmo salar (Atlantic salmon)	IIa, Va (in freshwater only)	III	-	-
Potamoschistus microps (common goby)	-	III	-	-
P. minutus (sand goby)	-	III	-	-
Vagrant				
Acipenser sturio (sturgeon)	IIa, IVa	III	I	5
Believed extinct				
Coregonus oxyrinchus (houting) (anadromous populations only)	IIa, IVa	III	-	-

Table 7.7.1
Protected species of rare marine fish in Britain.

indication and measure of environmental conditions and water quality.

The estimated total population of British marine fishes is 330, of which about 150 are recorded from the North Sea. Of these about 15 to 20 are of significant commercial value and about 55 are uncommon. Within the uncommon species, nine are scheduled and/or protected by National, EC or international conventions and legislation (Table 7.7.1). These are *Lampetra fluviatilis, Petromyzon marinus, Alosa alosa, Alosa fallax, Coregonus oxyrinchus, Salmo salar, Pomatoschistus microps, Pomatoschistus minutus* and *Acipenser sturio*. There is some doubt as to whether *Pomatoschistis microps* and *P. minutus* should be included under the Bern Convention (Potts & Swaby 1991).

In addition to the fully marine fishes, there are important estuaries opening into the North Sea. These provide essential feeding and breeding grounds for many estuarine and marine fishes as well as migration routes for catadromous and anadromous species. While only 41 species are estimated to be physiologically dependent on brackish estuarine conditions, there is some variation between different races at different levels of the zoogeographic distribution. In addition to the purely estuarine fishes there are 140 marine vagrants which use estuaries as feeding grounds or as shelter zones avoiding hostile coastal conditions (as in storms) or predators (Potts & Swaby 1993). The biomass of fish in the North Sea far exceeds birds and has greater economic importance.

Distributional records show that there are interesting trends between the southern North Sea and Shetland with regard to the relative numbers of species on the limits of their distribution.

7.8   RARE VASCULAR PLANTS

A 'nationally rare' vascular plant is defined as one which occurs in 15 or fewer 10 km Ordnance Survey grid squares in Britain. A 'nationally scarce' species is defined as one which occurs in 16–100 10 km grid squares. In Britain there are about 1,423 native species, 317 of which are nationally rare (Perring & Farrell 1983) and 307 of which are nationally scarce (Farrell 1989).

A total of 121 nationally rare and scarce species are found in coastal habitats in Britain (Farrell 1991). Of these 121 species 33 nationally rare and 72 nationally scarce species are found within the North Sea coastal margin, making a total of 105 species. This represents 7.4% of the native British flora and 16.8% of the nationally rare and

Figure 7.8.1
Habitats of nationally rare and scarce plant species in Britain.

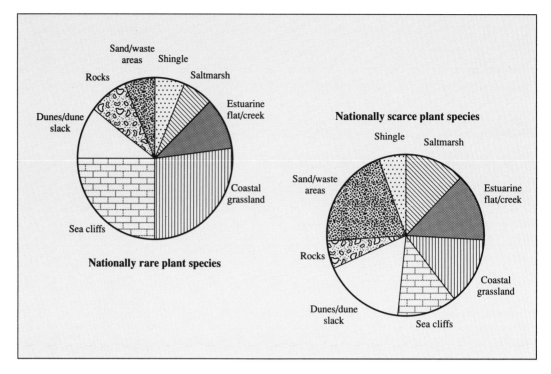

Nationally rare plant species

Nationally scarce plant species

Rare plant species	Distribution on North Sea	No. of 10 km² records in GB	Habitat
Carex recta	Northern	3	Estuarine flat
Epipactis dunensis	Northern	9	Dune/dune slack
Oxytropis halleri	Northern	11	Coastal grassland
*Gnaphalium luteoalbum***	Eastern	1	Dune/dune slack
Limonium bellidifolium	Eastern	5	Saltmarsh
Spartina alterniflora	Southern	1	Estuarine flat
*Petrorhagia nanteuillii***	Southern	1	Sandy shore/waste area
Limonium recurvum	Southern	1	Sea cliff
Geranium purpureum ssp. *forsteri*	Southern	2	Shingle
*Bupleurum baldense***	Southern	2	Sea cliff
*Centaurium tenuiflorum***	Southern	2	Coastal grassland
Matthiola incana	Southern	4	Sea cliff
*Melampyrum arvense***	Southern	5	Sea cliff
*Orobanche loricata***	Southern	5	Sea cliff
Orobanche purpurea	Southern	7	Coastal grassland
Orobanche maritima	Southern	9	Sea cliff
Gastridium ventricosum	Southern	9	Coastal grassland
*Ophrys sphegodes***	Southern	10	Sea cliff
*Chenopodium vulvaria***	Southern	15	Sandy shore/waste area
*Halimione pedunculata***	South-eastern	1	Saltmarsh
*Orobanche caryophyllacea***	South-eastern	2	Dune/dune slack
*Lactuca saligna***	South-eastern	4	Coastal grassland
*Corrigiola litoralis***	South-western	1	Lagoon
*Scirpus triquetrus***	South-western	1	Estuarine flat
*Polygonum maritimum***	South-western	1	Shingle
*Romulea columnae***	South-western	1	Coastal grassland
Allium ampeloprasum	South-western	2	Rocks
*Rumex rupestris***	South-western	3	Rocks
*Ononis reclinata***	South-western	4	Coastal grassland
Geranium purpureum ssp. *purpureum*	South-western	6	Shingle
Aster linosyris	South-western	7	Coastal grassland
*Teucrium scordium***	Scattered	3	Dune/dune slack
Eleocharis parvula	Scattered	6	Estuarine flat
Atriplex longipes	Scattered	7	Saltmarsh
** Species listed on Schedule 8 of the Wildlife and Countryside Act.			

Table 7.8.1a
The distribution and habitat of rare coastal vascular plant species on the North Sea coastal margin.

Scarce plant species	Distribution on North Sea	No. of 10 km² records in GB	Habitat
Carex maritima	Northern	26	Sandy shore/waste area
Primula scotica	Northern	28	Coastal grassland
Centaurium littorale	Northern	42	Dune/dune slack
Juncus balticus	Northern	47	Dune/dune slack
Mertensia maritima	Northern	48	Shingle
Cochlearia scotica	Northern	76	Sandy shore/waste area
Lathyrus japonicus	Eastern	16	Shingle
Corynephorus canescens	Eastern	16	Dune/dune slack
Festuca juncifolia	Eastern	27	Dune/dune slack
Ruppia cirrhosa	Eastern	32	Estuarine creek
Marrubium vulgare	Southern	14	Sea cliff
Centaurium capitatum	Southern	19	Coastal grassland
Orobanche maritima	Southern	22	Coastal grassland
Poa bulbosa	Southern	23	Sandy shore/waste area
Carex punctata	Southern	23	Sandy shore/waste area
Juncus acutus	Southern	25	Sandy shore/waste area
Vicia bithynica	Southern	25	Sea cliff
Alopecurus bulbosus	Southern	26	Saltmarsh
Suaeda fruticosa	Southern	30	Shingle
Oenothera stricta	Southern	32	Dune/dune slack
Brassica oleracea	Southern	33	Sea cliff
*Gentianella anglica***	Southern	36	Sea cliff grassland
Trifolium suffocatum	Southern	40	Dune
Trifolium squamosum	Southern	41	Coastal grassland
Arum italicum	Southern	43	Sea cliff woodland
Medicago polymorpha	Southern	43	Sandy shore/waste area
Vulpia membranacea	Southern	44	Dune/dune slack
Bupleurum tenuissimum	Southern	58	Saltmarsh
Inula crithmoides	Southern	62	Saltmarsh
Orobache hederae	Southern	64	Sea cliffs
Limonium binervosum	Southern	70	Rocks
Althaea officinalis	Southern	73	Saltmarsh
Thesium humifusum	Southern	73	Sea cliff grassland
Trifolium ornithopodioides	Southern	85	Sandy shore/waste area
Oenanthe pimpinelloides	Southern	94	Coastal grassland
Chenopodium botryoides	South-eastern	17	Estuarine flat
Polypogon monspeliensis	South-eastern	18	Saltmarsh
Spartina maritima	South-eastern	25	Estuarine creek
Frankenia laevis	South-eastern	25	Saltmarsh
Salicornia pusilla	South-eastern	32	Saltmarsh
Parapholis incurva	South-eastern	36	Estuarine creek
Salicornia perennis	South-eastern	37	Saltmarsh
Trifolium glomeratum	South-eastern	37	Sandy shore/waste area
Vulpia ambigua	South-eastern	40	Sandy shore/waste area
Puccinellia rupestris	South-eastern	51	Sandy shore/waste area
Puccinellia fasciculata	South-eastern	52	Estuarine creek
Hordeum marinum	South-eastern	59	Coastal grassland
Adiantum capillus-veneris	South-western	21	Rocks
Scilla autumnalis	South-western	28	Coastal grassland
Lotus hispidus	South-western	35	Coastal grassland
Erodium moschatum	South-western	37	Sandy shore/waste area
Parentucellia viscosa	South-western	66	Coastal grassland
Lavatera arborea	South-western	70	Sandy shore/waste area
Euphorbia portlandica	South-western	74	Dune/dune slack
Asplenium billotii	South-western	76	Rocks
Erodium maritimum	South-western	77	Dune/dune slack
Vicia lutea	Scattered	19	Sea cliffs
Ophioglossum azoricum	Scattered	19	Coastal grassland
Zostera angustifolia	Scattered	29	Estuarine flat
Silene nutans	Scattered	32	Sea cliffs
Hippophae rhamnoides	Scattered	36	Dune/dune slack
Zostera noltii	Scattered	43	Estuarine flat
Limonium humile	Scattered	49	Saltmarsh
Fumaria capreolata	Scattered	62	Sandy shore/waste area
Polygonum raii	Scattered	66	Sandy shore/waste area
Zostera marina	Scattered	74	Estuarine flat
Carex divisa	Scattered	79	Estuarine flat
Ranunculus baudotii	Scattered	83	Estuarine flat
Crambe maritima	Scattered	88	Shingle
Raphanus maritimus	Scattered	89	Sandy shore/waste area
Equisetum variegatum	Scattered	89	Dune/dune slack
Euphorbia paralias	Scattered	92	Dune/dune slack

** Species listed on Schedule 8 of the Wildlife and Countryside Act.

Table 7.8.1b
The distribution and habitat of scarce coastal plant species on the North Sea coastal margin.

scarce elements. These are located in eight main habitat types:
i)   estuarine mudflat or creek
ii) saltmarsh
iii) vegetated shingle
iv) sandy shores, waste areas, open spaces
v)   rocks
vi) dunes and dune slacks
vii) sea cliffs
viii)coastal grassland.

Coastal grassland and sea cliffs support the most nationally rare species (8 and 7 respectively), whilst sandy shores, waste areas and open spaces have the most nationally scarce species (13) (see Figure 7.8.1).

The majority of nationally rare species have a southern or south-western distribution within the North Sea coastal margin. The majority of nationally scarce plant species have a southern, scattered or south-eastern distribution.

Tables 7.8.1a and 7.8.1b show the number and distribution of the 10 km grid squares which contain nationally rare and scarce plants on the North Sea coast. The majority of these plants occur in the south-east and southern England. This is related to the fact that the total number of plant species which occur is much larger in eastern and southern England than it is on other parts of the North Sea coast, therefore it is not surprising that more rare or scarce species occur there. The North Sea coast (with the exception of Shetland and Orkney), being generally more continental than oceanic in climate, harbours more nationally rare and scarce plant species than more northern and western coasts.

ACKNOWLEDGEMENTS

This chapter was originally compiled by Barbara Smith and Charlotte Johnston. Information, comments and revisions were kindly provided by the following people and organisations:

Birds: Mark Tasker (JNCC, Offshore Animals) and Nick Davidson (JNCC, Coastal Review Unit).

Marine mammals: Dr John Harwood of the NERC Sea Mammal Research Unit (who provided distribution maps of breeding grey and common seals for 1989 and updated the text in 1993); Dr Paul Thompson of the University of Aberdeen (Department of Zoology); Dr Hans Kruuk (ITE), Dr C. Mason, University of Essex; Mr and Mrs J. Green, Vincent Wildlife Trust; Dr P. Evans (Oxford University), Mark Tasker (JNCC) and Dr Don Jeffries (previously of the JNCC). Mr Thijs Kuiken of the Institute of Zoology, the Zoological Society, provided further information on diseases and pollution.

Amphibians and reptiles: Dr Arnie Cooke and Tony Gent (English Nature) who also commented on draft text.

Fishes: Dr Geoff Potts (Marine Biological Association of the United Kingdom).

Rare plants: Lynne Farrell (English Nature), who also commented on draft text.

REFERENCES

ALLPORT, G., O'BRIEN, M., & CADBURY C.J. 1986. Breeding redshank. Survey on saltmarshes 1985 - RSPB report. *Nature Conservancy Council, CSD Research Report, No. 649.*

ANDERSON, S. 1988. *The grey seal.* Aylesbury, Shire Publications (Shire Natural History Series, No. 26).

ASPINALL, S.J., & TASKER, M.L. 1990. *Coastal birds of east Dorset.* Peterborough, Nature Conservancy Council.

ASPINALL, S.J., & TASKER, M.L. 1992. *Birds of the Solent.* Peterborough, Joint Nature Conservation Committee.

BAKER, J.R., JONES. A.M., JONES, T.P., & WATSON, H.C. 1981. Otter *Lutra lutra* mortality and marine oil pollution. *Biological Conservation, 20*: 311-321.

BLAKE, B.F., DIXON, T.J., JONES, P.H., & TASKER, M.L. 1985. Seasonal changes in the feeding ecology of guillemots *Uria aalge* off north and east Scotland. *Estuarine and Coastal Shelf Science, 20*: 559-568.

BONNER, W.N. 1972. The grey seal and common seal in European waters. *Oceanography and Marine Biology Annual Review, 10*: 461-507.

CARTER, I.C., WILIAMS, J.M., WEBB, A., & TASKER, M.L. 1993. *Seabird concentrations in the North Sea: an atlas of vulnerability to surface pollutants.* Aberdeen, Joint Nature Conservation Committee.

CHANIN, P. 1985. *The natural history of otters.* London, Croom Helm.

CHANIN, P., & JEFFRIES, D.J. 1978. The decline of the otter *Lutra lutra* L. in Britain: an analysis of hunting records and discussion of causes. *Biological Journal of the Linnean Society, 10*: 305-328.

DAVIDSON, N. *et al.* (1991) *Nature conservation and estuaries in Great Britain.* Peterborough, Nature Conservancy Council.

DUNNET, G.M., FURNESS, R.W., TASKER, M.L., & BECKER, P.H. (1990). Seabird ecology in the North Sea. *Netherlands Journal of Sea Research, 26*: 387-425.

EBBINGE, B.S. (1985). Factors determining the population size of arctic breeding geese wintering in western Europe. *Ardea, 73*: 123-128.

EVANS, P.G.H. 1987. *The natural history of whales and dolphins.* Beckenham, Christopher Helm.

EVANS, P.G.H. 1990a. Cetaceans. The Marine Forum for Environmental Issues. *North Sea Report 1990.*

EVANS, P.G.H. 1991. Whales, dolphins and porpoises: Order Cetacea. *In: Handbook of British Mammals,* ed. by Gordon B. Corbet and S. Harris. Oxford, Blackwell Scientific Publications.

EVANS, P.G.H., HARDING, S., TYLER, G., & HALL, S. 1986. *Analysis of cetacean sightings in the British Isles, 1958-1985. Nature Conservancy Council, CSD Report,* No. 892.

EVANS, P.R. & PIENKOWSKI, M.W. 1983. Implications for coastal engineering projects of studies, at the Tees estuary, on the effects of reclamation of intertidal land on shorebird populations. *Water, Science and Technology, 16,* 347-354.

FARRELL, L. 1989. Vascular plants. In: *Guidelines for selection of biological SSSIs,* Part C, Chapter 11. Peterborough, Nature Conservancy Council.

FARRELL, L. 1991. Rare and scarce vascular plants of coastal habitats. In: *Nature conservation and estuaries in Great Britain,* ed. by N. Davidson *et al.* 1991. Peterborough, Nature Conservancy Council.

FOSTER-TURLEY, P., MACDONALD, S.M., & MASON, C.F. 1990. *Otters: an action plan for their conservation.* Gland, IUCN.

FRAZER, D. 1983. *Reptiles and amphibians in Britain.* London, Collins.

FURNESS, R.W., & HISLOP, J.R.G. 1981. Diets and feeding ecology of the great skua *Catharacta skua* during the breeding season in Shetland. *Journal of Zoology, London, 195*: 1-23.

GALBRAITH, H. 1983. The diet and feeding ecology of breeding kittiwakes *Rissa tridactyla. Bird Study, 30*: 109-120.

GOSS-CUSTARD, J.D. 1985. Foraging behaviour of wading birds and the carrying capacity of estuaries. In: *Behavioural Ecology: ecological consequences of adaptive behaviour.* 25th symposium of the British Ecological Society, Reading 1984, pp. 169-188.

GREEN, R. 1991. The impact of hunting, poaching and accidents on otter survival and measures to protect individual animals. In: Reutler, C. & Rochert, R. (eds). *Proceedings of the 5th International Otter Colloquium, Habitat 6*: 171-190.

GREEN, J., & GREEN, R. 1980. *Otter survey of Scotland 1977-1979.* London, Vincent Wildlife Trust.

GREEN, J., & GREEN, R. 1987. *Otter survey of Scotland 1984 –1985.* London, Vincent Wildlife Trust.

GUBBAY, S. 1988. *Coastal directory for marine nature conservation.* Ross-on-Wye, Marine Conservation Society.

HALL, A.J., LAW, R.J., WELLS, D.E., HARWOOD, J., ROSS, H., KENNEDY, S., ALLCHIN, C.R., CAMPBELL, L.A., & POMEROY, P.P. 1992. Organochlorine levels in common seals (*Phoca vitulina*) which were victims and survivors of the 1988 phocine distemper epizootic. *Sci. tot. Envir., 15*: 145-162.

HALL, A.J., POMEROY, P.P., & HARWOOD, J. 1992. The descriptive epizootiology of phocine distemper in the UK during 1988/89. *Sci. tot. Envir., 15*: 31-44.

HAMMOND, P.S., MCCONNELL, B.J., & FEDAK, M.A. In press. Grey seals off the east coast of Britain: Distribution and movements at sea. *Symposium of the Zoological Society of London.*

HAMMOND, P.S., & PRIME, J.H. (1990). The diet of British grey seals *Halichoerus grypus*. In: Population biology of sealworm (*Pseudoterranova dicipiens*) in relation to its intermediate and seal hosts, ed. by W.D. Bowen. *Bull. Can. J. Fish. & Aquat. Sci.: 222.*

HAMMOND, P.S., & THOMPSON, P.M. (1991). Minimum estimate of the number of bottlenose dolphins (*Tursiops truncatus*) in the Moray Firth, N.E. Scotland. *Biological Conservation, 56*: 79-87.

HARRIS, M.P. & WANLESS, S. 1990. Breeding success of British kittiwakes *Rissa tridactyla* in 1986-88: evidence for changing conditions in the northern North Sea. *Journal of Applied Ecology, 27*: 172-187.

HARWOOD, J. 1990. What have we learned from the 1988 seal epidemic? *Biologist, 37(1)*: 7-8.

HARWOOD, J., HIBY, L., THOMPSON, D., & WARD, A. 1991. Seal stocks in Great Britain. Surveys conducted between 1986 and 1989. *NERC News, January*: 11-15. Natural Environment Research Council.

HIBY, L., DUCK, C., & THOMPSON, D. 1993. Seal stocks in Great Britain: surveys conducted in 1991. *NERC News (January 1993)*: 20-31. Natural Environment Research Council.

INSKIPP, T., & BARZDO, J. 1987. *World checklist of threatened mammals.* Peterborough, Nature Conservancy Council.

JEFFRIES, D.J. 1989. The changing otter population of Britain 1700-1989. *Linnean Society. Biological Journal, 38*: 61-69.

JEFFRIES, D.J., GREEN, J., & GREEN, R. 1984. *Commercial fish and crustacean traps: a serious cause of otter* Lutra lutra *(L) mortality in Britain and Europe.* London, Vincent Wildlife Trust.

KENDALL, M.D., SAFIEH, B., HARWOOD, J., & POMEROY, P.P. 1992. Thymulin plasma concentrations, the thymus and organochlorine contaminant levels in seals infected with phocine distemper virus. *Sci. tot. Envir., 15*: 133-144.

KIRBY, J.S., FERNS, J.R., WATERS R.J., & PRYS-JONES, R.P. 1991. *Wildfowl and Wader Counts 1990-91.* The Wildfowl and Wetlands Trust, Slimbridge.

KLINOWSKA, M. 1991. *Dolphins, Porpoises and Whales of the World. The IUCN Red Data Book.* Gland, IUCN.

KRUUK, H. 1989. Illuminating otters. *BBC Wildlife Magazine, 7*: 496-501.

KRUUK, H., & BALHARRY, D. 1990. Effects of sea water on thermal insulation of the otter, *Lutra lutra. Journal of Zoology, London, 220*: 405-415.

KRUUK, H., & CONROY, J.W.H. 1987. Surveying otter *Lutra lutra* populations: A discussion of problems with spraints. *Biological Conservation, 41*: 179-183.

KRUUK, H., & CONROY, J.W.H. 1991. Mortality of otters

Lutra lutra in Shetland. *Journal of Applied Ecology, 28:* 83-94.

KRUUK, H., CONROY, J.W. H., & MOORHOUSE, A. 1991. Recruitment to a population of otters *Lutra lutra* in Shetland, in relation to fish abundance. *Journal of Applied Ecology, 28:* 95-101.

KRUUK, H., & MOORHOUSE, A. 1990. Seasonal and spatial differences in food selection by otters *Lutra lutra* in Shetland. *Journal of Zoology, London, 221:* 621-637.

KRUUK, H., & MOORHOUSE, A. 1991. The spatial organisation of otters *Lutra lutra* in Shetland. *Journal of Zoology, London, 224:* 41-57.

KRUUK, H., MOORHOUSE, A., CONROY, J.W.H., DURBIN, L. & FREARS, S. 1989. An estimate of numbers and habitat preferences of otters *Lutra lutra* in Shetland, UK *Biological Conservation, 49,* 241-254.

KRUUK, H., WANSINK, D., & MOORHOUSE, A. 1990. Feeding patches and diving success of otters *Lutra lutra* in Shetland. *Oikos, 57:* 68-72.

LACK, P. 1986. *Atlas of the wintering birds in Britain and Ireland.* Calton, Poyser.

LENTON, E.J., CHANIN, P.R.F., & JEFFRIES, D.J. 1979. *Otter survey of England 1977-1979. Report to the Nature Conservancy Council.* Huntingdon, Nature Conservancy Council.

LLOYD, C., TASKER, M.L., & PARTRIDGE, K. 1991. *The status of seabirds in Britain and Ireland.* London, Poyser.

MACDONALD, S.M., & MASON, C.F. 1980. Observations on the marking behaviour of a coastal population of otters. *Acta Theriologica, 25:* 245-253.

MACDONALD, S.M., & MASON, C.F. In press. *Status and conservation needs of the otter* Lutra lutra *in the Western Palearctic.* Strasbourg, Council of Europe, Nature and Environment Series.

MASON, C.F. 1989. Water pollution and otter distribution – a review. *Lutra, 32:* 97-131.

MASON, C.F., & MACDONALD, S.M. 1980. The winter diet of otters *Lutra lutra* on a Scottish sea loch. *Journal of Zoology, 192:* 558-561.

MASON, C.F., & MACDONALD, S.M. 1986. *Otters: ecology and conservation.* Cambridge, Cambridge University Press.

MASON, C.F., & MACDONALD, S.M. 1987. The use of spraints for surveying otter *Lutra lutra* populations: an evaluation. *Biological Conservation, 41:* 167-177.

MASON, C.F., & MACDONALD, S.M. In press, a. Impact of organochlorine pesticide residues and PCBs on otters *Lutra lutra:* a study from western Britain. *Science of the Total Environment.*

MASON, C.F., & MACDONALD, S.M. In press, b. Impact of organochlorine pesticide residues and PCBs on otters *Lutra lutra* in eastern England. *Science of the Total Environment.*

McCONNELL, B.J., CHAMBERS, C., NICHOLAS, K.S.,

& FEDAK, M.A. 1992. Satellite tracking of grey seals (*Halichoerus grypus*). *Journal of Zoology, London,* 226: 271-282.

MONAGHAN, P. UTTLEY, J.D., & BURNS, M.D. 1992. Effects of changes in food availability on reproductive effort in arctic terns *Sterna paradisea. Ardea, Vol. 80* (special publication): 71-80.

MOSER, M.E. 1987. A revision of population estimates for waders (*Charadrii*) wintering on the coastline of Britain. *Biological Conservation, 39:* 153-164.

MOSER, M.E., & PRYS-JONES, R.P. 1990. Waders. *In: Marine Forum for environmental issues. North Sea Report 1990.* London, Marine Forum.

MOSER, M.E., & SUMMERS, R.W. 1987. Wader populations on non estuarine coasts of Britain and Northern Ireland - results of the 1984-1985 Winter Shorebird Count. *Bird Study, 34:* 71-81.

NATURAL ENVIRONMENT RESEARCH COUNCIL 1984. *Interactions between grey seals and UK fisheries.* Cambridge, Sea Mammal Research Unit, Natural Environment Research Council.

NATURAL ENVIRONMENT RESEARCH COUNCIL 1987. *Tracking seals at sea. Report for 1986-87, 24.* Swindon, Natural Environment Research Council.

NATURAL ENVIRONMENT RESEARCH COUNCIL 1989. *Seal epidemic of 1988. Report for 1988-89, 33.* Swindon, Natural Environment Research Council.

NATURE CONSERVANCY COUNCIL 1983. *The ecology and conservation of amphibian and reptile species endangered in Britain.* London, Nature Conservancy Council.

NATURE CONSERVANCY COUNCIL 1989. *Breeding failures of seabirds: Shetland in perspective. Ornithology note, No. 16.* Peterborough, Nature Conservancy Council.

NORFOLK NATURALISTS TRUST 1989. *The report of the north Norfolk otter project 1986-1987.* London, Vincent Wildlife Trust.

NORTHRIDGE, S. 1988. *Marine mammals and fisheries: a study of conflicts with fishing gear in British waters. A report commissioned by Wildlife Link's seals group.* London, Wildlife Link.

NORTHRIDGE, S. 1990. Seals. *In: North Sea Report,* 85-88. London, The Marine Forum for Environmental Issues.

PERRING, F.H., & FARRELL, L. 1983. *British Red Data Book 1. Vascular plants,* 2nd ed. Lincoln, Royal Society for Nature Conservation.

PIENKOWSKI, M.W., & EVANS, P.R. 1984. Migratory behaviour of shorebirds in the western palaearctic. *In: Behaviour of marine animals, Vol. 6 Shorebirds,* ed. by J. Burger and B.L. Olla. New York, Plenum Press.

PIERSMA, T. ed. 1986. Breeding waders in Europe. A review of population size estimates and a bibliography of information sources. *Wader Study Group Bulletin, 48 (supplement).*

POTTS, G.W., & SWABY S.E. 1991. Evaluation of the conservation requirements of rare British marine fishes. Final Report. *Nature Conservancy Council, CSD Report, No. 1228.*

POTTS, G.W., & SWABY, S.E. 1993. Review of the status of estuarine fishes. *English Nature Research Reports, No. 34.* Peterborough, English Nature.

PRATER, A.J. 1981. *Estuary birds of Britain and Ireland.* Calton, Poyser.

PRATER, A.J. 1989. Ringed plover *Charadrius hiaticula*, breeding population in the United Kingdom in 1984. *Bird Study, 36:* 154-159.

PRESTT, I., COOKE, A.S., & CORBETT, K.F. 1974. British amphibians and reptiles. *In: The changing flora and fauna of Britain,* ed. by D.L. Hawkesworth. London.

PRIME, J.H., & HAMMOND, P.S. (1990). The diet of grey seals from the southwestern North Sea assessed from analyses of hard parts found in faeces. *Journal of Applied Ecology, 27:* 435-447.

RAFFAELLI, D., HULL, S., & MILNE, H. 1989. Long-term changes in nutrients, weed mats and shorebirds in an estuarine system. *Cahiers de Biologie Marin, 30:* 259-270.

REED, T.M. 1985. Estimates of British breeding wader populations. *Wader Study Group Bulletin, 45:* 11-12.

REES, E.I.S., & TASKER, M.L. 1990. *Birds of the Irish Sea and its shores – a conservation evaluation. The Irish Sea, An Environmental Review Part 1, Nature Conservation.* Irish Sea Study Group. Liverpool, Liverpool University Press.

REIJNDERS, P.J.H. 1984. Man-induced environmental factors in relation to fertility changes in pinnipeds. *Environmental Conservation, Vol. 11 (1).* Switzerland, The Foundation for Environmental Conservation.

ROSS, A. 1988. *Controlling nature's predators on fish farms.* Ross-on-Wye, Marine Conservation Society.

SALMON, D.G. 1990. Wildfowl. *In: Marine Forum for environmental issues. North Sea Report 1990.* London, Marine Forum.

SHARROCK, J.T.R. 1976. *The atlas of breeding birds in Britain and Ireland.* Calton, Poyser.

SMIT, C.J., & PIERSMA, T. 1989. Numbers, midwinter distribution and migration of wader populations using the east Atlantic Flyway. *In: Flyways and reserve networks. IWRB, Proceedings of the third meeting of the conference of contracting parties, Regina, Canada.* 24-36. Canadian Wildlife Service/IWRB.

SMITH, K.W. 1983. The status and distribution of waders breeding on wet lowland grassland in England and Wales. *Bird Study, 30:* 177-192.

SMITH, K.W. 1988. BTO/WSG breeding wader monitoring scheme-the story so far. *Wader Study Group Bulletin, 53:* 3.

STRACHAN, R., BIRKS, J.D.S., CHANIN, P. R. F., & JEFFRIES, D. J. 1990. *Otter survey of England 1984–1986.* Peterborough, Nature Conservancy Council.

STROUD, D.A., MUDGE, G.P., & PIENKOWSKI, M.W. 1990. *Protecting internationally important bird sites. A review of the EC Special Protection Area network in Britain.* Peterborough, Nature Conservancy Council.

SUBRAMANIAN, A.N., TANABE, S., TATSUKAWA, R., SAITO, S., & MIKAZAKI, N. 1987. Reduction in the testosterone levels by PCBs and DDE in Dall's porpoises of the northwestern North Pacific. *Marine Pollution Bulletin, 18 (12):* 643-646.

TASKER, M.L., & PIENKOWSKI, M.W. 1987. *Vulnerable concentrations of birds in the North Sea.* Peterborough, Nature Conservancy Council.

TASKER, M.L., & WEBB, A. 1990. Seabirds. *The Marine Forum for Environmental Issues 1990 North Sea Report.* London, Marine Forum for Environmental Issues.

TASKER, M.L., WEBB, A., HALL, A.J., PIENKOWSKI, M.W., & LANGSLOW, D.R. 1987. *Seabirds in the North Sea.* Peterborough, Nature Conservancy Council.

TASKER, M.L., WEBB, A., HARRISON, N.M., & PIENKOWSKI, M.W. 1990. *Vulnerable concentrations of marine birds to the west of Britain.* Peterborough, Nature Conservancy Council.

THOMPSON, P.M. 1989. Seasonal changes in the distribution and composition of common seal (*Phoca vitulina*) haul-out groups. *Journal of Zoology, 217:* 281-294.

THOMPSON, P.M., FEDAK, M.A., MCCONNELL, B.J., & NICHOLAS, K.S. 1989. Seasonal and sex-related variation in the activity patterns of common seals (*Phoca vitulina*). *Journal of Applied Ecology, 26:* 521-535.

THOMPSON, D., HAMMOND, P.S., NICHOLAS, K.S., & FEDAK, M.A. 1991. Movements, diving and foraging behaviour of grey seals *Halichoerus grypus. Journal of Zoology, London, 224:* 223-232.

THOMPSON, P.M., & HARWOOD, J. 1990. Methods for estimating the population size of common seals *(Phoca vitulina). Journal of Applied Ecology, 27:* 924-938.

THOMPSON, P.M., & MILLER, D. 1990. Summer foraging activity and movements of radio-tagged common seals (*Phoca vitulina*) in the Moray Firth, Scotland. *Journal of Applied Ecology, 27(2):* 492-501.

THOMPSON, P.M., & ROTHERY, P. 1987. Age and sex differences in the timing of moult in the common seal *Phoca vitulina. Journal of Zoology, 212:* 597-603.

WATSON, H. 1978. *Coastal otters Lutra lutra in Shetland.* London, Vincent Wildlife Trust.

WEBB, A., HARRISON, N.M., LEAPER, G.M., STEELE, R.D., TASKER, M.L., & PIENKOWSKI, M.W. 1990. *Seabird distribution west of Britain.* Peterborough, Nature Conservancy Council.

WEIR, V. 1988. *The otter,* 2nd edition. London, Vincent Wildlife Trust.

WOOD, M.S. ed. 1979. *Otters 1979. Second report of the Joint Otter Group.* Lincoln, Society for the Promotion of Nature Conservation.

Chapter 8

JNCC COASTAL AND ESTUARIES REVIEWS

8.1 COASTAL REVIEW UNIT

The Coastal Review Unit (CRU) works within the Coastal Conservation Branch of the Joint Nature Conservation Committee. The work of the CRU in providing coastal information is outlined below, and the following section describes the earlier Nature Conservancy Council's Estuaries Review. The CRU is continuing the Estuaries Review work as part of its role.

The role of the CRU includes the collection, collation and dissemination of comprehensive and consistent information about the coastal zone and man's impact upon it. This is a key element in underpinning the development of Coastal Zone Management (CZM) strategies. An important feature of the work is the development of an information system capable of covering the whole coastal zone, from hard rocky shores to extensive soft tidal flats; and from subtidal marine systems through tidally inundated saltmarshes to wholly terrestrial maritime habitats such as sand dunes. A second key part of the approach is data collation on a wide range of human activities taking place on the coast as a baseline for identifying the location and type of activities which may conflict with its sustainable use.

The data sets which are being collated or linked will come eventually from many sources, including computerised datasets held within the JNCC, and from other conservation bodies and organisations. These have been collected at many scales and levels of detail, from information on individual sites to national vegetation surveys of sand dunes, shingle structures and saltmarshes. Packaging this to provide a consistent UK resource data set amenable to analysis is a major task, particularly when it includes information on human uses and impacts. It is also essential to establish links between the great variety of other data sets, such as those for the marine part of the zone and on species concentrations (e.g. migratory birds, rare plants and invertebrates) if a complete picture is to be obtained. To this end the unit is currently undertaking a wide-ranging information systems review. This will focus on data handling for the UK, but the methodology will also be applicable to wider European initiatives.

Collation and linking of datasets is of course not the end-point of the process and there are a variety of products ranging from nationwide reviews of habitats and activities to detailed inventories of sites and electronic databases. Some of these are being produced in collaboration with other conservation agencies and include UK-wide distribution analyses of human activities on estuaries and the scale and pattern of water-based recreational activities on British estuaries.

The CRU is nearing completion of another inventory project, *An inventory of UK estuaries* (Buck 1993). This publication will give a standardised summary of the location, wildlife, conservation status and human activities of each of the 163 UK estuaries and is designed to be widely available for use as background to CZM plans and as a baseline for resource monitoring. The British volumes of this inventory are well advanced and a Northern Ireland volume is now being developed in collaboration with the Department of the Environment (Northern Ireland) and the RSPB.

This data gathering exercise builds on the work of the Estuaries Review (Davidson *et al.* 1991a), which itself has laid firm foundations for policy development. For example, its findings are now providing the starting-point for several initiatives including the development of estuary management plans as part of English Nature's Estuaries Initiative and for similar programmes by Scottish Natural Heritage and the Countryside Council for Wales.

This type of summary inventory, compiled from the more detailed data holdings of the Coastal Review, illustrates an important point about the data handling methodology. Complex datasets can generate both detailed analyses and simpler inventory listings. It is also important to recognise that the approach uses existing information to help inform the decision-making process.

8.2   ESTUARIES REVIEW

INTRODUCTION

Britain has a larger area of estuarine (intertidal and subtidal) habitat (almost 530,000 ha) than any other single European country. The importance of estuaries like the Wash is recognised in conservation terms by national and international designations. However, concern over increasing pressures on estuaries and their wildlife from many human activities prompted the Nature Conservancy Council to initiate the Estuaries Review as the basis for an overall conservation strategy for estuaries in Britain. The Estuaries Review started in September 1988 with a remit to provide an overview of the wildlife importance of estuaries and the pressures affecting them.

A great deal is known about estuaries and what affects the various habitats and the wildlife. However, much of the information is piecemeal and scattered, often referring only to single sites. The Estuaries Review redresses the limitations of this information by looking at three main topics:

❖ wildlife interest
❖ conservation status
❖ human activities.

Information has been drawn largely from existing sources, both published and unpublished. The report highlights the extent of knowledge which exists about estuarine wildlife and areas where further information is required for effective estuarine conservation.

The Estuaries Review report *Nature conservation and estuaries in Great Britain* (Davidson *et al.* 1991a) provides a national (GB) overview of the resource, its wildlife interest, conservation status and human activities and forms the basis for the development of individual estuarine strategies. The main report is supplemented by an illustrated summary document (Davidson *et al.* 1991b). Site by site summaries for all estuaries which are covered by the review will also be published by the Joint Nature Conservation Committee in seven volumes in 1993 (Buck 1993).

Further work based on Estuaries Review data is being produced by the JNCC as part of the work of the Coastal Review Unit. This includes further analyses of the national distribution of human activities around estuaries.

WHAT IS AN ESTUARY?

To encompass all facets contributing to estuarine wildlife conservation, a broad definition of the estuarine resource has been used within the Estuaries Review: partially enclosed soft tidal shore and its surroundings, open to saline water from the sea and receiving fresh water from rivers, land run-off or seepage. This definition encompasses extensive open, marine-influenced shores such as the barrier beach systems of Lindisfarne and the North Norfolk coast, but deep-water sea lochs with predominantly rocky shores are excluded. The 155 British sites selected for inclusion in the Estuaries Review are shown in Davidson *et al.* (1991a). Along the North Sea coastal margin 89 sites (57.4% of the GB total) fall within this definition and the distribution of these is given in Figure 8.1.1.

For each site a core area was selected within the intertidal and sub-tidal zones along with a surrounding terrestrial envelope of maritime and sub-maritime habitats. The area and shoreline length for each site was measured and details are given in the review. Revised and expanded listings of estuary measurements are given in Volume 1 of the inventory of UK estuaries (Buck 1993). There is over 261,000 ha of intertidal and subtidal land in these estuaries along the North Sea coastal margin (49% of the GB total).

CONSERVATION INTEREST OF ESTUARIES

A key feature of estuaries in Britain is their complex and often highly productive mosaic of wildlife habitats which includes marine features, intertidal mud, sandflats and saltmarshes. The surrounding habitats – sand dunes, shingle and coastal grazing marshes – are an integral part of the overall wildlife interest. For each feature of wildlife interest the text within the Estuaries Review follows a broadly similar pattern. A general description of the ecological and behavioural characteristics of the wildlife that are relevant to their conservation is followed by an analysis of the size and distribution of the wildlife resource around the review sites. The topics covered in the review are listed below:

❖ Estuarine habitats
❖ Terrestrial invertebrates
❖ Marine communities
❖ Fish
❖ Amphibians and reptiles
❖ Birds
❖ Mammals.

The natural interest of estuarine ecosystems varies regionally, and as far as possible variation has been described both in terms of the British resource and in a European and international context. Major pressures and threats to the particular features

Figure 8.1.1
Estuaries Review sites which
lie along the North Sea
coastal margin (after
Davidson *et al.* 1991b).
Based upon the 1975 Ordnance Survey
1:1,250,000 map with the permission
of the Controller of Her Majesty's
Stationery Office © Crown Copyright.

of interest are described as are the current methods for conserving the habitat or species. In particular, the chapter on human activities (Chapter 11) and the overall analysis of conservation status focuses on the needs and issues of the different components of the wildlife resource.

The amount of detail contained within each section is variable, reflecting the extent of current knowledge available for different features. For example, the distribution and movements of birds on estuaries have been the subjects of extensive studies by a wide range of groups, whereas information on the distribution of marine communities and terrestrial invertebrates is much less detailed.

The international significance of estuaries for their wetland habitats and bird populations is recognised in conservation terms by their identification as wetlands of international importance under the Ramsar Convention and as Special Protection Areas (SPA). These areas are described in more detail in Chapter 10 of this directory and further in the Estuaries Review. Of the 89 estuarine sites discussed within the Review, seven sites have been designated and 26 further sites have been proposed as Ramsar/SPA sites.

SOURCES OF INFORMATION

Information on wildlife and habitats was taken from the large volume of data held within the country agencies. The major source of information for non-breeding waders and wildfowl on different British estuaries was collated from the monthly counts undertaken by the Birds of Estuaries Enquiry (see Section 7.2). Much of the information on human activities used in the Estuaries Review was collected from other primary sources through discussions with the appropriate members of NCC regional staff and where necessary from outside organisations. The assessment of human activities, given within the Estuaries Review examines the number, distribution and characteristics of estuaries affected by a particular activity.

Staff at JNCC were involved in the overall coordination of the project, providing advice and information.

ACKNOWLEDGEMENTS

This section was produced by Nick Davidson, JNCC.

REFERENCES

BUCK, A.L. 1993. *An inventory of UK estuaries*. 7 volumes. Joint Nature Conservation Committee, Peterborough.

DAVIDSON, N.C. *et al.* 1991a. *Nature conservation and estuaries in Great Britain*. Nature Conservancy Council, Peterborough.

DAVIDSON, N.C. *et al.* 1991b. *Estuaries, wildlife and man. (A summary of nature conservation and estuaries in Great Britain.)* Nature Conservancy Council, Peterborough.

Chapter 9

OTHER SOURCES OF INFORMATION

9.1 NCC COASTWATCH PROJECT

The Coastwatch survey was initiated in 1985 and designed for volunteer participation. It was intended to collect basic information on the extent of various intertidal and coastal habitat types and the scale of various human coastal uses and activities on them for the whole coast of Great Britain.

The survey, which covered the area between low water mark and the inland limit of maritime influence and extended into estuaries, sea-lochs and inlets to the point of normal tidal limit, has now been completed. The information collected is being used to assist with selecting sites for more detailed survey work, to assess broad environmental changes and to evaluate areas for their nature conservation importance.

The Coastwatch database is currently being incorporated into the JNCC Coastal Review Unit's database development. Further analysis of the results of the survey will be undertaken to contribute to a comprehensive description of the coast.

DATA COLLECTION

Coastwatch consisted of two surveys:

❖ The Habitat Mapping Survey. The distribution and extent of habitat types such as rocky, sandy and muddy shores, saltmarshes, sand dunes and cliff slopes are represented on large-scale maps using a colour code. The land use adjacent to the coast was also recorded, as this may affect coastal habitats in some way. Measurements were then made from the maps of the area or length of the coastal habitats, the total length of the coast at the high water mark and of the various adjacent landward transitions.

❖ The Coastal Uses and Activities Survey. Selected observable coastal impacts, such as types of coastal constructions, pollution and the number of people engaged in various coastal pastimes, were noted on prepared recording sheets. Both surveys used 1:10,000 scale Ordnance Survey maps for data recording. A group of four 1 km grid squares, a tetrad, forms the mapping unit.

Coastwatch surveys were undertaken while walking the coast or, where access is difficult, by boat.

9.2 NORWICH UNION COASTWATCH UK

Norwich Union Coastwatch UK is a joint initiative with Farnborough College of Technology in association with the Marine Conservation Society. It is the country's largest independent beach and coastal survey carried out by a network of volunteers and a part of Coastwatch Europe, a survey carried out in 16 participating countries, including all the North Sea coastal states.

The aims of the project are to raise public awareness of our coastlines, gather reference data and aid coastal protection measures.

The Coastwatch survey is carried out during the same fortnight each autumn and provides a snapshot picture of the state of the coast at that time, including land use adjacent to the shore, presence of litter, inflows (with information on water quality and nitrate levels), sewage pollution incidents, microbiological parameters and other coastal pollution problems or threats. In 1992 500 coastal sites and over 2,000 km (more than 15%) of the UK coastline were covered, including 1,296.5 km on the North Sea coast.

Further information on this project is available from Kathy Pond, Norwich Union Coastwatch UK, Farnborough College of Technology, Boundary Road, Farnborough, Hampshire, GU14 6SB.

9.3 ATLAS OF COASTAL SITES SENSITIVE TO OIL POLLUTION

The Nature Conservancy Council produced a set of coastal maps and schedules. These are used to guide local authorities, the Marine Pollution Control

Unit (MPCU), oil companies and all those involved in dealing with oil pollution incidents. The Atlas contains 77 full-colour maps at 1:100,000 scale covering the coast of Britain. Each map shows:

❖ coastal habitat type (including intertidal zone, saltmarsh, sand dune and cliff)

❖ boundaries of sites of nature conservation interest

❖ boundaries of counties and districts

❖ symbols to indicate important bird and seal concentrations, and sites of marine biological importance

❖ sites of international importance for birds.

The maps are supported by detailed schedules, which give:

❖ a general description of the coastal area

❖ a detailed breakdown of the nature conservation features of importance, including a sensitivity analysis, and a list of statutory protected sites and other important nature conservation areas

❖ means of access to the coast

❖ sites suitable for disposal of oily wastes and other information on waste disposal.

Copies of the Atlas or individual maps from it, together with information schedules, are available from English Nature, Northminster House, Peterborough PE1 1UA. The Atlas costs £700; maps cost £15 each.

9.4 REPORT OF THE MANS (MANAGEMENT ANALYSIS OF THE NORTH SEA) PROJECT

The MANS project was initiated by the Dutch Government in 1987 in response to a growing awareness of the need to make coherent planning and other decisions in the light of an integrated vision of the sustainable functioning and utilisation of the North Sea's natural systems. The object of the project has been defined as 'The development of a set of analytical tools to facilitate the comparison and evaluation of policy alternatives with respect to the use, physical planning and management of the North Sea.'

From this general objective a number of secondary objectives were defined:

❖ make an inventory of relevant available knowledge, data and (mathematical) models

❖ identify additional requirements in knowledge, data and models and, where possible, meet these requirements

❖ carry out specific, management-orientated, policy analysis studies to support the formulation of policy plans and decision-making

❖ define, initialise and stimulate research programmes and projects.

The MANS project is structured around several topics or themes, as follows:

i) Risk analysis of calamitous oil and chemical spills

ii) The discharge of toxic and hazardous substances, their up-take in the food chain and their effect on ecology

iii) Eutrophication and its effects on the algae of the North Sea

iv) Physical planning of sea use

v) Biomass and the effects of human influences on the ecosystem

vi) Economic analysis

vii) Database management modelling system which brings together all the available models and databases so that an integrated analysis of this information can be made

viii) Legal and institutional matters.

For each of the above themes a main report has been produced, supported, where appropriate, by additional sub-reports. In addition an overall summary report has been published, which contains a summary of all the work done under the different themes, describes the interrelations between the various themes and provides an integrated analysis of the theme.

Of particular relevance to the UK North Sea coastal margin is a report on data investigations for the United Kingdom (Cole-King 1990).

9.5 BRITISH MARINE FISHES DATABASE

Developing from the growing concern on the status of marine fishes and the state of the environment, the Marine Biological Association has established a British Marine Fishes Database (BMFD) of information covering aspects of the biology and ecology of marine fishes. The data on each fish is divided into 18 topic headings including a summary, picture, and distribution map. The database will also included details of capturing techniques, transport, maintenance and management of captive stock, and other topics not normally included in the scientific literature. A section on the conservation status of the less common species is included with an assessment of the major threats likely to influence population numbers. A bibliography of key references is included with each species. The data is continually reviewed by experts and undergoes regular updating.

The database is a focal point for fish records and is currently being used as a tool for monitoring the distribution and abundance of uncommon species in response to environmental change. Particular attention is being paid to estuarine species and those on the edge of their range. The BMFD will also contribute to programmes of education, conservation and research.

For further details contact Dr G.W. Potts or Ms S.E. Swaby, Marine Biological Association, Citadel Hill, Plymouth, PL1 2PB. Tel. 0752 222772.

9.6 UNITED KINGDOM DIGITAL MARINE ATLAS PROJECT

The United Kingdom Digital Marine Atlas (UKDMAP) was developed by the British Oceanographic Data Centre, Natural Environment Research Council (NERC), with funding by NERC, the Ministry of Agriculture, Fisheries and Food, Scottish Office Agriculture and Fisheries Department, the former Nature Conservancy Council, Joint Nature Conservation Committee and the National Rivers Authority.

The UKDMAP is a reference work on all aspects of the coastline and seas around the British Isles, generally covering the area 45°N to 65°N, 15°W to 15°E which includes the whole of the North Sea. It will be of use to the scientific, educational, government and commercial sectors. It is not a full Geographical Information System (GIS), but is rather a combination of a traditional printed atlas and a series of geo-referenced catalogues and indices of material related to the marine environment. It contains a wide diversity of themes, with a variety of presentation methods, including contoured plots of physical, chemical and geological parameters, colour-coded distribution charts of sea-use, biological and fisheries information, oceanographic data catalogues and geo-referenced directories which present detailed information on demand. The Atlas system has been developed to run on IBM-compatible PCs.

Further information and copies of the UKDMAP are available from the British Oceanographic Data Centre, Proudman Oceanographic Laboratory, Bidston Laboratory, Birkenhead, Merseyside L43 7RA.

9.7 MAFF'S UKDMAP-BASED COASTAL DIRECTORY

For more than five years MAFF's Directorate of Fisheries Research (DFR) has seen the need for a computerised directory of the resources and uses of the seaward coastal zone. The need stems, in the main, from the responsibility of the Fisheries Laboratories to give policy makers in MAFF reliable information at short notice about any aspect of the waters of the Territorial Sea.

UKDMAP (see Section 9.6) has been chosen as the format for the Directory because of its compatibility with all IBM-type PCs, its demonstrated capability, its potential for development and because it is user-friendly. Its format will be used in a large-scale sense routinely in this application.

The north-east coast of England between Berwick and Flamborough Head has been chosen as the 'pilot' area and much of this data is already in UKDMAP format. It is anticipated that this will become widely available in updates of the full UKDMAP in the foreseeable future.

ACKNOWLEDGEMENTS

The NCC Coastwatch section was written by Clare Brewster, Teresa Bennett and Roger Mitchell of the Nature Conservancy Council. Information for the other sections was provided by Kathy Pond (Norwich Union Coastwatch), Peter Simmonds (former NCC, Site & Pollution Policy Branch), the MANS Report, Dr Geoff Potts (Marine Biological Association), the British Oceanographic Data Centre and Dr Stephen Lockwood (MAFF).

REFERENCES

COLE-KING, A.J. 1990. *Alg 2: Data Investigation United Kingdom, MANS (Management Analysis North Sea)*. Rijkswaterstaat and Department of Maritime Studies, University of Wales, Cardiff.

REES, G., & POND, K. 1993. *Norwich Union Coastwatch UK 1992 Survey Report*. Norwich Union.

Chapter 10

SITE PROTECTION

10.1 INTRODUCTION

This chapter describes the main bodies responsible for protecting sites. The most important types of protection are considered in turn.

CENTRAL GOVERNMENT ORGANISATIONS

Section 10.2 includes site lists and maps for the following types of site protection, with a description of the type of protection afforded:
❖ National Nature Reserves
❖ Marine Nature Reserves
❖ Sites of Special Scientific Interest
❖ Marine Consultation Areas
❖ Areas of Outstanding Natural Beauty
❖ Heritage Coast
❖ National Scenic Areas
❖ National Parks
❖ Environmentally Sensitive Areas
❖ Areas of Special Protection
❖ Special Protection Areas and Ramsar sites
❖ World Heritage sites
❖ Biosphere Reserves
❖ Several and Regulating Orders, static gear reserves.

LOCAL GOVERNMENT ORGANISATIONS

Section 10.3 includes a summary of the planning system regarding coastal development in Scotland and England, plus site lists and maps for the following types of site protection:
❖ Local Nature Reserves and Country Parks
❖ Regional Landscape Designations.

VOLUNTARY AND PRIVATE ORGANISATIONS

Section 10.4 includes site lists and maps of voluntary and private types of site protection conferred by National Trust for Scotland and National Trust, Royal Society for the Protection of Birds (RSPB) and local Wildlife Trusts.

10.2 CENTRAL GOVERNMENT ORGANISATIONS

INTRODUCTION

Site protection on the North Sea coast is administered by several central government organisations. Protected status includes statutory designations operating at national and international levels and both statutory and non-statutory nature reserves. Each of these is described below in relation to the body responsible for the legislation.

NATURE CONSERVATION AGENCIES

Prior to April 1991 the **Nature Conservancy Council** (NCC) was the Government's main statutory adviser on nature conservation. Under the Wildlife and Countryside Act 1981 it was responsible for the establishment of National Nature Reserves, notification of Sites of Special Scientific Interest (SSSI) and selection of Marine Nature Reserves. It also nominated some inshore areas in Scotland as Marine Consultation Areas, which are not protected by legislation. All these designations are to protect and conserve the habitats and species within the defined areas. The NCC also identified sites of Nature Conservation Review (NCR) status – see Ratcliffe (1977) – and Geological Conservation Review (GCR) sites. These are non-statutory, identifying sites which are nationally important examples of their type for the habitats or species they contain, or for their geological and physio-graphic interest.

Areas of Special Protection were recommended by the NCC to the Secretary of State for the Environment (England), or to the Secretary of State for Scotland, under the 1981 Act. The NCC was also responsible for advising on European and worldwide protection measures (see below).

The Environmental Protection Act 1990 established separate agencies for England, Scotland and Wales to replace the NCC. These each took over the responsibilities of the NCC statutory site designations outlined above. The new Nature Conservancy Council for England, known as **English Nature**, was established in April 1991. In Wales the Countryside Commission was combined with part of the former NCC to form the **Countryside Council for Wales** (CCW, established in April 1991). Similarly, the Natural Heritage (Scotland) Bill (1991) resulted in the Countryside Commission for Scotland being merged with the NCC in Scotland to form **Scottish Natural Heritage** (SNH, established in April 1992).

Under the arrangements arising from the Environment Protection Act (EPA), the **Joint Nature Conservation Committee** (JNCC) was established. It is a committee of the three country agencies set up under the EPA – English Nature, SNH and CCW – together with representatives from Northern Ireland and the United Kingdom and independent members. It is the means through which the Councils must carry out their 'special' functions relating to wider environmental issues. These are defined in section 133 of the Act and include setting common scientific standards, undertaking and commissioning research, dissemination of knowledge about nature conservation and giving advice on wider nature conservation matters which affect the whole of Great Britain or the UK. JNCC also has the UK responsibility for European and international commitments for wildlife.

COUNTRYSIDE COMMISSION, COUNTRYSIDE COUNCIL FOR WALES AND SCOTTISH NATURAL HERITAGE

As noted above, the Countryside Commission and the NCC merged in Wales to form the Countryside Council for Wales and in Scotland to form Scottish Natural Heritage. The Countryside Commission is now responsible for England alone.

These three countrywide organisations designate or identify areas which have particular scenic value, and which need protection from adverse or excessive development. In England and Wales these areas are National Parks and Areas of Outstanding Natural Beauty (AONB), both of which are statutory designations, and Heritage Coasts (HC). Heritage Coasts, while identified by the

Commission, are defined on development plans by local planning authorities in consultation with the Commission. In Scotland the legislative framework differs from that in England, so a different designation, National Scenic Area, applies. Local planning authorities must take account of the scenic value of these areas when considering planning applications for development within them. There are no National Parks in Scotland. The ten National Parks in England and Wales were designated in the 1950s by the National Parks Commission, the predecessor of the Countryside Commission. Two areas of equivalent status exist on the North Sea coast. These are the Broads, administered by the Broads Authority, and the New Forest, administered by the New Forest Committee. These areas are designated as exceptionally fine stretches of relatively wild countryside.

EUROPEAN COMMUNITY (EC)

Three directives of the European Community have particular relevance to the conservation of sites in Britain. These are described below.

The **EC Directive on the Conservation of Wild Birds** (Directive 79/409) requires member states to take special conservation measures to protect the habitats of rare or vulnerable species (listed in Annex 1 of the Directive) and of regularly occurring migratory birds. These measures include the designation of Special Protection Areas (SPAs) where appropriate. Designation of Special Protection Areas under the Directive is undertaken by the Department of the Environment and the Scottish Office, in consultation with the JNCC and the relevant country agency.

The **EC Directive concerning Urban Waste Water Treatment** adopted on 12 May 1991 (91/271/EC) allows for protection of the environment from the adverse effects of discharges of waste water. It recommends secondary sewage treatment for waste water discharges to all coastal areas not specifically notified as 'less sensitive'. It also recommends more stringent waste water treatment in areas notified as 'sensitive'. Discharges to 'less sensitive' areas may only receive primary treatment. 'Sensitive' and 'less sensitive' areas have yet to be defined, but it seems likely that SSSIs and some other conservation areas and areas liable to eutrophication such as estuaries would be defined as 'sensitive' and therefore waste water discharged to them may require further treatment.

The **EC Directive on the Conservation of Natural Habitats and of Wild Fauna and Flora** (92/43/EEC) was notified to the UK Government on 5 June 1992. The aim of the Habitats and Species Directive, as it has become known, is to 'contribute towards ensuring bio-diversity through the conservation of natural habitats and of wild fauna and flora ... in Member States ... Measures taken pursuant to this Directive shall be designated to maintain or restore, at favourable conservation status, natural habitats and species of wild fauna and flora of Community interest.'

Member states are required to produce a list of sites of community importance to be designated as Special Areas of Conservation (SAC). The Directive requires Member States to implement conservation measures for each SAC involving, 'if need be', appropriate management plans, as well as 'statutory, administrative or contractoral measures' to manage the sites for conservation. SACs will combine to form a network of sites known as Natura 2000.

Guidance on the selection of sites is given in Annex I of the Directive (which sets out a list of habitat types of Community interest) and Annex II (which lists species of Community interest). Within these lists, some habitats and species have priority status. Annex III presents a set of criteria for selecting sites. Priority habitats and species will automatically be accepted by the European Commission as sites of Community Importance, as will all Special Protection Areas designated under the EC directive on the Conservation of Wild Birds.

WORLDWIDE ORGANISATIONS

World Heritage sites and Biosphere Reserves are declared by UNESCO (United Nations Educational, Scientific and Cultural Organisation). These are respectively sites of 'natural and cultural treasures' and sites representing significant examples of biomes throughout the world (Countryside Commission 1989b).

The **Convention on Wetlands of International Importance especially as Waterfowl Habitat**, known as the 'Ramsar Convention', was adopted at a meeting of countries concerned with wetland and waterfowl conservation held in Ramsar, Iran in 1971. The UK government signed the Convention in 1973 and the UK Parliament ratified it in 1976. The Convention requires contracting parties to identify and take special measures to protect internationally important wetlands. It also requires contracting parties to promote, as far as possible, the 'wise' use of all wetlands in their territory.

The Council of Europe Convention on the conservation of European wildlife and natural habitats, known as the **Berne Convention,** covers the protection of mammals, birds, amphibians, reptiles, freshwater fish, invertebrates and plants. The UK ratified the Berne Convention on 28 May 1982. Parties to the Convention are required to take appropriate and necessary legislative measures to ensure the conservation of the habitats of the wild fauna and flora, particularly those specified in Appendices I (rare plants) and II (rare animals) of the Convention. In addition the Convention gives special attention to the protection of areas of importance to migratory species, in particular those areas used for wintering, staging, feeding, breeding and moulting. This has special significance for the conservation of the North Sea coastal margin, which supports internationally important populations of several species of migratory bird.

Britain is a party to the **Convention on the Conservation of Migratory Species of Wild Animals** known as the **Bonn Convention.** The Bonn Convention provides for strict protection of a number of endangered animals listed in its Appendix I. The Convention also provides the framework for a series of agreements between range states for the conservation and management of species listed in Appendix II. For the Convention to be effective, all states of a region need to join and then negotiate agreements, but at the time of writing this directory no agreements have yet been negotiated.

FISHERIES

Legislation controlling aspects of fisheries protection is administered by the Ministry of Agriculture, Fisheries and Food (MAFF) in England, the Welsh Office Agriculture Department (WOAD) and the Scottish Office Agriculture and Fisheries Department (SOAFD) in Scotland. Specific areas of coastal waters, for example, may be subject to Fishery Orders (Several and Regulating Orders) which confer the rights of management or cultivation of natural or non-natural beds of shellfish in order to regulate harvesting or to improve their level of production. These departments are also responsible for enacting by-laws to control fisheries within Marine Nature Reserves. The Inshore Fishing (Scotland) Act 1984 enables the Secretary of State for Scotland to make orders regulating fishing in waters off the coast of Scotland. These orders may prohibit all fishing, fishing of particular species, or a particular method of fishing. They may apply for specified periods or throughout the year. In 1985 an order for the Prohibition of Fishing and Fishing Methods in Scottish Inshore Waters SI962 was made. It identified areas where there were restrictions on the use of mobile gear (nets). These became known as static gear reserves and are specifically concerned with the control of trawling, Danish seine or similar, purse seine and ring net or dredge. The order reduces conflict between fishermen using static gear and those operating mobile gear. In 1989 a similar order SI 2307 was introduced which further identified areas of the Scottish coast in which types and methods of fishing were prohibited. In particular, SI 2307 restricted the areas in which suction dredges could be operated.

MINISTRY OF DEFENCE

In addition to the government organisations with a specific responsibility for the conservation of the North Sea coastal margin, the Ministry of Defence (MOD) owns sites covering more than 320 km of coastline around the United Kingdom. Many of these sites have been designated as Sites of Special Scientific Interest. It is MOD policy that, where a site has significant importance in terms of its natural history, a Conservation Group is established to record, monitor and protect it. Examples of some of those sites owned by the MOD which fall within the boundary of this Directory include:

Cape Wrath, situated in northern Scotland, which boasts the highest cliffs on the British mainland and one of the major seabird cliff breeding stations in Britain;

The Wash, significant for populations of wildfowl and waders as well as harbouring large concentrations of seals, has RAF Holbeach, RAF Donna Nook and RAF Wainfleet situated around its coasts;

Foulness Island, at the extreme south-east of Essex, provides one of the main early wintering grounds for dark-bellied brent geese in north-west Europe and is of great importance for numerous other species of bird;

Dungeness, well known for its extensive shingle spit and unusual populations of holly trees, includes the Cinque Ports Training Areas;

Thorney Island in West Sussex, with a population of rare grass-poly *Lythrum hyssopifolia*, is one of many notable sites on the south coast of England;

Dorset has several important coastal sites encompassing heathland habitats.

These examples illustrate the diversity of coastal habitat types under MOD stewardship; for all these sites and many others extensive information exists, and can be made available for academic study.

TYPES OF PROTECTION

National Nature Reserves

National Nature Reserves (NNR) may be declared by the country agencies under section 19 of the National Parks and Access to the Countryside Act 1949, or section 35 of the Wildlife and Countryside Act 1981.

The areas declared as NNRs represent some of the most important natural and semi-natural ecosystems in Great Britain, and are managed for the purposes of the conservation of the habitat, and providing special opportunities for scientific study of the habitats, communities and species represented within them (Countryside Commission 1989b).

National Nature Reserve land may be owned or leased by the country agencies, managed under a nature reserve agreement, or 'held and managed by an approved body and declared under section 35 (1)(c) of the Wildlife and Countryside Act 1981' (Nature Conservancy Council 1989b). An 'approved body' may be a local Wildlife Trust, National Park authority, or a county, regional or district council. Access to National Nature Reserves on the North Sea coast is by permit only, obtainable from the regional office of English Nature and Scottish Natural Heritage, but public rights of way are maintained.

The distribution of National Nature Reserves along the North Sea coastal margin is shown in Figure 10.2.1. NNRs are listed in Table 10.2.1. See Table 10.2.2 for a summary of sites and areas.

Marine Nature Reserves

The Wildlife and Countryside Act 1981 makes provisions for the setting up of Marine Nature Reserves. The Act states that reserves may be established to the limits of UK territorial waters and include both the sea and the seabed. Marine Nature Reserves may be designated by the Secretary of State, to be managed by English Nature, SNH or CCW, for the purposes of:

❖ conserving marine flora or fauna or geological or physiographical features of special interest in the area

❖ providing, under suitable conditions and control, special opportunities for the study of, and research into, matters relating to marine flora and fauna and the physical conditions in which they live, or for the study of geological and physiographical features of special interest in the area (Wildlife & Countryside Act 1981, section 36).

The procedures for establishing Marine Nature Reserves involve extensive consultation between the new conservation agencies (formerly the Nature Conservancy Council) and the considerable number

National Nature Reserve	County/Region	Area (ha)
1 Dunnet Links	Highland	465
2 Hermaness	Shetland Isles	964
3 Keen of Hamar	Shetland Isles	30
4 Noss	Shetland Isles	313
5 Nigg and Udale Bays	Highland	640
6 Sands of Forvie and Ythan Estuary	Grampian	973
7 St. Cyrus	Grampian	92
8 Tentsmuir Point	Fife	515
9 Isle of May	Fife	57
10 St. Abb's Head	Borders	77
11 Lindisfarne	Northumberland	3,278
12 Saltfleetby to Theddlethorpe Dunes	Lincolnshire	440
13 Gibraltar Point	Lincolnshire	414
14 The Wash	Lincolnshire	97
15 Scolt Head Island	Norfolk	737
16 Holkham	Norfolk	3,925
17 Winterton Dunes	Norfolk	109
18 Hickling Broad	Norfolk	487
19 Ludham Marshes	Norfolk	73
20 Benacre	Suffolk	231
21 Walberswick	Suffolk	514
22 Orfordness to Havergate	Suffolk	225
23 Hamford Water	Essex	688
24 Colne Estuary	Essex	576
25 Dengie	Essex	2,011
26 Blackwater Estuary	Essex	1,031
27 The Swale	Kent	216
28 Pevensey Levels	East Sussex	52
29 North Solent	Hampshire	763
30 Arne, The Moors	Dorset	9
31 Studland Heath	Dorset	631
32 Hartland Moor	Dorset	321
33 Axmouth to Lyme Regis Undercliffs	Devon	748

Table 10.2.1
Distribution of National Nature Reserves on the North Sea coast.

of organisations which have an interest in or jurisdiction over a proposed Marine Nature Reserve.

Once established, Marine Nature Reserves will be protected through by-laws, the majority of which are likely to be drawn up by other bodies, but on the basis of advice from the country agencies. This situation has arisen because the NCC's successor bodies are restricted in what by-laws they can pass.

There are only two statutorily designated Marine Nature Reserves in Britain – Lundy Island in the Bristol Channel and Skomer Island off south-west Wales. There are none on the North Sea coast. There are six proposed Marine Nature Reserves in various states of preparation for designation. One of these, St. Abb's Head, is on the North Sea coast. St. Abb's Head and the Eyemouth area is already a voluntary marine reserve, managed by a committee which includes members from the Scottish Wildlife Trust, local councils, SCUBA diving groups, the Marine Conservation Society and fishermen's associations. There are a number of other voluntary marine protected areas on the North Sea coast (Gubbay 1988).

National Nature Reserves declared up to 31 March 1989			
	Total	Scotland	England
North Sea Coast	33	10	23
Britain	234	68	121
Area of National Nature Reserves in hectares			
	Total	Scotland	England
North Sea Coast	21,702	4,126	17,576
Britain	165,833	112,241	41,312

Table 10.2.2
Number and area of National Nature Reserves on the North Sea coast and total in Britain.

Sites of Special Scientific Interest (SSSI)

Sites of Special Scientific Interest (SSSI) represent some of the best examples of Britain's natural features. English Nature, CCW and SNH have a statutory duty under the Wildlife and Countryside Act 1981 to notify land-owners or occupiers of a site which, in their opinion, 'is of special interest by reason of any of its flora, fauna, or geological or

Figure 10.2.1
Distribution of National
Nature Reserves on the North
Sea coast.
Based upon the 1975 Ordnance Survey
1:1,250,000 map with the permission
of the Controller of Her Majesty's
Stationery Office © Crown Copyright.

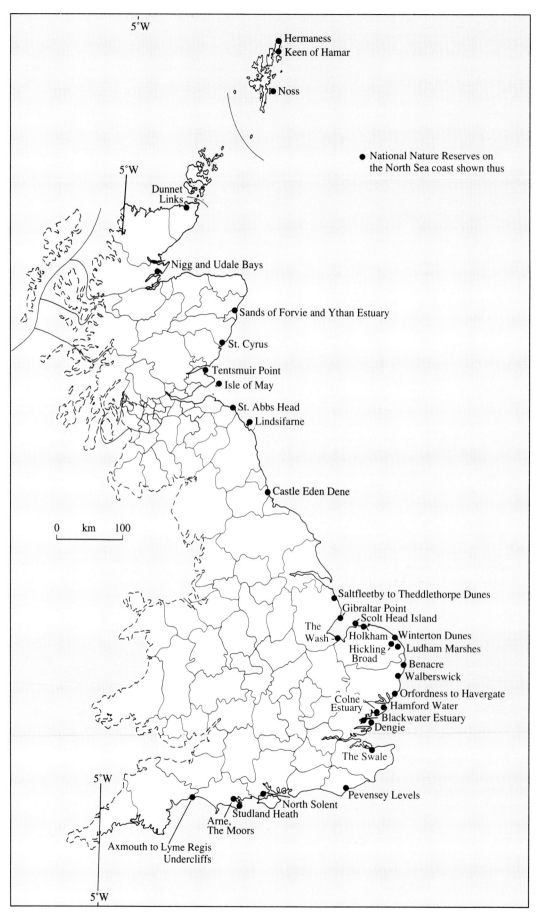

physiographical features'. SSSIs on the North Sea Coast will be listed and shown in map form in the Regional reports which accompany this directory.

Marine Consultation Areas

The Nature Conservancy Council introduced the concept of Marine Consultation Areas (MCA) in Scotland in 1986. MCAs have, as yet, no statutory locus but identify areas which are considered by Scottish Natural Heritage as deserving particular distinction in respect to the quality and sensitivity of their marine environment. In the absence of legislation allowing for protection of sub-tidal habitats and communities, other than that for Marine Nature Reserves, their selection allows bodies which consult with Scottish Natural Heritage to be aware of marine conservation issues within particular areas.

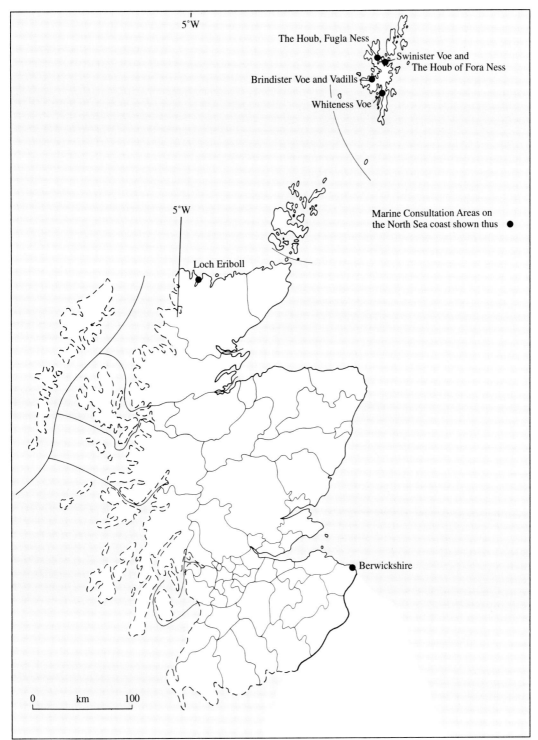

Figure 10.2.2
Distribution of Marine Consultation Areas on the North Sea coast (after Nature Conservancy Council 1990).
Based upon the 1975 Ordnance Survey 1:1,250,000 map with the permission of the Controller of Her Majesty's Stationery Office © Crown Copyright.

211

Initially, fourteen MCAs were identified in Scotland on the basis of available scientific information. This list has been augmented to 29, in the light of further survey work carried out as part of the Marine Nature Conservation Review. Of the 29 MCAs identified in Scotland there are six within the North Sea coastal area, four of which are in the Shetland Islands (Figure 10.2.2).

For each MCA a citation is produced indicating the various elements which comprise its nature conservation interest. Citations distinguish the sub-tidal and inter-tidal nature conservation interest and that of marine and maritime birds and mammals. A document containing the citations was circulated to organisations with an interest in the marine resources within the identified areas (NCC 1990).

The Department of the Environment and the Welsh Office published proposals for sixteen MCAs on the coasts of England and Wales in February 1992 (DoE/Welsh Office 1992). Of these, nine fell within the North Sea coastal area. However, as a result of the spread of coastal management plans and new marine management initiatives instigated by English Nature, including the promotion of 'Sensitive Marine Areas', DoE has now withdrawn its MCA proposals, since they would duplicate existing work. The identification of Sensitive Marine Areas was announced by English Nature (1993) as this document went to press and could not, therefore, be covered here.

Areas of Outstanding Natural Beauty

Between 1956 and 1991, 39 AONBs were designated in England and Wales by the Countryside Commission and its predecessor, the National Parks Commission. These areas cover 13.5% of the countryside of England and Wales. In Scotland,

National Scenic Areas are designated by Scottish Natural Heritage.

The primary purpose of the AONB designation is to conserve natural beauty; recreation is not an objective of designation, as it is for National Parks. However, AONBs should be used to meet the demands for recreation as far as is consistent with the conservation of natural beauty and the needs of agriculture, forestry and other users. In pursuing the primary objective of designation, account is taken of the need to safeguard agriculture, forestry and other rural industries, and of the economic and social needs of local communities. Although these are national objectives, the day to day administration of AONBs rests with the local authorities, split between county and district authorities, ideally with joint working (Countryside Commission 1989a).

Twenty of the 39 AONBs adjoin the coast, thirteen of them on the North Sea coast (see Figure 10.2.3 and Table 10.2.3). The total area covered by AONBs in England and Wales is 20,439 square miles (52,937 km^2), 7,342 miles (19,016 km) of which occur on or are adjacent to the North Sea coast.

A Directory of Areas of Outstanding Natural Beauty was produced for the Countryside Commission in 1989 giving details of all the AONBs in England and Wales. It provides the following information for each AONB:

i) A boundary map of each area, showing adjoining AONBs, Heritage Coast and National Park boundaries

ii) Size, date of designation, local authorities concerned

iii) A description of the main features of the landscape including other designations such as SSSI, Local Nature Reserve, etc.

iv) Brief details of pressures on the landscape

Table 10.2.3
Areas of Outstanding Natural Beauty on the North Sea coast.
*This figure includes parts of AONBs outside the North Sea area, fronting the Bristol Channel, and the entirely inland area of Bodmin Moor.

Area of Outstanding Natural Beauty	Confirmation of order	Area (ha)
1 Northumberland Coast	1958	13,500
2 Norfolk Coast	1968	45,100
3 Suffolk Coast and Heaths	1970	40,500
4 Kent Downs	1968	87,800
5 High Weald, Kent	1983	146,000
6 Sussex Downs	1966	98,300
7 Chichester Harbour, Dorset	1964	7,400
8 Isle of Wight	1963	18,900
9 South Hampshire Coast	1967	7,700
10 Dorset	1959	112,900
11 East Devon	1963	26,800
12 South Devon	1960	33,700
13 Cornwall	1959 and 1983	95,800*

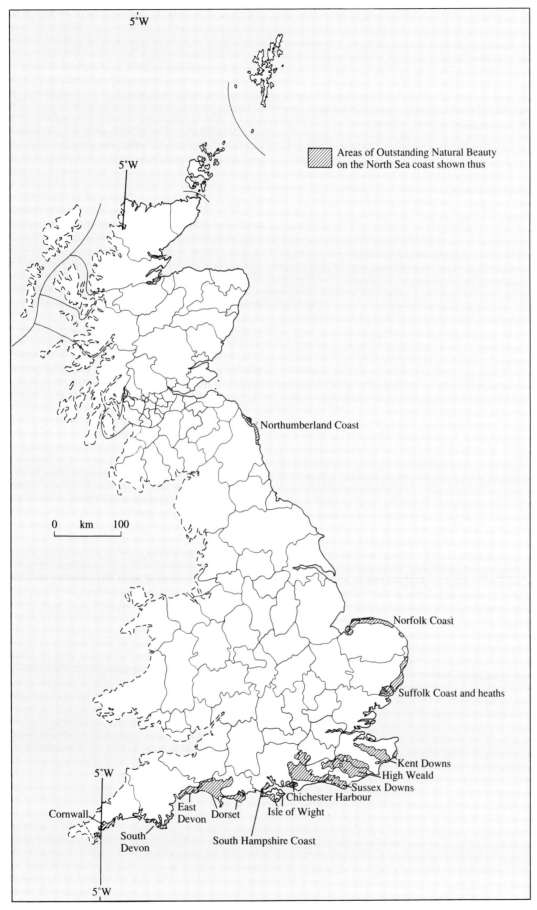

Figure 10.2.3
Distribution of Areas of
Outstanding Natural Beauty
(England only) on the North
Sea coast (after Countryside
Commission 1989a).
Based upon the 1975 Ordnance Survey
1:1,250,000 map with the permission
of the Controller of Her Majesty's
Stationery Office © Crown Copyright.

Areas of Outstanding Natural Beauty
on the North Sea coast shown thus

Northumberland Coast

0   km   100

Norfolk Coast

Suffolk Coast and heaths

Kent Downs
High Weald
Sussex Downs
Chichester Harbour
East   Isle of Wight
Devon   Dorset
Cornwall
South   South Hampshire Coast
Devon

5°W

v) Statutory policies concerning the designation, such as local structure plans and district local plan policies

vi) Details of formal management programmes, joint committees or statements of intent concerning the AONB itself

vii) Management mechanisms and staffing

viii) Details of wardening and county officer duties

ix) Active conservation organisations and contact address.

Heritage Coast

Heritage Coasts are selected by the Countryside Commission in England and CCW in Wales; the designation does not exist for Scotland. Heritage Coast covers 34% of the coastline (Countryside Commission 1989b), and most of the land is in private ownership with a large proportion owned by the National Trust. The designation originated in 1970 as an aid to planning authorities, recommending that selected sections of undeveloped coastline of high scenic quality should be given a special protective designation as Heritage Coast.

The areas selected should:

a) comprise a coastline of exceptionally fine scenic quality

b) exceed 1 mile in length

c) be substantially undeveloped

d) contain features of special significance and interest, whether natural or man-made (Countryside Commission 1970).

Heritage Coast is not a statutory designation and defining a particular area as Heritage Coast does not confer on that site any specific protection. However, management plans for a number of areas of Heritage Coast have been drawn up by their relevant local authorities, and Heritage Coasts are indicated on local and structure plans. In this way they are approximately equivalent to the Scottish 'Areas of Great Landscape Value' (see Section 10.3). Some sites have a Heritage Coast Officer who may enforce by-laws, perform maintenance work, gather information on the site and inform the public about the particular interest of the site.

The distribution of Heritage Coast sites along the North Sea coastal margin is given in Figure 10.2.4, their length is given in Table 10.2.4 and they are listed in Table 10.2.5. For most, both the lateral and inland boundaries are defined; a few are only identified by their coastal length.

The Heritage Coast Forum has produced a Heritage Coast Directory (Heritage Coast Forum 1989), which gives basic information as follows:

i) A map showing all Heritage Coasts in England and Wales

Table 10.2.4
Number and length of Heritage Coasts on the North Sea coast and total in Britain.

Heritage Coasts in Britain	No. of areas	Length (km)
North Sea coast	18	661
Britain	43	1,493

Table 10.2.5
Heritage Coasts defined on the North Sea coast.

Heritage Coast		County	Date defined	Length of coastline (km)
1	North Northumberland	Northumberland	1973	96
2	N Yorkshire and Cleveland	N Yorks & Cleveland	1981	57
3	Flamborough Head	N Humberside	1979 & 1989	19
4	Spurn	N Humberside	1988	18
5	North Norfolk	Norfolk	1975	64
6	Suffolk	Suffolk	1979 & 1987	57
7	South Foreland	Kent	1975	7
8	Dover - Folkestone	Kent	1975	7
9	Sussex	Sussex	1973	13
10	Hamstead	Isle of Wight	1974 & 1988	11
11	Tennyson	Isle of Wight	1974 & 1988	34
12	Purbeck	Dorset	1981	50
13	West Dorset	Dorset	1984	41
14	East Devon	Devon	1984	27
15	South Devon	Devon	1986	75
16	Rame Head	Cornwall	1976 & 1986	8
17	Gribbin Head - Polperro	Cornwall	1976 & 1986	24
18	The Roseland	Cornwall	1976 & 1986	53

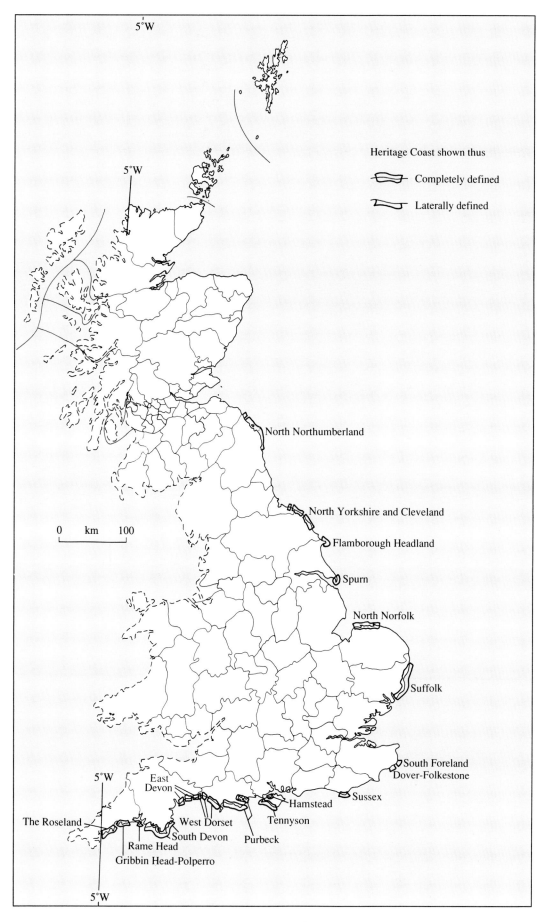

Figure 10.2.4
Distribution of Heritage Coasts defined on the North Sea coast (England only). After Heritage Coast Forum 1989.

Based upon the 1975 Ordnance Survey 1:1,250,000 map with the permission of the Controller of Her Majesty's Stationery Office © Crown Copyright.

Heritage Coast shown thus

Completely defined

Laterally defined

5°W

5°W

5°W

North Northumberland

North Yorkshire and Cleveland

Flamborough Headland

Spurn

North Norfolk

Suffolk

South Foreland
Dover-Folkestone

Sussex

East Devon

Hamstead

Tennyson

West Dorset

Purbeck

The Roseland

South Devon

Rame Head

Gribbin Head-Polperro

5°W

5°W

ii) An entry for each section of coast giving grid references for the lateral limits, a brief description of the site, its status and date of definition, relevant management and local plans, addresses for contacts concerning management of the coastal area and other comments, including whether the site overlaps with other designations such as SSSI, Area of Outstanding Natural Beauty, nature reserve, etc.

Addresses of people and organisations with responsibilities and interest in Heritage Coasts are given, and there is a small section on coastal management schemes in areas not defined as Heritage Coast. Hampshire County Council published details of such a scheme for coastal conservation and management in 1992. A full list of Heritage Coasts is given in Table 10.2.5.

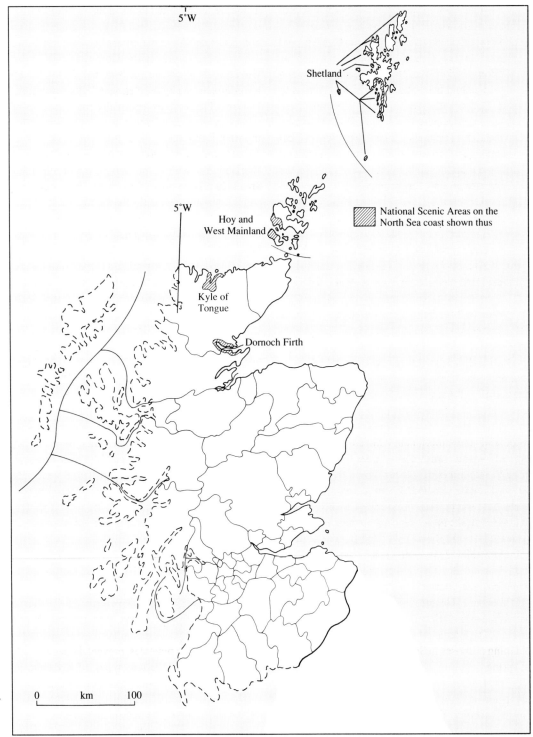

Figure 10.2.5
Distribution of National Scenic Areas on the North Sea coast (after Countryside Commission for Scotland 1989).
Based upon the 1975 Ordnance Survey 1:1,250,000 map with the permission of the Controller of Her Majesty's Stationery Office © Crown Copyright.

National Scenic Areas

National Scenic Areas are designated by Scottish Natural Heritage (SNH) as the best of Scotland's landscapes, deserving special protection in the Nation's interest. Special development control measures for the 40 National Scenic Areas in Scotland were introduced by the Scottish Development Department in 1980. Prior to this there were two categories of existing arrangements, under various planning acts, which sought to secure the conservation of scenic interest in Scotland:

i) Five areas were suggested by the Scottish National Parks Survey Committee for designation as National Parks in the 1940s. When it was decided not to extend the National Parks and Access to the Countryside Act 1949 to Scotland, these areas were designated as National Park Direction Areas. This designation meant that relevant local planning authorities were required to submit all planning applications within these areas to the Secretary of State for scrutiny

ii) Planning authorities designated in their development plans Areas of Great Landscape Value where the authorities themselves chose to operate special development control policies to conserve scenic and landscape interest of these areas (see section on Regional Landscape Designations in Scotland).

None of the areas considered under these development controls was in the North Sea coastal area.

National Scenic Areas are areas which have 'features which are most frequently regarded as beautiful'. This means that 'richly diverse landscapes which combine prominent landforms, coastline, sea and freshwater lochs, rivers, woodland and moorlands with some admixture of cultivated land are generally the most prized' (Countryside Commission for Scotland 1978). They are selected by a subjective assessment of the best scenic areas in terms of their diversity of landscape, the presence of spectacular landforms or seascapes and the rarity of the type of scenery being considered. In general, large towns are not included, but if a town is present within an area under consideration it is not specifically excluded. The areas are selected in order to be conserved as part of the national heritage. The seaward boundary of National Scenic Areas is the same as that for planning purposes in Scotland, i.e. mean low water of spring tides.

Forty National Scenic Areas have been identified in Scotland, four of which are on the North Sea coast. These are shown in Figure 10.2.5 and Table 10.2.6.

National Scenic Area	Region	Area (ha)
1 Shetland (several areas)	Shetland	15,600
2 Hoy and West Mainland	Orkney	14,800
3 Kyle of Tongue	Highland	18,500
4 Dornoch Firth	Highland	7,500

Table 10.2.6
National Scenic Areas on the North Sea coast.

National Parks

There are ten National Parks in England and Wales designated by the National Parks Commission and confirmed by the Government between 1951 and 1957. The Countryside Commission is the Government's adviser on National Parks, which are administered by the National Parks authorities. National Parks are exceptionally fine stretches of relatively wild countryside, including mountains, moorland and heath. The National Parks cover 14,100 km² (1,410,000 ha) of the total area of England and Wales, and the greater part of their area is in private ownership. Of these, five contain some coastline, but only the North York Moors National Park has any coastline on the North Sea coast (Figure 10.2.6). The North York Moors National Park Authority is a department of North Yorkshire County Council and is therefore part of the local authority. The purpose of the National Park Authority is to preserve and enhance the Park's natural beauty and to promote public enjoyment of it, while having regard for the social and economic well-being of those living within it. The policies and objectives of the Park are set out in the National Park Plan which was last reviewed in 1991.

National Parks are not declared in Scotland due to legislative differences between the countries. There are also two areas in England which, although not National Parks, have similar status (the Broads in Norfolk and the New Forest in Hampshire). A small part of the New Forest falls within the South Hampshire Coast AONB. The two non-National Park areas each abut the North Sea coast, but their primary scenic interest is terrestrial or freshwater.

Environmentally Sensitive Areas

The Environmentally Sensitive Area (ESA) scheme is one of the programmes through which the Government seeks to encourage environmentally sensitive farming practices, prevent damage which might result from certain types of agricultural intensification, and restore traditional landscapes. It targets specific areas of high conservation value and provides incentives to farmers and landowners to protect and enhance the environmental features

Figure 10.2.6
Distribution of National
Parks and areas of similar
status on the North Sea coast
(after Countryside
Commission 1989b).
Based upon the 1975 Ordnance Survey
1:1,250,000 map with the permission
of the Controller of Her Majesty's
Stationery Office © Crown Copyright.

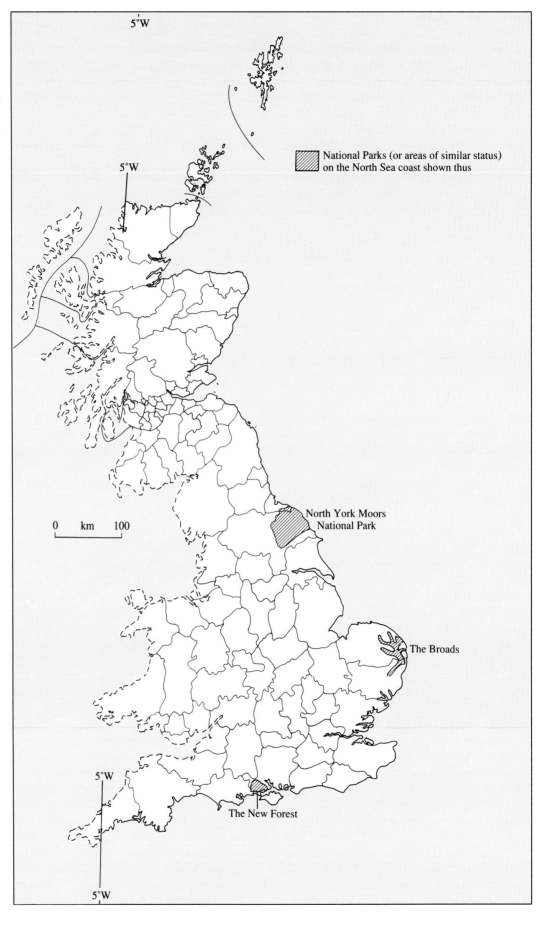

National Parks (or areas of similar status)
on the North Sea coast shown thus

North York Moors
National Park

The Broads

The New Forest

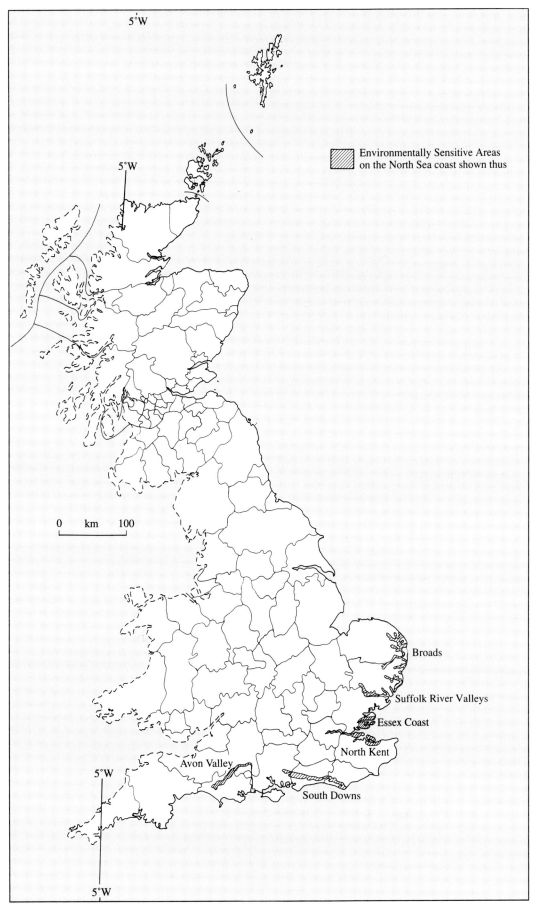

Figure 10.2.7
Distribution of
Environmentally Sensitive
Areas on the North Sea coast
(after MAFF 1989).
Based upon the 1975 Ordnance Survey
1:1,250,000 map with the permission
of the Controller of Her Majesty's
Stationery Office © Crown Copyright.

Table 10.2.7
Environmentally Sensitive
Areas on the North Sea coast.

Environmentally Sensitive Area	Date	Area (ha)
1 Norfolk Broads	1987	29,870
2 Suffolk River Valleys	1988	32,149
3 South Downs	1987/1988	53,343
4 North Kent Marshes	1993	14,700
5 Avon Valley	1993	5,200

of their land. This is achieved by making payments available for land management in accordance with one of a number of set prescriptions.

The legislative framework for the ESA scheme is contained in Article 19 of Council Regulation (EEC) No. 797/85, as amended, and the Agricultural Act 1986. The EC Regulation permits Member States to make payments to farmers in designated areas of high conservation value in order to encourage farming practices favourable to the environment. Section 18 of the 1986 Act specifies how this is to be implemented within the UK.

The selection of an area for designation as an ESA is based on candidate areas meeting three main criteria which are:
❖ each area must be of national environmental significance
❖ its conservation must depend upon adopting, maintaining or extending particular farming practices and operations
❖ each area must represent a discrete and coherent unit of environmental interest.

ESAs are designated by the Ministry of Agriculture (MAFF) and the Scottish Office Agriculture and Fisheries Department (SOAFD), in consultation with the Department of the Environment, the Countryside Commission and the country agencies.

Sixteen ESAs have been designated in England, two in Wales, five in Scotland and one in Northern Ireland. None of the ESAs in Scotland include coastal lands and only five in England have land which borders the North Sea coastal margin (see Figure 10.2.7 and Table 10.2.7).

A further six ESAs were declared in England in 1993 although only two of these, the Essex Coast and the Avon Valley, border the North Sea coast.

The Agriculture Act 1986 requires Ministers to keep the effects of designation under review and from time to time to publish information about the effects. Reports published by the Department of Agriculture and Fisheries for Scotland (1989) and the Ministry of Agriculture, Fisheries and Food (1989) describe the development of Environmentally Sensitive Areas in Scotland and England and give a description of those areas currently designated.

Areas of Special Protection

Under the Wildlife and Countryside Act (1981) the Secretary of State may, by order, make provision with respect to any area for the protection of an individual wild bird species which is under threat

Site	Location	Order
Sanctuaries designated under the Protection of Birds Act		
Island of Fetlar	Shetland	Wild Birds Order 1968
Kinloss Airfield	Moray	Wild Birds Order 1978
Island of Inchmickery	Firth of Forth	Wild Birds Order 1963
Bass Rock, Craigleith, Fidra, the Lamb, Eybroughty	Firth of Forth	Wild Birds Order 1930
Farne Islands	Northumberland	Wild Birds Order 1964
Coquet Island	Northumberland	Wild Birds Order 1978
Fairburn Ings	N Yorkshire	Wild Birds Order 1980
Hornsea Mere	Yorkshire	Wild Birds Order 1980
Humber Estuary	Yorkshire/Lincolnshire	Wild Birds Order 1955, 1963
Gibraltar Point	Lincolnshire	Wild Birds Order 1971
Cley Marshes	Norfolk	Wild Birds Order 1966
Havergate Island	Suffolk	Wild Birds Order 1961
Poole Harbour	Hampshire	Wild Birds Order 1978
Exe Estuary	Devon	Wild Birds Order 1951
Tamar Lake	Devon	Wild Birds Order 1960
Areas of Special Protection designated under the Wildlife and Countryside Act		
Easington Lagoons	Humberside	
Needs Ore Point	Hampshire	
Berry Head	Devon	

Table 10.2.8
Sites of protection for birds designated as sanctuaries under the Protection of Birds Act and as Areas of Special Protection under the Wildlife and Countryside Act.

from human activity. Areas needing protection under the above Act are recommended to the Secretary of State by the country agencies with advice from JNCC. The designation of an Area of Special Protection (ASP) prevents the disturbance and destruction of birds for which the area is identified by prohibiting access to the site and by making it unlawful to damage or destroy either the birds or their nests. Provision is made within the order for authorised persons to continue their normal activities on the site and all owner/occupiers are consulted before any order is made.

Areas of Special Protection replace the orders under the 1954 to 1967 Protection of Birds Acts which were repealed and amended under the Wildlife and Countryside Act (1981). The former Acts provided for Sanctuaries to be established for the protection of individual species. Existing Bird Sanctuary Orders in 1981 were transferred to the new legislation as indicated by the Wildlife and Countryside Act.

Sites designated under section 3 (1) of the Wildlife and Countryside Act (1981) as Areas of Special Protection are listed in Table 10.2.8 along with those sites covered by the Protection of Birds Act (1954) Sanctuary Order.

Special Protection Areas and Wetlands of International Importance

Special Protection Areas (SPA)

The European Council of Ministers adopted the Directive on the Conservation of Wild Birds (Directive 79/409) on 2 April 1979 in response to a need to provide conservation measures for those birds which move between different member countries of the European Community. The UK, as a member country, is bound to conserve bird habitats as a means of maintaining populations. Habitat protection is achieved by the establishment of a

network of protected areas for birds – Special Protection Areas. Members are required to take special measures to conserve the habitats, including designation of Special Protection Areas, of two groups of birds – listed rare or vulnerable species (Article 4.1 79/409/EEC) and regularly occurring migratory species (Article 4.1 79/409/EEC).

The articles which govern this directive and information relevant to the conservation of 48 species that occur regularly in Britain (and are listed in Annex 1 of the EC directive) are given in Stroud *et al.* (1990).

The domestic legislation intended to allow implementation of the Birds Directive varies from country to country. In Britain legislation is incorporated in the Wildlife and Countryside Act (1981). Sites of international importance are identified by the JNCC and the appropriate country agency (English Nature, Scottish Natural Heritage or the Countryside Council for Wales) and are, or will be, designated as SSSIs. Legislation for designation of SSSIs does not extend below intertidal areas and therefore it is not yet possible to designate the many offshore and inshore areas that meet the requirements for Special Protection Area status. However, those marine areas which are important for birds are currently being identified and their protected status reviewed (Tasker *et al.* in preparation).

There are currently 40 SPAs designated within the United Kingdom, a total of 134,440 hectares. There are ten sites totalling 83,983 hectares (62%) present on the North Sea coastal margin. A further 177 sites of international importance have been identified in Britain as potential SPAs. Sites which lie along the North Sea coastal margin are shown in Figure 10.2.8 and listed in Table 10.2.9. Those areas marked with an asterisk are also designated, in whole or in part, as Ramsar sites. A full list of proposed and designated SPA sites is given in Stroud *et al.* (1990).

Special Protection Area	District/County	Date	Area (ha)
Forth Islands	East Lothian & Fife	26 April 1990	92
Farne Islands	Northumberland	17 July 1985	97
Coquet Island	Northumberland	17 July 1985	21
The Wash*	Lincolnshire & Norfolk	30 March 1988	63,135
North Norfolk Coast*	Norfolk	20 January 1989	7,701
Orfordness - Havergate	Suffolk	31 August 1982	117
The Swale*	Kent	31 August 1982	5,677
Pagham Harbour*	West Sussex	30 March 1988	616
Chichester & Langstone Harbours*	West Sussex & Hampshire	28 October 1987	5,764
Chesil Beach & the Fleet*	Dorset	17 July 1985	763

Table 10.2.9
Special Protection Areas on the North Sea Coast. (Those areas marked with an asterisk are also designated, in whole or in part, as Ramsar sites.)

Figure 10.2.8
Distribution of Special
Protection Areas and
Wetlands of International
Importance (Ramsar) sites on
the North Sea coast (after
Stroud *et al.* 1990).

Based upon the 1975 Ordnance Survey
1:1,250,000 map with the permission
of the Controller of Her Majesty's
Stationery Office © Crown Copyright.

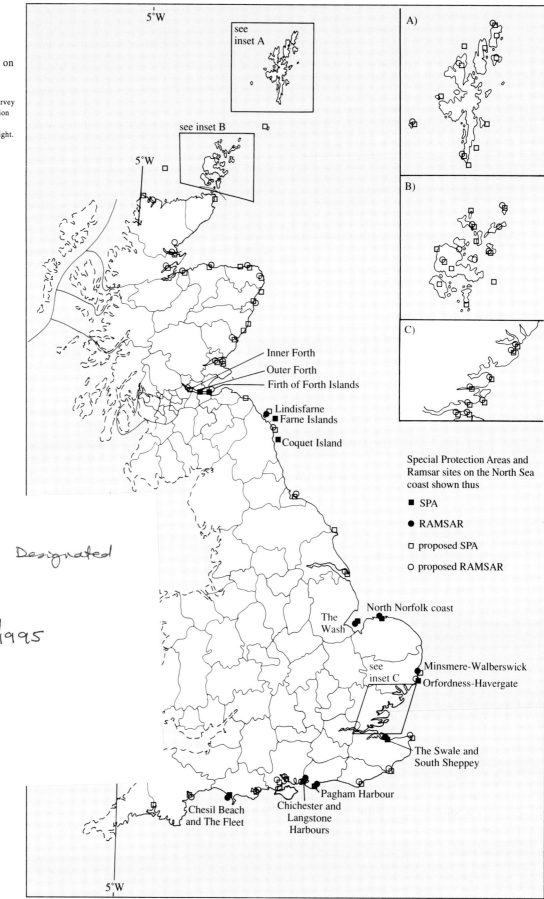

Montrose Designated
SPA
Ramsar
by end 1995

Special Protection Areas and
Ramsar sites on the North Sea
coast shown thus

■ SPA

● RAMSAR

□ proposed SPA

○ proposed RAMSAR

Ramsar site	Region/County	Date	Area (ha)
Lindisfarne	Northumberland	5 January 1976	3,123
The Wash	Lincolnshire & Norfolk	30 March 1988	63,124
North Norfolk Coast	Norfolk	5 January 1976	1,597
Ouse Washes	Cambridgeshire & Norfolk	5 January 1976	2,276
Minsmere & Walberswick	Suffolk	5 January 1976	1,697
The Swale	Kent	17 July 1985	5,790
Pagham Harbour	West Sussex	30 March 1988	616
Chichester & Langstone Harbours	West Sussex & Hampshire	28 October 1987	5,749
Chesil Beach & the Fleet	Dorset	17 July 1985	763

Table 10.2.10
Ramsar sites on the North Sea Coast.

Wetlands of International Importance (Ramsar sites)

The importance of wetlands, especially as a waterfowl habitat, and the need for an international perspective to encourage their conservation was recognised by the Convention on Wetlands of International Importance. This Convention was adopted at a meeting, at Ramsar in Iran (1971), of countries concerned with wetland and waterfowl conservation. The objectives are to stem the progressive encroachment on, and loss of, wetlands. A wetland is defined as being an area of marsh, fen, peatland or water that is static or flowing, fresh, brackish or marine (down to 6 m depth at low water).

The Convention was signed by the UK Government in 1973 and ratified in 1976. Countries which are signatory to the Convention accept a commitment to promote both the conservation of particular sites and the wise use of wetlands. There is a requirement to designate wetlands in accordance with agreed criteria (Articles 1 to 5) for inclusion in a list of 'Wetlands of International Importance'.

The nature conservation agencies are responsible for identifying sites worthy of designation as Wetlands of International Importance (Ramsar sites). The responsibility for identifying sites lies with the Secretary of State for the Environment (in England and Wales) and the Secretary of State for Scotland.

The UK has designated 39 Ramsar sites out of 154 that had been identified by NCC, covering a total of 129,180 ha. Of this area 84,780 ha (67%) lies along the North Sea coast.

Ramsar Sites which lie along the North Sea coastal margin are listed in Table 10.2.10 and are shown along with proposed sites in Figure 10.2.8. A full list of the proposed and designated Ramsar sites is given in Stroud *et al.* (1990).

The Nature Conservancy Council published a review of the proposed network of Special Protection Areas for birds in Great Britain (Stroud *et al.* 1990). This report presents information on both identified sites of international importance and the rationale for their selection. It also provides background information on the populations, status and habitats of Annex 1 and a selection of other migratory species of major conservation importance which regularly occur in Britain.

World Heritage sites

World Heritage sites are 'natural and cultural treasures of exceptional interest and universal value' (Countryside Commission 1989). They are declared by UNESCO under the World Heritage Convention of 1972, which the UK signed in 1984.

There are no World Heritage natural sites on the North Sea coast, the only two natural sites in Britain being St. Kilda off the west coast of Scotland and the Giant's Causeway in Northern Ireland.

Biosphere Reserves

Biosphere Reserves were devised by UNESCO as project number 8 of their Man and the Biosphere (MAB) ecological programme, and were launched in 1970. Criteria and guidelines for selection of sites were produced by a UNESCO task force in 1974. They are protected areas representing significant examples of biomes throughout the world. They have particular value as benchmarks or standards for the measurement of long-term changes in the biosphere as a whole. In some cases, as in the UK, their designation coincides with another such as nature reserve, National Park or similar.

The North Norfolk coast is the only North Sea coast Biosphere Reserve, from a British total of 13.

Several and Regulating Orders, Static Gear Reserves

Several and Regulating Orders are administered by the Ministry of Agriculture, Fisheries and Food in England (MAFF), and by the Scottish Office Agriculture and Fisheries Department (SOAFD) in Scotland. They apply to areas of intertidal and subtidal land, and regulate shellfish fisheries in these areas. Regulating Orders apply to cooperatives or Sea Fisheries Committees, who may authorise fishing in these areas themselves under the orders.

Several Orders apply to either individuals or groups, giving them exclusive rights to the fishery for the specified shellfish within that area.

A list of Regulating and Several Orders applying to the North Sea coast up to August 1990 is given in

	Location	Grantee	Size (ha)	No. in group	Expiry date
Regulating Orders					
Boston Deeps Fishery Order 1930 (Oysters, mussels)	The Wash, Boston side, Lincolnshire	Eastern Sea Fisheries Committee	31,598	-	1992
Lynn Deeps Fishery Order 1932 as varied (Oysters, mussels)	The Wash, Lynn side, Norfolk	Eastern Sea Fisheries Committee	27,713	-	1992
Solent Oyster Fishery Order 1980 (Oysters)	The Solent, Hampshire	Southern Sea Fisheries Committee	17,195	-	2010
Poole Fishery Order 1915 as varied and extended (Oysters, mussels, cockles, clams)	Poole Harbour, Dorset	Southern Sea Fisheries Committee	3220	-	2015
River Teign Mussel Fishery Order 1966 (Mussels)	Teignmouth, Devon	Teign Musselmens Society Ltd	156	-	2026
Truro Port Fishery Order 1936 as varied (Oysters, mussels)	Between Truro and Falmouth, Cornwall	Carrick District Council	1,101	-	2014
Several Orders					
Boston Several Fishery Order 1930 (Oysters, mussels, cockles)	The Wash, Boston side, Lincolnshire	Eastern Sea Fisheries Committee	7,689	-	1992
River Nene Fishery Order 1986 (Oysters, mussels, cockles, clams)	The Wash, Norfolk	Eastern Sea Fisheries Committee	28.4	-	2016
Lynn Several Fishery Order 1932 as varied (Mussels)	The Wash, King's Lynn side, Norfolk	Eastern Sea Fisheries Committee	3,068	-	1992
Hunstanton Le Strange Fishery Order 1947 (Oysters, mussels, cockles)	The Wash, Hunstanton, Norfolk	Mr B. Le Strange	298	1	2027
Brancaster Staithe Fishery Order 1979 (Oysters, mussels, cockles)	Burnham Deepdale, Norfolk	Brancaster Staithe Fishermens Society	53	15	1994
Overy Creek Mussel and Cockle Fishery Order 1969 (Mussels, cockles)	Holkham Bay, Norfolk	D.L. & F.V.J. Lane	4	2	1999
Wells Harbour Shell Fishery Order 1972 (Oysters, mussels, cockles, clams)	Wells-next-the-sea, Norfolk	Wells Harbour Commissioners	8.5	-	2032
Blakeney Harbour Mussel Fishery Order 1966 (Mussels)	Blakeney Point, Norfolk	Blakeney Harbour Mussel Society Ltd	42	8	2026
Falkenham Creek Reach Oyster Fishery Order 1976 (Oysters)	Falkenham near Felixstowe, Suffolk	Mr R.C. Brinkley	22	1	2006
Horsea Island Oyster Fishery Order 1963 (Oysters)	Horsea Island near Walton-on-the-Naze, Essex	Mrs N.C. Backhouse	25	1	2023
Old Hall Farm Creek Oyster Fishery Order 1972 (Oysters)	Old Hall Creek near Tollesbury, Essex	Mr M.V. Frost	5	1	2002
Tollesbury & Mersea (Blackwater Fishery Order) 1938 (Oysters)	River Blackwater, Essex	The Tollesbury & Mersea Native Oyster Fishery Co. Ltd.	894	4	1998
Emsworth Channel Fishery Order 1975 (Oysters, mussels, clams)	Chichester Harbour, Hants. / W Sussex	Emsworth Harbour Fishermens Federation Ltd	49	49	2005
Portchester Channel Oyster Fishery Order 1986 (Oysters)	Portsmouth Harbour, Hampshire	Portsmouth Harbour Oyster Society Ltd	200	43	1993
Southampton Water (Chilling) Oyster Fishery Order 1984 (Oysters)	Southampton Water, Hampshire	Brownwich Reach Oystermen Ltd	445	30	1991
Marchwood Clam Fishery Order 1972 (Clams)	Southampton Water, Hampshire	Newtown Oyster Fishery Co. Ltd	6	3	2002
Calshot Oyster Fishery Order 1982 (Oysters)	The Solent, Hampshire & IOW	Calshot Oyster Fishermen Ltd	223	45	1995
Stanswood Bay Oyster Fishery Order 1988 (Oysters)	The Solent, Hampshire & IOW	Stanswood Bay Oystermen Ltd	262	42	1995
Portland Harbour Fishery Order 1989 (Oysters, scallops, mussels)	Portland Harbour, Dorset	Portland Oyster Fishermen	150	29	2000
Waddeton Oyster Fishery Order 1972 (Oysters)	Galmpton near Tor Bay, Devon	Mr M.L. Goodson	12	2	1997
Yealm Fishery Order 1914 as extended (Oysters, mussels)	Wembury near Plymouth, Devon	Mr R.A. Maskell	6	1	1994

Table 10.2.11
Regulating and Several Orders applying to the North Sea coast up to August 1990.

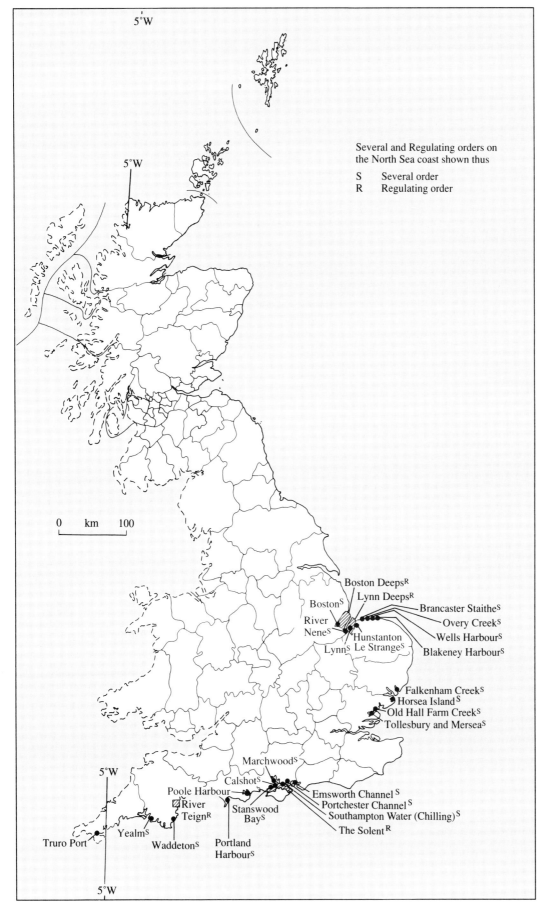

Figure 10.2.9
Distribution of Several and
Regulating Orders along the
North Sea coastal margin.
Based upon the 1975 Ordnance Survey
1:1,250,000 map with the permission
of the Controller of Her Majesty's
Stationery Office © Crown Copyright.

Several and Regulating orders on
the North Sea coast shown thus

S   Several order
R   Regulating order

Boston Deeps[R]
Lynn Deeps[R]
Boston[S]
Brancaster Staithe[S]
River
Nene[S]
Overy Creek[S]
Wells Harbour[S]
Hunstanton
Lynn[S] Le Strange[S]
Blakeney Harbour[S]

Falkenham Creek[S]
Horsea Island [S]
Old Hall Farm Creek[S]
Tollesbury and Mersea[S]

Marchwood[S]
Calshot[S]
Poole Harbour
Emsworth Channel [S]
Portchester Channel [S]
River
Teign[R]
Stanswood
Bay[S]
Southampton Water (Chilling) [S]
The Solent [R]
Yealm[S]
Truro Port
Waddeton[S]
Portland
Harbour[S]

0   km   100

225

Table 10.2.11 and their locations shown in Figure 10.2.9. There are no such Orders currently applying in Scottish waters on the North Sea coast.

The Inshore Fishing (Scotland) Act 1984 enables the Secretary of State for Scotland to make orders regulating fishing in waters off the coast of Scotland. These orders may prohibit all fishing, fishing of particular species or use of a particular method of fishing. They may apply for specified periods or throughout the year. In 1985 an order for the Prohibition of Fishing and Fishing Methods in Scottish Inshore Waters, SI 962, was made. It identified areas where there were restrictions on the use of mobile gear (nets). These became known as static gear reserves and are specifically concerned with the control of trawling, Danish seine or similar, purse seine and ring net or dredge. The order reduces conflict between fishermen using static gear and those operating mobile gear. In 1989 a similar order, SI 2307, was introduced which further identified areas of the Scottish coast in which types and methods of fishing were prohibited. In particular, SI 2307 restricted the areas in which suction dredges could be operated.

10.3 LOCAL GOVERNMENT ORGANISATION

INTRODUCTION

The principal control over land in the UK is through the operation of the planning system. However, this system does not control all development or activity on land. Some activities are not defined as development, such as afforestation, trunk roads and motorways or power stations, which are the responsibility of the relevant government department. Most harbour authorities have a significant degree of autonomy to operate under statutory powers set out in local Acts of Parliament or by means of orders made under the Harbours Act 1964. In other instances private Acts may provide a method of giving developers the authorisation for activities outside the scope of the planning system.

THE PLANNING SYSTEM

The town and country planning system is designed to regulate the development and use of land in the public interest. It is an important instrument for protecting and enhancing the environment and reconciling the interests of conservation and development. The principal planning legislation is contained in the Town and Country Planning Act 1990.

The powers provided by the 1990 Act are exercised by local planning authorities. The two most important functions of planning authorities are the preparation of development plans and the control of development through the determination of planning applications. In shire counties the planning responsibilities are shared between the county council and district councils. Elsewhere, London borough councils, some Scottish regions and metropolitan districts are the sole planning authorities. In certain circumstances planning powers can be vested in other bodies, such as National Parks (under provisions in the Local Government Act 1972) and the Broads Authority (under the Norfolk and Suffolk Broads Act 1988).

For maritime local planning authorities in England the administrative area, and hence the limits of control, normally ends at mean low water mark. In Scotland, the limit of jurisdiction is normally low water mark of spring tides, although there are notable exceptions such as Shetland, whose administrative area extends to the limit of territorial waters.

Development plans

Planning decisions must be in accordance with the development plan unless other material considerations indicate otherwise. Such plans set out the land use policies and proposals that will apply in an area. There are three main types of development plan:
❖ **Structure plans,** in which shire counties set out key strategic policies as a framework for local planning. They have to have regard, among other things, to national and regional policies. These plans have to include policies on the conservation of the natural beauty and amenity of the land, the improvement of the physical environment and management of traffic. They are also advised to include policies on: new housing, green belts and conservation, the rural economy, the urban economy including employment-generating and wealth-creating development, strategic transport and highways, minerals, waste disposal, tourism, recreation and leisure and energy generation, including renewable energy.

Authorities are advised to ensure that the interactions between policies are fully considered and that policies form an integrated whole (e.g. by forming an overall strategy for the coast).

Structure plans must have regard to environmental as well as social and economic considerations. Authorities are also advised that they should take all these considerations into account when preparing detailed development plans.
❖ **Local plans,** district councils and National Parks authorities have to prepare plans covering the whole

of their areas. These local plans set out more detailed policies for development control and proposals for specific sites. Local plans are required to be in general conformity with the structure plan.

County councils and National Parks authorities are required to produce a minerals local plan and a waste disposal local plan, with the exception of counties in Wales where the districts include waste policies in local plans.

❖ **Unitary development plans (UDPs),** prepared by London boroughs and metropolitan districts and combining the functions of both structure and local plans. They include minerals and waste policies.

In Scotland, structure plans are prepared by regional and island councils and, unlike England and Wales, continue to require the approval of the Secretary of State. Local plans are prepared by district councils, except in Borders, Dumfries and Galloway and Highland where they are prepared by the regional councils and in Orkney, Shetland and Western Isles by the Islands Council. There are no separate minerals planning authorities or UDPs.

Development control

A primary aim of the planning system is to facilitate acceptable and appropriate development and to strike the right balance between that development and the environment. The government sees the planning system, and development plans in particular, as contributing to ensuring that development and growth are sustainable. A fundamental feature is that development may not take place without planning permission. In most circumstances express (specific) planning permission is required upon application to the local planning authority, usually the district council (in the case of minerals or waste, permission needs to be sought from the mineral planning authority or waste disposal authority, respectively, which is usually the county council). Where the development plan is material to the development proposal, the decision whether or not to grant planning permission must be made in accordance with the plan, unless material considerations indicate otherwise.

National guidance

National guidance on relevant planning considerations is issued by the government in a variety of ways. Until 1988 the most frequent and influential forms of policy guidance were Circulars and Development Control Policy Notes (DCPN). Since then, however, the government has been issuing national guidance in the form of Planning Policy Guidance notes (PPG) and Minerals Planning Guidance notes (MPG). These are progressively replacing the guidance given in earlier Circulars and DCPNs and are intended to provide clearer, more accessible and more systematic policy guidance.

These documents are an important factor in defining 'material considerations' and influencing the way in which the planning system operates. Indeed, the Courts have held that these policy statements must be taken into account, where relevant, in decisions on planning applications.

Regional Planning Guidance

Regional Planning Guidance is also given by the government where issues apply across regions or parts of regions and need to be considered on a scale wider than a single county or district. The primary function of such guidance is to provide the framework for the preparation of structure plans. Strategic guidance is provided for metropolitan areas.

Within England and Wales there are nine planning regions, of which six have a coastline bordering the North Sea coastal margin. The way the guidance is prepared varies from region to region. The guidance for East Anglia, for example, follows the regional strategy which the Standing Conference of the East Anglian Local Authorities (SCEALA) submitted to the Secretary of State. The note addresses a range of topics of relevance to forward planning in the region. These include: environment and conservation (including the need to take into account sea-level rise); economic development; transportation; population and housing land; the development framework; retail development; land resources; sport and recreation; minerals and waste disposal.

Policy guidance of relevance to the coast

Most Government Circulars, PPGs and MPGs are relevant to planning in the coastal zone because of the enormous variety of land uses and activities which take place along the coastline. However, amongst the most relevant are:

❖ **DoE Circular 12/72 (WO 36/72) The Planning of the Undeveloped Coast,** which advised on the planning and management of the undeveloped coast: '... purely protective and restrictive policies applied more or less uniformly across wide expanses of the coast are not the answer'. Circular 12/72 para. 5.

The Circular also encouraged local authorities to consider defining and managing Heritage Coasts, in conjunction with the Countryside Commission. Local planning authorities were advised to include appropriate planning policies within development plans.

❖ **DoE Circular 17/82 (MAFF LDW 1/82; WO 15/82) Development in Flood Risk Areas**, which reinforces the need for liaison between planning authorities and the water authorities (now the NRA) when considering development proposals in flood risk areas. There is specific reference to tidal flooding:

'A particularly important point arises in relation to development of land which is protected from inundation by the sea. Clearly such land would be extremely vulnerable in the event of any embankment or sea wall being breached. For example, tidal surges might involve the loss of life as well as the destruction of property. Planning authorities are therefore asked to bear this point particularly in mind when considering development proposals for land protected in this way' (Circular 17/82 para. 7).

The government has recently issued a revised circular for public consultation (see below).

❖ **Doe Circular 2/85 Planning Control over Oil and Gas Operations**, which advises local planning authorities of their role in regulating the landward oil and gas exploration and development programme. The circular also contains details of the procedures for handling licence applications for landward areas that fall outside local authority jurisdiction (e.g. estuaries).

❖ **MPG 6 Guidelines for Aggregates Provision in England and Wales** (DoE 1989), which advises local planning authorities of the need to make every effort to identify and safeguard, in their development plans, suitable locations for marine aggregate wharfs.

❖ **PPG 14 Development on Unstable Land** (DoE 1990), which advises local planning authorities and developers of the need to take instability into account. This guidance is of particular importance in the coastal zone and, hence, has been the subject of recent research, commissioned by the DoE, into ways that landslide problems can be treated in development plans and considered in planning applications (see below).

❖ **DoE Circular 17/91 (WO 62/91) Water Industry Investment: Planning Considerations**, in which guidance is given about the planning implications of the proposed water industry investment programme to meet EC and national water quality standards. Local planning authorities are advised that they should handle applications for the proposed works expeditiously in order to enable the schemes to be completed on time.

❖ **PPG 17 Sport and Recreation** (DoE 1991) which describes the role of the planning system in assessing opportunities and needs for sport and recreation. Of significance to the coastal zone, the PPG includes advice on the use of redundant or disused land to alleviate the widespread shortage of leisure boat mooring facilities, without causing significant detriment to the natural environment. Planning authorities are advised that where conflict arises in designated areas of landscape value (e.g. National Parks and Heritage Coasts) the conservation and enhancement of natural beauty must prevail over encouragement of recreational activities.

❖ **PPG 7 The Countryside and the Rural Economy** (DoE 1992), which provides advice on the preparation of planning policies for designated areas, including National Parks and AONBs.

❖ **PPG 20 on Coastal Planning** (DoE 1992). This PPG was heralded by the Department of the Environment as representing the most important government statement on planning our coast for 20 years. It sets out comprehensive planning guidance for both the open coast and estuaries of England and Wales. Its most important feature is its recommendation that local authorities draw up development plans which protect the best of the coastline by directing development to areas that are already built up and limiting coastal development to that which genuinely requires a coastal location. The PPG proposes a new precautionary approach to developing coastal areas at risk from flooding, erosion and landslip. The PPG also encourages local authorities and other interested groups to develop coordinated plans for stretches of the coast, particularly estuaries.

The effective operation of the local authority development planning and control system is a key component of the future of the North Sea coastal margin. Such powers are, however, limited because the area of local authority jurisdiction extends only to low water mark. These powers, whilst effective for terrestrial-based developments, may not therefore extend to all parts of a functional coastal system such as an estuary. Resolving the complications that arise from the great number of consent authorities operating in the marine environment, as compared to the relatively simple system operating in the terrestrial environment, may therefore be crucial for safeguarding the future of the North Sea's coastal wildlife and natural features.

In addition to their role as planning authorities, local authorities have a wide range of responsibilities which affect the management and conservation of the coast. These include responsibility for coast protection works including the design and funding of some major engineering projects and the provision of tourism and leisure facilities.

Planning decisions are taken by a local planning committee of elected members, advised by local planning officers. It is also a function of local authorities to declare Local Nature Reserves and Country Parks, as well as areas to be protected from unsympathetic planning, such as Areas of Great

Landscape Value, Areas of Scenic Value, Areas of Regional Landscape Significance and Sites of Nature Conservation Interest.

Exceptions to the above general principles are:

i) In parts of Scotland the Island Councils and some Regional Councils have both structure and local planning as well as development control functions. Both Highland Region and Borders Region include part of the North Sea coast.

ii) In England the Metropolitan Borough Councils also have all the planning functions mentioned in i) above. They are required to produce 'Unitary Development Plans' which have separate parts, broadly fulfilling the roles of structure and local

plans respectively. North Tyneside, South Tyneside and Sunderland Metropolitan Boroughs in Tyne and Wear all have stretches of North Sea coast.

LOCAL NATURE RESERVES AND COUNTRY PARKS

Local Nature Reserves are established by local authorities under section 21 of the National Parks and Access to the Countryside Act 1949, in consultation with the Country Agencies. Country Parks are declared by local authorities under

Local Nature Reserve or Country Park	Region/District or County	Responsible Authority	Area (ha)
1 Balmedie Country Park	Grampian/Gordon	Grampian RC	72
2 Montrose Basin reserve	Tayside/Angus	Angus DC	1,012
3 Eden estuary reserve	Fife/NE Fife	NE Fife DC	700
4 Aberlady Bay reserve	Lothian/E Lothian	E Lothian DC	582
5 John Muir Country Park	Lothian/Berwickshire	E Lothian DC	675
6 Druridge Bay Country Park	Northumberland	Northumberland CC	306
7 Marsden Cliffs reserve	Tyne & Wear	S Tyneside MBC	1 km
8 Filey North Cliff reserve	N Yorkshire	Scarborough BC	46
9 Breydon Water reserve	Norfolk	Norfolk CC	453
10 Landguard reserve	Suffolk	Suffolk CC/SWT	15.6
11 Cudmore Grove Country Park	Essex	Essex CC	14.4
12 Marsh Farm Country Park	Essex	Essex CC	96
13 Hadleigh Country Park	Essex	Essex CC	136
14 Nor Marsh reserve	Kent	Gillingham BC/RSPB	102
15 Eastcourt Meadows reserve	Kent	Gillingham BC	24
16 Grazen Salts reserve	Kent	Dover DC	4.8
17 Folkestone Warren reserve	Kent	Shepway DC	140
18 Rye Harbour reserve	E Sussex	E Sussex CC	356
19 Hastings Country Park Nature Trail	E Sussex	Hastings BC	Various
20 Beachy Head Nature Trail	E Sussex	Eastbourne BC	2 km
21 Seaford Head reserve	E Sussex	Lewes DC	112
22 Cuckmere Haven reserve	E Sussex	E Sussex CC/Lewes DC	392
23 Pagham Harbour reserve	W Sussex	W Sussex CC	440
24 Hook-with-Warsash reserve	Hampshire	Hants CC	226.7
25 Royal Victoria Country Park	Hampshire	Hants CC	58
26 Calshot Marshes reserve	Hampshire	Hants CC	48
27 Lepe & Calshot Country Park	Hampshire	Hants CC	49.5
28 Keyhaven - Lymington Marshes reserve	Hampshire	Hants CC/HIOWWT	277.6
29 Fort Victoria County Park	Isle of Wight	IoW CC	20
30 Stanpit Marsh reserve	Dorset	Christchurch BC	48.7
31 Hengistbury Head reserve	Dorset	Bournemouth BC	100
32 Upton Country Park	Dorset	Poole BC	22.3
33 Durlston Country Park	Dorset	Dorset CC	104.4
34 Radipole Lake reserve	Dorset	RSPB/Weymouth & Portland BC	89
35 Dawlish Warren reserve	S Devon	DWT/Teignbridge DC	70
36 Sugarloaf Hill & Saltern Cove reserve	S Devon	Torbay BC	43
37 Berryhead Country Park	S Devon	Torbay BC	43
38 SW Peninsula Coast Path	S Devon	Devon CC	150 km

Key	CC	County Council	SWT	Suffolk Wildlife Trust
	DC	District Council	RSPB	Royal Society for the Protection of Birds
	RC	Regional Council	HIOWWT	Hampshire & Isle of Wight Wildlife Trust
	BC	Borough Council	IoW	Isle of Wight
	MBC	Metropolitan Borough Council	DWT	Devon Wildlife Trust

Table 10.3.1
Local Nature Reserves and Country Parks on the North Sea coast.

Figure 10.3.1
Distribution of Local Nature
Reserves and Country Parks
on the North Sea coast (after
Nature Conservancy Council
1989a and Anon. 1989).
Based upon the 1975 Ordnance Survey
1:1,250,000 map with the permission
of the Controller of Her Majesty's
Stationery Office © Crown Copyright.

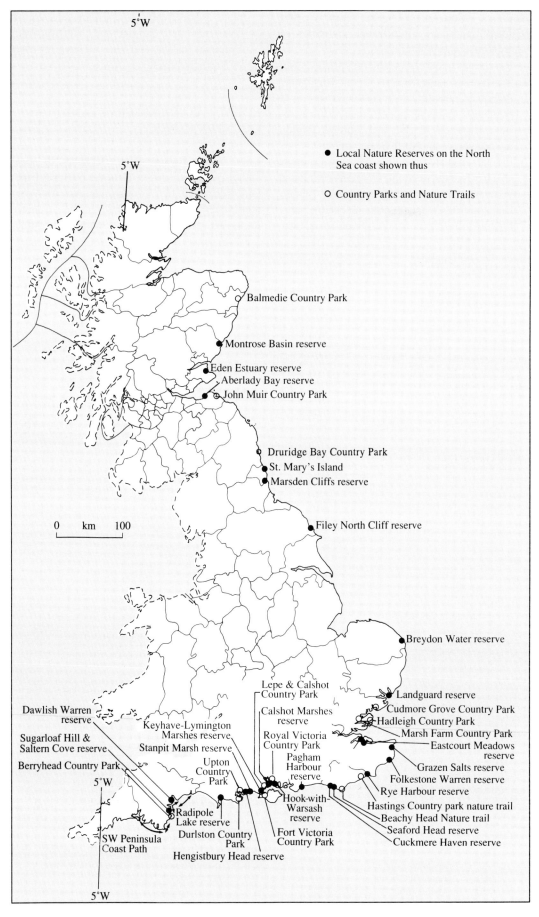

section 7 of the Countryside Act 1968, but not necessarily for their nature conservation interest.

Several of the Local Nature Reserves in Britain are owned by local authorities, but managed in conjunction with a voluntary body such as a local Wildlife Trust (see Section 10.4). The distribution of Local Nature Reserves and Country Parks along the North Sea coastal margin is given in Figure 10.3.1 and they are listed in Table 10.3.1. The number of Local Nature Reserves along the North Sea coastal margin is shown in Table 10.3.2.

REGIONAL LANDSCAPE DESIGNATIONS

Areas of Great Landscape Value (Figure 10.3.2 and

Number of Local Nature Reserves (up to March 1989)		
	Total	North Sea coast
Scotland	6	3
England	145	23

Table 10.3.2
Local Nature Reserves in Scotland and England.

Table 10.3.3) originated in a 1949 Technical Broadsheet, updated by Circular 2/1962. Areas where development was imminent were suggested as initial sites for designation by planning authorities to provide a strong presumption against development within that area. Local circumstances and the absence of further central guidance since 1962 means that regional landscape designations vary in title, date of establishment, scale and objectives from one planning authority to another (Cobham Resource Consultants 1988).

	Designated area name	Region	Designation	Area (ha)
1	Sea cliffs at Westray	Orkney	ASV	338
2	Sea cliffs at Yesnaby	Orkney	ASV	605
3	Sea cliffs at Hoy	Orkney	ASV	672
4	Leirinmore	Highland	AGLV	<100
5	Loch Eriboll	Highland	AGLV	<100
6	Sandside Bay	Highland	AGLV	<100
7	Holborn Head	Highland	AGLV	<100
8	Duncansby Head	Highland	AGLV	<100
9	Sutors of Cromarty	Highland	AGLV	<100
10	Rosemarkie Burn, Fortrose	Highland	AGLV	<100
11	Culbin	Grampian	ARLS	2,181
12	Cullen/Portsoy	Grampian	ARLS	524
13	Macduff/Quarryhead	Grampian	ARLS	3,325
14	Rattray	Grampian	ARLS	920
15	Longhaven/Cruden Bay	Grampian	ARLS	628
16	Collieston/Balmedie	Grampian	ARLS	1,212
17	Downies/Stonehaven	Grampian	ARLS	312
18	Stonehaven/Todhead Point	Grampian	ARLS	563
19	St. Cyrus	Grampian	ARLS	224
20	Lunan Bay and coast	Tayside	AGLV	3,258
21	Tay coast	Fife	AGLV	17,599
22	Tentsmuir shore	Fife	AGLV	17,595
23	East Neuk coast	Fife	AGLV	13,837
24	Burntisland coastal area	Fife	AGLV	3,620
25	Cramond Island, Cow & Calves, and Inchmickery	Lothian	AGLV	<100
26	Longniddry to Dirleton coast	Lothian	AGLV	1,615
27	North Berwick Law	Lothian	AGLV	123
28	Islands of Bass Rock, Craigleith and The Lamb	Lothian	AGLV	251
29	North Berwick to Tyninghame	Lothian	AGLV	1,555
30	Dunbar to Dunglass Burn	Lothian	AGLV	785
31	Berwickshire coastline	Borders	AGLV	1,232

Key: ASV= Areas of Scenic Value
ARLS= Areas of Regional Landscape Significance
AGLV= Areas of Great Landscape Value

Table 10.3.3
Regional landscape designations on the Scottish North Sea coast.

Figure 10.3.2
Distribution of regional
landscape designations on the
North Sea coast (after
Cobham Resource
Consultants 1988).

Based upon the 1975 Ordnance Survey
1:1,250,000 map with the permission
of the Controller of Her Majesty's
Stationery Office © Crown Copyright.

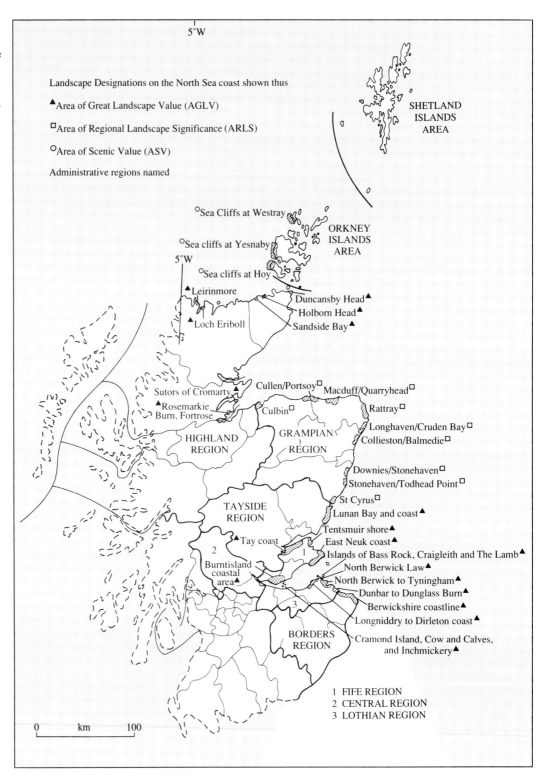

Landscape Designations on the North Sea coast shown thus

▲ Area of Great Landscape Value (AGLV)

□ Area of Regional Landscape Significance (ARLS)

○ Area of Scenic Value (ASV)

Administrative regions named

SHETLAND ISLANDS AREA

○ Sea Cliffs at Westray

ORKNEY ISLANDS AREA

○ Sea cliffs at Yesnaby

○ Sea cliffs at Hoy

▲ Leirinmore

▲ Loch Eriboll

Duncansby Head ▲
Holborn Head ▲
Sandside Bay ▲

Sutors of Cromarty ▲
Cullen/Portsoy □ Macduff/Quarryhead □

▲ Rosemarkie Burn, Fortrose   Culbin □   Rattray □

HIGHLAND REGION

GRAMPIAN REGION

Longhaven/Cruden Bay □
Colliesten/Balmedie □

Downies/Stonehaven □
Stonehaven/Todhead Point □

St Cyrus □

TAYSIDE REGION

Lunan Bay and coast ▲

Tentsmuir shore ▲

East Neuk coast ▲

▲ Tay coast

Islands of Bass Rock, Craigleith and The Lamb ▲

North Berwick Law ▲

North Berwick to Tyningham ▲

Burntisland coastal area ▲

Dunbar to Dunglass Burn ▲

Berwickshire coastline ▲

Longniddry to Dirleton coast ▲

BORDERS REGION

Cramond Island, Cow and Calves, and Inchmickery ▲

1 FIFE REGION
2 CENTRAL REGION
3 LOTHIAN REGION

0   km   100

10.4 VOLUNTARY AND PRIVATE ORGANISATIONS

INTRODUCTION

A variety of national and local organisations protect sites of nature conservation or scenic interest on the North Sea coast by ownership, leasing them from the owners, or by managing them by agreement with the owners. The organisations which own the largest areas of land on the North Sea coast are the National Trust in England and the Royal Society for the Protection of Birds (RSPB). Both these organisations also lease and manage further areas of land. In several cases their land is managed by local wildlife groups. A few nature reserves are owned privately,

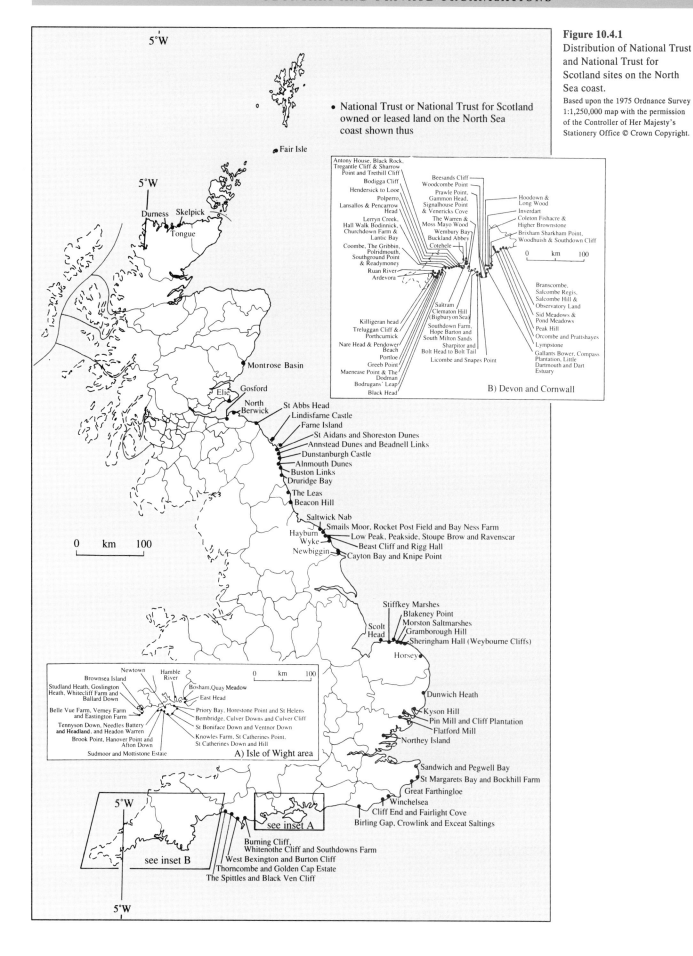

Figure 10.4.1
Distribution of National Trust and National Trust for Scotland sites on the North Sea coast.
Based upon the 1975 Ordnance Survey 1:1,250,000 map with the permission of the Controller of Her Majesty's Stationery Office © Crown Copyright.

• National Trust or National Trust for Scotland owned or leased land on the North Sea coast shown thus

Table 10.4.1
Distribution of National Trust and National Trust for Scotland sites on the North Sea coast.

Name of National Trust for Scotland sites	Region/District or County	Owned or conservation agreement
1 Fair Isle	Shetland Islands	O
2 Durness	Highland/Sutherland	CA
3 Tongue	Highland/Sutherland	CA
4 Skelpick	Highland/Sutherland	CA
5 Elie	Fife/NE Fife	CA
6 Gosford	Lothian/E Lothian	CA
7 North Berwick	Lothian/E Lothian	CA
8 St. Abb's Head	Borders/Berwickshire	O
Name of National Trust sites	**Region/District or County**	**Owned or conservation agreement**
9 Lindisfarne Castle	Northumberland	O
10 Farne Islands	Northumberland	O
11 St. Aidans and Shoreston Dunes	Northumberland	O
12 Annstead Dunes and Beadnell Links	Northumberland	O
13 Dunstanburgh Castle	Northumberland	O
14 Alnmouth Dunes	Northumberland	O
15 Buston Links	Northumberland	O
16 Druridge Bay	Northumberland	O
17 The Leas	Tyne and Wear	O
18 Beacon Hill	Durham	O
19 Saltwick Nab	N Yorkshire	O
20 Smails Moor, Rocket Post Field and Bay Ness Farm	N Yorkshire	O
21 Low Peak, Peakside, Stoupe Brow & Ravenscar	N Yorkshire	O
22 Beast Cliff & Rigg Hall	N Yorkshire	O
23 Hayburn Wyke	N Yorkshire	O
24 Cayton Bay & Knipe Point	N Yorkshire	O
25 Newbiggin	N Yorkshire	O
26 Scolt Head	Norfolk	O
27 Stiffkey Marshes	Norfolk	O
28 Blakeney Point	Norfolk	O
29 Morston Saltmarshes	Norfolk	O
30 Gramborough Hill	Norfolk	O
31 Sheringham Hall (Weybourne Cliffs)	Norfolk	O
32 Horsey	Norfolk	O
33 Dunwich Heath	Suffolk	O
34 Kyson Hill	Suffolk	O
35 Pin Mill and Cliff Plantation	Suffolk	O
36 Flatford Mill	Suffolk	O
37 Northey Island	Suffolk	O
38 Sandwich and Pegwell Bay	Kent	O
39 St. Margaret's Bay & Bockhill Farm	Kent	O
40 Great Farthingloe	Kent	O
41 Winchelsea	E Sussex	O
42 Cliff End & Fairlight Cove	E Sussex	O
43 Birling Gap, Crowlink & Exceat Saltings	E Sussex	O
44 East Head	W Sussex	O
45 Bosham, Quay Meadow	W Sussex	O
46 Hamble River	Hampshire	O
47 Priory Bay, Horestone Point & St. Helens	Isle of Wight	O
48 Bembridge, Culver Downs & Culver Cliff	Isle of Wight	O
49 St. Boniface Down & Ventnor Down	Isle of Wight	O
50 Knowles Farm, St. Catherine's Point, St. Catherine's Down & Hill	Isle of Wight	O
51 Sudmoor and Mottistone Estate	Isle of Wight	O
52 Brook Point, Hanover Point & Afton Down	Isle of Wight	O
53 Tennyson Down, Needles Battery & Headland, & Headon Warren	Isle of Wight	O
54 Newtown	Isle of Wight	O
55 Brownsea Island	Dorset	O
56 Studland Heath, Goslingston Heath, Whitecliff Farm and Ballard Down	Dorset	O

Table 10.4.1 ...continued.

57	Belle Vue Farm, Verney Farm & Eastington Farm	Dorset	O
58	Burning Cliff, Whitenothe Cliff & Southdown Farm	Dorset	O
59	West Bexington & Burton Cliff	Dorset	O
60	Thorncombe & Golden Cap Estate	Dorset	O
61	The Spittles & Black Venn Cliff	Dorset	O
62	Branscombe, Salcombe Regis, Salcombe Hill & Observatory Land	Devon	O
63	Sid Meadows & Pond Meadows	Devon	O
64	Peak Hill	Devon	O
65	Orcombe & Prattshayes	Devon	O
66	Lympstone	Devon	O
67	Brixham Sharkham Point, Woodhuish & Southdown Cliff	Devon	O
68	Coleton Fishacre & Higher Brownstone	Devon	O
69	Inverdart	Devon	O
70	Hoodown & Long Wood	Devon	O
71	Gallants Bower, Compass Plantation, Little Dartmouth & Dart Estuary	Devon	O
72	Beesands Cliff	Devon	O
73	Woodcombe Point	Devon	O
74	Prawle Point, Gammon Head, Signalhouse Point & Venericks Cove	Devon	O
75	Lincombe & Snapes Point	Devon	O
76	Sharpitor & Bolt Head to Bolt Tail	Devon	O
77	Southdown Farm, Hope Barton & South Milton Sands	Devon	O
78	Clematon Hill (Bigbury on Sea)	Devon	O
79	The Warren and Moss Mayo Woods	Devon	O
80	Wembury bay	Devon	O
81	Saltram	Devon	O
82	Buckland Abbey	Devon	O
83	Cotehele	Cornwall	O
84	Antony House, Black Rock, Tregantle Cliff and Sharrow Point & Trethill Cliff	Cornwall	O
85	Bodigga Cliff	Cornwall	O
86	Hendersick to Looe	Cornwall	O
87	Polperro	Cornwall	O
88	Lansallos & Pencarrow Head	Cornwall	O
89	Lerryn Creek, Hall Walk Bodinnick, Churchdown Farm & Lantic Bay	Cornwall	O
90	Coombe, The Gribbin, Polridmouth, Southground Point & Readymoney	Cornwall	O
91	Black Head	Cornwall	O
92	Bodrugan's Leap	Cornwall	O
93	Maenease Point & The Dodman	Cornwall	O
94	Greeb Point	Cornwall	O
95	Portice	Cornwall	O
96	Nare Head & Pendower Beach	Cornwall	O
97	Treluggan Cliff & Porthcurnick	Cornwall	O
98	Killigeran Head, Zone Point & St. Anthony Head	Cornwall	O
99	St. Mawes, St. Just-in-Roseland, Tregear Vean & Turnaware Point	Cornwall	O
100	Ardevora	Cornwall	O
101	Trelissick	Cornwall	O
102	Ruan River	Cornwall	O
103	Rosemullion Head & Mawnan Glebe	Cornwall	O

and may be managed in conjunction with a local Wildlife Trust.

NATIONAL TRUST AND NATIONAL TRUST FOR SCOTLAND

The National Trust for Scotland was established in 1931 (National Trust for Scotland Order Confirmation Act 1935) for the purposes of promoting the permanent preservation of Scotland's heritage of fine buildings, beautiful landscape and historic places, and to encourage public enjoyment of them.

The Trust is an independent charity and depends on donations, legacies and subscriptions for support. With over 100 properties owned throughout

Scotland, only St. Abb's Head and Fair Isle fall within the scope of this directory.

Land that is not owned by the Trust can be protected by a Conservation Agreement under power given to the National Trust for Scotland by a 1938 Act of Parliament. Conservation agreements are entered into voluntarily by landowners who wish areas to come under a form of protection which is not full Trust ownership. The aim is to ensure the conservation of the amenity of the site in perpetuity. As the agreement is binding on the title of the property it is automatically passed on to any subsequent owner. The sites may not have any particular nature conservation value as the assessment of conservation interest may be based on landscape features.

The distribution of National Trust for Scotland properties and land managed under Conservation Agreements along the North Sea coast is given in Figure 10.4.1.

The National Trust is an independent organisation with charitable status which was founded in 1895 to protect land and buildings for the nation. The Trust owns and safeguards 228,713 ha of land in England, Wales and Northern Ireland of which 45,488 ha occur on the North Sea coastal margin (Figure 10.4.1). A large number of properties are bequeathed to the Trust.

In 1965, due to increasing concern about the loss of attractive, unspoilt coastline, the National Trust launched a campaign (Enterprise Neptune) to raise funds to enable the purchase of coastal areas. This campaign was relaunched in 1985 and the length of coastline which is now protected is 825 km (512 miles), of which 306 km (190 miles) lie on the North Sea coast.

Land owned by the Trust is protected by an Act of Parliament (1907) which gives power to declare land and buildings inalienable with the result that these properties cannot be sold or mortgaged. Other lands are leased by the National Trust but are not inalienable and do not receive the same permanency of protection.

A complete list of National Trust and National Trust for Scotland sites is given in Table 10.4.1.

ROYAL SOCIETY FOR THE PROTECTION OF BIRDS

The Royal Society for the Protection of Birds (RSPB) is a voluntary organisation whose main concern is the protection and conservation of wild birds and their habitats. The Society developed from the Fur and Feather Group which was set up in 1889 to protest against the trade in bird feathers for millinery. In 1891 the group widened its interests and was renamed the Society for the Protection of Birds. Soon afterwards, in 1904, it was granted a Royal charter, becoming the Royal Society for the Protection of Birds.

A major policy of the RSPB is to acquire land on which it can establish reserves. Within these areas the Society can provide some protection to both the wild birds and the habitats which are important to them as feeding, breeding and overwintering grounds. At present the RSPB manages more than 120 reserves in the whole of Britain, covering over 56,000 ha. Forty-nine of these reserves (over 25,000 ha) include coastal habitats; those on the North Sea coast are shown in Figure 10.4.2 and listed in Table 10.4.2. The area of reserves on the North Sea coast is approximately 17,520 ha. The RSPB is the largest wildlife conservation body in Europe and as of March 1993 was supported by approximately 875,000 members. Most of its reserves are wardened and open to visitors, but a few are closed to avoid disturbing the bird populations.

Selection of RSPB reserve sites

In recent years it has become clear that a large number of bird habitats are under threat or have already been destroyed. As a result the RSPB developed a policy of selecting reserves based on habitat types, eventually hoping to own a representative selection of the habitats important to wild birds in this country. Twenty ornithological habitat types have been defined, six of which relate to coastal areas:

i)   Rocky islets and stacks
ii) Rocky coasts, cliffs and cliff-tops
iii) Sand dunes/shingle/low offshore islands
iv) Mud/sand-flats/saltmarsh
v)   Brackish water/mud
vi) Coastal grazing marsh.

Each habitat is considered to have a distinctive bird community whereby the combination of species in one habitat does not occur in any of the others. Species that are common, rare or only breed occasionally in this country are considered as well as wintering and passage birds. Special emphasis may be placed on sites holding:

❖ species whose breeding or wintering population forms 10% or more of the north-west European, European or world population

❖ scarce breeding species with up to 100 pairs in the UK

❖ some species particularly under threat

❖ species in one of the above categories but wintering in the UK outside its normal breeding range.

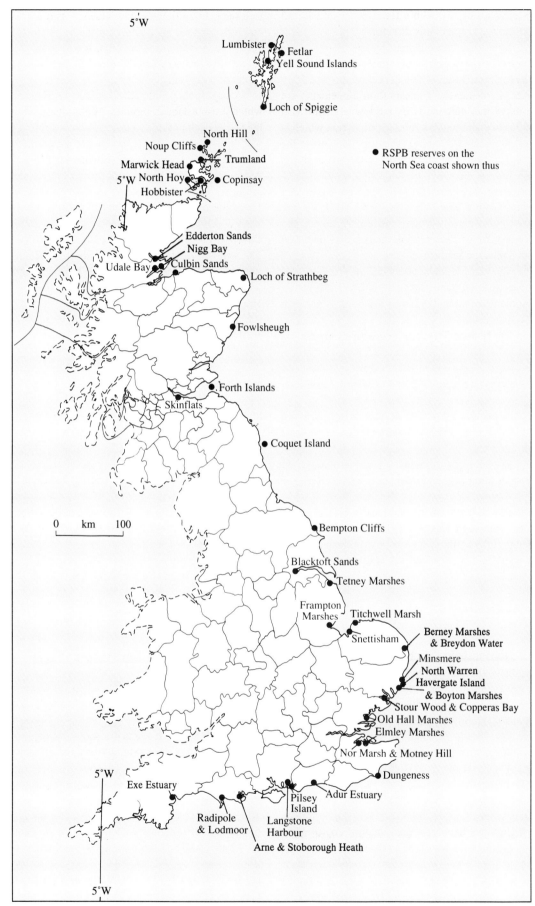

Figure 10.4.2
Distribution of RSPB reserves on the North Sea coast (after Royal Society for the Protection of Birds 1989).

Based upon the 1975 Ordnance Survey 1:1,250,000 map with the permission of the Controller of Her Majesty's Stationery Office © Crown Copyright.

Table 10.4.2
RSPB reserves on the North Sea coast (after Royal Society for the Protection of Birds 1989).

RSPB reserve	Region/District or County	Area (ha)
1 Lumbister	Shetland	1,761
2 Fetlar	Shetland	706
3 Yell Sound Islands	Shetland	162
4 Loch of Spiggie	Shetland	119
5 North Hill	Orkney	206
6 Noup Cliffs	Orkney	14
7 North Hoy	Orkney	3,946
8 Marwick Head	Orkney	19
9 Copinsay	Orkney	152
10 Hobbister	Orkney	759
11 Trumland	Orkney	433
12 Nigg Bay	Highland	113
13 Edderton Sands	Highland	87
14 Udale Bay	Highland	318
15 Culbin sands	Grampian	862
16 Loch of Strathbeg	Grampian	1,050
17 Fowlsheugh	Grampian	11
18 Skinflats	Lothian	413
19 Forth Islands	Lothian	7
20 Coquet Island	Northumberland	7
21 Bempton Cliffs	Humberside	24
22 Blacktoft Sands	Humberside	186
23 Frampton marshes	Lincolnshire	528
24 Tetney marshes	Lincolnshire	1,260
25 Snettisham	Norfolk	1,319
26 Titchwell marsh	Norfolk	206
27 Berney marshes & Breydon Water	Norfolk	529
28 Minsmere	Suffolk	829
29 Havergate Island & Boyton marshes	Suffolk	179
30 North Warren	Suffolk	212
31 Stour Wood & Copperas Bay	Essex	353
32 Old Hall Marshes	Essex	452
33 Nor Marsh & Motney Hill	Kent	102
34 Elmley marshes	Kent	282
35 Dungeness	Kent	874
36 Adur Estuary	West Sussex	10
37 Pilsey Island	West Sussex	18
38 Langstone Harbour	Hampshire	555
39 Lodmoor	Dorset	61
40 Radipole	Dorset	89
41 Arne & Stoborough Heath	Dorset	623
42 Exe Estuary	Devon	96

Having defined the habitat types, the following criteria are considered when selecting land for reserves (criteria were under review in 1987):
❖ the sites must include one or more of the listed habitat types
❖ the habitat or habitats must have a typical community of birds, or alternatively, the potential for the development of such a community
❖ there must be the capability for habitat control and management permitting the maintenance and improvement of the associated bird community
❖ it must be of national importance to birds or capable of being made so through management
❖ it should have been declared an SSSI, or if not it must satisfy the criteria under which the Country Agencies declare such sites (Hammond 1983).

Legal protection

It is an aim of the RSPB that all of its reserves should have SSSI status and therefore the protection afforded to these areas (see Section 10.2). Some of the reserves also have some protection by virtue of the fact that they are nationally or internationally important, lying within National Nature Reserves, listed as potential Ramsar sites, or Special Protection Areas under the EC Birds Directive (see Section 10.2). In other instances the main protection is through ownership. The majority of sites listed in Table 10.4.2 are wholly or partly owned by the Society. In some cases the land is leased and, in these instances, the Society aims to obtain a minimum of 21 years' tenure together with appropriate management rights.

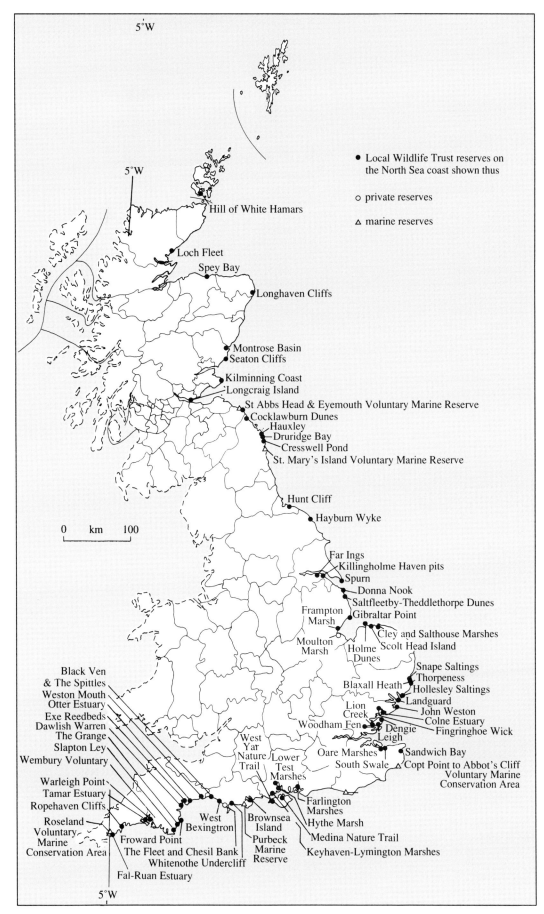

Figure 10.4.3
Distribution of local Wildlife
Trust and other reserves on
the North Sea coast.
Based upon the 1975 Ordnance Survey
1:1,250,000 map with the permission
of the Controller of Her Majesty's
Stationery Office © Crown Copyright.

5°W

5°W

● Local Wildlife Trust reserves on
   the North Sea coast shown thus

○ private reserves

△ marine reserves

Hill of White Hamars

Loch Fleet
Spey Bay

Longhaven Cliffs

Montrose Basin
Seaton Cliffs
Kilminning Coast
Longcraig Island
St Abbs Head & Eyemouth Voluntary Marine Reserve
Cocklawburn Dunes
Hauxley
Druridge Bay
Cresswell Pond
St. Mary's Island Voluntary Marine Reserve

Hunt Cliff
Hayburn Wyke

Far Ings
Killingholme Haven pits
Spurn
Donna Nook
Saltfleetby-Theddlethorpe Dunes
Frampton Gibraltar Point
Marsh
Cley and Salthouse Marshes
Moulton Scolt Head Island
Marsh Holme
Dunes
Snape Saltings
Thorpeness
Blaxall Heath Hollesley Saltings
Landguard
Lion John Weston
Creek Colne Estuary
Woodham Fen Dengie Fingringhoe Wick
Leigh
Oare Marshes Sandwich Bay
South Swale Copt Point to Abbot's Cliff
Voluntary Marine
Conservation Area

0   km   100

Black Ven
& The Spittles
Weston Mouth
Otter Estuary
Exe Reedbeds
Dawlish Warren
The Grange
Slapton Ley
Wembury Voluntary

Warleigh Point
Tamar Estuary
Ropehaven Cliffs
Roseland
Voluntary
Marine
Conservation Area
Froward Point
The Fleet and Chesil Bank
Whitenothe Undercliff
Fal-Ruan Estuary

West Bexingtron
Brownsea Island
Purbeck Marine Reserve

West
Yar
Nature
Trail
Lower
Test
Marshes

Farlington
Marshes
Hythe Marsh
Medina Nature Trail
Keyhaven-Lymington Marshes

5°W

Table 10.4.3
Local Wildlife Trust and
other reserves on the North
Sea coast.

Reserve name	Region/County	Management responsibility	Area (ha)
1 Hill of White Hamars	Orkney Islands/Hoy	SWT Head Office	40
2 Loch Fleet	Highland/Sutherland	SWT Head Office	1,163
3 Spey Bay	Highland/Moray	SWT Morayshire Members Group	-
4 Longhaven Cliffs	Grampian/Banff & Buchan	SWT Aberdeen & Kincardine Branch	50
5 Montrose Basin*	Tayside/Angus	SWT Angus & Dundee Branch/Angus DC	1,012
6 Seaton Cliffs	Tayside/Angus	SWT Angus & Dundee Branch	11
7 Kilminning Coast	Fife/NE Fife	SWT Fife & Kinross Branch	8
8 Longcraig Island	Fife/Dunfermline	SWT Fife & Kinross Branch	0.8
9 St. Abb's Head	Borders/Berwickshire	SWT Fife & Kinross Branch	97
10 St. Abb's and Eyemouth voluntary marine reserve	Borders/Berwickshire	Local Management Committee	1,030 (50 m)
11 Blackhall	Durham	Durham WT	32
12 Hawthorn Dene	Durham	Durham WT	67
13 Cocklawburn Dunes	Northumberland	Northumberland WT	6
14 Hauxley	Northumberland	Northumberland WT	32
15 Druridge Bay*	Northumberland	Northumberland WT/North. CC/NT	12 km
16 Cresswell Pond	Northumberland	Northumberland WT	10
17 St Mary's Island voluntary marine reserve	Northumberland	North Tyneside Council	-
18 Hunt Cliff	Cleveland	Cleveland WT	7.5
19 Hayburn Wyke	N Yorkshire	NT/Yorkshire WT	14
20 Spurn	Humberside	Yorkshire WT	112
21 Far Ings	S Humberside	Lincolnshire TNC	55
22 Killingholme Haven Pits	S Humberside	Lincolnshire TNC	32
23 Donna Nook	Lincolnshire	Lincolnshire TNC/MoD	1,106
24 Saltfleetby-Theddlethorp Dunes	Lincolnshire	EN/Lincolnshire TNC/MoD	478
25 Gibraltar Point	Lincolnshire	Lincolnshire TNC	429
26 Frampton Marsh	Lincolnshire	RSPB/Lincolnshire TNC	537
27 Moulton Marsh	Lincolnshire	S Lincolnshire Nature Reserves Ltd/AWA	25
28 Scolt Head Island	Norfolk	EN/NT/Norfolk NT	738
29 Holme Dunes	Norfolk	Norfolk NT	160
30 Cley and Salthouse Marshes	Norfolk	Norfolk NT	312
31 Thorpeness	Suffolk	Suffolk WT	63
32 Snape Saltings	Suffolk	Suffolk WT	6.7
33 Blaxall Heath	Suffolk	Suffolk WT	41
34 Hollesley Saltings	Suffolk	Suffolk WT	15
35 Landguard*	Suffolk	Suffolk WT/Suffolk CC	15.6
36 Hogmarsh	Essex	EWT	5
37 Skippers Island	Essex	EWT	94
38 Howlands Marsh	Essex	EWT	73
39 Colne Point	Essex	EN/EWT	246
40 Fingringhoe Wick	Essex	EWT	50
41 Rat Island	Essex	EWT	14
42 Bonners Saltings & Ray Island	Essex	EWT	24
43 Bradwell Shell Bank	Essex	EWT	81
44 Lion Creek	Essex	EWT	7
45 Woodham Fen	Essex	EWT	8
46 Shoebury Old Ranges	Essex	EWT/Southend BC	9
47 Two Tree Island	Essex	EWT/EN	255
48 Canvay Point	Essex	EWT	28
49 Vange Marsh	Essex	EWT	1
50 Fobbing Marsh	Essex	EWT	76
51 John Weston	Essex	EWT	8
52 Colne Estuary	Essex	EN/EWT	608
53 Fingringhoe Wick	Essex	EWT	50
54 Dengie	Essex	EN/EWT	3,025
55 Lion Creek	Essex	EWT	4.7
56 Woodham Fen	Essex	EWT	8
57 Leigh	Essex	EN/EWT	267
58 Oare Marshes	Kent	Kent TNC	67
59 South Swale	Kent	Kent TNC	423
60 Sandwich Bay	Kent	Kent TNC/RSPB/NT	455
61 Seven Sisters voluntary marine conservation area	E Sussex	SSVMCA working group	-

62	Sinah Warren	Hampshire	Hants & IoW WT	5
63	Farlington Marshes	Hampshire	Hants & IoW WT	120
64	Lower Test Marshes	Hampshire	Hants & IoW WT	110
65	Hythe Marsh	Hampshire	Hants & IoW WT	8.8
66	Keyhaven-Lymington Marshes	Hampshire	Hants CC/Hants & IoW NT	277.6
67	Medina Nature Trail	Isle of Wight	IoW NHAS	3.2-4.8 km
68	West Yar Nature Trail	Isle of Wight	IoW NHAS	8 km
69	Brownsea Island	Dorset	Dor TNC/NT	100
70	Purbeck Marine Reserve	Dorset	Dor TNC	650
71	Whitenothe Undercliff	Dorset	NT	46
72	The Fleet and Chesil Bank	Dorset	Strangways Estate	800
73	West Bexington	Dorset	Dor TNC	16
74	Black Ven and The Spittles	Dorset	NT	64.4
75	Weston mouth	Devon	Dev WT	-
76	Otter Estuary	Devon	Dev WT	18
77	Exe Reedbeds	Devon	Dev WT	-
78	Dawlish Warren*	Devon	Dev WT/Teignbridge DC	70
79	Forward Point	Devon	NT	22.8
80	Slapton Ley	Devon	FSC/WMCA Advisory Committee	190
81	Wembury voluntary marine conservation area	Devon	Dev WT	6 km
82	Warleigh Point	Devon	Dev WT	31
83	Tamar Estuary	Cornwall	Corn TNC	400
84	Ropehaven Cliffs	Cornwall	Corn TNC	20
85	Fal-Ruan Estuary	Cornwall	Corn TNC	100
86	Roseland voluntary marine conservation area	Cornwall	Corn TNC	-

Table 10.4.3 ...continued.

Key			
NT	Naturalists' Trust	BC	Borough Council
WT	Wildlife Trust	CC	County Council
TNC	Trust for Nature Conservation	NT	National Trust
SWT	Scottish Wildlife Trust	EN	English Nature
IoWNHAS	Isle of Wight Natural History and Archaeological Society	RSPB	Royal Society for the Protection of Birds
		MoD	Ministry of Defence
DC	District Council	*	Site included on Local Nature Reserves map
FSC	Field Studies Council	-	Information not available

LOCAL WILDLIFE TRUSTS

Forty-seven local Wildlife Trusts come together to form RSNC (Royal Society for Nature Conservation), the Wildlife Trusts Partnership, which operates nationwide. Sixteen of these Trusts, from the Scottish Wildlife Trust (SWT) in Scotland to the Cornwall Trust for Nature Conservation in the south-west, have some coastal frontage on the North Sea. The Wildlife Trusts manage nearly 2,000 nature reserves, encompassing more than 56,000 ha. Many are owned or leased, and some are managed under agreement with the owners. SWT and other Trusts hold records of undesignated Wildlife Sites.

More than half of the Wildlife Trust nature reserves are SSSIs and almost one-fifth are identified as sites of national importance in 'A Nature Conservation Review' (Ratcliffe 1977). Many of the sites may be owned or managed in conjunction with other bodies such as the RSPB, Nature Conservancy Council, Ministry of Defence or local or district councils (see Sections 10.2 and 10.3). An indication of the tenure is given in Table 10.4.3.

The distribution of local Wildlife Trust sites along the North Sea coast is given in Figure 10.4.3.

VOLUNTARY MARINE RESERVES

Voluntary marine reserves or conservation areas may be set up by representatives of the users of a subtidal area or an area of shore in order to initiate management of that area. Management may have a variety of purposes, from conservation of a marine biologically important area to use for educational purposes. These reserves or conservation areas usually have a management committee or steering group composed of users of the area, interested members of the public, fishermen, harbour authorities and local Wildlife Trusts.

ACKNOWLEDGEMENTS

Prepared by Charlotte Johnston from information provided by the following people, many of whom also commented on the draft text.

Ray Woolmore (Countryside Commission) on Areas of Outstanding Natural Beauty, Heritage Coasts and National Parks. Richard Ferguson (Countryside Commission for Scotland) on National Scenic Areas, National Parks and Country Parks.

Joe Burgon, Keith Alexander and Cathy Jackson (National Trust) provided information on National Trust land. John Mayhew (National Trust for Scotland) provided information on National Trust for Scotland sites. Caroline Steel and Trina Paskell (RSNC) supplied information on local Wildlife Trust reserves. Mick Rebane and Alasdair Somerville (Scottish Wildlife Trust) supplied information on Scottish Wildlife Trust reserves. Lennox Campbell (RSPB) provided information on RSPB sites.

Section 10.3 was written by Graham King with additional material by Jonathan Cox.

Information on Several and Regulating Orders was supplied by Ministry of Agriculture, Fisheries and Food, Directorate of Fisheries Research.

David Blatchford and Graham Culley (English Nature) and Murray Ferguson (JNCC) provided information and commented on draft text.

REFERENCES

ANON. 1989. *MacMillan Guide to Britain's Nature Reserves, 1989.* London, MacMillan.

COBHAM RESOURCE CONSULTANTS 1988. *The effectiveness of landscape designations in Scotland. A review study.* A report for the Countryside Commission for Scotland and the Scottish Development Department.

COUNTRYSIDE COMMISSION 1970. *The coastal heritage. A conservation policy for coasts of high quality scenery.* HMSO, Countryside Commission.

COUNTRYSIDE COMMISSION 1989a. *Directory of Areas of Outstanding Natural Beauty.* Cheltenham, Countryside Commission, National Parks and Planning Branch.

COUNTRYSIDE COMMISSION 1989b. *Protected areas in the United Kingdom* 5th ed. (map), Cheltenham, Countryside Commission.

COUNTRYSIDE COMMISSION 1991. *Heritage coasts. Policies and priorities 1991.* Cheltenham, Countryside Commission CCP305.

COUNTRYSIDE COMMISSION/COUNTRYSIDE COUNCIL FOR WALES 1991. *Areas of Outstanding Natural Beauty. A policy statement 1991.* Cheltenham, Countryside Commission CCP356.

COUNTRYSIDE COMMISSION FOR SCOTLAND 1978. *Scotland's scenic heritage.* Perth, Countryside Commission for Scotland.

COUNTRYSIDE COMMISSION FOR SCOTLAND 1989. Update of territorial figures. Unpublished information. Countryside Commission for Scotland.

DEPARTMENT OF AGRICULTURE AND FISHERIES FOR SCOTLAND 1989. *Environmentally sensitive areas in Scotland. A first report.* Edinburgh, Department of Agriculture and Fisheries for Scotland.

DEPARTMENT OF THE ENVIRONMENT AND THE WELSH OFFICE 1992. *Marine Consultation Areas. A description.*

ENGLISH NATURE 1993. *Managing England's marine wildlife.* Peterborough, English Nature.

EUROPEAN ECONOMIC COMMUNITY 1985. *On improving the efficiency of agricultural structures. Article 19: National aid in Environmentally Sensitive Areas.* Council Regulation (EEC) No. 797/85.

HAMMOND, N. 1983. *RSPB Nature Reserves.* Sandy, Royal Society for the Protection of Birds.

HERITAGE COAST FORUM 1989. *Heritage Coast Directory.* Manchester, Heritage Coast Forum Secretariat.

GUBBAY, S. 1988. *Coastal directory for marine nature conservation.* Ross-on-Wye, Marine Conservation Society.

IRVING, R. 1987. *The Hampshire Coast. A compendium of sites of nature conservation importance.* Winchester, Hampshire County Council.

MINISTRY OF AGRICULTURE, FISHERIES AND FOOD 1989. *Environmentally sensitive areas.* London, HMSO.

NATURE CONSERVANCY COUNCIL 1989a. *Local nature reserves. (Library information sheet No. 6).* Peterborough, Nature Conservancy Council.

NATURE CONSERVANCY COUNCIL 1989b. *15th Report. 1 April 1988–31 March 1989.* Peterborough, Nature Conservancy Council.

NATURE CONSERVANCY COUNCIL 1990. *Marine Consultation Areas: Scotland.* Edinburgh, Nature Conservancy Council.

ROYAL SOCIETY FOR THE PROTECTION OF BIRDS 1983. *RSPB nature reserves.* Sandy, Royal Society for the Protection of Birds.

ROYAL SOCIETY FOR THE PROTECTION OF BIRDS 1989. *RSPB: Where to go birdwatching. A guide to RSPB nature reserves.* London, BBC Books.

SCOTTISH WILDLIFE TRUST 1988. *Reserves handbook.* Edinburgh, Scottish Wildlife Trust.

SMITH, A.E. 1982. *A nature reserves handbook. A guide to a selection of the nature reserves of the Nature Conservation Trusts and the Royal Society for Nature Conservation.* Lincoln, Royal Society for Nature Conservation.

STROUD, D. A., MUDGE, G. P., & PIENKOWSKI, M. W. 1990. *Protecting internationally important bird sites. A review of the EEC Special Protection Area network in Great Britain.* Peterborough, Nature Conservancy Council.

TASKER, M.L. *et al.* (in prep.) Review of marine proposed Special Protection Areas. *Joint Nature Conservation Committee Report.*

Chapter 11

ACTIVITIES

11.1 INTRODUCTION

The Directory was never intended to be a major source of information on man's activities within the North Sea and at its coastal margins, and this chapter only provides a brief outline of some of the more significant of these. Indeed, an attempt to cover this huge subject properly would probably run to several volumes, each one the size of this publication. The previous chapters do, however, give brief accounts of effects of man's activities upon specific natural coastal features, species and habitats and should be consulted for further information. Other important sources of data on activities are noted at the end of this section, notable among these being the Estuaries Review (Davidson *et al.* 1991) and English Nature's Marine Conservation Handbook (Eno 1991).

11.2 NORTH SEA OIL AND GAS DEVELOPMENTS

INTRODUCTION

The North Sea is a very important area for offshore oil and gas production. This production extends to the coastal margin with attendant onshore production sites and related developments. However, onshore production is modest in terms of cost and scale when compared with the offshore industry.

The main offshore activity is within the United Kingdom and Norwegian sectors of the North Sea, with smaller developments in Danish and Dutch waters. Offshore exploration of the United Kingdom waters began in 1964 when 51 companies were awarded licences to operate in 348 exploration blocks. The discovery of the Gronigen gas field in the Netherlands stimulated exploration for gas in the southern North Sea with several very large gas discoveries being made in the late 1960s. Interest in the central and northern areas was increased by the Ekofisk oil field discovery in the Norwegian sector.

The areas over which coastal states have jurisdiction were detailed by agreement in the 1960s and 1970s. In the United Kingdom the Crown has rights to all gas and oil found within the UK sector and licences for oil and gas exploration and production have been issued by the Department of Energy in phases called 'rounds'.

Onshore oil discoveries have been small compared to offshore oil and gas fields, the largest being the development of the discovery at Wytch Farm, Poole Harbour in Dorset. Onshore developments require, in addition to a development licence, planning permission from the Local Planning Authority and permission from landowners and occupiers.

By the end of 1991 a total of 1,738 exploration wells had been started in the UK sector of the North Sea. Within the United Kingdom Continental Shelf there were around 5,800 km of pipelines associated with the production of oil and gas at the end of 1991. Production of crude oil during 1991 was 91.3 million tonnes and production of natural gas was 55.2 billion m³.

The 1958 Geneva Convention on the Continental Shelf allows states to create 500 m radius safety zones around fixed platforms and drilling rigs when operating on their shelves and to regulate navigation within these zones. These zones minimise the risk of collision by other users of the sea. In some more complex fields these zones are linked together to form larger development areas.

DISTRIBUTION

The main areas of production within the North Sea are the east Shetland basin, which is predominantly an oil production area, a central area in which both oil and gas are produced, and the southern basin which is mainly a gas production region. The distribution of the main oil and gas fields in the North Sea is shown in Figure 11.2.1.

Figure 11.2.1
Distribution of the main oil and gas developments in the North Sea and along the North Sea coastal margin.

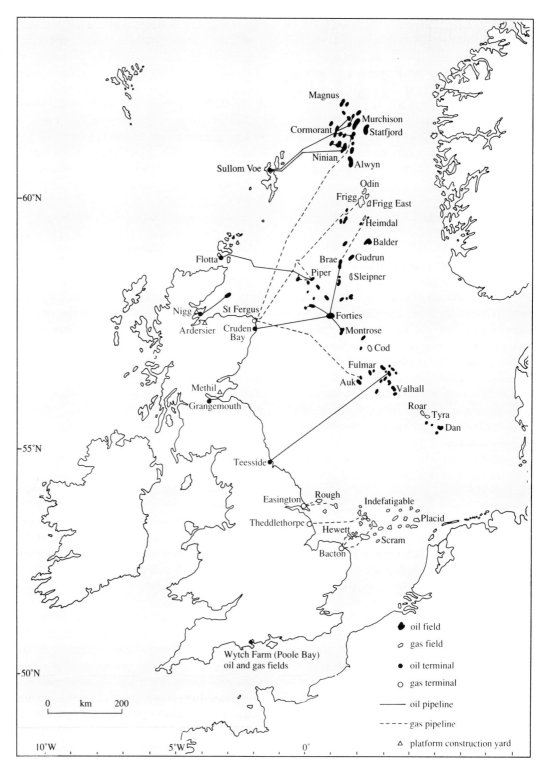

OIL SPILLS

All spills of oil from offshore installations must be reported to the Department of Trade and Industry. The Marine Pollution Control Unit (MPCU) of the Department of Transport has, since 1986, carried out surveillance flights over the North Sea to observe any oil spills from ships and offshore installations.

Offshore operators must have in place contingency plans to deal with any spillage of oil from their installations. Resources for dealing with an oil spill are available from the United Kingdom Offshore Operators Association (UKOOA), specialist companies and MPCU.

In 1991 the total discharge of oil from offshore installations in UK waters (including the Irish Sea) was 14,300 tonnes, of which 9,400 tonnes were contained in oil-based mud cuttings (most of this oil remains on the seabed with the cuttings), 4,700 tonnes were discharged with produced water and 200 tonnes were the result of spills (Department of Trade and Industry 1992). A more important source of surface oil is spills from shipping. Oil spills pose a threat to marine life and particularly to seabirds (McIntyre 1988), especially those species which surface dive or are flightless during moult (see Section 7.2).

CHEMICALS

The Department of Energy operates a voluntary chemical notification scheme for the use and discharge of chemicals offshore. This involves chemical manufacturers providing information on the composition and toxicity of their products for review by the Directorate of Fisheries Research of the Ministry of Agriculture, Fisheries and Food. They make recommendations as to whether the products may be discharged into the sea and if so, in what quantities. UKOOA has urged all its member companies to observe these recommendations.

FISHERIES

Offshore production installations provide a substratum for a variety of fauna and flora to colonise and provide shelter for numerous fish species. Studies on the effect of hydrocarbons on fish eggs and larvae have been undertaken in conjunction with government authorities. Research programmes covering the independent monitoring of hydrocarbon levels in the vicinity of offshore installations, pipelines and terminals are funded by government.

ABANDONED INSTALLATIONS

The Petroleum Act 1987 provides a framework for the safe and orderly abandonment of disused installations and pipelines on the UK Continental Shelf. The Act empowers the Secretary of State for Energy to require owners of installations and pipelines to submit abandonment programmes for his approval following full consultation with all relevant interested parties, including fishing organisations. The standards to be taken into account when a decision is made regarding the removal of a disused offshore installation will be consistent

with the guidelines adopted by the International Maritime Organisation (IMO). These recommend that removal should be performed in such a way as to cause no significant adverse effects upon navigation or the marine environment. Application of the IMO guidelines will result in the entire removal of all installations in the shallow waters of the southern basin of the North Sea. In the deeper waters of the central and northern sectors, partial removal will be permitted in certain circumstances. Each case will be considered on its individual merits.

COASTAL DEVELOPMENT

In common with any construction on green field sites, the development of oil refineries and construction yards on coastal land has resulted in the disturbance of natural faunal and floral communities. Under licence, and after treatment to meet environmental quality objectives for the particular waterway, refineries discharge ballast water and process water to tidal estuaries and/or coastal waters.

SOURCES OF INFORMATION

Information is available from surveys and studies carried out by the countries bordering the North Sea. Data have been collected for the International Conferences on the Protection of the North Sea and in addition the Paris Commission has collated data on discharges in the North Sea since 1985. The Department of Trade and Industry and the United Kingdom Offshore Operators Association both hold information on block licences, the number of production platforms and drilling wells and the length of pipeline in the North Sea.

Regular monitoring of changes to communities on the seabed within the vicinity of installations are carried out by environmental monitoring teams on contract to the oil producers (e.g. Matheson, Kingston, Johnston & Gibson 1986) and by Government Departments.

A review of the environmental effects of the industry is provided by Hartley & Clark (1987).

The Paris Convention for the 'prevention of marine pollution from land based sources' exists in order to control pollution from all countries which have coastlines bordering the North Atlantic Ocean. The convention applies to all man-made structures and islands and therefore also covers fixed oil platforms.

11.3 DUMPING OF WASTE AT SEA

INTRODUCTION

Four types of material have been dumped at sea by the UK: sewage sludge, dredge spoil, solid industrial waste and liquid industrial waste. The dumping of liquid industrial waste in the North Sea by the UK had ceased by 1992. The largest North Sea sewage sludge dumping site is the Barrow Deep, followed by Spurn Head, Harwich, Southampton, Exeter and Plymouth (Lee & Ramster 1981). The dumping of sewage sludge is to be phased out by 1998 (Oslo Commission 1989b).

Licensed industrial waste dump sites are concentrated on the north-east coast of England, off the Humber Estuary, east of the Thames Estuary and off the central Channel coast. Solid industrial wastes consist primarily of stone material from mining operations and flyash from coal-burning power stations, which are considered to be relatively inert. The dumping of these is to be phased out before the year 2000 (Anon. 1990).

By far the greatest quantity of material dumped at sea is dredge spoil (MAFF 1989), and there are a large number of licensed sites for its disposal around the North Sea coast. Most of this originates from excavating docks, harbours, channels, marinas, etc. and includes both the maintenance dredging of existing coastal features and capital dredging to deepen existing channels or create new facilities.

Dumping takes place at a number of offshore and inshore sites licensed by the Ministry of Agriculture, Fisheries and Food (MAFF) Marine Environmental Protection Division, which maintains a database of dump sites and dumping licences. Each site is generally set aside for the dumping of one type of material only and licences run for fixed periods. MAFF and the Scottish Office Agriculture and Fisheries Department (SOAFD) are also responsible for designating these dump sites. Applications are considered on the basis of whether dumping at sea is the only realistic means of disposal of the waste. There are currently no plans to end the dumping of dredge spoil.

IMPACTS

The impacts of dumping have greatest impact on benthic communities, and are described in Sections 5.5 and 5.6. Where dumping takes place on the coast or close inshore, the supply of material may affect patterns of coastal erosion and accretion. Cessation of coastal mine waste dumping in north-east England with the closure of collieries, for example, may lead to increased coastal erosion as previously deposited coal waste is lost from the upper beach.

SOURCES OF INFORMATION

The Marine Environment Protection Division of MAFF maintains a database containing all licensing information, including area coordinates, permitted tonnages and permitted concentrations of contaminants in dumped material. Summary statistics are published periodically by MAFF and by the Oslo Commission (1989a). MAFF also publishes the results of monitoring of individual sites (Eagle *et al.* 1978; Murray *et al.* 1980).

11.4 AGGREGATES DREDGING

INTRODUCTION

Dredging of marine aggregates takes place at a number of sites around the North Sea of England. In 1990, approximately 19 million tonnes of sand and gravel were dredged from the North Sea and English Channel waters, under licence from the Crown Estate Commissioners, who own most of the seabed around the UK (CEC 1988). This consists of approximately 11 million tonnes from the east coast areas (CEC 1991).

In considering licence applications, the Crown Estate consults statutory bodies as part of obtaining what is termed the 'Government View' (Department of the Environment 1989).

IMPACTS

As would be expected, the impacts of marine aggregates dredging principally concern benthic communities, which are described in Section 5.5, and fisheries (International Council for the Exploration of the Sea 1979). Cases of coastal erosion have resulted in the past from the removal of offshore sediments, the most notable of these being the loss of the village of Hallsands in Start Bay in 1917. Hydraulics Research Ltd studies of aggregate licence applications assess whether dredging will affect the adjacent coastline.

SOURCES OF INFORMATION

Nunney & Chillingworth (1986) have produced a review of the industry for the DoE.

11.5 COAST PROTECTION AND SEA DEFENCE WORKS

INTRODUCTION

Over the centuries man has sought to control the influence of the tide and storms. This has involved two main activities – firstly, movement seaward by the enclosure of low-lying areas to take advantage of natural accretionary processes and, secondly, prevention of erosion. Each of these processes has involved the construction of a variety of artificial barriers. These are considered in more detail below.

SEA DEFENCE

Sea defences consist of earth banks or other sea walls designed to prevent the incursion of the sea, generally over previously inter-tidal areas. As tidal lands have been enclosed in this way some large areas of land have been created. In some areas these amount to many thousands of hectares. Much of the high quality agricultural land in Cambridgeshire, south Lincolnshire and the coastal areas of Essex and north Kent has been formed in this way. These areas are characterised by flat alluvial landscapes usually with a sea wall forming a seaward barrier preventing incursion and flooding of the land by the sea.

COAST PROTECTION

Coast protection features come in a variety of forms. Most commonly they include concrete sea walls which form major industrial or urban complexes, or consist of revetments or groynes designed to slow down the erosion of coastal cliffs or beaches by the sea. Coast protection structures are erected to control the erosive forces of the sea along otherwise natural coastlines. The distinction between these and sea defences is not always clear – the latter are, however, generally designed to gain land from the sea and to protect the artificial coastline.

In England the responsibility for the construction and maintenance of sea defence and coast protection structures is shared amongst three organisations. The National Rivers Authority has responsibility for the maintenance of sea defences, while coast protection structures are the responsibility of local authorities which obtain financial support from MAFF.

Approaches to sea defence and coast protection

In the past a solid engineering design, in the form of a concrete sea wall or imported rock armourment

for example, was often advocated for sea defence and coast protection structures. These structures generally had an unattractive appearance and often caused damage to wildlife habitats and natural features. In many instances the adoption of such hard engineering solutions has disrupted natural movements of sediment and exacerbated problems of coast erosion on adjacent, unprotected, coastlines.

In recent years English Nature and others have been advocating the development of soft engineering solutions to sea defence and coast protection schemes (English Nature 1991). Such solutions depend on an understanding of the natural sediment characteristics of a coastline to develop a system of groynes, bars and reefs that harness the ability of the coastline to develop natural features, such as an increased beach level or the accretion of mudflats and salt marshes, to protect the coast. Although such solutions are not applicable in all cases, the NRA Anglian Region has developed a sea defence project, covering large sections of the east coast of England, using these ideas. (See also MAFF 1993a & b.)

The importance of isostatic change and landform

Two factors are of importance in determining the extent of coastal protection. Firstly, the isostatic adjustment following the last glaciation: land in the north is generally rising faster than sea level, whereas in the south the land is sinking. Secondly, the nature of the landform itself: in Scotland the rocks are generally harder than in the south, and thus there is less erosion. In addition, many areas are not suitable for enclosure of tidal swamplands as is the case in the flatter alluvial areas of south-east England. There are fewer reclaimed areas in Scotland and therefore less land liable to flooding and requiring sea defences to be built or maintained.

Coast protection features are therefore markedly predominant in south and south-east England (Figure 11.5.1). A few embankments exist in the major estuaries of Scotland, but these are not shown on the figure.

REGIONAL VARIATION ON THE NORTH SEA COAST

By comparison with England, much of the North Sea coast of Scotland is free from artificial structures designed to protect the land (Figure 11.5.1). This is partly due to the more resilient nature of the rocks forming the coastline. In addition, relative sea level is falling as a consequence of isostatic adjustment following the last glaciation. Even where erosion has been taking place there are fewer people and

Figure 11.5.1
Distribution of coastal
protection along the North
Sea coastal margin.
Based upon the 1975 Ordnance Survey
1:1,250,000 map with the permission
of the Controller of Her Majesty's
Stationery Office © Crown Copyright.

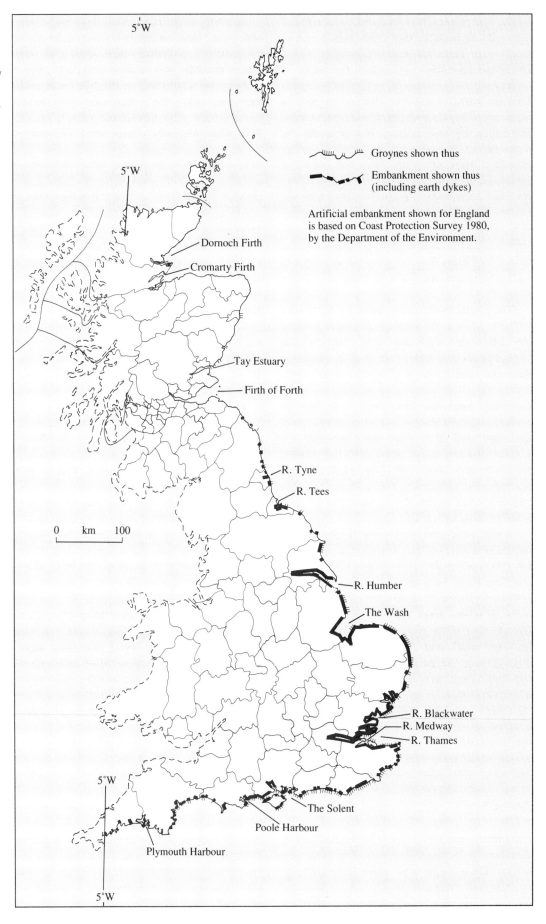

buildings to protect. There are also fewer areas of enclosed tidal land. Some of the estuaries, such as the Firth of Forth and the Tay, have protected shores, though this is very much an exception.

Moving further south, the extent of protected features increases until south-east England is reached, notably East Anglia, where 60% or more of the coast is protected in one way or another. In this area, relative sea level is rising due to the combined effects of a sinking coastline and rising mean sea level. Combined with this the softer rocks are more susceptible to erosion. Sea walls in the Humber form the first extensive artificial coastline and, along with the Wash, represent sea banks erected as part of major tidal land enclosure. In the case of the former this was partly for industry and agriculture, and the latter predominantly for agriculture.

The coastlines of Norfolk and Suffolk are very different. They consist mostly of eroding boulder clay cliffs or mobile soft sedimentary habitats, such as sand dunes or shingle. As a consequence, over the last 40 years or so a major part of the coast (some 80% in Norfolk) has received some form of coastal protection measures. These include groynes to prevent longshore drift and revetments to protect the base of some of the more unstable cliffs.

The Thames basin, similarly, has a high proportion of its coast bordered by earth or concrete sea defences. As with the Wash, these have been largely erected in response to enclosure of tidal lands to create agricultural areas.

A mixture of groynes and sea walls characterize the remaining area of the south-east, though there are also much more extensive areas of 'natural' coastline. From the Solent westwards, continuous and extensive areas of estuaries are bordered by sea walls. In several areas, including Kimmeridge in Dorset, clay cliffs pose problems as frequent landslips cause loss of cliff-top lands. In some areas this involves the need to carry out expensive stabilisation work in order to protect property sited on the cliff-top.

Elsewhere on the south coast, further to the west where harder rocks predominate, there are fewer smaller alluvial landscapes and coast protection and sea defence are much less prevalent.

IMPACTS

Historically, man has created and protected land by the erection of hard sea defences or coast protection works. These impose an essentially artificial structure on the transition between the land and the sea which has a number of other consequences.

Eroding sea cliffs often form important sources of sediment for accretionary features further along the coast. These features themselves may form important sea defences. In many areas the alignment of the coast has been held artificially by man-made structures, making the maintenance of the present line of defence more difficult and costly to sustain. This most frequently occurs when sections of eroding cliffs are protected by groynes and other structures. The unprotected ends may suffer accelerated rates of erosion and often the solution adopted is to extend the 'hard' defences further along the coast. This may have the effect of 'pushing' the problem into another authority's jurisdiction.

Where concrete sea walls with vertical or near vertical faces are constructed, there is some evidence that they may exacerbate beach loss. When combined with effects of other scouring action, even massive defences can be undermined.

In the south-east, particularly where the land is sinking relative to sea level, the saltmarshes which often fringe the sea banks are eroding. This reduces the ameliorating effect of the saltmarsh on wave attack and results in the undermining of sea defences. A major programme of refurbishment is already underway (notably in East Anglia) to reinstate those defences, which were repointed and reinforced following the 1953 storm surge. This is essential if major flooding is to be avoided. Part of this programme recognises the importance of natural sea defences such as sand dunes and saltmarshes, and most important of all, a high, wide beach.

Artificial protection of the 'soft' chalk shores of the south-east has had a major effect on the specialised marine communities of these areas. Unique assemblages of algae occur in the splash zones of chalk cliffs. The construction of revetments to prevent cliff erosion removes the upper shore and splash zone habitat, replacing it with concrete, unsuitable for moisture-loving unicellular algae. Tittley (1985) drew attention to the implication of coastal protection in the south-east for the phycological importance of the area. Of the 130 km of chalk shore in Britain (0.6% of the coastline) 27.3% is modified by coastal protection (Tittley 1987).

The essential conflict here is that without the maintenance of the sea defence or coast protection structure, the land protected from erosion or flooding may be lost. The creation of an artificial barrier inevitably disturbs natural features, some of which may themselves provide important sea defences. Reinstatement of the 'natural' coastline may be the best option, but is unlikely to be attainable except in a few cases because of the investment value of the protected land. However, a better understanding of man's impacts on natural processes for both nature conservation and physical protection of the coast will be essential to accommodate sea level rise attributable to isostatic change and predicted from global warming (McKirdy 1987 and 1989).

11.6 GENERAL DEVELOPMENT

INTRODUCTION

Many activities and developments take place along the coastal margin and in the inshore waters of the North Sea. It is not possible to consider all the activities which impinge upon these areas and their environmental interest within this directory. This section only serves to indicate the distribution of some major developments.

URBAN DEVELOPMENT AND INDUSTRY

Large coastal urban areas, industrial sites and ports and harbours are all located in a narrow fringe of land bordering the sea. Associated discharges from these developments (sewage, waste chemicals and oils) plus run-off from agricultural land, results in an impairment in the quality of sea water in some coastal areas. The sewage from 31 million people (7.3 million m³ per day), along with 5 million m³ of industrial effluent per day, is estimated to flow into the North Sea (Couper 1989). The current planning system only takes account of the natural environmental interest of coastal habitats in certain instances where a number of localised initiatives have attempted to integrate development (see Chapter 10 and Section 11.2).

Compared with the northern North Sea coastline, development pressure is much greater in the south-east and along the south coast. This is reflected in the population densities which occur along the North Sea coastal margin. The distribution of major urban areas and the population density for each region or county are given in Figure 11.6.1.

LAND CLAIM

The enclosure of intertidal areas for development has taken place in a number of sites along the east coast, particularly in estuaries. An example is Teesmouth which has been subjected to various land claim projects since 1850. Steel-works, chemical and petrochemical industries and port related developments have resulted in a decline in the intertidal area from almost 3,000 ha in 1850 to

400 ha. Details of this can be found in the Estuaries Review Document (Davidson *et al.* 1991).

PORT AND HARBOUR DEVELOPMENT

The number and size of ports required by a country is related to the volume of trade and amount of maritime activity. Most ports are located in deep rivers, estuaries, bays and more recently on artificial man-made islands. The authorities which control ports are of three types – companies, local authorities and trusts, and these operate with statutory powers under private Acts of Parliament. By its very nature, the location of a port generates other development. Ports may act as distributional centres and often have large industrial sites associated with them. As centres for trade, efficient lines of communication are required and consequently road and rail networks are often developed on the surrounding coastal area.

Port developments along the North Sea coastal margin in Britain have assumed greater importance in recent years as trade with other European Community member countries has increased. In Britain major international ports are concentrated in the south and south-east of England and this is also where the most recent major port developments have taken place – Felixstowe, Dover, Hull Portsmouth and Ramsgate have all expanded in recent years. There are also many small ports along the east coast which deal with domestic coastal trade. The distribution of ports and docks along the North Sea coastal margin is given in Figure 11.6.2.

TERRESTRIAL SOURCES OF POLLUTION

In England the National Rivers Authority is responsible for monitoring and licensing a variety of pollution discharges to coastal waters and maintains information on coastal water quality, river pollution loads and locations of marine sewage outfalls. The Department of the Environment (in England and Wales) and the Scottish Office provide information on water quality data for their regions (DoE 1985 and Scottish Office Environment Department 1992). General information on inputs of contaminants to the North Sea is given in Grogan (1984).

RECREATION

Sailing is popular in Britain, and the south coast provides numerous harbours, marinas and sheltered areas which allow sailing to take place by the ever-

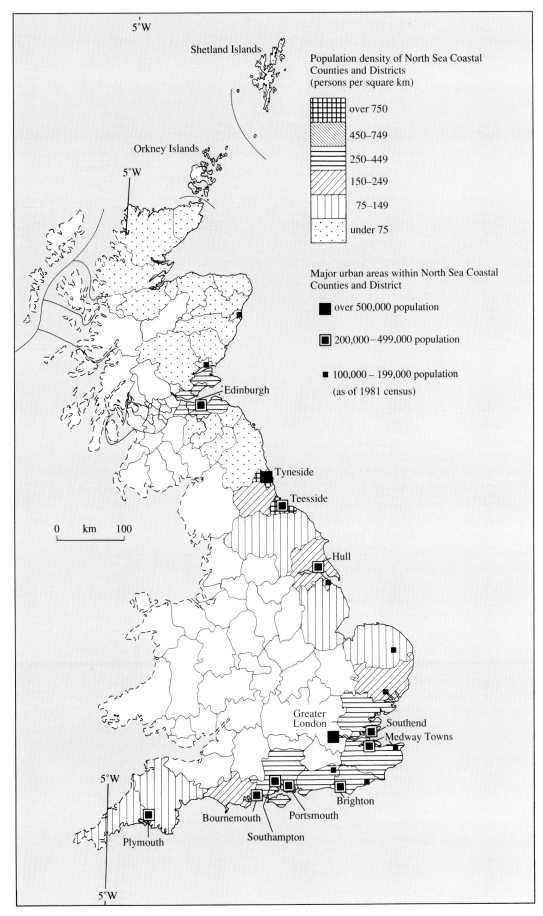

Figure 11.6.1
Population density for each
region/county along the
North Sea coastal margin.
Based upon the 1975 Ordnance Survey
1:1,250,000 map with the permission
of the Controller of Her Majesty's
Stationery Office © Crown Copyright.

Population density of North Sea Coastal
Counties and Districts
(persons per square km)

over 750
450–749
250–449
150–249
75–149
under 75

Major urban areas within North Sea Coastal
Counties and District

over 500,000 population

200,000 – 499,000 population

100,000 – 199,000 population
(as of 1981 census)

Shetland Islands

Orkney Islands

Edinburgh

Tyneside

Teesside

Hull

Greater
London

Southend

Medway Towns

Brighton

Bournemouth

Portsmouth

Southampton

Plymouth

Figure 11.6.2
Distribution of ports and
docks along the North Sea
coastal margin.

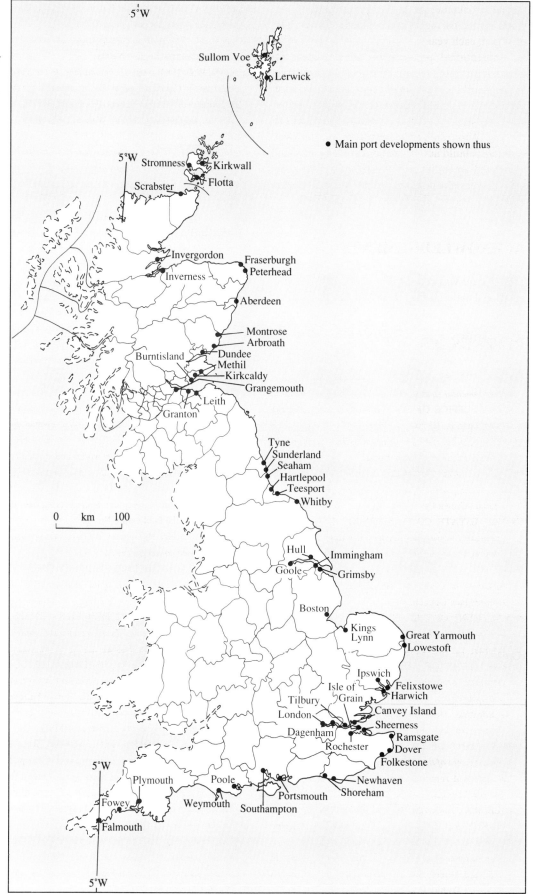

increasing number of boat owners. One of the world's principal regattas takes place at Cowes, Isle of Wight, each year.

Recreational pressure on coastal areas is increasing as more leisure time becomes available and as sporting interests change. To allow more individuals to pursue their interests (such as water sports and diving), greater access to coastal areas is required. This results in increased pressure on local councils to build new car parks, caravan parks and associated amenities and coastal paths. In some areas, increased access is contributing to the erosion of coastal features such as sand dunes.

ACKNOWLEDGEMENTS

This chapter was compiled by Graham King with additional material from Jonathan Cox.

REFERENCES

ANON. 1990. *This common inheritance: Britain's environmental strategy.* Cmnd 1200. London, HMSO.

CENTRAL OFFICE OF INFORMATION 1990. *Britain 1990.* London, HMSO.

COUPER, A.D. *ed.* 1989. *The Times atlas and encyclopedia of the sea.* London, Times Books.

CROWN ESTATE COMMISSIONERS 1988. *Licensing and management of marine aggregate dredging.* London, Crown Estate Office.

CROWN ESTATE COMMISSIONERS 1991. *Marine aggregates crown estate licences: summary of statistics.* London, Crown Estate Office.

DAVIDSON, N.C. *et al.* 1991. *Nature conservation and estuaries in Great Britain.* Peterborough, Nature Conservancy Council.

DEPARTMENT OF THE ENVIRONMENT 1985. *River quality in England and Wales.* [incl. map series.] London, HMSO.

DEPARTMENT OF THE ENVIRONMENT 1989. Offshore dredging for minerals: review of the procedure for determining production licence application. *Department of the Environment News Release* No. 265.

DEPARTMENT OF TRADE AND INDUSTRY 1992. *Development of the oil and gas resources of the United Kingdom. A report to Parliament by the Minister for Energy.* London, HMSO.

EAGLE, R.A., HARDIMAN, P.A., NORTON, M. G., & NUNNY, R.S. 1978. *The field assessment of dumping wastes at sea: a survey of the sewage sludge disposal area in Lyme Bay.* Ministry of Agriculture, Fisheries and Food, Directorate of Fisheries Research, Fisheries Research Technical Report No. 49.

ENGLISH NATURE 1991. *A guide to the selection of coast protection works for geological SSSIs.*

ENO, N.C. *ed.* 1991. *Marine conservation handbook,* 2nd ed. Peterborough, English Nature.

GROGAN, W.C. 1984. *Input of contaminants to the North Sea from the United Kingdom.* Report prepared for the Department of the Environment. Edinburgh, Institute of Offshore Engineering, Herriot Watt University.

HARTLEY, J.P., & CLARK, R.B. *eds.* 1987. *Environmental effects of North Sea oil and gas developments. Proceedings of a Royal Society discussion meeting held on 19 and 20 February 1986.* Cambridge, Cambridge University Press.

INTERNATIONAL COUNCIL FOR THE EXPLORATION OF THE SEA 1979. *Report of the ICES Working Group on effects on fisheries of marine sand and gravel extraction.* Copenhagen. (CM1979/E:3.)

LEE, A.J., & RAMSTER, J.W. *eds.* 1981. *Atlas of the seas around the British Isles.* Lowestoft, Ministry of Agriculture, Fisheries and Food, Directorate of Fisheries Research.

MATHESON, I., KINGSTON, P.F., JOHNSTON, C.S., & GIBSON, M.J. 1986. *Statfjord field environmental study. Proceedings, workshop on oil based drilling fluids.* Trondheim, Statfjord Unit.

McINTYRE, A.D. 1988. Pollution in the North Sea from oil-related industry – an overview. *In: Environmental protection of the North Sea,* ed. by P.J. Newman and A.R. Agg. Oxford, Heinemann Professional Publishing.

McKIRDY, A.P. 1987. Protective works and geological conservation. *In: Planning and engineering geology,* ed. by M.G. Culshaw, F.G. Bell, C.J. Cripps and M. O'Hara. London, Geological Society (Engineering Geology Special Publication No. 4).

McKIRDY, A.P. 1989. New moves in coastal management. *Earth science conservation,* 26: 21-22.

MINISTRY OF AGRICULTURE, FISHERIES AND FOOD 1989. *Report on the disposal of waste at sea 1986 and 1987.* London, HMSO.

MINISTRY OF AGRICULTURE, FISHERIES AND FOOD 1993. *Coastal defence and the environment: A guide to good practice.* London, HMSO.

MINISTRY OF AGRICULTURE, FISHERIES AND FOOD 1993. *Coastal defence and the environment: A strategic guide for managers and decision makers in the National Rivers Authority, Local Authorities and other bodies with coastal responsibilities.* London, HMSO.

MURRAY, L.A. , NORTON, M.G., NUNNY, R.S., & ROLFE, M.S. 1980. *The field assessment of dumping wastes at sea: 6. The disposal of sewage and industrial waste off the River Humber.* Ministry of Agriculture, Fisheries and Food, Directorate of Fisheries Research, Fisheries Research Technical Report No. 55.

NUNNEY, R.S., & CHILLINGWORTH, P.C.H. 1986. *Marine dredging for sand and gravel.* Department of the Environment. (Minerals Planning Research Project No. PECD 7/1/163 - 99/84.)

OSLO COMMISSION 1989a. *Thirteenth Annual Report on the Activities of the Oslo Commission.* London, Oslo and Paris Commissions.

OSLO COMMISSION 1989b. *Review of sewage sludge disposal at sea.* London, Oslo and Paris Commissions.

SCOTTISH OFFICE ENVIRONMENT DEPARTMENT. 1992. *Water quality survey of Scotland 1990.* Edinburgh, The Scottish Office.

TITTLEY, I. 1985. *Chalk cliff algal communities of Kent and Sussex, South-east England.* (Contractor: Department of Botany, British Museum [Natural History]). Nature Conservancy Council, South East Region.

TITTLEY, I. 1987. Public Inquiry on 23 June 1987, Ramsgate Harbour access road, western undercliff and Pegwell Bay. Proof of Evidence by I. Tittley.

Chapter 12

GENERAL REFERENCES

Listed below are a number of key references which give a general overview on some aspects of the British coastline.

BARNES, R.S.K. *ed.* 1977. *The coastline.* Chichester, John Wiley and Sons.

COUNTRYSIDE COMMISSION 1970. Nature Conservation at the Coast. *Coastal Preservation and Development Special Study Reports, Vol. 2.* London, HMSO.

DAVIDSON, N.C., LAFFOLEY, D. d'A., DOODY, J.P., WAY, L.S., GORDON, J., KEY, R., DRAKE, C.M., PIENKOWSKI, M.W., MITCHELL, R., & DUFF, K. L. 1991. *Nature conservation and estuaries in Great Britain.* Peterborough, Nature Conservancy Council.

ENGLISH NATURE 1993. *Managing England's marine wildlife.* Peterborough, English Nature.

ENGLISH NATURE 1993. *Important areas for marine wildlife around England.* Peterborough, English Nature.

ENO, N.C. *ed.* 1991. *Marine Conservation Handbook,* 2nd ed. Peterborough, English Nature.

GUBBAY, S. 1988. *Coastal directory for marine nature conservation.* Ross-on-Wye, Marine Conservation Society.

HMSO 1988. Ministerial Declaration, issued by the Department of the Environment of the United Kingdom, April 1988. *Second International Conference on the Protection of the North Sea, London, 24-25 November 1987.* London, HMSO.

INSTITUTE OF OFFSHORE ENGINEERING, 1988. *A review of the future of offshore and coastal industry in Scottish waters and its potential impact on the marine environment. A report to the Nature Conservancy Council.* Edinburgh, Institute of Offshore Engineering, Heriot Watt University.

LEE, A.J., & RAMSTER, J.W. *eds.* 1981. *Atlas of the seas around the British Isles.* Lowestoft, Ministry of Agriculture, Fisheries and Food, Directorate of Fisheries Research.

MILLS, D.J.L., HILL, T.O., THORPE, K., & CONNOR, D.W. *eds.* 1993. Atlas of marine biological surveys in Britain. *Joint Nature Conservation Committee Report,* No. 167. (Marine Nature Conservation Review Report, No. MNCR/OR/17.). Peterborough, Joint Nature Conservation Committee.

NEWMAN, P.J., & AGG, A.R. *eds.* 1988. *Environmental protection of the North Sea.* London, Heinemann Professional Publishing.

NORTH SEA 2000: Environment and Sea Use Planning Conference, 16–18 August 1989, Edinburgh. Conference pre-prints. Edinburgh, Institute of Offshore Engineering, Heriot Watt University.

RATCLIFFE, D.A. *ed.* 1977. *A nature conservation review – The selection of biological sites of national importance to nature conservation in Britain, Vols. 1 & 2.* Cambridge, Cambridge University Press.

SIDE, J. DE GROOT, S., & SMITH, H. *eds.* 1991. Proceedings of North Sea 2000: Environment and Sea Use Planning Conference, 16-18 August 1989, Edinburgh. *Ocean and Shoreline Management, 16.*

The following are more general texts on the natural history of Britain's coastline.

BELLAMY, D. *et al.* 1982. *Discovering the countryside with David Bellamy – coastal walks.* RSNC. London, Hamlyn.

GREENPEACE 1987. *Coastline, Britain's threatened heritage.* London, Kingfisher.

HYWELL-DAVIES, J., & THOM, V. 1984. *The Macmillan guide to Britain's nature reserves.* London, Macmillan.

SOOTHILL, E., & THOMAS, M.J. 1987. *The natural history of Britain's coasts.* London, Blandford Press.

SOPER, T. 1984. *A natural history guide to the coast.* Exeter, Webb & Bower in association with the National Trust.

INDEX

dolphins. *See* cetaceans

dredging **16, 246.** *See also* **hydraulic dredging; mineral extraction**

impact on inshore sediment habitats   118–119

dumping **105, 246.** *See also* **waste disposal**

impact on benthic communities   246

impact on sublittoral substrata   110

E

EC directives   206–207. *See also* **international conventions**

concerning Urban Waste Water Treatment   206

on Conservation of Wild Birds   153–155

on the Conservation of Natural Habitats and of Wild Fauna and Flora   206–207

on the Conservation of Wild Birds   206, 221, 238

effluent disposal. *See* **waste disposal**

enclosure of saltmarshes   7

energy

Department of Energy   119

English Nature. *See* **statutory bodies**

Environmental Protection Act 1990. *See* **legislation (national)**

Environmentally Sensitive Areas. *See* **site protection**

erosion

impact on coastal saline lagoons   74

impact on hard rock cliffs   28

impact on saltmarshes   62

impact on sand dunes   54

impact on soft rock cliffs   22–23

of the Norfolk and Lincolnshire coast   21

sediment transport and deposition   5

Estuaries Initiative   197

Estuaries Review   136, 197, 243

F

Field Studies Council

Oil Pollution Research Unit   81

fish species   137–139. *See also* **shellfish**

cod   139–140

haddock   140–142

herring   139

mackerel   137–139

plaice   144

rare species   188–189

saithe   143–144

salmonids   145–146

sandeel   145

sole   145

sprats   139

whiting   142–143

fisheries management   135–152, 188–189

fishing. *See also* **hydraulic dredging; Ministry of Agriculture, Fisheries and Food**

British Marine Fisheries Database   202–203

Common Fisheries Policy   135

impact of offshore oil and gas   245

impact on birds   167

impact on cetaceans   183–184

impact on otters   180

impact on rocky shores   110

impact on seals   176

impacts of beam trawling on offshore habitats   127

legislation   223–226

protective legislation of fisheries   207–208

foreshore exposure platforms   28–32

regional variation in   31–32

forestry. *See also* **coastal woodlands**

impact of afforestation on sand dunes   8, 55

former shorelines. *See* **sea level change**

G

gas industry. *See* **oil and gas development**

geochemistry

offshore   39–40

Geological Conservation Review (GCR)   3, 23, 205

geological history of the North Sea   17–18

geology and geomorphology   5, 17. *See also* **sea cliffs**

offshore   33

bathymetry   33

geochemistry   39–40

seabed rock and geology   35–38

sediments   35

grazing

impact on saltmarshes   63

impact on sand dunes   55

impact on shingle structures   70

grazing marshes. *See* **coastal grazing marshes**

H

habitats   5-16, 41–80, 81-134. *See also* **entries for individual habitats**

formation of   5

protection of. *See* **site protection; EC directives**

hard rock cliffs. *See* **sea cliffs**

Heritage Coasts / Heritage Coast Forum. *See* **site protection**

herptiles   8, 185–188

amphibians   185–187

reptiles   187

human disturbance. *See also* **recreation**

impact on birds   167, 168–169

hunting

impact on otters   179

hydraulic dredging

impact on sediment communities   105, 119

I

Institute of Terrestrial Ecology (ITE)   181

International Bottom Trawl Survey (IBTS)   135

international conventions. *See also* **EC directives**

Berne (Council of Europe, on wildlife and habitats)   183, 207

Bonn (migratory species)   183, 207